NATIONAL GEOGRAPHIC

ALMANAC
2019

Zebras run free in Namibia's NamibRand Nature Reserve.

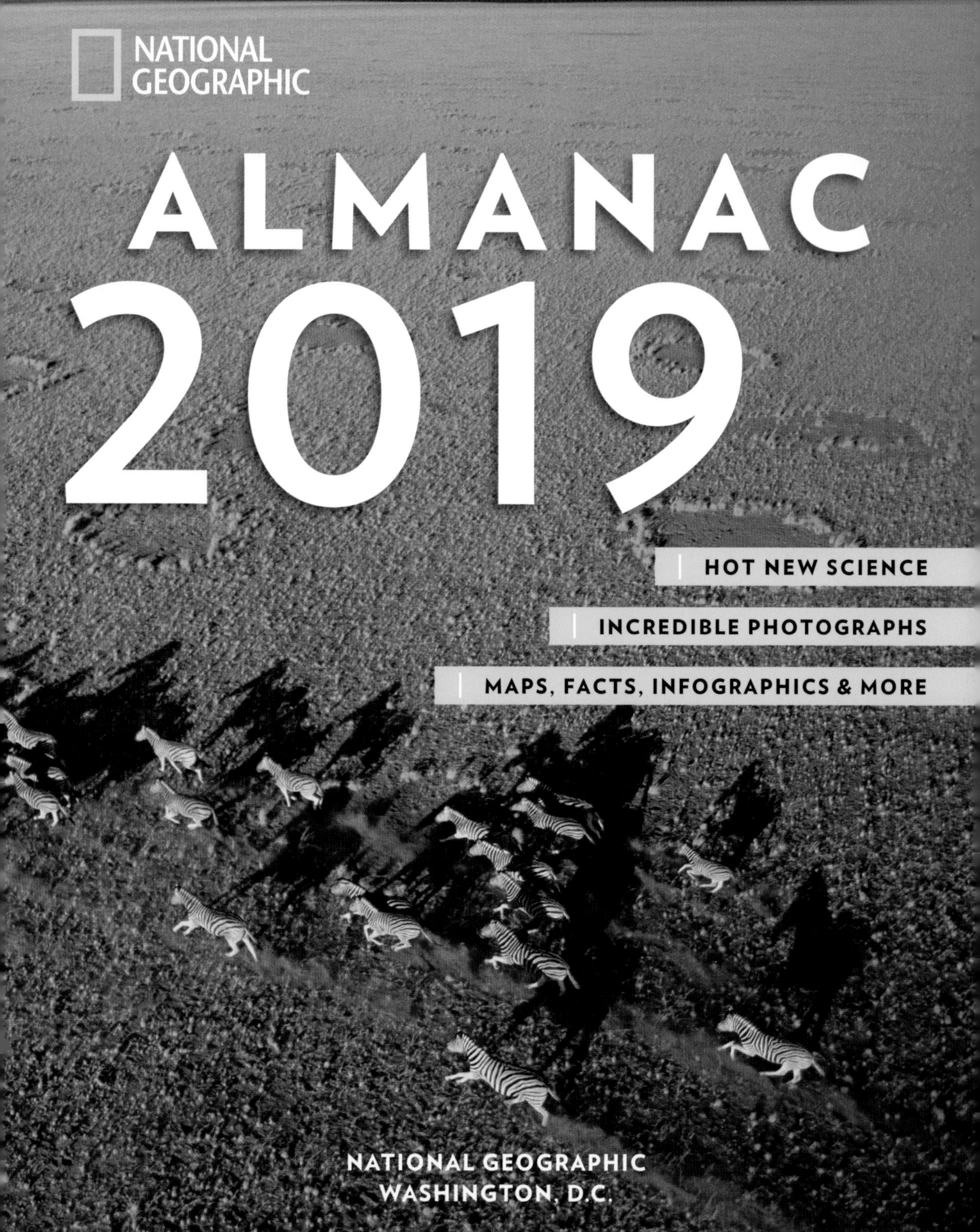

NATIONAL GEOGRAPHIC

ALMANAC
2019

HOT NEW SCIENCE

INCREDIBLE PHOTOGRAPHS

MAPS, FACTS, INFOGRAPHICS & MORE

NATIONAL GEOGRAPHIC
WASHINGTON, D.C.

CONTENTS

A trekker explores Alaska's Mendenhall Glacier.

A jaguar peers through tall grass in Brazil's Pantanal.

The Curiosity rover eyes Mars's Mount Sharp.

Dancers wear stilts and masks at a Dogon funeral in Mali.

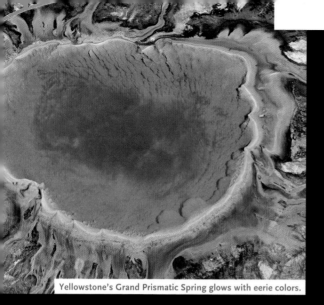
Yellowstone's Grand Prismatic Spring glows with eerie colors.

A green-cheeked conure, a parrot species, cocks its perky head.

ALWAYS
MORE TO LEARN

A climber glories in the panorama of Italy's Brenta Dolomites.

Cara Santa Maria and an albino raven at the California Wildlife Center

As a correspondent on National Geographic Channel's *Explorer,* I have the opportunity to travel the world and experience its incredible geography, wildlife, and people. It never ceases to amaze me just how many secrets planet Earth holds for us, waiting to be unlocked by our curiosity and ingenuity. Human beings have always been an inquisitive bunch, and it is this very nature that propels us forward—our insatiable hunger for knowledge is a catalyst for progress.

Unfortunately, such advancements are not without their costs. As we learn more and more about the deleterious effects our own actions have on climate, biodiversity, and the overall health of our home planet, we are driven to develop innovative solutions to these global problems. We must strike a delicate balance between our quest for knowledge and our responsibility to Mother Nature, ensuring that the decisions we make today will pave the way for a lasting, beautiful future on Earth and beyond.

It is in this spirit that I am pleased to present National Geographic's *Almanac 2019,* a compendium of adventure, science, photography, and wonder that will spark your curiosity and excite your senses. This book celebrates trailblazing scientists and explorers, and the contributions they've made to our understanding of the universe. It will inspire and challenge you through its diverse pages of stunning imagery and epic storytelling.

At the beginning of each section, I will test your knowledge through various Quizmaster pages, asking questions that range from the trivial to the profound. Your curiosity will guide you through the chapters that follow, where you will gain insights from world-renowned experts with firsthand experience of nature's surprises. From history to humanity to the wonders of the cosmos, we'll leave no stone unturned and no interest "unpiqued."

Founded 130 years ago, the National Geographic Society has always been guided by a central mission, promoting "the power of exploration, science, and storytelling to change the world." I am honored to be a small part of this endeavor. Whether it is travel to Machu Picchu, exploration of Jupiter's moons, or an investigation of the medicinal effects of snake venom, getting lost in these pages will surely ignite your passion for discovery and adventure. It is my most sincere desire that the *Almanac* inspires you to dig deeper and go further in your own personal quest for knowledge.

My own interests in the human brain and its untold mysteries were instilled in me as a young child and reinforced throughout my professional journey. I am lucky enough to have a job that sustains and strengthens my love for science every single day. Projects like this book remind me that it takes a village—in fact, an entire planet—to progress together toward a more prosperous and harmonious future. Deep down, we are all scientists. The human experience is one of exploration, fascination, inquisitiveness, and awe. I am pleased to welcome you on this journey into the depths of our world. Together, we can make a difference.

TRENDING 2019

EXTREMES | PLASTIC | TO THE MOON

City of the future: Singapore's Supertrees combine nature and technology, greenery and light.

GENE EDITING | CITIES

QUIZ MASTER

The Journey Starts Here What are the most exciting things happening in science and discovery today? As we put this almanac together, we asked ourselves that question—and here are our answers: the perfect place to begin!

—CARA SANTA MARIA, *Our Favorite Nerd*

p17

WHAT WORLD CAPITAL IS DUE TO BECOME THE FIRST NATIONAL PARK CITY?

p33

HOW COLD CAN IT GET IN THE DRY VALLEYS OF ANTARCTICA?

p29

WHAT ENTITY ENACTED AN OUTER SPACE TREATY IN 1967?

p24

WHAT FOOD HAS ALREADY BEEN IMPROVED VIA CRISPR GENE-EDITING TECHNIQUES— RADISHES, BRUSSELS SPROUTS, OR MUSHROOMS?

HOW MUCH DOES VIRGIN GALACTIC CHARGE TO ROCKET INTO EARTH ORBIT?

p25

WHY IS CHINA'S MOON MISSION CALLED CHANG'E?

p24

NAME THE CAPITAL OF MONGOLIA.

p33

IN WHAT OCEAN WERE THE FIRST **EXTREMOPHILES** LIVING NEAR HYDROTHERMAL VENTS DISCOVERED?

p16

WHAT **FOUR** NATIONS HAVE **MOON** MISSIONS, PAST AND PRESENT?

p24

WHAT IS THE **LIMIT OF BACTERIA THAT NASA ALLOWS OUTSIDE ITS INTERPLANETARY SPACECRAFT?**

p17

WHEN WAS THE **HUMAN** GENOME **FIRST** SEQUENCED: 3 YEARS AGO, 10 YEARS AGO, **OR 20** YEARS AGO?

p26

WHAT PERCENTAGE OF THE WORLD'S GAS AND OIL GOES INTO MAKING PLASTIC?

p21

WHAT IS MEXICO'S NAICA MINE, NEAR CHIHUAHUA, FAMOUS FOR?

p14

WHAT'S A CHEMICAL COMPATIBILIZER FOR— DIVING SAFELY TO THE OCEAN BOTTOM, RECYCLING PLASTIC, OR BREATHING IN THE MOON'S ATMOSPHERE?

p21

EXTREMES

LIFE ON THE EDGE

Think life is fragile? Think again. Rugged explorers and amazingly engineered robots are reaching the deepest, highest, driest, strangest, and most extreme environments on our planet, and we are finding new life-forms everywhere. Whether conditions are boiling hot, crushingly deep, parchingly dry, or chemically toxic, life has found a way. Discoveries are redefining where ecosystems exist and pushing the boundaries of what it means to be alive. Creatures that are rewriting the history of life on Earth also offer tantalizing glimpses of what life might look like on another planet.

Selenite crystals in Mexico's Naica mine harbor bacteria and keep them alive, though dormant, in these extreme conditions.

RESEARCHERS PROBING LAKE WHILLANS, 2,625 FEET UNDER THE ICE IN ANTARCTICA, FOUND ALMOST 4,000 SPECIES OF MICROBES ALIVE DESPITE THE INHOSPITABLE ENVIRONMENT.

TAKING IT TO THE MAX

REVISING OUR DEFINITIONS OF LIFE

A hydrothermal vent in the Mariana Trench

HYDROTHERMAL VENTS

THE BLACK BOILING SEA

In 1977, geologists exploring the Pacific Ocean floor along the Galápagos Rift stumbled onto an alien landscape that reshaped our definition of life. Over a mile below the surface, in pitch black, deep-sea explorers discovered a living world filled with extremophiles—crabs, worms, shrimp, and bacteria that clustered around a boiling, billowing hydrothermal vent, where temperatures can reach 750°F (399°C). How could there be life-forms bathing in the heavy metal ash of a black smoker? Their metabolic systems were chemosynthetic, generating energy by consuming the chemicals spewing from the vents. Today, hydrothermal vents remain fascinating to both scientists and the public—oceanic oases that also suggest the potential of life-forms hidden beneath the oceans of other worlds.

CRYSTAL COCOONS

TIME-TRAVELING MICROBES

A quarter mile beneath the rocky landscape of Chihuahua, Mexico, inside the Naica mine, are the famous crystal caves, where temperatures range around 150°F (65°C) with up to 99 percent humidity. Giant crystals 30 feet long erupt from the walls. But the real secrets may be deeper within. Inside these crystals are microbial worlds, undisturbed for 50,000 years. Genetically distinct from anything else on Earth, these microbes have survived encased in crystal, deprived of light and oxygen for all this time. Yet when scientists brought them out of the cave and into the laboratory, they found the microbes were dormant, not dead. For scientists, the idea is vexing—and tantalizing: If life could survive for so long on Earth, could similar life-forms be hiding beneath the surface of Mars, Venus, or the moons of Jupiter?

Mexico's Cave of the Crystals

Gondola Ridge and the Mackay Glacier in Antarctica

ANTARCTIC EXTREMES

A FROZEN WORLD

The Dry Valleys of Antarctica are the most punishing place on a punishing continent. Temperatures drop to -90° F (-68°C) and the winds can reach 200 miles an hour, enough to carve holes in the rocks. In a land covered in sheets of ice, these valleys are the driest place on Earth. The region has no liquid water and what little ice exists came as frozen vapor on the intense wind. But here too life has found a way. Lichens and moss, even microscopic worms called nematodes, can grow inside sheltered rocks. This is the closest analog on Earth to the surface of Mars, and it offers clues to life-forms as well as experimental locations to model human habitation of the red planet.

EXTREMOPHILE LIFE-FORMS HAVE BEEN FOUND THRIVING AMID TOXIC WASTE, ORGANIC SOLVENTS, AND HEAVY METALS, WHERE MOST LIFE WOULD PERISH.

NASA's James Webb Telescope in a "clean tent"

DON'T SPREAD GERMS

A THREAT TO THE SOLAR SYSTEM?

Earth is teeming with life—in our clouds, our soil, and our water. As we search for life on other planets, we need to be sure we didn't bring it with us. To do this, NASA has created an Office of Planetary Protection to protect us from the solar system and, equally important, to protect the solar system from us. To keep human missions from infecting the planets they visit, the goal is to keep the craft so clean that fewer than 300,000 bacteria can be found on its exterior. That may sound like a lot, but the skin on your hands can contain 4.6 million bacteria! To keep spacecraft clean on the way to launch, NASA builds them in specially designed clean rooms, exposing them to intense heat, radiation, chemicals, and other protocols to sterilize them.

PLASTIC

RETHINKING THE MIRACLE MATERIAL

Plastics are a wondrous group of materials. They can be as soft as a pair of nylons or as solid as a sewer pipe. What's more, they're easy to create—and hard to break down. This is great for manufacturing and durability but hard on planet Earth. Now we find ourselves trying to reshape our love affair with disposable plastics through changing what they're made from, how they are used, and where they end up. Technological breakthroughs promise ways that we can make the most of this miracle material without it harming the environment.

Ocean currents collect floating mounds of plastic waste like this one 15 miles off the coast of Roatán, Honduras, in the Caribbean.

THE FIRST PLASTICS WERE INVENTED IN 1869 TO CREATE SUBSTITUTES FOR IVORY.

THE STUFF THAT WILL NOT GO AWAY

MODERN WONDER, FUTURE SCOURGE

A sea turtle bypassing plastic entangled with seaweed

OCEAN WOES

FLOATING FLOTSAM

The North Pacific Subtropical Gyre is an oceanic dead spot—a calm eye at the heart of currents flowing around the vast ocean. It's also the last stop on an oceanic spin cycle, trapping any debris that falls in or floats away. Old shoes, milk jugs, grocery bags, and more create a plastic and seawater soup. Our love of plastics has changed the Pacific gyre into the Great Pacific Garbage Patch, a virtual sea of abandoned plastic. Clever engineers are developing new technologies to gather and isolate this floating debris to help clean the ocean—one important step in the worldwide process of reducing plastic waste in our landscapes and seas. The best method to reduce the garbage patch remains the simplest: Use less plastic.

MICROPLASTICS

AN INVISIBLE PROBLEM

Plastics aren't just all around you. They're also in you and on you. They come from plastic microbead ingredients in commercial products—toothpastes, exfoliants, and other items—that have been on the market for decades. Some countries like the United States and the United Kingdom are now banning microbeads in personal products but leaving commercial and industrial use untouched. As such, the ocean receives a dump truck's worth of plastic pollution every minute. Other microplastics form when plastic waste breaks apart into small pieces in the environment. Unlike larger ocean debris, these microscopic pieces can't be collected by any net, and they often wind up entering the food chain.

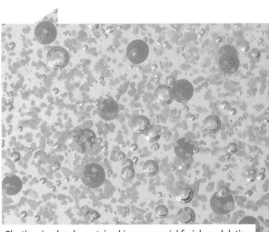

Plastic microbeads contained in commercial facial scrub lotion

Plastic materials being sorted for recycling

SCIENTISTS HAVE DISCOVERED SPECIES OF BACTERIA THAT CAN BREAK DOWN PETROLEUM-BASED PLASTICS.

RECYCLING PLASTIC

RETHINKING REUSE

There are literally thousands of types of plastic on the planet, and recycling it used to be a slow, meticulous process. Many types of plastic can't be recycled together, separating like oil and water. Recycling programs often lose money, due to the need to sort and clean each piece of plastic recycled. Thank goodness, new technologies are enabling recycling plants to sort plastics more efficiently before shredding and melting them down into the tiny beads that are then used to make new products. Chemists are also creating chemical "compatibilizers" that let different plastics be recycled together and new catalysts that speed up the process of shredding and remelting. Chemistry made plastics possible—and new chemistry may help turn the plastic tide.

A WORD FROM

Reduce, Reuse, Rethink   Maybe it isn't plastic that is to blame, but our inability to understand the material. How we use it, what we're using it for, and, more importantly, how we dispose of it so that it doesn't end up in our oceans. If you really want to get involved, you look at it and say let's make waste a resource, and you start to reduce, reuse, recycle, and rethink. You fundamentally start to change your perception of your role on this planet to lessen your human fingerprint.

—**DAVID DE ROTHSCHILD,** *inventor of Plastiki, a boat made of plastic bottles*

Biodegradable and hence compostable plastic cups

BIOPLASTICS

THE NEXT "MATERIAL OF THE FUTURE"?

Plastics are a key by-product of the world's oil and gas industry. Over 4 percent of all global oil and gas production goes to make plastic products, many designed for disposability: straws and spoons, cups and wrappers. It's a troubling paradox of our modern world: The things we plan on throwing away are made of the material least likely to decompose. Now materials scientists believe they have an answer: bioplastics. Made from pulped plants instead of fossil fuels, bioplastics use the sugar in corn, beets, or sugarcane to create the long chains of molecules needed to make plastic. Because they are made from organic plant material, they can be composted after use and turned into soil. Bioplastic cups, cutlery, and even trash bags are already on the market—and making a difference.

TO THE MOON

ANOTHER GIANT LEAP

In 1969, the United States sent astronauts to the moon and made history. For the first time, humans were leaving our warm and comfortable home to set foot elsewhere in the solar system. Today other countries and even private companies are exploring a return to the moon. As these countries take their first steps toward the moon and beyond, to explore Mars and elsewhere, humanity faces questions about how we protect worlds not our own and how we preserve the history made there.

Every Full Moon
HAS A NAME

JANUARY
Wolf Moon, Old Moon

FEBRUARY
Snow Moon, Hunger Moon

MARCH
Worm Moon, Sap Moon, Crow Moon

APRIL
Pink Moon, Grass Moon, Fish Moon

MAY
Flower Moon, Planting Moon

JUNE
Strawberry Moon, Rose Moon

JULY
Buck Moon, Thunder Moon, Hay Moon

AUGUST
Sturgeon Moon, Red Moon

SEPTEMBER
Harvest Moon, Corn Moon

OCTOBER
Hunter's Moon

NOVEMBER
Beaver Moon, Frost Moon

DECEMBER
Cold Moon, Long Night's Moon

A supermoon rises over Mongolia, as seen from the International Space Station.

"HAVING SOME PERMANENT PRESENCE ON ANOTHER HEAVENLY BODY . . . AND THEN GETTING PEOPLE TO MARS AND BEYOND—THAT'S THE CONTINUANCE OF THE DREAM OF APOLLO THAT I THINK PEOPLE ARE REALLY LOOKING FOR."

—ELON MUSK, CEO OF SPACEX AND TESLA

OUR OWN SATELLITE

BACK TO THE MOON, THIS TIME TO STAY

China's first moon rover launch, 2013

THE MOON GODDESS

THE NEXT SPACE RACE

In 2013, China's Chang'e 3 lander and its Yutu rover achieved the first soft landing on the moon since Russia's Luna 24 mission in 1976. There's more to come, since the moon is becoming 2019's hottest ticket. More Chang'e missions, named after the Chinese moon goddess, are headed back. Chang'e 4 and Chang'e 5 will explore the unknown regions on the far side of the moon. India's Chandrayaan program (its name from the Sanskrit for "moon vehicle") set a craft in moon orbit and will target a landing soon. With four key nations intent on moon exploration—China, Russia, India, and the U.S.—international cooperation may be the best way to make more footprints in the lunar dust.

LUNAR LEGACIES

HISTORIC PRESERVATION OFF-PLANET

The lunar landing sites of the Apollo program are safe from disruption now, and several organizations want to keep them that way. A proposal by researchers at New Mexico State University would create the first off-planet historic parks. They would protect the various lunar landers that have been left on the moon's surface by prohibiting future missions from utilizing those sites for landing or even visiting. The action raises fascinating questions of sovereignty: Although the lunar landers belong to the nation that launched them, under the United Nations' 1967 Outer Space Treaty, no country can claim land on the moon, even for the sake of preservation. For now, NASA has issued guidelines to keep Apollo's landing sites off-limits, until more formal protection can be created.

Apollo 17's lunar module and rover

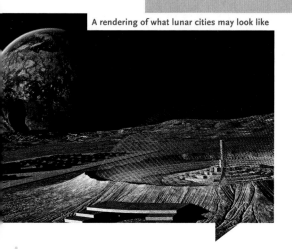
A rendering of what lunar cities may look like

THE GOOGLE LUNAR X PRIZE OFFERED $30 MILLION FOR A MOON LANDING, TRAVEL, AND VIDEO TRANSMISSION BY 2018—BUT NO ONE SUCCEEDED.

A Tesla Roadster en route to Mars

GET YOUR TICKETS NOW

TRANSPLANETARY TOURISM?

Private companies like SpaceX, Virgin Galactic, and Space Adventures are developing the translunar tourism businesses of the future. Virgin Galactic's new SpaceShip Two craft is being tested to carry six commercial astronauts into orbit at a cost of $250,000 each, and Virginia-based Space Adventures has patrons willing to spend millions of dollars on visits to the International Space Station. Space Adventures even has options for a full spacewalk, if you can afford it. SpaceX plans to start with a week-long lunar flyby for some lucky duo, following the arc of Apollo 8 and powered by its reusable Falcon Heavy rocket. Thus far, no commercial itineraries venture farther than these—out beyond Earth's orbit—but the race is on.

ON THE WAY TO MARS

INTERPLANETARY PIT STOP

Reaching the moon will be an epic challenge, but for futurists, the moon is merely a stepping-stone on man's journey across the solar system. These scientists envision the moon as a testing site, construction yard, and refueling stop for missions to Mars and beyond. The moon is a perfect test bed for space exploration—beyond the atmosphere and gravity of Earth, with all the requirements a rocket program would need. Lunar ice can be harvested to create hydrogen fuel for rockets. Rare elements—like helium-3, used in nuclear power plants, or rare earth metals, used in electronics—can be mined. Even the metals for construction are here. Futurists envision our small satellite as a lunar pit stop where astronauts can fuel, supply, and maybe even create the next step in interplanetary travel.

GENE EDITING

REWRITING THE GENOME

Geneticists first published a rough draft of the human genetic code nearly two decades ago, and even before that scientists had been trying to manipulate it. With emerging technologies like the "genetic scissors" known as CRISPR (clustered regularly interspaced short palindromic repeats), we can now target and edit specific stretches of DNA for desired results. So far these techniques have been used to reduce the spread of malaria from mosquitoes, identify early signs of infection, treat cancer, and respond to genetic defects. Laboratories worldwide are exploring new applications.

Zhong Zhong and Hua Hua, two macaques created in 2018 by Chinese researchers, are genetically identical, both cloned from the same donor culture of fetal monkey cells.

THE SOLUTION TO ANTIBIOTIC-RESISTANT BACTERIA MAY LIE IN GENE EDITING. RESEARCHERS ARE WORKING ON TECHNIQUES THAT TRIGGER SELF-DESTRUCT SEQUENCES IN THE BACTERIA'S DNA.

DNA REVOLUTION

HOW IT WORKS IN NATURE

Researchers studying how viruses infect bacteria discovered a natural immune system that cuts the invader's DNA.

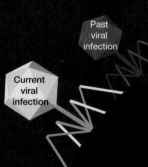

Past viral infection

Current viral infection

Ventral tegmental area (VTA)
Dopamine is produced here and flows outward along neurons distributed throughout the brain's reward system.

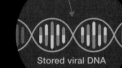

1. Genetic memory card
When a virus attacks, a bacterium captures and stores a segment of the intruder's DNA sequence.

Stored viral DNA

How to Hack DNA

Some bacteria have evolved a powerful system, called CRISPR, to fight viral infections. When a virus strikes, a bacterium captures and stores a short, identifying sequence of the virus's DNA—a sort of genetic "memory card." If the same virus attacks future generations of the bacteria, they use the memory card to guide a killer enzyme to the identical sequence in the new invader and cut it away. Scientists have co-opted this natural molecular machinery not only to turn off the action of a gene, but also to insert new genetic code into living organisms, including humans. CRISPR has sparked an explosion of research—and a heated ethical debate.

2. A new attack
When the virus invades again, the bacterium generates a copy of the memory card, called guide RNA, to seek out the matching sequence in the attacking virus's genome.

Guide RNA

CRISPR-Cas9

Cutting enzyme (Cas9)

3. Arming the defense
The guide RNA recruits an enzyme, Cas9. The CRISPR-Cas9 pair scans the viral double helix, looking for a telltale marker to the DNA sequence stored in memory.

Marker

4. Cutting the code
When the marker is found, CRISPR-Cas9 unzips the sequence. If it's a match, the viral DNA is cut. It then degrades and is prevented from reproducing.

HOW IT'S HARNESSED IN THE LAB

Scientists realized they could adapt this mechanism to disable genes or insert DNA into any organism.

Hacking the system
Scientists can begin to understand gene function by turning a gene on and off. To do this, they program CRISPR-Cas9 structures in a lab to snip DNA and disable genes that affect health and crops.

Customized genomes
Synthetic DNA sequences can also be engineered in the lab and spliced in at the site of the cut, introducing desired traits into an organism, such as resistance to a parasite.

Unlimited possibilities
With CRISPR, scientists can alter and edit any genome that has been sequenced—quickly, cheaply, and efficiently.

APPLICATIONS FOR CRISPR TECHNOLOGY

Treating Disease
Genome-editing technology is revealing which DNA sequences are involved in diseases such as AIDS.

Altering Ecology
The spread of vector-borne illnesses like malaria could be reduced by introducing disease-resistant genes into wild insect populations.

Transforming Food
CRISPR could be used to develop drought-resistant or otherwise hardier crops. CRISPR mushrooms that don't brown have already been approved in the U.S.

Editing Humans?
Experiments with nonviable embryos show that much work will have to be done—and many questions answered—before CRISPR can be used to edit humans.

CITIES

THE EMERGENCE OF *HOMO URBANUS*

In 2008, humanity crossed a revolutionary milestone as we became a majority urban species. At the same time, new technologies and new ways of thinking are changing our understanding of cities and what it means to live an urban lifestyle. Traffic lights communicate with smart cars, old subways become new green space, and whole patches of steel and concrete transform into national parks. The cities of the future are being created today, and the world will change as a result.

A futuristic vision of Manhattan mixes old and new with lots of green.

PROJECTIONS SUGGEST WE WILL ADD 2.4 BILLION PEOPLE TO THE WORLD'S POPULATION BY 2050, WITH NEARLY 90 PERCENT OF THE INCREASE HAPPENING IN THE CITIES OF ASIA AND AFRICA.

IT'S AN URBAN WORLD

REVOLUTIONIZING OUR WAY THROUGH CITY STREETS

View of London from Greenwich Park

GREEN CITIES

TRANSFORMING THE CONCRETE JUNGLE

As green technologies become all the rage, scientists are starting to understand the values of green spaces as well. Studies reveal that even small parks can help increase health, social interaction, community support, and even general happiness. Whole cities can be defined by their green spaces: the National Mall in Washington, D.C., Central Park in New York, or the Tuileries Gardens in Paris, for example. Now new cities are getting into the act. Atlanta, Georgia, has transformed its old rail line into a massive greenbelt around the city. Mexico City has created vertical gardens to scrub the air of pollution, while Singapore has created new Supertrees—massive structures supporting more than 150,000 plants in an urban oasis.

SMART CITIES

A NEW DIGITAL LANDSCAPE

What happens when the grid meets the cloud? When the infrastructure that runs our cities collides with the big data that sort out our lives? The answer is being discovered in two different corners of the world. Oslo, Norway, connected all of the city's streetlamps to a digital command center that controls timers, dimmers, and energy supply. Within a single year, city managers cut the lighting costs for the city by 20 percent while improving service and response times. In San Diego, California, a similar project is going even further, integrating cameras, microphones, and pollution detectors into the city's smart streetlight system. The next step is to integrate autonomous vehicles and traffic flow—all urban improvements that will power the future while protecting the planet.

How self-driving cars could navigate streets

Rooftop gardens turn urban space greener.

CITY AS PARK

LONDON'S GOING GREEN
London is already one of the greenest cities on the planet, with almost half its area dedicated to gardens, parks, or open space. Now visionaries are making plans to increase that area and transform the entire metropolis into the first National Park City. The idea would empower the city to celebrate its unique ecology as much as its iconic architecture. The National Park map would help people find urban farms and community gardens, as well as nature hikes and kayak rentals, and connect people with the natural world that's all around them. Other cities are getting in on the action too, transforming abandoned areas or yesterday's infrastructure into the urban parks of tomorrow.

POP!

CITIES OF THE FUTURE
- San Fransokyo in *Big Hero 6* (2014)
- NeoSeoul in *Cloud Atlas* (2012)
- Mega-City One in *Dredd* (2012)
- The Capital in *Hunger Games* (2012)
- Bregna in *Aeon Flux* (2005)
- Zion in *The Matrix* (1999)
- Neo-Tokyo in *Akira* (1988)
- Mingo City in *Flash Gordon* (1980)
- City of Domes in *Logan's Run* (1976)
- Metropolis in *Metropolis* (1927)

THE NUMBER OF CITY DWELLERS IN SUB-SAHARAN AFRICA, WITH THE WORLD'S HIGHEST RATE OF URBANIZATION, WILL DOUBLE BETWEEN 2000 AND 2030.

Rocinha, in Rio de Janeiro, is Brazil's largest favela.

SLUM SMARTS

NATURAL COMMUNITIES
Shanty town. Slum. The wrong side of the tracks. Home. Whatever you call it, every metropolis has them: densely crowded neighborhoods with poor sanitation, inadequate water, and unstable housing. It's estimated that by 2030, two billion people will live in slums around the world. Some urban planners see promise in these neighborhoods, though. Slums have tightly focused local economies. They are walkable communities with social cohesion. Creating microcities—deliberately planned communities—right in the middle of slums might help bridge the gap between urban haves and have-nots. A company appropriately called Utopia is working in Ulaanbaatar, the capital of Mongolia, to create a microcity linked to the city's financial, social, and medical services. If successful, this microcity concept could save cities from the inside out.

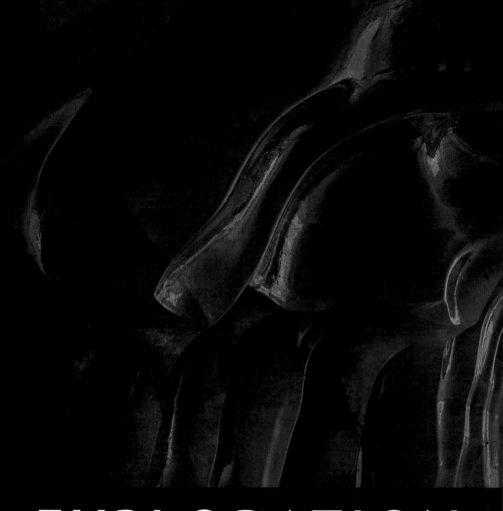

EXPLORATION & ADVENTURE

EXPLORATION | EXTREMES

Icy archway: Hikers emerge from an ice cave as they explore Alaska's Black Rapids Glacier.

QUIZ MASTER

Intrepid Explorer? Does your spirit carry you to all corners of the globe? Which are you—sophisticated traveler or courageous adventurer? Either way, you'll journey to even more destinations in this chapter.

—CARA SANTA MARIA, *Our Favorite Nerd*

IN WHAT AFRICAN COUNTRY WAS MAD MAX: FURY ROAD FILMED?

p84

THROUGH WHAT THREE **AFRICAN COUNTRIES** DOES THE OKAVANGO RIVER FLOW?

p43

WHEN DID SOCCER BECOME AN OLYMPIC SPORT?

p61

WHICH OF THESE SITES DID **HIRAM BINGHAM** DISCOVER: CHICHÉN ITZÁ, **MACHU PICCHU,** OR **TEOTIHUACAN?**

p68

WHAT 16TH-CENTURY **CHINESE SCIENTIST** INVENTED A ROCKET CHAIR?

WHAT IS THE WORLD'S LARGEST FRESH WATER LAKE?

p54

WHEN DID THE FIRST AMERICAN **CLIMBING** TEAM SUMMIT **MOUNT** EVEREST?

p53

p62

NAME THE **EASTERNMOST** NATIONAL PARK IN THE UNITED STATES.

p73

IF YOU WANT TO GO **SAND** TOBOGGANING, **WHAT'S** THE BEST DESTINATION IN **TEXAS?**

p47

OF THE SEVEN **ANCIENT** WONDERS OF **THE WORLD,** HOW MANY CAN STILL BE **VISITED AND** WHICH ONES ARE THEY?

p64

WHAT IS THE **EXTREME SPORT** THAT ALEX HONNOLD IS FAMOUS FOR— **SKY DIVING,** FREE SOLOING, **HIGHLINING,** FREE DIVING, OR PARASAILING?

p50

IN WHAT CENTURY AND CONTINENT **DO WE FIND** EVIDENCE OF EARLIEST **USE OF A COMPASS?**

p38

WHAT ARE **GREEN** BOMBERS AND WHY ARE THEY **CALLED THAT?**

p44

WHAT DO ALL THESE CITIES HAVE IN COMMON: **DYERSVILLE, IOWA;** RAVELLO, ITALY; SWAKOPMUND, **NAMIBIA; AND HAMILTON,** NEW ZEALAND?

p84

EXPLORATION
TIME LINE

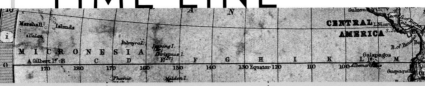

PREHISTORY	2000 to 1 BC	AD 1 to 1000	1000 to 1500

PREHISTORY

■ **80,000 ya***
Homo sapiens moves out of Africa.

■ **ca 75,000 ya**
Modern humans reach Southeast Asia.

■ **ca 65,000 ya**
Humans reach Australia.

■ **ca 15,000 BC**
First settlements appear in North America.

■ **ca 8000 BC**
Dogs help pull sleds over snow.

■ **ca 6300 BC**
Earliest known boat is made.

■ **ca 2300 BC**
The earliest known maps are produced in Mesopotamia.

* *years ago*

2000 to 1 BC

■ **ca 2000 BC**
Austronesians settle on various islands in the South Pacific.

■ **ca 700 BC**
Celts are introducing Iron Age technology to Europe.

■ **240 BC**
Greek mathematician Eratosthenes calculates the circumference of the Earth.

■ **ca 115 BC**
Early trade agreements form between Chinese and European powers.

AD 1 to 1000

■ **150**
Ptolemy maps the world in his *Geography*.

■ **271**
A compass is first used in China.

■ **ca 400**
Polynesian seafarers settle the Hawaiian Islands.

■ **ca 600**
Silk Road is in full use, with China absorbing influences from the West.

■ **1000**
Viking longships under the command of Leif Eriksson cross the Atlantic and reach North America.

1000 to 1500

■ **1050**
Arab astronomers and navigators introduce the astrolabe to Europe.

■ **1271**
Marco Polo sets off on a four-year, 7,500-mile journey from Venice, Italy, to Shangdu, China.

■ **1331**
Arab traveler Ibn Battuta visits East Africa as part of a long voyage through the Islamic world.

■ **1492**
Christopher Columbus lands on a Caribbean island that he names Hispaniola.

■ **1499**
Italian navigator Amerigo Vespucci explores the northeast coastline of South America.

| 1500 to 1750 | 1750 to 1900 | 1900 to 1950 | 1950 to PRESENT |

1500 to 1750

■ 1513
Ponce de León arrives in today's Florida, first of the Spanish conquistadors in the Americas.

■ 1519
Ferdinand Magellan begins his circum-navigation of the globe.

■ 1535
Jacques Cartier travels up St. Lawrence River to site of today's Montreal.

■ 1595
Gerardus Mercator's first atlas is published.

■ 1607
The English establish Jamestown on the James River in North America.

■ 1722
The Dutch land on Easter Island.

1750 to 1900

■ 1768
Britain's Capt. James Cook begins exploring the Pacific Ocean.

■ 1799
The Rosetta Stone is discovered in Egypt.

■ 1804–1806
Lewis and Clark run an expedition across the western territory of what is now the United States.

■ 1841
The first wagon trains to cross the Rocky Moun-tains arrive in California.

■ 1891
Construction begins on the Trans-Siberian Railroad.

1900 to 1950

■ 1901
The city of Fairbanks is settled on the Alaskan frontier.

■ 1904
Much of Chichén Itzá is discovered, in Mexico.

■ 1909
Cmdr. Robert E. Peary and Matthew Henson lead the first expedition to the North Pole.

■ 1937
Amelia Earhart disappears during an attempt at a flight around the world.

■ 1946
Richard E. Byrd leads an expedition to the South Pole.

1950 to PRESENT

■ 1953
Edmund Hillary and Tenzing Norgay reach Mount Everest's summit.

■ 1957
The U.S.S.R. launches Sputnik 1, setting off a space race with America.

■ 1960
Jacques Piccard becomes the first human to visit the Challenger Deep, the deepest point in the ocean.

■ 1969
Apollo 11 lands men on the moon.

■ 1990
The Hubble Space Telescope is put into operation.

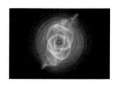

■ 2004
NASA's Spirit and Opportunity rovers land on Mars.

NAT GEO EXPLORERS
AROUND THE WORLD

GROUNDBREAKERS AND CHANGEMAKERS IN THE FIELD

National Geographic scientists, conservationists, and storytellers
are innovators who are making a difference and changing the world.

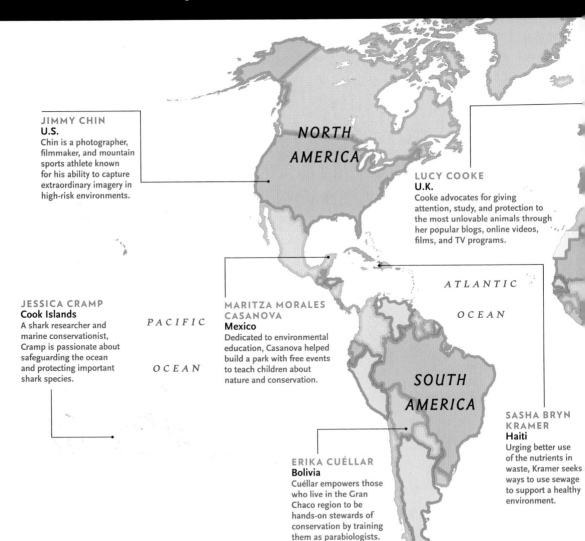

JIMMY CHIN
U.S.
Chin is a photographer, filmmaker, and mountain sports athlete known for his ability to capture extraordinary imagery in high-risk environments.

NORTH AMERICA

LUCY COOKE
U.K.
Cooke advocates for giving attention, study, and protection to the most unlovable animals through her popular blogs, online videos, films, and TV programs.

JESSICA CRAMP
Cook Islands
A shark researcher and marine conservationist, Cramp is passionate about safeguarding the ocean and protecting important shark species.

PACIFIC

OCEAN

MARITZA MORALES CASANOVA
Mexico
Dedicated to environmental education, Casanova helped build a park with free events to teach children about nature and conservation.

ATLANTIC

OCEAN

SOUTH AMERICA

SASHA BRYN KRAMER
Haiti
Urging better use of the nutrients in waste, Kramer seeks ways to use sewage to support a healthy environment.

ERIKA CUÉLLAR
Bolivia
Cuéllar empowers those who live in the Gran Chaco region to be hands-on stewards of conservation by training them as parabiologists.

"EVERY NATIONAL GEOGRAPHIC EXPLORER IS INFINITELY CURIOUS ABOUT OUR PLANET, COMMITTED TO UNDERSTANDING IT, AND PASSIONATE ABOUT HELPING MAKE IT BETTER."

—GARY KNELL, CEO, NATIONAL GEOGRAPHIC PARTNERS

JØRN HURUM
Norway
Hurum excavates specimens from one of the biggest locations of Jurassic marine reptiles in the world, connecting new dots in the evolutionary story.

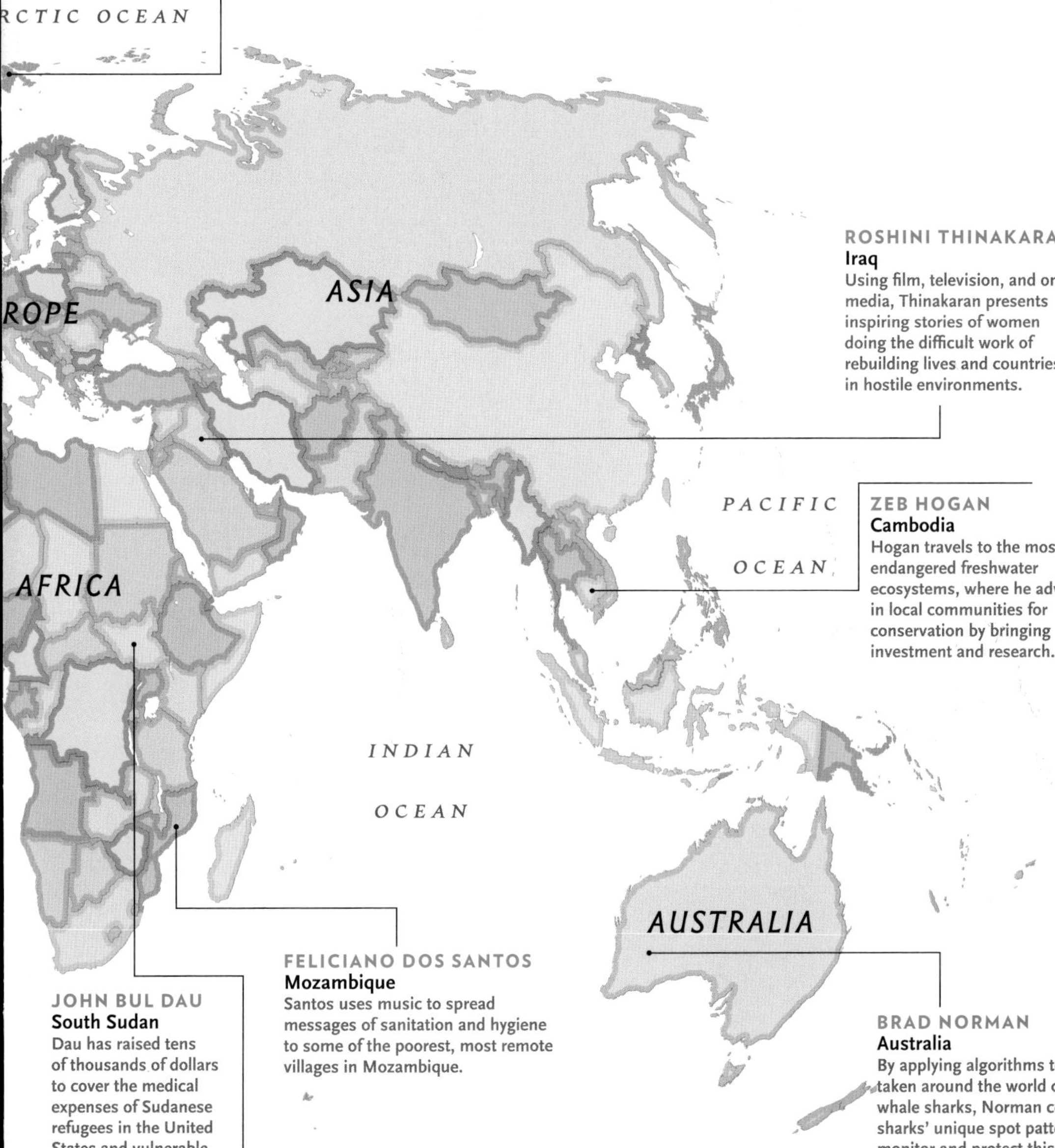

RCTIC OCEAN
ROPE
ASIA
AFRICA
PACIFIC OCEAN
INDIAN OCEAN
AUSTRALIA

ROSHINI THINAKARAN
Iraq
Using film, television, and online media, Thinakaran presents inspiring stories of women doing the difficult work of rebuilding lives and countries in hostile environments.

ZEB HOGAN
Cambodia
Hogan travels to the most endangered freshwater ecosystems, where he advocates in local communities for conservation by bringing investment and research.

JOHN BUL DAU
South Sudan
Dau has raised tens of thousands of dollars to cover the medical expenses of Sudanese refugees in the United States and vulnerable children in South Sudan.

FELICIANO DOS SANTOS
Mozambique
Santos uses music to spread messages of sanitation and hygiene to some of the poorest, most remote villages in Mozambique.

BRAD NORMAN
Australia
By applying algorithms to snapshots taken around the world of massive whale sharks, Norman compares sharks' unique spot patterns to monitor and protect this highly elusive, migratory, and threatened species.

STEVE BOYES
CONSERVATIONIST

IN LOVE WITH THE LAND

Steve Boyes first traveled to the nearly untouched Okavango Delta in Botswana to become a safari guide and camp manager. African parrot conservation kept him coming back. Now he works tirelessly to explore and protect the delta and the animals flourishing there.

Boyes and his team paddle, pole, and portage through central Africa each year.

The greater Okavango River Basin is the largest freshwater wetland in southern Africa and the main source of water for a million people. Its delta—which National Geographic Fellow Steve Boyes describes as "the beating heart of our planet"—is one of Africa's richest places for biodiversity. The world's largest remaining elephant population makes its home here, as do lions, cheetahs, wild dogs, and hundreds of species of birds. Now, due in part to Boyes's campaign combining high-quality research and community-based conservation action, the delta is a UNESCO World Heritage site, a designation protecting it indefinitely from agriculture and extractive industry.

PRESERVING A RARE HABITAT

In 2010, Boyes made the first documented journey across the Okavango Delta. It was surprisingly pristine because regional wars had made it difficult to reach the river, which runs from the highlands of Angola, through Namibia, and into the Kalahari Desert in Botswana, where it flattens out into the delta. Each subsequent year, he returns to a different 200-plus-mile section of the delta to gather data with a growing team of experts, photographers, and local guides.

The goal? For the team to generate data, maps, and media that help identify opportunities not just for conservation, but also for tourism development, which helps local communities diversify their economies even as they establish a wildlife reserve. "It's not just about the adventure," he says. "How do you convince billions of people around the world that have no opportunity to even see nature or stars to care enough about it to conserve it?"

> " THIS IS ONE OF THOSE LAST CHANCES TO SAVE A WILD RIVER, THE LAST CHANCE TO SAVE THE ELEPHANTS, THE LAST CHANCE TO SAVE THE LAST WETLAND WILDERNESS IN AFRICA—OR IN THE WORLD."

When at home in South Africa, Boyes teaches forest rehabilitation.

KEY DATES

Boyes's
ACHIEVEMENTS

■ **2009**
Founded the Wild Bird Trust and serves as scientific director

■ **2015**
Launched the Okavango Wilderness Project and embarked on a four-month, 1,578-mile expedition of the Okavango River; Okavango Delta designated 1,000th UNESCO World Heritage site

■ **2016**
Secured $10 million commitment from National Geographic Society for the Okavango Wilderness Project

■ **2017**
Conducted first round of dives in delta's source lakes, revealing 96 fish species

■ **2018**
Documentary *Into the Okavango* has its world premiere at Tribeca Film Festival

EXPLORING DEEP OCEANS

95 PERCENT OF EARTH'S LARGEST HABITAT IS UNEXPLORED

Deepsea Challenger sub carries James Cameron to Challenger Deep.

NEW TECHNOLOGY

A DIFFERENT KIND OF SPACECRAFT

The ocean, many say, is the next frontier for humans to explore, map, and exploit. This sentiment takes on urgency when one considers how the negative effects of our presence—pollution, climate change, mining, and fishing—are changing the seas and the creatures in them. Though we are eager to mount expeditions into space as quickly as possible, the cosmos will remain largely unchanged in the meantime. We may, however, have only centuries or even decades to explore our oceans before they are irreversibly altered—as widespread coral reef die-offs make evident. Demand is growing for submersible remotely operated vehicles, cameras, and other instruments that are resilient enough to withstand the pressures, temperatures, and trip durations that make some destinations inhospitable to humans.

DEEP-SEA CREATURES

LUMINOUS LIFE

As scientists explore the deeper reaches of the sea, they discover previously unknown luminous species, such as "green bombers"—deep-sea swimming worms that release sacs of bright green light when attacked—which were identified and described by marine biologists at the Monterey Bay Aquarium Research Institute. They estimate that three-quarters of the animals dwelling in depths up to two and half miles have bioluminescence. Near the surface are jellyfish, followed deeper down by worms and then larvaceans, a zooplankton resembling tadpoles. Some upcoming challenges in this growing field of research include measuring bioluminescence and understanding how these creatures will be affected by changing oxygen levels due to climate change.

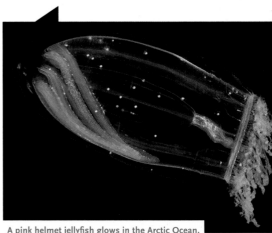

A pink helmet jellyfish glows in the Arctic Ocean.

Giant tube worms cluster near a vent in the Galápagos Rift.

THERMAL VENTS

UNEXPECTED COLONIES

The study of hydrothermal vent ecosystems has redefined our understanding of the requirements for life. It was thought that all life on Earth depended on the sun's energy, through photosynthesis. But in 1977, while exploring the Galápagos Rift, scientists came across hydrothermal vents and, shockingly, a robust local community of creatures. Despite extreme temperatures and pressures, toxic minerals, and lack of sunlight, life was thriving because it generated food via chemosynthesis: the absorption of chemicals found in vent water to make organic carbon. Since then, 550 active hydrothermal vent sites have been identified.

Continued exploration of these ecosystems is also challenging models of how life began on Earth. Some scientists say that Charles Darwin's pond-and-lightning model should be replaced by the high-pressure environment found near a vent. In fact, the oldest fossils of living organisms ever found, which could be over four billion years old, come from rock in northern Quebec, Canada, that was once on the ocean floor and likely near a hydrothermal vent.

KEY DATES

Modern Exploration of
DEEP SEAS

■ **1872–1876**
H.M.S. *Challenger* circles the globe conducting research for the Royal Society of London, laying the groundwork for modern oceanography.

■ **1943**
Jacques Cousteau and Émile Gagnan engineer the Aqua-Lung, forever changing the course of human-sea interaction.

■ **1961**
The Scripps Institution of Oceanography develops the Deep Tow System, the forerunner of all remotely operated unmanned oceanographic systems.

■ **1977**
Hydrothermal vents are discovered, along with an ecosystem that survives without the energy of the sun, by a team led by Robert Ballard.

■ **2010**
The first ever Census of Marine Life catalogs the diversity, abundance, and distribution of marine species in an online database.

GET OUT INTO YOUR COUNTRY

WONDERS AND THRILLS BOTH NEAR AND FAR

Adventure enthusiasts from all over the world travel to the United States to explore stunning national parks, trek iconic trails, and immerse themselves in America's vast wilderness. Each state has its own unique landscape, packed with outdoor activities for every skill level. Don't overlook some obvious choices, for the changing seasons often bring new displays of beauty and experiences to well-known locales.

POP!

ROAD TRIP PLAYLIST

- "Big Sky Country," Chris Whitley
- "The Distance," Cake
- "Edge of Town," Middle Kids
- "Horizon," Tycho
- "Light Enough to Travel," The Be Good Tanyas
- "Lovely Day," Bill Withers
- "Ocean to City," High Highs
- "On the Road Again," Willie Nelson
- "Plan the Escape," Bat for Lashes
- "Wish You Were Here," Pink Floyd

The Navajo name for Arizona's awe-inspiring Antelope Canyon is Tse' bighanilini—"the place where water runs through rocks."

The remote Alvord Desert in Oregon is a dry lake bed.

ARIZONA

Smooth sandstone canyons attract hikers and photographers to Antelope Canyon on the Navajo Indian Reservation in Arizona. Made up of multiple canyons, the area provides hikes for all skill levels.

CALIFORNIA

Jedediah Smith Redwoods State Park in Northern California is home to trees that date back thousands of years and are only able to thrive in the state's North Coast. Take a scenic drive, snorkel in the Smith River, or camp among the majestic trees.

GEORGIA

The calm waters of the Chattahoochee River ("river of painted rocks") support rafting and trout fishing. Nearby trails are used by bird-watchers, mountain bikers, and lovers of the outdoors.

INDIANA

Autumn colors are bright around Forested Lake at Mount Saint Francis Sanctuary in Indiana. Found in the state's southern hills, the property— managed by the religious community from which it gets its name—offers paths traversing almost 400 acres.

MAINE

Fly-fishing is a favorite activity at Maine's Baxter State Park, which also rents canoes and kayaks for fishing (on an honor system) at ponds throughout the park. Rock climbing and bouldering spots are among the region's most challenging. The Appalachian Trail's northern terminus is located on Mount Katahdin.

MISSOURI

Elephant Rocks State Park, Missouri, is a sight to behold. Visitors will find 1.5-billion-year-old granite boulders, known as Nature's Circus Elephants, inside the park. The "leader of the herd" is a 27-foot-tall and 680-ton granite giant.

NEW HAMPSHIRE

Frankenstein Cliff (not as scary as it sounds) in New Hampshire's Crawford Notch State Park is a popular destination for ice climbers. Stunning ice falls, with routes to match every visitor's skill level, are usually found here from December to March.

OREGON

Oregon's barren Alvord Desert attracts campers who crave solitude and find beauty in rugged desert terrain and wide-open skies. Nearby Mann Lake draws anglers eager to catch cutthroat trout.

PENNSYLVANIA

Hyner View State Park has one of the most scenic overlooks in Pennsylvania, with a glorious view of the Susquehanna River. The six-acre park is also popular with hang gliders, who sail over the river's west branch.

TENNESSEE

Churning white-water rapids draw professional and recreational kayakers to the Caney Fork River Gorge in Tennessee's Rock Island State Park. Highlights are the ruins of an old mill and an unusual waterfall—created by the nearby dam—that comes through the walls of a gorge.

TEXAS

The dynamic desert dunes of Monahans Sandhills State Park in Texas grow and change each season, making each trip different from the last. Visitors can rent toboggans and disks for sand surfing, but bring your own horse for the equestrian trails.

UTAH

Hikers of all ages can explore the landscape created by two cinder cone volcanoes—including lava tubes and a lava flow trail—at Utah's Snow Canyon State Park. The park receives enough rainfall to feature wildflowers in spring and fall.

VIRGINIA

Fly-fishers on the New River near Blacksburg, Virginia, have the chance to catch nearly every major freshwater game fish in the state. Tubing, canoeing, and kayaking are popular activities, as is the rail-to-trail path in the New River Trail State Park.

WISCONSIN

The Apostle Islands National Lakeshore—a 21-island archipelago in Wisconsin known as the Jewels of Lake Superior—is home to thousands-year-old ice caves open to visitors for winter exploration.

BEST OF @NATGEO

OUR FAVORITE ADVENTURE PHOTOS

@shonephoto | ROBBIE SHONE
Spelunkers amid white calcite and stalactites during a caving expedition in Križna jama in Slovenia

@ladzinski | KEITH LADZINSKI
Highliner Caio Afeto balances above the clouds during a coastal storm in Rio de Janeiro.

@paulnicklen | PAUL NICKLEN
A diver and a giant ocean sunfish perform a blue-water ballet off the coast of British Columbia.

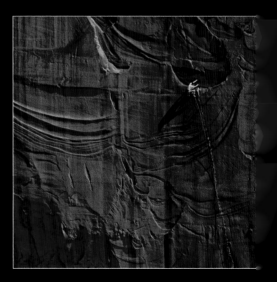

@coryrichards | CORY RICHARDS
Rock climber Alex Honnold scales the sandstone in Day Canyon, outside of Moab, Utah.

> **" A GREAT PHOTOGRAPH IS ONE THAT FULLY EXPRESSES WHAT ONE FEELS, IN THE DEEPEST SENSE, ABOUT WHAT IS BEING PHOTOGRAPHED."** —ANSEL ADAMS, PHOTOGRAPHER

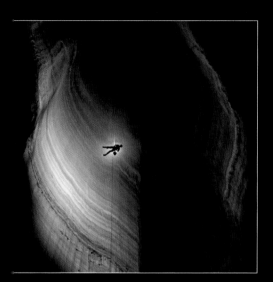

@salvarezphoto | STEPHEN ALVAREZ
A caver descends into Fantastic Pit, a nearly 600-foot-deep shaft in Georgia's Pigeon Mountain.

@shaulschwarz | SHAUL SCHWARZ
BASE jumpers take flight from Kjerag, a 3,300-foot cliff in Norway.

@jimmy_chin | JIMMY CHIN
An ice climber scales a rarely formed tunnel in the Ghost River Wilderness Area in Alberta.

@timlaman | TIM LAMAN
A climber free solos below the Channel Falls in the heart of Indonesia's Gunung Palung National Park.

ALEX HONNOLD
CLIMBER

DOING THE UNTHINKABLE

On June 3, 2017, renowned rock climber Alex Honnold became the first person ever to free solo climb the famous El Capitan rock face. Free soloing is when a climber is alone and uses no ropes or any other equipment (except shoes and a chalk bag) that aids or protects him as he climbs, leaving no margin of error.

> **" I'VE PUSHED MY** COMFORT ZONE **AND MADE IT BIGGER AND BIGGER UNTIL THESE OBJECTIVES THAT SEEMED TOTALLY** CRAZY **EVENTUALLY FELL WITHIN THE REALM OF THE** POSSIBLE.**"**

Alex Honnold dangles expertly 20 feet above deep water on the east coast of Oman, free soloing with might and muscle along this rocky shoreline.

Alex Honnold completed what may be the greatest feat of pure rock climbing in the history of the sport. He ascended the peak of Yosemite National Park's El Capitan in three hours, 56 minutes, taking the final moderate pitch at a near run. At 9:28 a.m., under a nearly cloudless sky, he pulled his body over the lip of the summit and stood on a sandy ledge the size of a child's bedroom. Honnold had begun his historic rope-less climb in the pink light of dawn at 5:32 a.m.

It's hard to overstate the physical and mental difficulties of a free solo ascent of the peak, considered by many to be the epicenter of the rock climbing world. As climber Tommy Caldwell, who has also made notable ascents in Yosemite, said of Honnold's success, "This is the 'moon landing' of free soloing."

PHYSICALLY AND MENTALLY READY

Honnold—who has climbed all over the world but calls Sacramento, California, home—was very familiar with this ascent. (A vertical expanse stretching more than a half mile up, it's higher than the world's tallest building, the Burj Khalifa in Dubai.) Back in June 2012 he free soloed all but 500 feet of the route as part of climbing the "triple" in Yosemite: a back-to-back climb of El Capitan, Half Dome, and Mount Watkins, the park's tallest formations.

Elite climbers have pointed to Honnold's unique ability to remain calm and analytical in such dangerous situations, a skill that he has developed over 20 years of climbing. There are other climbers in Honnold's league physically, but his tolerance for scary situations is so remarkable that neuroscientists have studied the parts of his brain related to fear to see how they might differ from the norm.

Honnold in the Bugaboos in eastern British Columbia, Canada

KEY DATES

Honnold's Career
HIGHS

■ **2007**
Free soloed Yosemite's Astroman and Rostrum in one day

■ **2009**
First ascent of Low's Gully gorge, Mount Kinabalu, Borneo

■ **2010**
First ascent of Rainbow Arch, Ennedi Desert, Chad

■ **2010 AND 2018**
Voted National Geographic's Adventurer of the Year—twice

■ **2012**
With Hans Florine, sets record time on Nose of El Capitan

■ **2014**
First ever to free solo University Wall, Squamish, British Columbia

■ **2017**
First ever to free solo El Capitan, Yosemite

A HISTORY OF CLIMBING EVEREST

PROPELLED BY AMBITION AND AWE

For generations, the mountain we know as Everest was a presence to be honored, not conquered. But once British mountaineers attempted to reach its summit in 1922, Everest became an irresistible challenge to climbers from all over the world, forever altering the lives of people living around it. Adventurers have brought wealth and high-tech gear to the region, but they've also introduced pollution and a demand for guides willing to endure dangerous treks. Many hope that, in light of recent tragedies, ambition will be tempered by care and caution.

A WORD FROM

The Need to Explore Climbing is kind of a strange pursuit — it's an endeavor where you can slowly build up your skills toward the goal of doing something that might seem impossible. But there's intense personal gratification in finding a mountain and becoming inspired by the aesthetics of an unclimbed line on that mountain . . . And what happens is that through the course of the pursuit there is so much to be learned about yourself. And the relationships and friendships with your climbing partners become very powerful . . . I really believe that as human beings we have an innate need to explore, to see what's around the corner.

—JIMMY CHIN, *photographer*

"The mountain remains unvanquished," wrote Barry Bishop after the 1963 American Everest expedition, shown here.

Setting Records on
EVEREST

■ **MAY 1953 (SOUTH FACE)**
Edmund Hillary (New Zealand) and
Tenzing Norgay (Nepal) accomplish
the first recorded summit of Everest.

■ **MAY 1963 (WEST RIDGE AND
NORTH FACE)**
First successful American expedition:
Team members Thomas Hornbein
and Willi Unsoeld traverse Everest
via West Ridge.

■ **MAY 1975 (SOUTH FACE)**
Junko Tabei (Japan) becomes first
woman to reach summit—just 12 days
after being injured in an avalanche.

■ **AUG. 1980 (NORTH FACE)**
Reinhold Messner (Italy) makes
first solo ascent—notably without
supplementary oxygen, as on his
previous summit in May 1978.

■ **SEPT. 1988 (SOUTH RIDGE)**
Jean-Marc Boivin (France) accomplishes
the first paraglider descent from the
summit, thus also clocking the fastest
descent ever.

■ **MAY 2010 (NORTH FACE)**
Jordan Romero (U.S.) becomes the
youngest person to summit, at 13 years
and 10 months old.

■ **MAY 2012 (NORTH FACE)**
Tamae Watanabe (Japan) becomes
oldest female to summit, at age 73 years
and 180 days—breaking her own record.

■ **MAY 2013**
Yuichiro Miura (Japan) reclaims title
of oldest man to summit, at age 80.

■ **MAY 2013**
Dave Hahn (U.S.) sets a new
record, 15, for number of ascents
by a non-Sherpa.

■ **APRIL 2014 (SOUTH FACE)**
Sixteen Sherpas die in an avalanche
on deadliest single day in Everest
history.

EARTH'S EXTREMES

PUTTING THE AWE BACK IN AWESOME

Sunrise over Lake Superior

WATER RECORDS

LARGEST FRESHWATER LAKE

Lake Superior stretches across 31,700 square miles of the United States and Canada, making it the largest lake by surface area. It was formed about 10,000 years ago.

LOWEST POINT

The Challenger Deep in the Pacific is the lowest point on Earth: 36,037 feet below sea level. Mount Everest could be sunk into its depths and still be covered by more than one mile of water.

DEEPEST LAKE

Russia's Lake Baikal is both the deepest lake, at 5,387 feet, and the oldest, at 25–30 million years old. It is part of a rift valley, where tectonic plates are breaking apart.

LARGEST RIVER

There is no competition here: The Amazon River and its tributaries flow through Peru, Bolivia, Venezuela, Colombia, Ecuador, and Brazil before emptying into the Atlantic Ocean. The next largest, India's "Mother Ganges," discharges a significantly lower volume of water than the Amazon does.

LONGEST RIVER

Calculating the length of rivers is a complicated and controversial process. Freshwater scientists often cannot agree on a river's precise source or on how far to extend its watershed boundaries. But most agree that the Nile, stretching through northeast Africa, is the longest in the world at 4,160 miles. The Amazon is a close second at 4,150 miles and the Yangtze clocks in at 3,880 miles long.

The Nile in Sudan

The Valle de la Luna in Chile's Atacama Desert

SCIENTISTS THINK THE DRY VALLEYS OF ANTARCTICA MAY BE THE CLOSEST OF ANY EARTH ENVIRONMENT TO THE PLANET MARS.

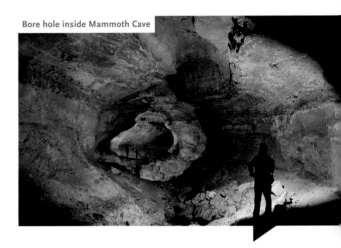

Bore hole inside Mammoth Cave

LAND RECORDS

DRIEST PLACE
Parts of the high plateau of the Atacama Desert in Chile and the Dry Valleys of Antarctica have never recorded a drop of rain. They are ringed by high mountains that prevent moisture from reaching the dry basins.

HIGHEST POINT
Mount Everest is the world's highest elevation, 29,035 feet above sea level—a figure that increases as the Indian subcontinent crashes into Asia. Hawaii's Mauna Kea is the world's tallest mountain, 33,000 feet from seafloor to summit.

WETTEST PLACE
Asian monsoons make the Indian state of Meghalaya the rainiest place in the world. The town of Mawsynram received about 83 feet of rain in 1985. In 1861, nearby Cherrapunji received 86.6 feet.

FARTHEST FROM THE OCEAN
About 200 miles north of Urumqi, a city in Xinjiang, China, is a "pole of inaccessibility"—a location that is "challenging to reach owing to its remoteness from geographical features that could provide access." The most remote pole of inaccessibility—the place farthest from the ocean—is also in Xinjiang, about 1,644 miles from the coast.

LONGEST CAVE SYSTEM
The Mammoth-Flint Ridge cave system in Kentucky stretches about 400 miles, nearly twice the length of the next longest cave system, Mexico's Sac Actun underwater cave.

HOTTEST PLACE
The temperature at Furnace Creek Station in Death Valley National Park, which straddles California and Nevada, reached 134°F (56.7°C) on July 10, 1913. However, the Danakil Depression—which reaches into Eritrea, Djibouti, and Ethiopia—has the highest average year-round temperature—93.92°F (34.4°C).

COLDEST PLACE
A region near Vostok Station, a Russian research station in Antarctica atop ice almost two and a half miles thick, set the world record on August 10, 2010, when the temperature dipped to minus 135.8°F (−93.2°C).

SYLVIA EARLE
MARINE BIOLOGIST

INSATIABLE CURIOSITY

Sylvia Earle is always seeking to better understand the unknown. The legendary oceanographer has been exploring the deep sea for more than four decades, leading countless underwater expeditions, conducting game-changing research on marine ecosystems, and setting a solo dive record.

Even a pier on Bonaire, a Dutch Caribbean island, supports marine life that fascinates Sylvia Earle.

A world-renowned marine conservationist and National Geographic Explorer-in-Residence, Sylvia Earle—known to colleagues as "Her Deepness"—has spent more than 7,000 hours underwater, led over a hundred expeditions, and served as the first female chief scientist for the National Oceanic and Atmospheric Administration (NOAA). She even led NASA's first all-female mission—when she and her team of aquanauts lived in and conducted research from Tektite II, an underwater lab used to simulate an extreme environment, for two weeks.

RECENT WORK AND ADVOCACY

At a conference in 2006, Earle chided Google Earth founder John Hanke for not including the ocean in its mapping project, saying, "You've done a great job with the dirt. But what about the water?" He and his team were inspired to fix that omission. Using a layers feature, Ocean in Google Earth reveals topographic maps of the seafloor, locations of shipwrecks and algal blooms, and even underwater volcanoes.

Only about 5 percent of the oceans, what Earle calls the "vital blue heart of our planet," is protected in any way. (The figure for land is closer to 12 percent.) So with the same drive and tenacity that she brings to her research, Earle is raising worldwide awareness of the urgent need for more marine protected areas, or "Hope Spots," via her nonprofit, Mission Blue. Today, nearly 90 Hope Spots covering more than 18.5 million square miles—over 44 percent of the ocean—have been designated around the world, further galvanizing support for ocean conservation.

> " WHAT'S HELD MY ATTENTION, AND WHAT SHOULD HOLD EVERYONE'S ATTENTION, IS THE SPLENDOR OF LIFE—ALL THESE CREATURES THAT ARE LIKE US IN SO MANY WAYS."

Earle founded companies that make equipment for deep-ocean environments.

KEY DATES

Earle's Oceanic ACHIEVEMENTS

1970
Led NASA's all-female aquanaut team

1979
Set a record for walking the ocean floor (1,250 feet deep) untethered for 2 hours

1990
Was appointed first female chief scientist at NOAA

1998
Named *Time*'s first Hero for the Planet

2009
Won $100,000 TED Prize and founded nonprofit Mission Blue

2017
Awarded the Rachel Carson Prize and featured in *Firsts: Women Who Are Changing the World*, a multimedia project from *Time*

...NG THE PROBLEM OF SNOW

...e last ice age, Stone Age hunters began strapping long pieces of ...their feet to travel farther and faster over snow in pursuit of the ...at flourished across Europe and Asia. Scientists continue to find ...e of early skiers' presence engraved in rock and preserved in bogs.

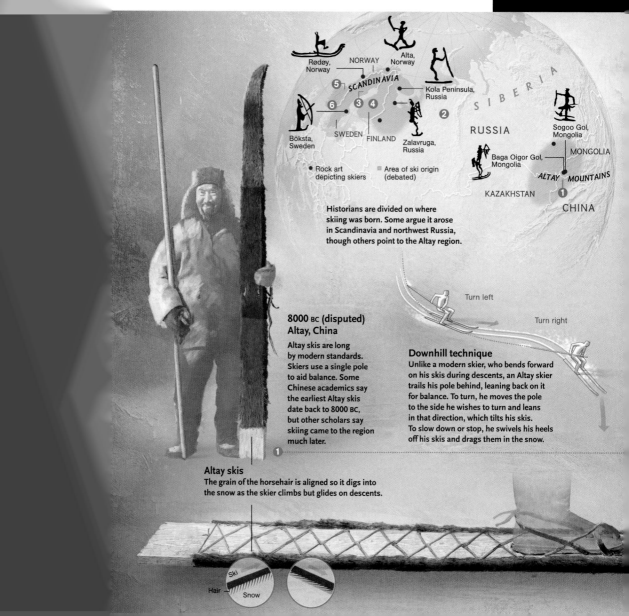

Røto øy,
Norway
NORWAY
Alta,
Norway

5 SCANDINAVIA

6   3   4

Böksta,
Sweden

SWEDEN   FINLAND

SIBERIA

Kola Peninsula,
Russia

2

RUSSIA

Zalavruga,
Russia

Sogoo Gol,
Mongolia

MONGOLIA

Baga Oigor Gol,
Mongolia

ALTAY   MOUNTAINS

KAZAKHSTAN

1

CHINA

● Rock art
depicting skiers

■ Area of ski origin
(debated)

Historians are divided on where
skiing was born. Some argue it arose
in Scandinavia and northwest Russia,
though others point to the Altay region.

8000 BC (disputed)
Altay, China

Altay skis are long
by modern standards.
Skiers use a single pole
to aid balance. Some
Chinese academics say
the earliest Altay skis
date back to 8000 BC,
but other scholars say
skiing came to the region
much later.

Turn left

Turn right

Downhill technique

Unlike a modern skier, who bends forward
on his skis during descents, an Altay skier
trails his pole behind, leaning back on it
for balance. To turn, he moves the pole
to the side he wishes to turn and leans
in that direction, which tilts his skis.
To slow down or stop, he swivels his heels
off his skis and drags them in the snow.

1

Altay skis

The grain of the horsehair is aligned so it digs into
the snow as the skier climbs but glides on descents.

Ski

Hair

Snow

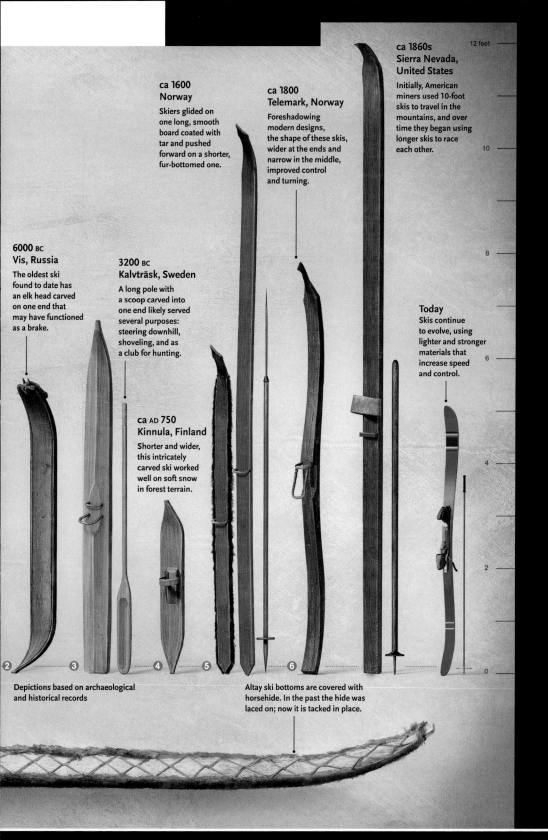

**ca 1600
Norway**

Skiers glided on one long, smooth board coated with tar and pushed forward on a shorter, fur-bottomed one.

**ca 1800
Telemark, Norway**

Foreshadowing modern designs, the shape of these skis, wider at the ends and narrow in the middle, improved control and turning.

**ca 1860s
Sierra Nevada, United States**

Initially, American miners used 10-foot skis to travel in the mountains, and over time they began using longer skis to race each other.

**6000 BC
Vis, Russia**

The oldest ski found to date has an elk head carved on one end that may have functioned as a brake.

**3200 BC
Kalvträsk, Sweden**

A long pole with a scoop carved into one end likely served several purposes: steering downhill, shoveling, and as a club for hunting.

Today

Skis continue to evolve, using lighter and stronger materials that increase speed and control.

**ca AD 750
Kinnula, Finland**

Shorter and wider, this intricately carved ski worked well on soft snow in forest terrain.

12 feet

10

8

6

4

2

0

Depictions based on archaeological and historical records

Altay ski bottoms are covered with horsehide. In the past the hide was laced on; now it is tacked in place.

THE WORLD'S FAVORITE SPORT

PLAYED BY THE HUMBLE AND CELEBRITIES ALIKE

Soccer's universality comes from its simplicity—the fact that the game can be played anywhere with anything. Urban children kick the can on concrete, and rural kids kick a rag wrapped around a rag wrapped around a rag, barefoot, on dirt. The sport's widespread popularity is nothing new: For instance, researchers have found more than 1,000 courts used by the Maya and Aztec. Today, FIFA, soccer's international governing body, is affiliated with more than 200 national associations, leading some to call it "the United Nations of Football."

France (in blue) and the United States stretch for the ball on day one of the 2016 Olympics in Rio de Janeiro.

Kicking the Ball
FOR MILLENNIA

CA 3000 BC
Evidence is found of a Chinese game involving goals known as *tsu chu*, which means "to kick a ball of leather."

CA 1400 BC
Maya play *pitz*, a soccer-like ball game on a court using a rubber ball.

CA AD 20
Chinese military manual mentions a game of "football for the power of soldiers," called *taju bingshi*.

CA 200
Athenaeus mentions *harpastum* (or *episkyros* in Greek), a rugby-like ball game played on a small court.

CA 640
Historian writes of *kemari*, a Japanese version of *tsu chu* that becomes popular among medieval nobility and elites.

OCTOBER 1863
England establishes the Football Association, the first governing body for the modern game, which (unlike rugby) forbids ball carrying.

MAY 1904
Seven countries found the Fédération Internationale de Football Association (FIFA).

OCTOBER 1908
The London Olympics include soccer.

JULY 1930
Thirteen national teams play in the first men's World Cup competition, held in Uruguay.

NOVEMBER 1991
Teams from 12 countries compete in China at the first Women's World Championship (later the Women's World Cup).

JULY 2010
The television audience for the World Cup final (the Netherlands lost to Spain) exceeds one billion viewers.

TRANSPORTATION
TIME LINE

PREHISTORY	1700 to 1 BC	AD 1 to 1000	1000 to 1700

PREHISTORY

■ **ca 65,000 ya***
Modern humans reach New Guinea and Australia by boat.

■ **ca 14,700 ya**
Humans are present in the Americas.

■ **ca 10,000 ya**
Dugout canoes are in use in Europe.

■ **ca 5500 BC**
Humans use bits and reins to manage horses for riding.

■ **ca 3500 BC**
The wheel is invented in Mesopotamia.

■ **ca 2500 BC**
Mesopotamians waterproof boats and buildings with tar.

* years ago

1700 to 1 BC

■ **ca 1700 BC**
Horses and chariots are introduced to Egypt.

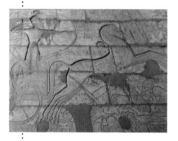

■ **691 BC**
Assyrians build an aqueduct to carry water to their capital, Nineveh.

■ **312 BC**
Rome builds its first major road, the Appian Way.

■ **110 BC**
Romans use rudimentary horseshoes.

AD 1 to 1000

■ **415**
In India, suspension bridges are built using iron chains.

■ **ca 660**
Camel herds support a nomadic way of life among people living in the Sahara.

■ **ca 700**
Europeans begin to adopt the use of stirrups for riding horses.

■ **ca 800**
Roads in Baghdad, Iraq, are paved with tar extracted from nearby oil fields.

■ **ca 860**
Viking longships venture as far west as Iceland.

1000 to 1700

■ **ca 1088**
Shen Kuo first describes a magnetic compass used for navigation.

■ **ca 1450**
The Inca construct a road system 20,000 miles long to unite their empire.

■ **1457**
The first four-wheel passenger coach is built in Hungary.

■ **1500**
Chinese scientist Wan Hu attempts to make a flying machine out of rockets tied to a chair.

■ **1692**
In France, the 32-mile Canal du Midi, linking the Mediterranean Sea with the Atlantic Ocean, is completed.

| **1700 to 1900** | **1900 to 1930** | **1930 to 1960** | **1960 to PRESENT** |

1700 to 1900

■ 1769
James Watt patents the modern steam engine.

■ 1783
French brothers Joseph and Jacques Montgolfier first demonstrate the hot air balloon.

■ 1869
The Suez Canal is completed in Egypt.

■ 1869
The U.S. Transcontinental Railroad is completed.

■ 1879
Karl Benz runs the first gas-powered automobile.

■ 1891
Construction begins on the Trans-Siberian Railroad.

1900 to 1930

■ 1903
Orville and Wilbur Wright fly a powered airplane at Kitty Hawk, North Carolina.

■ 1904
The first portion of the New York City subway opens.

■ 1908
The first Model T Ford comes off the assembly line.

■ 1909
French aviator Louis Blériot flies across the English Channel.

■ 1927
Charles Lindbergh flies the *Spirit of St. Louis* nonstop from New York to Paris.

1930 to 1960

■ 1933
The first modern airliner, the Boeing 247, enters service.

■ 1937
The *Hindenburg* dirigible bursts into flames when attempting to dock after a transatlantic flight.

■ 1939
Inventor Igor Sikorsky builds the first helicopter.

■ 1945
James Martin designs the ejector seat.

■ 1947
American airman Charles "Chuck" Yeager makes the first supersonic flight.

■ 1958
Australian engineer David Warren invents the "black box" flight data recorder.

1960 to PRESENT

■ 1961
Soviet cosmonaut Yuri Gagarin becomes the first man in space.

■ 1969
The British-French supersonic airliner Concorde takes its maiden flight.

■ 1969
NASA's Apollo 11 makes the first piloted moon landing.

■ 1998
English inventor David Baker patents the Land Shark, a high-speed amphibious car.

■ 2010
Self-driving cars make their first test drives on public streets.

ICONIC
DESTINATIONS

JOURNEYS THAT SHOULD BE ON EVERY BUCKET LIST

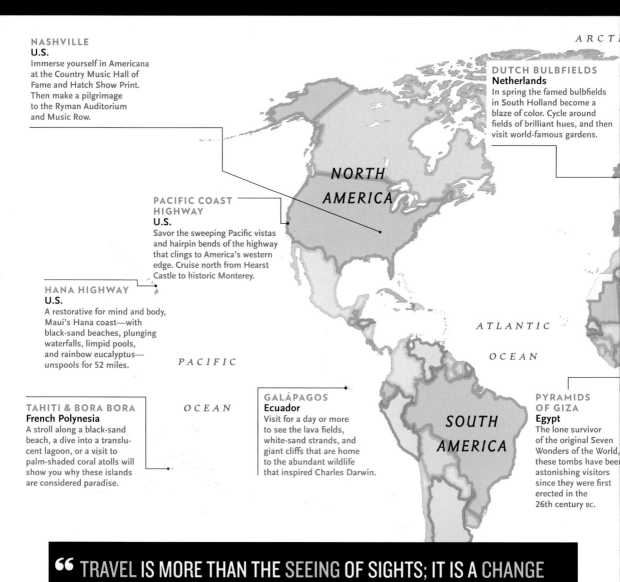

NASHVILLE
U.S.
Immerse yourself in Americana at the Country Music Hall of Fame and Hatch Show Print. Then make a pilgrimage to the Ryman Auditorium and Music Row.

DUTCH BULBFIELDS
Netherlands
In spring the famed bulbfields in South Holland become a blaze of color. Cycle around fields of brilliant hues, and then visit world-famous gardens.

PACIFIC COAST HIGHWAY
U.S.
Savor the sweeping Pacific vistas and hairpin bends of the highway that clings to America's western edge. Cruise north from Hearst Castle to historic Monterey.

HANA HIGHWAY
U.S.
A restorative for mind and body, Maui's Hana coast—with black-sand beaches, plunging waterfalls, limpid pools, and rainbow eucalyptus— unspools for 52 miles.

TAHITI & BORA BORA
French Polynesia
A stroll along a black-sand beach, a dive into a translucent lagoon, or a visit to palm-shaded coral atolls will show you why these islands are considered paradise.

GALÁPAGOS
Ecuador
Visit for a day or more to see the lava fields, white-sand strands, and giant cliffs that are home to the abundant wildlife that inspired Charles Darwin.

PYRAMIDS OF GIZA
Egypt
The lone survivor of the original Seven Wonders of the World, these tombs have been astonishing visitors since they were first erected in the 26th century BC.

NORTH AMERICA

SOUTH AMERICA

ARCT[I]

ATLANTIC

OCEAN

PACIFIC

OCEAN

> **66** **TRAVEL** IS MORE THAN THE **SEEING** OF SIGHTS; IT IS A **CHANGE** THAT GOES ON, DEEP AND PERMANENT, IN THE IDEAS OF **LIVING.**"
>
> —**MIRIAM BEARD,** HISTORIAN AND ACTIVIST

BOLSHOI EXPRESS
Russia
Get a taste of Russian extravagance aboard the overnight *Bolshoi (Grand) Express* between Moscow and St. Petersburg. Service starts at first class.

GREAT WALL
China
This is the world's largest human-made military structure and one of its oldest. Climb the Mutianyu section of wall and take in views of far-off misty green hills.

GREEK ISLANDS
Greece
Azure Aegean waters, terraced hillsides, olive groves, blue-domed churches, and whitewashed villages overlooked by windmills bring visitors unfailing delight.

MOUNT FUJI
Japan
Contemplate the sacred volcano and its serene setting while soaking in the hot springs or taking a leisurely bike ride at Lake Kawaguchi, one of the Fuji Five Lakes.

A N

R O P E

ASIA

PACIFIC

OCEAN

AFRICA

TAJ MAHAL
India
The shimmering Taj Mahal is a monument to human skill as well as to an emperor's love. Visit it at sunrise to watch the white marble change color with the light.

INDIAN

OCEAN

AUSTRALIA

KILIMANJARO
Tanzania
The trek up Africa's highest mountain passes through five distinct temperate zones, from rain forest to tundra. Uhuru Peak affords an infinite horizon line.

SYDNEY OPERA HOUSE
Australia
A masterful feat of architecture, the building's profile resembles pearly billowing sails, an illusion achieved with multiple interlocking shells set on a pedestal.

TRAVEL SMART

TIPS TO MAKE THE JOURNEY EASIER

Pack light and smart.

Research airport transportation options.

BEFORE YOU GO

RELIABLE TRAVEL ADVICE

Solicit advice from friends, relatives, and colleagues. Someone who knows your destination well may be in your social media network. Guidebooks or posts from a professional reviewer are the next best choice.

BOOKING YOUR TRIP

Competent travel agents really are worth their weight in gold. But if you're booking your own trip, take extra care, especially if venturing abroad: Check dates and times, airports, and names on your documents. It is crucial that you understand the terms of your purchase and any passport or visa requirements.

PACKING UP

Before you go, research your luggage options, how to protect your bags en route, and your rights when they're lost. Being prepared will save additional grief.

GETTING THERE

ROAD TRIP

Take a car (yours or a rental) if you have the time and want the freedom to explore. Pack a map in case GPS isn't available. If train or bus travel appeals to you, look into the peculiarities of that mode of travel on your route before booking your trip.

HANDLING SECURITY

The Transportation Security Administration (TSA) is an inevitable part of the air travel experience. You can get through the screening process with your nerves and your dignity intact as long as you plan ahead and know what to expect.

MAKING THE MOST OF YOUR LAYOVER

Hate searching for an outlet so you can charge your devices? Bring a small power strip that works as an extension cord and lets others plug in too.

Get immersed in local shops and stalls.

WHEN YOU ARRIVE

IDEAL LODGING

Not excited about a standard hotel stay? Informal and alternative choices include B&Bs, home swaps, glamping, hostels, and, of course, Airbnb. Decode which conveniences you can live without and make your choice accordingly.

KEEP CONNECTED

Call your provider to find out whether your cell phone is "locked." If it is, you can't just swap out your SIM card to one that works in the country you're visiting. You may need to buy an unlocked phone, which you'll be able to use on any compatible network.

MANAGING MONEY

If you're traveling abroad, carry at least one credit card (preferably two) and some local currency. Both payment forms have risks and rewards, but both will serve you well. Mind the fine print and fees, and call the company in advance of your trip to avoid having a card suspended by its fraud monitoring department.

FINDING FOOD

Food can easily become one of the most disappointing parts of a vacation, so plan ahead and avoid falling back on "first available" choices. Be open to cooking when possible and to packing picnics for the road.

Posh Airport
ENHANCEMENTS

■ CHANGI
The new 10-story Jewel expansion at Singapore's SIN has a hedge maze and a giant bouncing net. Indoor playgrounds, rides, and a reading corner make it family-friendly.

■ HONG KONG
At HKG, you'll find a nine-hole golf course, one of Asia's biggest IMAX screens, virtual car racing and basketball, and a Muji store.

■ INCHEON
Seoul's ICN boasts a year-round skating rink, an 18-hole golf course and driving range, and a culture center with Korean crafts and music.

■ MUNICH
No surprise: MUC has an on-site brewery, Airbräu, and an Audi showroom. It also hosts indoor surfing and mountain bike events.

■ SAN FRANCISCO
SFO has an aviation museum, a branch of the Steinhart Aquarium, and a public transit stop right in the airport.

■ SCHIPHOL
Amsterdam's AMS houses an oxygen bar with aromatherapy, a library, and two 24/7 mini museums: Rijksmuseum (art) and Nemo (science).

■ VANCOUVER
YVR takes advantage of its expansive spaces with large-scale native art and aquarium exhibits that are home to over 5,000 creatures.

■ ZURICH
Healthy travelers will like ZRH's on-site grocery store and the chance to get some fresh air by renting in-line skates, bikes, or walking poles.

■ DETROIT
Move in style from one concourse to another through DTW's Light Tunnel, illuminated glass panels that throb in time with space-age music.

MACHU PICCHU

JAW-DROPPING BEAUTY AND ENGINEERING

In July 1911, Yale explorer Hiram Bingham III set off in search of ancient ruins in Peru. A local boy led him through dense forest, up and down incredibly steep inclines, to reach one of the greatest archaeological finds of the 20th century: Machu Picchu ("old peak"), an Inca city built in the mid-15th century at the remarkable altitude of nearly 8,000 feet above sea level, high above the city of Cusco. The stunning stonework, terraced farmland, and aqueducts are even more impressive considering they were built without mortar, metal tools, or the wheel.

Bingham saw about 20 buildings, though the site actually had about 500.

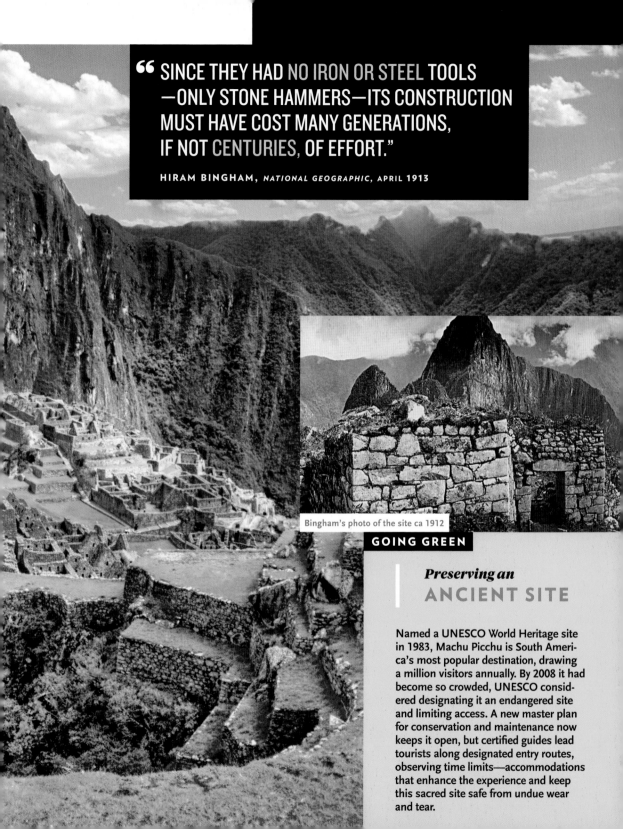

> **" SINCE THEY HAD NO IRON OR STEEL TOOLS —ONLY STONE HAMMERS—ITS CONSTRUCTION MUST HAVE COST MANY GENERATIONS, IF NOT CENTURIES, OF EFFORT."**
>
> HIRAM BINGHAM, *NATIONAL GEOGRAPHIC*, APRIL 1913

Bingham's photo of the site ca 1912

GOING GREEN

Preserving an
ANCIENT SITE

Named a UNESCO World Heritage site in 1983, Machu Picchu is South America's most popular destination, drawing a million visitors annually. By 2008 it had become so crowded, UNESCO considered designating it an endangered site and limiting access. A new master plan for conservation and maintenance now keeps it open, but certified guides lead tourists along designated entry routes, observing time limits—accommodations that enhance the experience and keep this sacred site safe from undue wear and tear.

GREATEST EXPEDITIONS

FOLLOW HISTORY'S PATHWAYS AROUND THE WORLD

Passengers traverse Switzerland's Landwasser viaduct.

BY TRAIN

SWISS ALPS AND ITALIAN LAKE DISTRICT

Climb aboard the unhurried *Glacier Express* and savor the panorama of snowcapped peaks, dense forests, rushing rivers, Alpine meadows, and mountain villages near Switzerland's southern borders.

CANADIAN ROCKIES

Take the *Rocky Mountaineer*'s dramatic route through the Canadian Rockies—rocky gradients, soaring pine trees, spiraling tunnels—from Vancouver to Banff.

SHINKANSEN TRANS-SIBERIAN RAILWAY

A weeklong Moscow-Beijing route via Mongolia weaves though the Russian hinterlands of Siberia, the wilderness of Mongolia, and the wastes of the Gobi, within sight of Lake Baikal and the Great Wall.

ACROSS LAND

MOROCCO'S CITIES OF LEGEND

A journey along age-old trade routes—from Ceuta (officially part of Spain) to the tiny fishing port of Tarfaya—immerses you in ancient cultures, exotic markets, and imposing mountain and desert scenery.

NEW ZEALAND NORTH TO SOUTH

The unspoiled (but accessible) landscape between Karamea and Jackson Bay includes two glaciers, exceptional ocean vistas, and alpine scenery.

PILGRIMAGE TO BHUTAN

One enchanted tour includes a trek into Trashi-yangtse, a stunning "lost" valley, with a monastery, a wildlife sanctuary, a shrine, and welcoming locals.

Prayer flags frame Bhutan's mythic Taktsang Monastery.

Sea Cloud II approaches St. Lucia's Pitons.

TOGETHER, TOURISTS FROM CHINA AND THE UNITED STATES SPEND ALMOST $400 BILLION A YEAR ON TRAVEL.

BY SEA

CARIBBEAN DREAMING

These legendary islands are synonymous with paradise: idyllic beaches, water sports, and rum cocktails. A cruise through the breathtaking waters offers luxury, shopping, and outdoor fun.

EPIC POLYNESIA

During one seven-day excursion around Tahiti and nearby islands, guests can kayak, dive, snorkel, hike, or sunbathe. Inland spots to visit include an archaeological site and a vanilla plantation.

ANTARCTIC CRUISING

You'll be comfortable aboard an ice-reinforced vessel as icebergs float past, some of them as large as ships themselves. Time your trip right to catch sight of seals, whales, and penguins.

Zebras and wildebeests graze in Tanzania's Serengeti National Park.

ON SAFARI

TANZANIA'S GREAT MIGRATION

On the ground, in the trees, along rivers, and in the sky—more than 1,000 bird species can be found here, and it's possible to see 100 species in a day. Birding is good year-round, but fall migration is spectacular.

BOTSWANA GAME RESERVE

On a guided safari, guests of the national parks shoot the "big five" of African wildlife—lion, leopard, buffalo, rhino, and elephant—with cameras rather than guns.

VICTORIA FALLS

On a microlight aircraft, there's not much between you and the tree-covered islands that dot the Zambezi River as it approaches Victoria Falls. Want to see wildlife? Book a flight over the nearby national park.

A WORD FROM

Always a New Day I never set out to make discoveries or describe new species or lost tribes; I set out to explore one more wild place. The test is that you wake up well before dawn and you are raring to get out of your tent, because there were unresolved stories that were unfolding the day before. Only going further will solve the riddle, answer your questions.

—**MIKE FAY,** *explorer*

U.S. NATIONAL PARKS

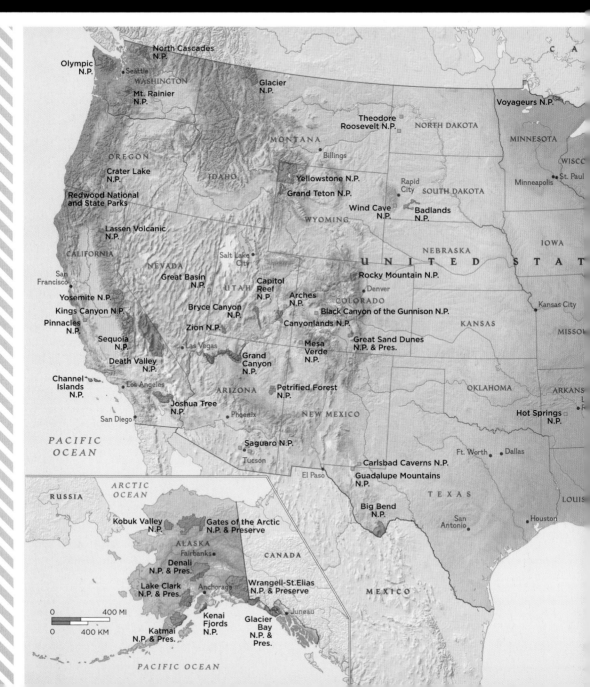

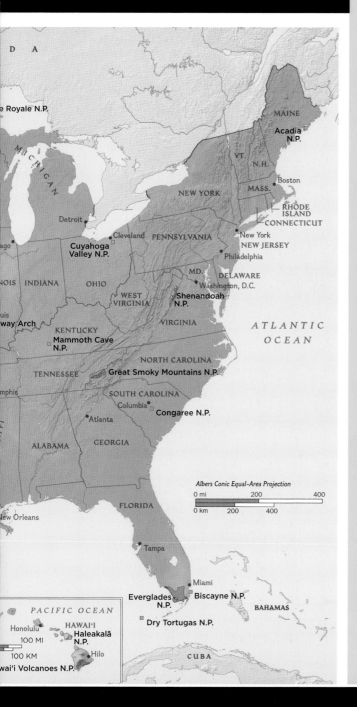

KEY DESTINATIONS

Secret Gems Among the U.S. PARKS

■ **CANYONLANDS (UT)**
Run the Colorado's white water in narrow slot canyons during the day and camp on beaches under an ocean of stars at night.

■ **CHANNEL ISLANDS (CA)**
Often likened to the Galápagos, these islands teem with wildlife. Visitors can scuba dive in kelp forests and kayak through sea caves.

■ **CONGAREE (SC)**
Stroll along elevated boardwalks under massive oaks, tupelos, and cypress trees.

■ **DRY TORTUGAS (FL)**
Most of this park is underwater, protecting corals and roughly 200 shipwrecks. Its seven tiny islands shelter nesting sea turtles.

■ **GATES OF THE ARCTIC (AK)**
Located above the Arctic Circle, this pristine wilderness is filled with jagged peaks, sweeping tundra, and abundant wildlife.

■ **GREAT BASIN (NV)**
Visit bristlecone pines—the world's longest living trees—and exquisite marble caves filled with stalactites and stalagmites.

■ **GUADALUPE MOUNTAINS (TX)**
This park is home to seven of Texas's tallest peaks, including the dramatic El Capitan.

■ **ISLE ROYALE (MI)**
This archipelago is accessible only by boat or seaplane. Stay at Rock Harbor Lodge, paddle the rocky coast, or hike to remote campsites.

■ **NORTH CASCADES (WA)**
Over 300 glaciers—roughly a third of all glaciers in the lower 48—are found in this nearly deserted alpine wonderland.

■ **WRANGELL-ST. ELIAS (AK)**
Our largest national park has 16 of America's tallest mountains, 5,000 square miles of glaciers, and the 7,000-foot Stairway Icefall.

REBUILDING THE WORLD TRADE CENTER

THE NEW WORLD TRADE CENTER

For decades the twin towers of the World Trade Center symbolized New York, the United States, wealth, achievement, and a global economy. Destroyed by terrorists on September 11, 2001, the twin towers' footprint now stands as the centerpiece of a new neighborhood of enterprise—and spirit. Two massive fountains, ringed by parapets inscribed with the names of all those lost, are part of the National September 11 Memorial & Museum. Under the memorial, the museum extends nine stories down to bedrock, with artifacts and exhibition spaces reflecting that day in history. Nearby buildings climb high again, with many still under construction.

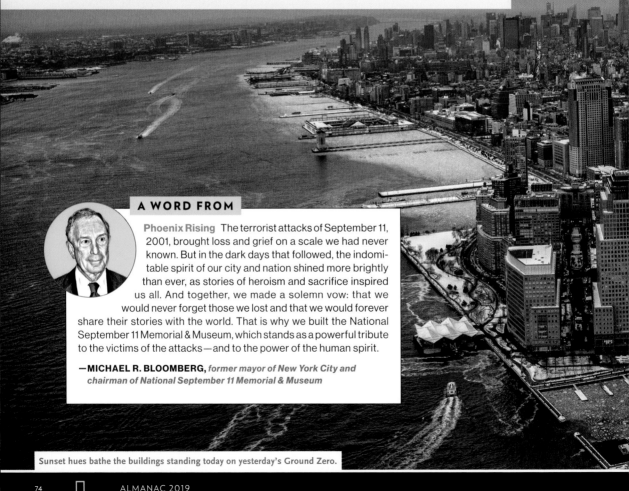

A WORD FROM

Phoenix Rising The terrorist attacks of September 11, 2001, brought loss and grief on a scale we had never known. But in the dark days that followed, the indomitable spirit of our city and nation shined more brightly than ever, as stories of heroism and sacrifice inspired us all. And together, we made a solemn vow: that we would never forget those we lost and that we would forever share their stories with the world. That is why we built the National September 11 Memorial & Museum, which stands as a powerful tribute to the victims of the attacks—and to the power of the human spirit.

—**MICHAEL R. BLOOMBERG,** *former mayor of New York City and chairman of National September 11 Memorial & Museum*

Sunset hues bathe the buildings standing today on yesterday's Ground Zero.

TALLEST IN WEST
With antenna, 1 WTC measures 1,776 feet—a symbolic number and one that makes this the tallest building in the Western Hemisphere.

ONE WORLD OBSERVATORY
This 360° observation deck is 1,250 feet up. The elevator to the top travels 102 stories in 47 seconds.

NOT JUST A PRETTY FACE
Much of the three million square feet of office space in 1 WTC is awash in natural light.

SEPT. 11 MEMORIAL
Monumental fountains, a public plaza, and a museum mark the spot where the original twin towers stood.

Milestones of
WTC HISTORY

1946
New York State legislature creates the World Trade Corporation.

1964
Port Authority names Minoru Yamasaki as lead architect of World Trade Center.

1968
Construction begins on north tower.

1969
Construction begins on south tower.

1974
French acrobat Philippe Petit walks wire strung between two towers.

1993
Terrorists detonate bomb in underground garage, killing six.

2001
Terrorists pilot hijacked jets into twin towers and into Pentagon; a fourth hijacked jet crashes in Pennsylvania.

2002
The "Last Column" is removed, signaling end to recovery efforts at site.

2004
Architect Michael Arad and landscape architect Peter Walker's memorial plaza design announced.

2005
Construction begins on Transportation Hub, designed by Santiago Calatrava.

2006
Ground broken for construction of One World Trade Center.

2011
Memorial opens with ceremony honoring families of victims and survivors.

2014
1 WTC opens for business when Condé Nast moves into offices.

BEST OF @NATGEO

OUR FAVORITE PHOTOS OF TRAVEL

@daveyoder | DAVE YODER
A boy jumps over a hot walkway at the popular seaside resort of Lido di Camaiore, on Italy's Ligurian coast.

@cookjenshel | DIANE COOK AND LEN JENSHEL
Fourth of July fireworks light the skies, visible from the High Line park in New York City.

@timlaman | TIMOTHY LAMAN
Making snow angels below the mountains at Grand Teton National Park

@geosteinmetz | GEORGE STEINMETZ
Water sports reach new heights in Miami Harbor with Aquajet jetpacks.

> **"TRAVEL IS FATAL TO PREJUDICE, BIGOTRY, AND NARROW-MINDEDNESS."**
>
> —MARK TWAIN, HUMORIST AND AUTHOR

@pedromcbride | PETE MCBRIDE
Burning Man brings a crowd of some 70,000 people to Nevada's Black Rock Desert.

@joeriis | JOE RIIS
Fire lights up a campsite on the elk migration trail in Yellowstone National Park.

@jr | JR
French street artist JR motorbikes with a friend along the Malecón in Havana, Cuba.

@amivitale | AMI VITALE
Thermal springs in Budapest, Hungary, offer a chance for traditional outdoor bathing.

HONG KONG

ASIA'S FRAGRANT HARBOR

Nowhere else can one experience a city so exuberantly complex in such a geographically tiny package as Hong Kong (Heung Gong means "fragrant harbor" in Cantonese), which packs seven million citizens into just 426 square miles, making it one of the most densely populated regions on the planet. This hyperactive city encompasses villages and bustling urbanity, looming mountain ranges, ribbons of coastline, and, stunningly, parks and preserves, which make up 40 percent of the cityscape. A British colony from 1942 until 1997, the city is again part of China.

CENTRAL PLAZA
The four neon bands at the top of this triangular 78-story building use colors to indicate the time in 15-minute increments.

BANK OF CHINA
Chinese-American architect I. M. Pei has explained that the building's trunk and sharp top point resemble bamboo, a symbol of strength.

HOPEWELL CENTRE
This circular skyscraper has a revolving restaurant that gives diners a 360° view of the city every 66 minutes.

A WORD FROM

A Race for Buns Time your visit to Hong Kong's tiny island of Cheung Chau for the first 10 days of the fourth lunar month. (In 2019, that means mid-May.) That's when the Cheung Chau Bun Festival takes place, with music, lion dances, and a parade. In times past, men grappled up the 60-foot bamboo towers, grabbing as many sticky buns as they could get. Nowadays no one climbs the towers, but celebrants hoist costumed children above their shoulders and honor Pak Tai, the Taoist god of the sea. Sticky buns for everyone.

—**GEORGE STONE,** *editor of* **National Geographic Traveler** *magazine*

The Tsim Sha Tsui pier in Kowloon has a full view of the brilliant Hong Kong skyline.

TWO INTERNATIONAL FINANCE CENTRE
Ascend to the observation deck on the 55th floor of this 88-story tower for a cool view of the city.

HONG KONG OBSERVATION WHEEL
This harbor-front attraction draws locals and tourists who want to capture this photogenic city from one of its 42 temperature-controlled gondolas.

What to Do in
HONG KONG

1 **VICTORIA PEAK** Get a great view of the skyline from 1,800 feet up. Go past the tram stop to see outlying islands too.

2 **HORSE RACES** Catch the thrill as part of a rapt crowd at one of the Hong Kong Jockey Club's two locations.

3 **CENTRAL MID-LEVELS ESCALATOR** Ride the world's longest outdoor covered escalator. Some exits are worth exploring.

4 **STREET MARKETS** Residents shop—and bargain—for everything from daily provisions to designer knockoffs.

5 **YUM CHA (DIM SUM)** Observe this Sunday morning social event and spectacle at teahouses and restaurants.

6 **HONG KONG TRAMWAYS** Climb aboard and ride the lines for great sightseeing. Little has changed since 1904.

7 **THE GREAT OUTDOORS** Hike, swim, and sample seafood on outlying islands, or catch a coastline-hugging bus (No. 6).

8 **TRADITIONAL VILLAGES** Many area villages are centuries old. In Tai O, see stilt houses and cruise in glass-bottomed boats.

9 **STAR FERRY** Around 8 p.m., take the ferry across the harbor and look back at the skyscraper-coordinated light show.

10 **TEN THOUSAND BUDDHAS MONASTERY** The 431 steps are flanked by golden statues, with various expressions and poses.

SUSTAINABLE TRAVEL

RESPONSIBLE AND SPECTACULAR: UNIQUE LODGES OF THE WORLD

Topas Ecolodge's infinity pool and bungalows have unsurpassed views.

MOUNTAIN

SA PA, VIETNAM
Topas Ecolodge—a cluster of mountain bungalows north of Hanoi—organizes treks into Hoang Lien National Park, a global biodiversity hot spot.

ARISTI, GREECE
Crystal rivers, deep gorges, and soaring peaks combine with village life at Aristi Mountain Resort & Villas.

COCHRANE, CHILE
The Lodge at Valle Chacabuco, in Chile, sits in the heart of Patagonia Park, a conservation initiative protecting nearly 200,000 acres.

HIGH ATLAS MOUNTAINS, MOROCCO
Kasbah du Toubkal is a tribute to Berber culture and hospitality built upon the ruins of an ancient kasbah.

DESERT

NORTHERN TERRITORY, AUSTRALIA
The Longitude 131° lodge is built into the curve of a sand dune, isolated from everything but the raw beauty of Uluru-Kata Tjuta National Park.

GOBI, MONGOLIA
The Three Camel Lodge, a scattering of traditional felt-covered Mongolian tents, celebrates the traditions of Mongolia's nomads while seeking to preserve its awe-inspiring surroundings.

TRUTH OR CONSEQUENCES, NEW MEXICO
Ted Turner's Sierra Grande Lodge is on over half a million acres of private wilderness, part of the conservation crusader's efforts to rewild America.

The spa at Sierra Grande Lodge includes pools fed by hot springs.

Lapa Rios sits amid some of the last remaining lowland tropical rain forest in Central America.

SEASIDE

OSA PENINSULA, COSTA RICA

The Lapa Rios Lodge has long been a conservation icon in this lowland tropical rain forest, where guests are sure to spot plenty of local wildlife.

FÉLICITÉ, SEYCHELLES

Guests at the Six Senses Zil Pasyon can kayak to Cocos Island National Park. The resort is committed to habitat restoration, ridding the island of invasive species, and propagating rare local plants.

TETIAROA, FRENCH POLYNESIA

The Brando is late actor Marlon Brando's eco-dream brought to life: a private tropical island run on 100 percent renewable energy sources, including solar power and coconut oil.

KENAI PENINSULA BOROUGH, ALASKA

Nestled amid old-growth Sitka spruces at the mouth of a miles-long fjord, the Tutka Bay Lodge is a wilderness lodge with deep roots and a culinary twist.

Tips for Eco-Conscious TRAVELERS

■ AVOID THE PLANE
Go to fewer places and stay longer.

■ GIVE—THE RIGHT WAY
Identify reputable local organizations that work on social welfare programs.

■ SAY NO TO PLASTIC
Opt for locally purified water in recyclable glass bottles (or drink coconut water), and carry tote bags to use while perusing street markets and shops.

■ RESEARCH TOUR OPERATORS
Ask about environmentally friendly practices, examples of supporting wildlife or culture, and employment of local guides.

■ SUPPORT LOCAL ECONOMIES
Purchasing locally made crafts has a direct and positive impact.

■ REFUSE WILDLIFE PRODUCTS
Be wary of souvenirs that create demand for endangered wildlife products.

EXPLORE
PATAGONIA

AN UNTAMED LANDSCAPE

One of the world's largest wilderness areas, Patagonia is pure, dramatic nature: craggy peaks that seem to signal the end of the Earth, waterfalls and glaciers seeping into lakes colored a startling blue, and panoramas of grassy foothills, each topped with a guanaco on the lookout for pumas. Patagonia's alluring roads and vistas have been traversed and explored by legendary figures like Ernesto "Che" Guevara, Bruce Chatwin, and Charles Darwin.

Revel in the beauty of rivers, lakes, and glaciers with a visit to Chile's Torres del Paine National Park.

Patagonia's northern end edges against the grassy Argentine Pampas and then stretches south to the remote islands of Tierra del Fuego scattered in the Beagle Channel. Whales frolic in the Atlantic waves breaking against Patagonia's eastern edge, and the Andes Mountains loom over glacial lakes on the Chile-Argentina boundary.

FROM SPIRES TO FJORDS

Península Valdés juts into the Atlantic, its beaches a playground for seals, sea lions, and penguins. Pods of southern right whales and orcas migrate just off shore at Punta Norte and in the Golfo Nuevo.

Patagonia is raw, cold, rugged, and at its most spectacular on the Chilean border along the Andes Mountains. At the heart of this landscape is the famous pinnacle Monte Fitz Roy, with a misty ring around its 11,073-foot summit. Its sheer granite surface looms over Lago Viedma on the northern edge of Parque Nacional Los Glaciares, home to nearly 50 major glaciers. The most impressive glacier of all is Perito Moreno, a three-mile-wide wall of aquamarine ice that rises almost 200 feet above Lago Argentino and emits a grinding roar as it shifts. This is one of Patagonia's essential sights, with bus-size chunks of ice shearing off the glacier and crashing into the lake's water.

To the south of the park is Torres del Paine, a dramatic triplet of mountain summits. Patagonia's end-of-the-earth feeling is at its strongest in Ushuaia, the world's southernmost city, pressed between the soaring tail of the Andes and the violent waves of the Beagle Channel. Its lonely port is a base for ships leaving for Antarctica.

> **" THERE ARE MOMENTS WHEN I THINK WITH PROFOUND LONGING OF THOSE WONDERFUL AREAS IN OUR SOUTH. PERHAPS ONE DAY, TIRED OF CIRCLING THE WORLD, I'LL RETURN TO ARGENTINA."**
>
> —CHE GUEVARA, *THE MOTORCYCLE DIARIES*

Jagged granite peaks long ago earned the nickname "Cleopatra's Needles."

GOING GREEN

Private Lands Set Aside FOR CONSERVATION

More than 2.5 million acres of privately owned wild land in Patagonia have been purchased and preserved by conservationists Kristine McDivitt Tompkins and her late husband, Doug (former CEOs of outfitters Patagonia and The North Face, respectively). The acquisition allowed them to help create five national parks and numerous reserves, such as the 715,000-acre Pumalín Park, which includes Pacific coast fjords in Chile's Palena Province; the 726,000-acre Corcovado National Park, south of Pumalín, which encompasses pristine coastline and an iconic volcano; and the 650,000-acre Patagonia Park, which has opened to the public and is now on the path to federal protection.

ON LOCATION
DESTINATIONS

VISIT THE SPOTS WHERE YOUR FAVORITE SCENES WERE FILMED

ARCT

STAR WARS:
THE LAST JEDI
Skellig Michael,
Ireland
Once home to a medieval
monastery and now a
UNESCO World Heritage
site, the dramatic ruins
on this isolated island
include the steep stairs
seen in the film.

NORTH
AMERICA

127 HOURS
Midway, Utah, U.S.
The Homestead Crater
is a rare geothermal spring
hidden inside a limestone
rock. It is on a resort
property where visitors
can swim, soak, or scuba dive.

FIELD OF DREAMS
Dyersville, Iowa, U.S.
Each year, about 65,000 people
make a pilgrimage to this town
of 4,000 to see the baseball
diamond made for the Oscar-
nominated movie—on a farm,
surrounded by fields of corn.

ATLANTIC

OCEAN

PACIFIC

POP!

MOVIE SETS YOU CAN VISIT

- **Contrabando, Texas:** *Lone Star*
- **Henry River Mill Village, North Carolina:** *The Hunger Games*
- **Mellieha, Malta:** *Popeye*
- **Płaszów Camp, Poland:** *Schindler's List*
- **Tozeur, Tunisia:** *Star Wars: A New Hope*
- **Wallilabou Bay, St. Vincent:** *Pirates of the Caribbean: The Curse of the Black Pearl*

SOUTH
AMERICA

QUANTUM OF SOLACE
Panama City, Panama
The National Institute of
Culture of Panama, found in
the Casco Viejo neighborhood,
was reconceived as a Bolivian
hotel in this James Bond film.

MAD MAX:
FURY ROAD
Swakopmund, Nami
Previous Mad Max films
were shot in Australia,
but this sequel was mad
in the stark Namib Dese
where enormous dunes
set a postapocalyptic mo

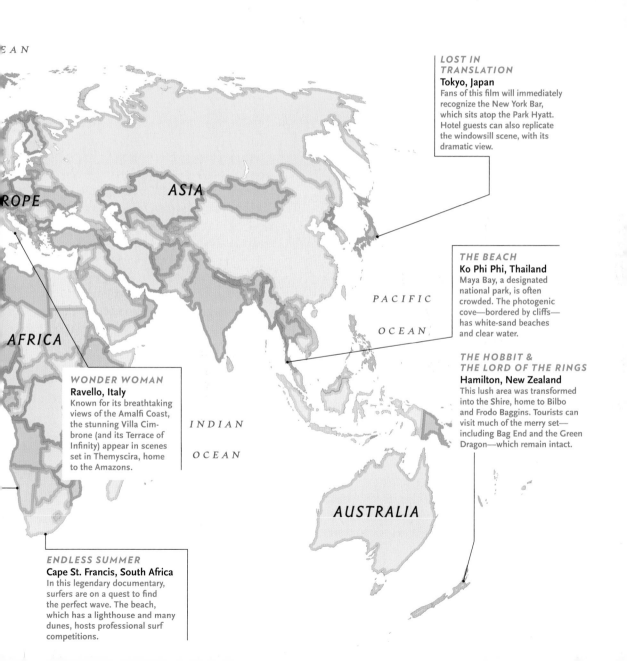

THE STAR WARS MOVIES HAVE BEEN FILMED ALL OVER THE WORLD, IN PLACES SUCH AS TUNISIA, ICELAND, NORWAY, CHINA, MALDIVES, GUATEMALA, JORDAN, AND ITALY.

LOST IN TRANSLATION
Tokyo, Japan
Fans of this film will immediately recognize the New York Bar, which sits atop the Park Hyatt. Hotel guests can also replicate the windowsill scene, with its dramatic view.

THE BEACH
Ko Phi Phi, Thailand
Maya Bay, a designated national park, is often crowded. The photogenic cove—bordered by cliffs—has white-sand beaches and clear water.

THE HOBBIT & THE LORD OF THE RINGS
Hamilton, New Zealand
This lush area was transformed into the Shire, home to Bilbo and Frodo Baggins. Tourists can visit much of the merry set—including Bag End and the Green Dragon—which remain intact.

WONDER WOMAN
Ravello, Italy
Known for its breathtaking views of the Amalfi Coast, the stunning Villa Cimbrone (and its Terrace of Infinity) appear in scenes set in Themyscira, home to the Amazons.

ENDLESS SUMMER
Cape St. Francis, South Africa
In this legendary documentary, surfers are on a quest to find the perfect wave. The beach, which has a lighthouse and many dunes, hosts professional surf competitions.

AMERICA'S BEST EATS

TASTY MEALS ARE ONE OF TRAVEL'S GREAT REWARDS

Tacos bring the flavors of Mexico north.

WEST COAST

FISH TACOS
Close to the sea and to Mexico, San Diego knows how to wrap excellent seafood in a tortilla: Fish is fried in beer batter or grilled over an open flame and then drenched in fiery salsa or topped with cabbage.

SAN FRANCISCO SOURDOUGH
Different yeasts, water, and even air contribute to unique tastes of fermented bread, and the San Francisco variety is known for its sharp acidity.

WEST COAST DOUGHNUTS
Savory or sweet, topped with chocolate or decked out in unexpected fixings like porcini mushrooms, the West Coast doughnut—of which Oregon is particularly proud—is a destination decadence.

MIDWEST

CHICAGO-STYLE HOT DOG
Hot dogs get signature treatment in cities like Chicago, where its "dragged-through-the-garden" beef dog is amped up with sweet relish, a pickle spear, hot pickled peppers (sport peppers), tomato wedges, diced onions, and a dash of celery salt and mustard.

JUICY LUCY
Minnesota's Juicy Lucy, invented in the 1950s, is a hamburger that contains a golden, molten, cheesy core tucked into the middle of a beef burger.

TART CHERRY PIE
Michigan's signature cherries are tart, so its beloved pies tend to run more sour than supersweet.

Cherries too tart for snacking are great in pies.

Cajun food emerged in areas settled by French Canadians.

Bagels are an example of local food gone national.

SOUTH

CAJUN FOOD
Commonly labeled "country" food, authentic Louisiana Cajun is big on pork, particularly boudin sausage; rice; cayenne pepper and paprika; and onion, garlic, bell pepper, and celery. It is considered less genteel than its Creole counterpart.

BARBECUE
Different locale, different barbecue. Chopped pork with a tomato-free vinegar sauce? You're probably in eastern North Carolina. Tangy dry-rub baby backs? Memphis. Molasses-based sauce? Kansas City.

KEY LIME PIE
Florida's official state pie features key limes, a tart fruit that's the size of a golf ball, has a yellow rind when ripe, and was introduced by Spaniards in the Keys.

A WORD FROM

Food as Community I always think of how food, for me, is a valuable tool for creating a relationship with people and with different cultures. Just as alliances in war build bonds between people who are different from each other, food and cooking can do the same … Food is a cultural fountain that doesn't just feed us but really tells the stories of faraway places.

—**JOSÉ ANDRÉS,** *chef and humanitarian*

NORTHEAST

BAGELS
The ultimate New York bagel is crisp on the outside without being crunchy, dense on the inside without being heavy, and plump without being oversize.

LOBSTER
Knowing how to eat a whole lobster is a skill Mainers seem to be born with, which doesn't make it any less messy. Don the requisite plastic bib, grab a claw cracker to get at that tasty claw meat, and dig in.

BOSTON CREAM PIE
This decadent dessert isn't a pie at all. It's a cake: two layers of golden sponge cake separated by a thick layer of rich, eggy pastry cream, all draped in chocolate and etched with white icing.

FULL-IMMERSION
FESTIVALS

LIKE NOWHERE ELSE

A yearning for authentic adventure influences travelers' itineraries, from informal lodging to attending events that are special to a certain place. At their best, these festivals welcome visitors with the hosts' unique approach to hospitality, communicate their culture's values, and impart their joie de vivre.

Burning Man is known for its large-scale sculptures, including the one it's named after.

World's Most Marvelous
FESTIVALS

1 **BURNING MAN** This temporary city (technically not a festival!) in the Nevada desert is a physical manifestation of a global community.

2 **CARNIVAL** Just before Lent, Rio holds a citywide costume party, with glitter, beads, balls, concerts, and the Samba Parade.

3 **DÍA DE LOS MUERTOS** In Mexico families welcome ancestors with glowing altars (*ofrendas*), skulls (*calaveras*), and parties.

4 **FESTIVAL FRINGE** Small venues in Edinburgh host this beloved open-access (read: uncurated) performing arts festival.

5 **FEZ FESTIVAL OF WORLD SACRED MUSIC** This event promotes peace with transcendent performances by diverse artists.

6 **GLASTONBURY FESTIVAL** The only thing better than this U.K. gathering's killer lineup is the £2 million it raises for NGOs.

7 **HOLI** Hindus in India and elsewhere celebrate winter's end with water and colored powders, symbolic of fire and spring.

8 **LA TOMATINA** At the world's biggest food fight, held in Spain, there are no losers. Get a ticket and some swim goggles.

9 **SYDNEY NEW YEAR'S EVE** One of the world's most spectacular fireworks productions is held on the waterfront.

10 **YI PENG FESTIVAL** In Chiang Mai, Thailand, thousands of glowing paper lanterns bear wishes and prayers aloft.

FURTHER

HIDDEN WORLDS UNDERGROUND

Earth holds wonders yet to be discovered, some unknown because inaccessible and others hidden from view by human activity. Hang Ken, part of a vast complex of caves in Vietnam's Phong Nha-Ke Bang National Park, was only revealed to the world in the last decade. Its limestone arches, vast stalagmites, and lightless pools harboring microscopic organisms have yet to be fully explored. Park rangers and tourist limits protect it and nearby caves from degradation. Those few lucky enough to visit commit to a few days off trekking and camp at water's edge.

Cavers illuminate the massive depths of Vietnam's Hang Ken.

GEOLOGISTS ESTIMATE THE HANG KEN CAVES TO BE THREE MILLION YEARS OLD, CARVED OUT BY RIVERS THAT STILL PLUNGE THROUGH DURING THE TORRENTIAL WET SEASON.

THIS PLANET
& BEYOND

Hawaii's Big Island, lava glows, oozes, and shoots up steam as it meets the sea.

THE SOLAR SYSTEM | THE UNIVERSE & BEYOND

QUIZ MASTER

Planetary Genius? How much do you know about our planet—Earth, sea, and sky? How about the solar system, universe, and beyond? Test your knowledge, and then read on for answers and general amazement.

—CARA SANTA MARIA, *Our Favorite Nerd*

p98

HOW MUCH OF OUR PLANET IS COVERED BY OCEAN?

PROJECTIONS SUGGEST ALL SUMMER ARCTIC SEA ICE WILL MELT BY WHAT YEAR?

HOW MUCH OF THE OCEAN IS CURRENTLY PROTECTED BY LAW?

p116

WHAT'S RARER, A SOLAR ECLIPSE OR A TRANSIT OF MERCURY?

p125

p116

THE DEADLIEST VOLCANIC ERUPTION OCCURRED IN WHAT CENTURY?

DID DINOSAURS EVER LIVE IN ANTARCTICA?

p130

WHAT COUNTRY WAS THE FIRST TO LAND ON THE MOON, AND IN WHAT YEAR?

p101

p109

WHAT'S THE BEST PLACE ON EARTH TO LISTEN FOR EARTHQUAKES?

p142

p101

WHAT PLANET WILL THE MISSION BEPICOLUMBO STUDY?

p128

HOW LONG AFTER THE BIG BANG DID STARS FIRST LIGHT UP?

WHAT PLANET CONTAINS THE LARGEST KNOWN CANYON IN THE SOLAR SYSTEM?

p134

OTHER THAN THE SUN, WHAT STAR IS CLOSEST TO EARTH?

p147

p153

WHAT'S A BLAZAR— A BLACK HOLE, A LASER, OR A STAR?

WHICH STAR IS NOT PART OF THE SUMMER TRIANGLE: VEGA, POLARIS, DENEB, OR ALTAIR?

p122

EARTH SCIENCE
TIME LINE

| 4.6 to 2.3 BYA | 2.3 BYA to 400 MYA | 400 to 200 MYA | 200 MYA to 20,000 YA |

■ 4.6 bya*
Planet Earth forms from the material that built the rest of the solar system.

■ 4.5 bya
Earth's moon forms out of space debris.

■ 4.3 bya
Liquid water appears on Earth.

■ 3.8 bya
Single-celled life emerges on Earth.

■ 3 bya
Earth's continental masses form.

■ 2.5–2.3 bya
Oxygen levels in the Earth's atmosphere rise.

* billion years ago

■ 2.1 bya
More complex multicellular organisms evolve.

■ 720–635 mya*
The temperature on Earth falls, and the entire planet is covered in ice.

■ 541 mya
Most major animal groups evolve in an event known as the Cambrian explosion.

■ 520 mya
Animals with bilateral symmetry first flourish on Earth.

■ 470 mya
Plant life first appears on land.

* million years ago

■ 360 mya
Amphibious life emerges from the water to live on land.

■ 251 mya
Massive numbers of marine and land species die off in the Permian extinction, the largest mass extinction in history.

■ 250 mya
A single supercontinent called Pangaea emerges.

■ 240 mya
The first dinosaurs appear on Earth.

■ 200 mya
The supercontinent Pangaea breaks up into separate landmasses.

■ 130 mya
Flowering plants, the most diverse group of land plants, emerge.

■ 65 mya
Dinosaurs go extinct in the aftermath of the Chicxulub asteroid impact.

■ 2.6 mya
Continents arrive at roughly their modern positions and a pattern of glacial and interglacial periods emerges.

■ 200,000 ya*
Homo sapiens first appear, and modern humans emerge.

* years ago

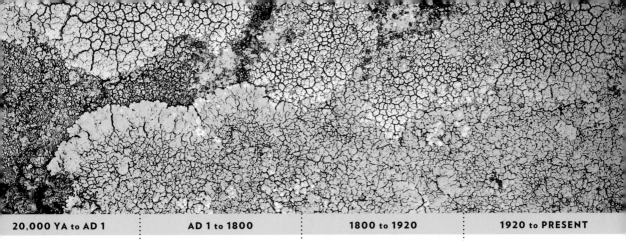

| 20,000 YA to AD 1 | AD 1 to 1800 | 1800 to 1920 | 1920 to PRESENT |

20,000 YA to AD 1

■ **11,700 ya**
The Holocene,
the current geological
age, begins.

■ **10,000 ya**
The last major
ice age ends.

■ **ca 499 BC**
Indian scientist Aryabhata
proposes that Earth
rotates on its axis.

■ **240 BC**
Eratosthenes calculates
the circumference
of the Earth.

AD 1 to 1800

■ **ca 1088**
Chinese scientist
Shen Kuo first describes
a magnetic compass
used for navigation.

■ **1490s**
Leonardo da Vinci begins
filling notebooks with
theories on astronomy,
Earth, physics, and more.

■ **1543**
Copernicus publishes
ideas on heliocentrism.

■ **1595**
Gerardus Mercator's
atlas of the world
is first published.

1800 to 1920

■ **1815**
Explosion of Mount
Tambora temporarily
changes Earth's climate.

■ **1831**
English explorer
James Ross locates
the position of the
north magnetic pole.

■ **1851**
Léon Foucault constructs
Foucault's pendulum
to show Earth's rotation.

■ **1912**
Alfred Wegener first
describes the theory
of continental drift.

■ **1913**
Charles Fabry and Henri
Buisson discover
the ozone layer.

1920 to PRESENT

■ **1935**
Charles Richter invents
the Richter scale
to measure earthquake
intensity.

■ **1960s**
Scientists first describe
plate tectonics.

■ **1960**
Jacques Piccard and Don
Walsh are first to visit
the deepest point in the
ocean, Challenger Deep.

■ **1970**
The inaugural Earth Day
is held on April 22.

■ **2017**
One of the largest
icebergs on record breaks
off from Antarctica's
Larsen C ice shelf.

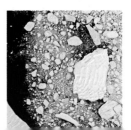

POLAR JET STREAM

A FORCE OF NATURE

The polar jet stream is a current of high-altitude air that separates low-pressure Arctic air from warmer, high-pressure air to the south. When it dips far south, it can deliver blasts of cold and snow to temperate latitudes; a north-jutting ridge promotes heat and drought.

Causes of Extreme Weather
Scientists are debating whether extremes are primarily due to the shifting cycles of the Pacific or to the melting of the Arctic.

Is It the Pacific?
Every few years or decades the eastern Pacific flips from a cold, food-rich body of water to something warmer—a cycle called the Pacific Decadal Oscillation.

Is It the Arctic?
Since satellites began regularly measuring Arctic sea ice in 1979, it has declined sharply in extent and thickness. Projections suggest that by 2040, it will have no sea ice left in summer.

The Arctic

The Arctic is warming faster than the rest of the planet, and loss of sea ice has global climatic effects. According to a controversial theory, Arctic warming is causing the jet stream to slow down and meander more. The result: unseasonable weather that sits in one place for a long time.

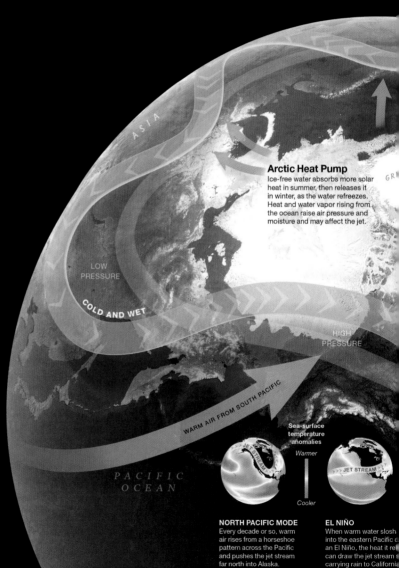

Arctic Heat Pump
Ice-free water absorbs more solar heat in summer, then releases it in winter, as the water refreezes. Heat and water vapor rising from the ocean raise air pressure and moisture and may affect the jet.

ASIA

GR

LOW PRESSURE

COLD AND WET

HIGH PRESSURE

WARM AIR FROM SOUTH PACIFIC

PACIFIC OCEAN

Sea-surface temperature anomalies

Warmer

Cooler

JET STREAM

JET STREAM

NORTH PACIFIC MODE
Every decade or so, warm air rises from a horseshoe pattern across the Pacific and pushes the jet stream far north into Alaska.

EL NIÑO
When warm water slosh into the eastern Pacific c an El Niño, the heat it re can draw the jet stream carrying rain to California

AS JET STREAMS MEANDER SLOWLY AROUND THE PLANET, THE WEATHER THEY CARRY LINGERS FOR A LONG TIME—AS HAPPENED WITH THE POLAR VORTEX COVERING MUCH OF NORTH AMERICA IN EARLY 2018.

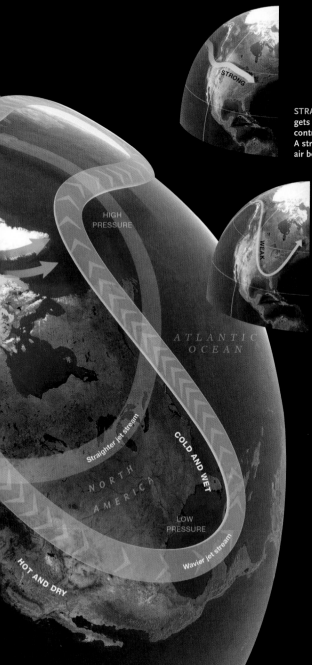

STRAIGHTER JET STREAM. The jet stream gets most of its energy from the temperature contrast between the air masses it separates. A strong jet is a straighter jet that keeps cold air bottled up in the Arctic.

WAVIER JET STREAM. As the Arctic warms faster than the midlatitudes, the temperature contrast decreases. That weakens the jet, letting Arctic air flow south—over eastern North America, for instance.

GOING GREEN

Jet Plane and Jet Stream INTERACTIONS

Eastward-bound aircraft gain speed and save fuel by flying inside a jet stream, but the relationship between climate and planes isn't mutually beneficial. Plane emissions contribute to human-generated climate change, and recent episodes of extreme heat grounded planes because they need cooler, heavier air to provide lift.

SHRINKING ANTARCTICA

STATE OF THE CONTINENT REFLECTS CLIMATE CHANGE

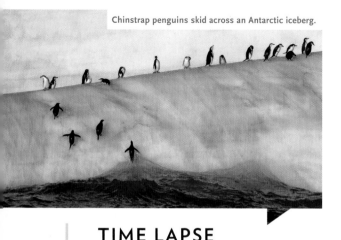

Chinstrap penguins skid across an Antarctic iceberg.

LANDSCAPE

EBB AND FLOE

Using data from 1992 to 2011, scientists measured ice sheet mass balance—how much snow was deposited on an ice sheet versus how much was lost, either due to surface melting or ice breaking off glaciers. Over those years, West Antarctica lost 65 billion tons of ice a year and the Antarctic Peninsula lost 20 billion tons a year. East Antarctica gained 14 billion tons of ice a year, however, a result of the higher rates of snowfall associated with climate change.

The rate at which ice melts and calves in the Amundsen Sea has quadrupled.

TIME LAPSE

A FAILING BUTTRESS

The floating Pine Island ice shelf, which supports a massive glacier, is failing. Warm ocean water is weakening it from below, reaching farther under the shelf than ever. Satellite pictures (below) captured the growth of a rift upstream, some 10 miles in from the Amundsen Sea. It sliced across the width of the shelf, releasing 225 square miles of ice. Even before it calved, a second rift more than 100 yards wide had formed a few miles up from the first.

Satellite images show a loss of ice about 10 times the size of Manhattan in just two months.

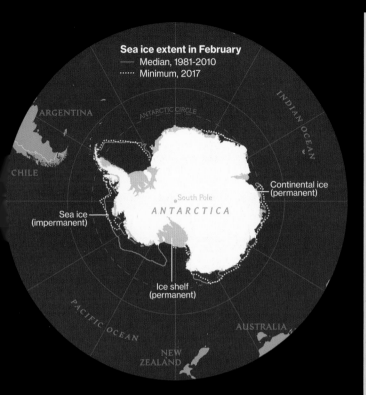

Sea ice extent in February
— Median, 1981-2010
······ Minimum, 2017

INDIAN OCEAN

ARGENTINA

ANTARCTIC CIRCLE

CHILE

Continental ice
(permanent)

South Pole

Sea ice
(impermanent)

ANTARCTICA

Ice shelf
(permanent)

PACIFIC OCEAN

AUSTRALIA

NEW
ZEALAND

CRISIS ON THE ICE

TRACKING THE MELTDOWN

Snow falling on Antarctica through the ages has piled up in domes of ice more than two miles thick. Most of that is likely safe for many centuries. But as the climate warms—water temperature here has risen by more than 1°F over recent decades—the continent's edges are crumbling. The natural flow of ice, down through coastal glaciers and floating ice shelves to the sea, is speeding up. By 2100 the ice loss may add several feet to global sea level rise.

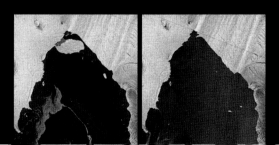

Exploration of the
7TH CONTINENT

1 **DINOSAURS LIVED HERE** when it was a more temperate climate and the continent was in our southwest Pacific Ocean.

2 **A METEORITE FROM MARS** that landed in Antarctica 13,000 years ago contains possible evidence of ancient life on Mars.

3 **THE BEST LISTENING SPOT FOR EARTHQUAKES** is here because there is no interference from the Earth's spinning motion.

4 **AN ACTIVE UNDERSEA VOLCANO** that sits off the Antarctic coast is just 900 feet from the water surface.

5 **ONCE PART OF NORTH AMERICA?** A lone granite boulder found on a glacier is very similar to rock found only in N.A.

6 **ICEBERGS ARE HOT SPOTS FOR AQUATIC LIFE** because they release nutrients from soil material into ocean waters.

7 **ANIMALS FROM AFRICA CAME TO ANTARCTICA** during a mass extinction event when it was part of the supercontinent Pangaea.

8 **GLACIERS ARE BEING ERODED ALONG THEIR FRONTS** by warmer ocean water due to climate change.

9 **A VALLEY DEEPER THAN THE GRAND CANYON** (with a depth of two miles) is hidden under the ice of West Antarctica.

10 **LIFE EXISTS THOUSANDS OF FEET UNDERWATER,** although no one knows what the tiny fish and other creatures there eat.

READING THE CLOUDS

Looking Up Though we've always had clouds above, we are still coming up with new ways to categorize and name them. Changes in technology, especially the sharing of photos, is also leading to new identifications.

FAIR-WEATHER CUMULUS
Small, puffy, white

CUMULIFORM
Puffy, humid air condensing

ORTHOGRAPHIC
Precipitation near mountains

CIRRUS
Thin and transparent

CIRROCUMULUS
White patches of high clouds

CIRROSTRATUS
High and thin, hazy

ALTOCUMULUS
Puffy clouds with darker patches

LENTICULAR
Lens-shaped, over mountains

ALTOCUMULUS CASTELLANUS
Tall, narrow

STRATOCUMULUS
Spread across large areas

STRATUS
Featureless gray layers

ALTOSTRATUS
Thin, gray, highest sheet-type

NIMBOSTRATUS
Low, dark, gloomy

CUMULUS CONGESTUS
Cauliflower-like

CUMULONIMBUS
Anvil shape, brings thunderstorms

ALTOCUMULUS MAMMATUS
Hanging pouches

THE INTERNATIONAL CLOUD ATLAS RECOGNIZED A NEW CLOUD TYPE IN 2017: THE ASPERITAS, DAPPLED LIKE THE SEA SEEN FROM UNDERWATER.

WILDER WEATHER

ANTICIPATING SEVERE EVENTS

Torrential hurricanes, devastating droughts, crippling ice storms, and raging heat waves—extreme weather phenomena claim lives and cause untold damage. Climate change influences severe weather by causing longer droughts and higher temperatures in some regions and more intense deluges in others, say climate experts. In mountainous and coastal settings worldwide, citizens are adjusting to new weather realities by strengthening warning, shelter, and protection systems.

Climate is a factor in, but not always a cause of, extreme weather events.

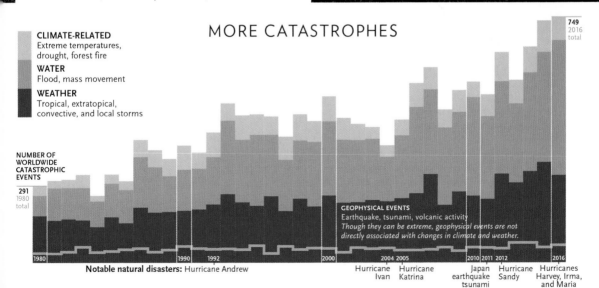

MORE CATASTROPHES

CLIMATE-RELATED
Extreme temperatures, drought, forest fire

WATER
Flood, mass movement

WEATHER
Tropical, extratopical, convective, and local storms

749
2016 total

NUMBER OF WORLDWIDE CATASTROPHIC EVENTS

291
1980 total

GEOPHYSICAL EVENTS
Earthquake, tsunami, volcanic activity
Though they can be extreme, geophysical events are not directly associated with changes in climate and weather.

1980   1990   1992   2000   2004 2005   2010 2011 2012   2016

Notable natural disasters: Hurricane Andrew   Hurricane Ivan   Hurricane Katrina   Japan earthquake tsunami   Hurricane Sandy   Hurricanes Harvey, Irma, and Maria

TORNADO

UNSTOPPABLE, POWERFUL STORMS WREAK HAVOC

Tornadoes are vertical funnels of rapidly spinning air. Their winds may top 250 miles an hour and can clear a pathway a mile wide and 50 miles long. Twisters are born in thunderstorms and are often accompanied by hail. Giant, persistent thunderstorms called supercells spawn the most destructive tornadoes. These violent storms occur in countries around the world, but the United States is a major hot spot, with about a thousand tornadoes every year—doing about $400 million in damage and killing as many as 70 people.

SPIN
When warm, humid air collides with cold, dry air, the warm air rises, causing an updraft, which may begin to rotate.

WIND SPEEDS
Measurements are estimations because anemometers cannot withstand the enormous force of tornadoes to record them.

A WORD FROM

Getting Close Although they mostly gain our attention for their adverse and sometimes tragic impacts upon humanity, tornadoes are fascinating, mesmerizing, and often stunningly beautiful phenomena. It takes a rare conspiracy of events to produce a tornado, and relatively few people ever get to witness one. As storm-chasing scientists, we strive to locate ourselves beneath rotating supercell thunderstorms in positions from where tornadogenesis, the formation process, and the rest of a tornado's ephemeral life cycle can be observed safely. Visual observations that we and other storm chasers record on video can then be analyzed alongside data from research radars and other scanning technologies to better understand the phenomenon.

—**ANTON SEIMON,** *geographer and storm chaser*

TOUCHDOWN
Water droplets from the rotating updraft's moist air can form a funnel cloud that grows and eventually descends.

With Doppler radar, warning time for tornadoes has more than doubled since the 1980s.

TIME OF DAY
Most tornadoes form in the late afternoon, because by then the sun has heated the ground and the atmosphere enough to produce thunderstorms.

DESTRUCTION
The Fujita scale measures intensity by matching storm damage to destruction at various observed wind speeds.

Deadliest Tornadoes in
U.S. HISTORY

1 **MAR. 1925: MO, IL, IN** This twister, known as the Tri-State Tornado, caused 2,027 injuries and 695 deaths.

2 **MAY 1840: LA, MS** At least 317 were killed and 109 hurt when this storm touched down along the Mississippi River.

3 **MAY 1896: MO, IL** Part of a larger outbreak, this event caused 1,000 injuries and 255 deaths in the St. Louis area.

4 **APR. 1936: MS** Though 700 people were hurt and 216 were killed in Tupelo, one-year-old Elvis Presley survived.

5 **APR. 1936: GA** The morning after Tupelo's tornado, another 203 died and 1,600 were injured in nearby Gainesville.

6 **APR. 1947: TX, KS, OK** Eventually reaching two miles wide, this twister hurt 970 and took the lives of 181.

7 **MAY 2011: MO** In Joplin, the costliest single tornado in U.S. history ($2.8 billion) took 158 lives and hurt 1,000.

8 **APR. 1908: LA, MS** This Dixie Alley tornado, which saw 770 injuries and 143 fatalities, traveled over 150 miles.

9 **JUNE 1899: WI** The New Richmond "cyclone" struck circusgoers, killing 117 and leaving another 200 injured.

10 **JUNE 1953: MI** One of eight in MI and OH that day, a tornado in Flint's Beecher suburb left 116 dead and 844 injured.

BE PREPARED
FOR TORNADOES

THINK THROUGH REACTIONS BEFORE, DURING, AND AFTER

Make safety plans ahead of time.

HOW TO PREPARE

INSIDE

Build an emergency kit and designate a safe room. Make a plan for communication and reunion during and after the tornado. Research risk and insurance policies. Gather helmets, goggles, and car seats for additional protection.

OUTSIDE

Learn the terms: "Watch" refers to conditions; "warning" means tornadoes have been spotted. Know warning signs, including a loud roar and large hail.

DON'TS

Don't go outside if a watch has been issued, unless you're in a mobile home and you can reach sturdier shelter immediately. Don't leave items such as grills, yard furniture, and trash cans outside your home.

HOW TO SURVIVE

INSIDE

Get to a safe room or a room with no windows on the lowest floor. Gather items such as your wallet, keys, prescriptions, and sturdy shoes only if time permits.

OUTSIDE

If you're in your car, stay inside (but not in the driver's seat) with your seat belt on; lower your head below the windows and cover it. If outside, lie down and cover your head; find a ditch or sloping area, if possible.

DON'TS

Don't open windows. Don't seek shelter on higher floors (inside) or under overpasses (outside); always get as low as you can. Don't try to outrun the tornado.

Stay in your car if you see a twister coming.

Beware of hazards after the storm passes.

HOW TO RECOVER

INSIDE
Leave immediately if you suspect a gas leak. Shut off the main circuit breaker if you suspect damage to the electrical system. Assess structural damage before picking through debris. Clean up hazardous materials.

OUTSIDE
Report hazards to utility companies and police. Dress appropriately if approaching debris and proceed with caution: Many tornado injuries occur after the event (e.g., stepping on nails).

DON'TS
Don't move injured people. Don't stop monitoring weather reports. Don't burn fuel (e.g., propane, charcoal) indoors. Don't go anywhere near downed power lines. Don't return home until you're told it's safe.

> **" CLOSE-KNIT COMMUNITIES ARE ONE OF OUR GREATEST ADVANTAGES WHEN IT COMES TO DEALING WITH NATURAL HAZARDS."**
>
> **—LEE DEPALO**, REGIONAL ADMINISTRATOR, FEMA

In Your Home
EMERGENCY KIT

1 **FOOD AND WATER** One gallon of water per person per day and shelf-stable food for 14 days (or three days' worth for evacuation)

2 **LIGHT SOURCES** At least one flashlight and spare batteries; battery-powered lantern; matches or butane lighters (use cautiously)

3 **RADIO AND PHONE** Crank- or battery-powered radio, preferably with weather radio scanner; cell phone, battery, and charger

4 **FIRST-AID KIT AND MEDICATIONS** Ready-made kit with emergency manual and a week's worth of unexpired prescription meds

5 **MULTIPURPOSE TOOL** A small, many-in-one tool comprising blades and hardware, including pliers and screwdrivers

6 **ATTENTION GETTERS** A whistle or shrill noisemaker and a brightly colored cloth, such as a bandanna, to use as a signal

7 **HYGIENE SUPPLIES** Toilet paper, soap, feminine hygiene items, and toothbrushes and toothpaste; makeup and deodorant optional

8 **IMPORTANT DOCUMENTS** Copies of birth certificates, passports, and insurance policies; local map; list of emergency contact numbers

9 **CASH AND CREDIT CARDS** Funds sufficient for several days, especially in case of power outages; spare credit card

10 **SENIOR, BABY, AND PET CARE** Items for certain household members, such as medications, diapers, wipes, prepared food, and cat litter

VOLCANO

WHEN EARTH ERUPTS

When we talk about volcanoes in the continental U.S., we probably think of Mount St. Helens, the "Mount Fuji of America," which erupted spectacularly in May 1980. We are less likely to think of Yellowstone, even with its geysers and hot mud, because although it is surrounded by mountains, it is not one itself. But our most famous national park sits squarely atop one of Earth's biggest volcanoes—a supervolcano—and it is not extinct. Volcanoes, as we tend to imagine them, form mountains. Supervolcanoes erase them.

Sleeping Giants

Beneath Yellowstone is a hellish column of superheated rock— mostly solid, some viscous, some molten. Experts say three major blasts, bigger than most known prehistoric eruptions, have shaken Yellowstone in its two million years atop the plume. The smallest of these ejected 280 times the volume of what Mount St. Helens projected.

The U.S. Geological Survey's Yellowstone Volcano Observatory monitors sensors and satellites, looking for changes in activity. Despite rumors, a supereruption like the one illustrated on the facing page is not imminent. For its part, the USGS puts the rough yearly odds of another massive Yellowstone blast at one in 730,000.

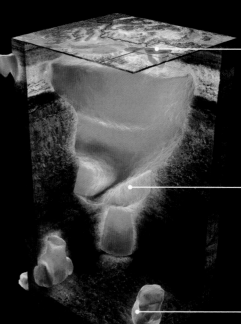

CALDERA
Buoyed by an expanding magma chamber, the caldera, formed by the last major eruption, has risen as much as 2.8 inches a year over the past decade.

PLUME
Beneath the caldera, a vast rocky zone of primordia heat emanates from the mantl This plume feeds a magma chamber brimming with volcanic fuel just a few miles below the surface.

HOT POCKETS
Current seismic data and geological conditions suggest there may be smaller pockets of hot rock associated with the Yellowstone plume.

POP!

MOVIES STARRING VOLCANOES

- *The Last Days of Pompeii* (1935)
- *Stromboli* (1950)
- *Krakatoa: East of Java* (1969)
- *St. Helens* (1981)
- *Joe Versus the Volcano* (1990)
- *Dante's Peak* (1997)
- *Volcano* (1997)
- *Supervolcano* (2005)
- *Disaster Zone: Volcano in New York* (2006)
- *Volcano Zombies* (2014)
- *Pompeii* (2014)
- *Ixcanul* (2015)

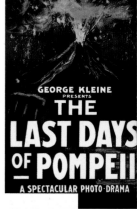

GEORGE KLEINE
PRESENTS
THE
LAST DAYS
OF POMPEII
A SPECTACULAR PHOTO·DRAMA

HOW DOES IT HAPPEN?

World's Deadliest
ERUPTIONS

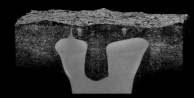

BEFORE THE ERUPTION Warning signs may appear years in advance. Pressure builds from below, driving seismic activity and doming of the land over the hot spot.

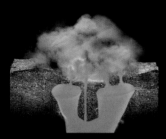

THE EARTH FRACTURES Gas-filled magma explodes upward; ash and debris soon rain down across hundreds of miles. Fiery ash flows clog rivers and carpet landscapes near and far.

ERUPTIONS CONTINUE Periodic blasts go on for weeks or even months, emitting pollutants and causing acid rain. Eventually, the land collapses and a new caldera is born.

1 **TAMBORA, INDONESIA**
Apr. 10, 1815: 92,000 killed
Largest in recorded history, with ejecta volume of 12 mi^3

2 **KRAKATAU, INDONESIA**
Aug. 26, 1883: 36,417 killed
Ash layer lowered temperatures and affected global climate.

3 **PELÉE, MARTINIQUE**
May 8, 1902: 29,025 killed
Most deaths direct result of eruption and not tsunami, etc.

4 **RUIZ, COLOMBIA**
Nov. 13, 1985: 25,000 killed
Mudflows caused by melting snow and ice buried thousands.

5 **UNZEN, JAPAN**
May 21, 1792: 14,300 killed
Eruption followed by earthquake, landslide, and tsunami

6 **LAKI, ICELAND**
June 8, 1783: 9,350 killed
Lava flows and explosions continued for eight months.

7 **KELUD, INDONESIA**
May 19, 1919: 5,110 killed
Still active with hundreds killed in 1951, 1966, 1990, and 2014

8 **GALUNGGUNG, INDONESIA**
Oct. 8, 1882: 4,011 killed
Crater lake ejected boiling water and mud during eruptions.

9 **VESUVIUS, ITALY**
Dec. 16, 1631: 3,500 killed
Fatal pyroclastic flows followed a 30-mile-high cloud.

10 **VESUVIUS, ITALY**
79: 3,360 killed
Ash-covered Pompeii is famous for perfectly preserved victims.

CARSTEN PETER
PHOTOGRAPHER

FOR HIM, EXTREME IS THE NEW NORMAL

Adventure photographer Carsten Peter, a two-time recipient of a World Press Photo Award, is no stranger to extreme conditions, such as rappelling into active volcanoes with turbulent lava lakes and superheated thermal caves. This passion was born at the edge of a volcano crater when on a family vacation as a teen.

Peter captures the action as lava shoots into the air from Mount Etna in Sicily.

The first time Carsten Peter tried to photograph an active volcano, he was too busy running away from flying rocks to remember to click the shutter. Now the German adventure photographer spends his National Geographic assignments going to extremes—braving toxic caverns and acid waterfalls to shoot within the deepest ice shafts on Earth, breaking altitude records while flying his motorized paraglider, and both chasing and being chased by tornadoes. Peter claims that he does not go looking for danger, but what inspired this enthusiastic quest for never-before-seen images from some of the world's scariest environments?

CAPTIVATED BY MOUNT ETNA

"I was 15 years old and on vacation in Italy with my parents. They took me to see Mount Etna," he says. "As soon as I saw it, I was drawn to the crater's edge. I was fascinated. My parents went back to the tour bus . . . but I couldn't leave. I edged closer, seeing the smoke inside, imagining the boiling magma below. At that moment I became infected."

Over the past few decades, Peter has traveled the world to examine volcanoes in places like Iceland, Ethiopia, Indonesia, Hawaii, the South Pacific, Kamchatka, Iceland, and the Democratic Republic of the Congo, using single-rope descending and climbing techniques developed by cave explorers. "The size and power of a volcano is like nothing else on Earth," he says. "You think you understand the Earth and its geology, but once you look down into a volcanic crater and see what's there, well, you realize you will never completely understand. It is that powerful. That big." He grins.

" IT'S NOT LIKE I'M ACTIVELY LOOKING FOR DANGER. I WANT TO SHOW PEOPLE THE WONDERS OF NATURE."

Recently, Peter explored lava tubes and caves near Mauna Loa.

BY CONTINENT

Partial List of Peter's HOT SPOTS

■ **AFRICA: Mount Nyiragongo**
Active volcano in Virunga Mountains, Democratic Republic of the Congo

■ **ANTARCTICA: Mount Erebus**
Earth's southernmost active volcano, with lava lakes deep inside ice caves

■ **ASIA: Klyuchevskoy**
Large active crater on Russia's Kamchatka Peninsula; highest active volcano in Eurasia

■ **EUROPE: Mount Etna**
On the east coast of Sicily, Europe's largest active volcano, first recorded eruption in 425 BC

■ **NORTH AMERICA: Yellowstone**
Last erupted 70,000 ya, but recent tremors including a measurable quake suggest eruptions in near future

■ **SOUTH AMERICA: Tungurahua**
Southeast of Quito, Ecuador, its name means "throat of fire" in native Quechua

BEST OF @NATGEO

OUR FAVORITE PHOTOS OF EXTREME WEATHER

@pedromcbride | PETE MCBRIDE
Earth tones resolve into all the colors of the rainbow as weather lifts over the Grand Canyon.

@ladzinski | KEITH LADZINSKI
A beautiful, fierce cumulonimbus cloud over the plains of eastern Wyoming

@jimmy_chin | JIMMY CHIN
Summer storm clouds roll through the Teton Range near the city of Jackson, Wyoming.

@haarbergphoto | ORSOLYA HAARBERG
Snow falls in a Scandinavian birch forest in winter, obscuring the treeline.

> ❝ CLIMATE IS WHAT ON AN AVERAGE WE MAY EXPECT. WEATHER IS WHAT WE ACTUALLY GET.❞
>
> —ANDREW JOHN HERBERTSON, GEOGRAPHER

@thomaspeschak | THOMAS PESCHAK
A sandstorm rages across a road in central Namibia. These storms are so powerful they can strip paint.

@randyolson | RANDY OLSON
A lightning storm creates a magnificent aerial backdrop to thousands of sandhill cranes coming in to roost in the shallows of Nebraska's Platte River.

@hoang_dai_thach | HOÀNG THẠCH
A fisherman watches a waterspout as a storm approaches Doc Let Beach in Vietnam.

@adamfergusonphoto | ADAM FERGUSON
A summer storm forms over an opal field in a remote area of South Australia.

MINERALS
REVEALED

How Hard Is It? More than 4,000 naturally occurring minerals have been found on Earth. Geologists classify them according to hardness, using the Mohs' scale (opposite). All rocks are made of mixtures of minerals.

JASPER
Hardness: 6–7

FELDSPAR
Hardness: 6–7

OLIVINE
Hardness: 6.5–7

GARNET
Hardness: 6.5–7.5

EPIDOTE
Hardness: 6–7

STAUROLITE
Hardness: 7–7.5

TOURMALINE
Hardness: 7–7.5

PYROXENE
Hardness: 5–6.5

TALC
Hardness: 1

HORNBLENDE
Hardness: 5–6

BIOTITE
Hardness: 2.5–3

MUSCOVITE
Hardness: 2–2.5

KAOLINITE
Hardness: 2–2.5

SERPENTINE
Hardness: 3–6

DOLOMITE
Hardness: 3.5–4

CALCITE
Hardness: 3

GYPSUM & ANHYDRITE
Hardness: 2 & 3–3.5

MALACHITE
Hardness: 3.5–4

CHALCOPYRITE
Hardness: 3.5–4

GALENA
Hardness: 2.5–3

PYRITE
Hardness: 6–6.5

FLUORITE
Hardness: 4

MAGNETITE
Hardness: 5.5

HEMATITE
Hardness: 5–6

QUARTZ
Hardness: 7

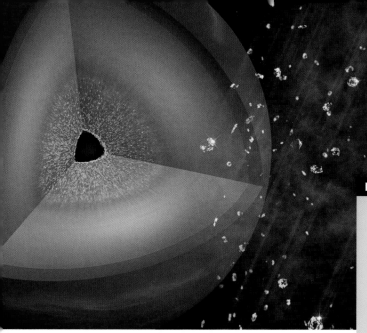

CREATING GEMS

DIAMONDS FROM HEAVEN?

Knowing that medieval alchemists sought, unsuccessfully, to change base metals into gold was no deterrent to the scientists who gathered at the SLAC National Accelerator Laboratory at Stanford to turn plastic into diamonds. Their experiment was an attempt to re-create what might take place inside our icy giant planets. In the lab, polystyrene stood in for hydrogen and carbon, and an intense optical laser played the role of the pressure and temperature found in the planets' cores. The result—diamond rain!—was otherworldly, indeed, though fleeting: The diamonds lived for only 50 quadrillionths of a second (5.0×10^{-14} sec.) and measured a few nanometers (1×10^{-9} m) in diameter. Once researchers figure out how to make them last longer, they may find other applications for them in medicine and technology.

> ## " IT WAS ONE OF THE BEST MOMENTS OF MY SCIENTIFIC CAREER."
>
> —DOMINIK KRAUS, DIAMOND RAIN PROJECT SCIENTIST

Mohs' Mineral
HARDNESS SCALE

1 **Easily scratched by fingernail, feels soapy or greasy** *Example: talc*

2 **Can be scratched by fingernail** Gold, 2.5–3.0. *Example: gypsum*

3 **Can be scratched by copper coin** Copper penny, 3.2. *Example: calcite*

4 **Can be scratched by knife** Platinum, 4–4.5; iron, 4–5. *Example: fluorite*

5 **Scratched by knife with difficulty** Pocketknife, 5.1; plate glass, 5.5. *Example: apatite*

6 **Can be scratched by steel file but not knife; scratches glass with difficulty** Steel needle, 6.5. *Example: feldspar*

7 **Scratches window glass** *Example: quartz*

8 **Scratches glass very easily** Varieties of beryl, 7.5–8. *Example: topaz, cubic zirconia, emerald, aquamarine*

9 **Cuts glass** *Example: corundum (ruby and sapphire)*

10 **Cuts glass so easily that it is used as a glass cutter** *Example: diamond*

SAVING THE WORLD'S
PRISTINE SEAS

THERE ARE PLACES IN THE WORLD WHERE MARINE LIFE ABOUNDS

National Geographic Explorer-in-Residence Enric Sala launched the Pristine Seas project in 2008 to explore and help save the last wild places in the ocean. Since then, thanks to this effort, 18 marine reserves have been created and nearly two million square miles of ocean have been protected.

THE OCEAN COVERS 70 PERCENT OF THE PLANET, YET ONLY 3 PERCENT OF THE OCEAN IS PROTECTED.

Manta rays glide through the pristine waters of Palau, in the South Pacific.

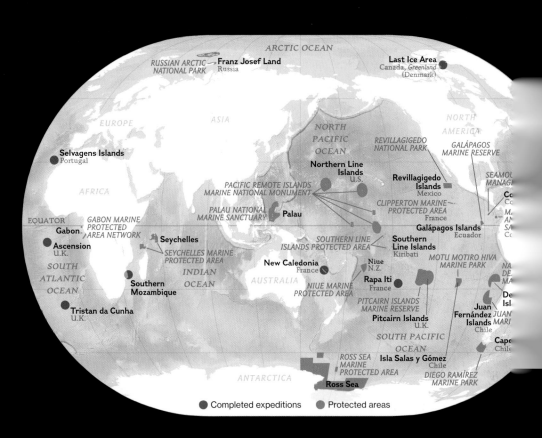

ARCTIC OCEAN

RUSSIAN ARCTIC → **Franz Josef Land**
NATIONAL PARK   Russia

Last Ice Area
Canada, *Greenland*
(Denmark)

EUROPE   ASIA   NORTH
                                  PACIFIC   NORTH
                                  OCEAN   AMERICA

Selvagens Islands   REVILLAGIGEDO   GALÁPAGOS
Portugal   NATIONAL PARK   MARINE RESERVE

                          **Northern Line   SEAMOU
                          Islands**   MANAGE
AFRICA   U.S.
           PACIFIC REMOTE ISLANDS   **Revillagigedo**   Co
           MARINE NATIONAL MONUMENT   **Islands**   Co
                                           Mexico
                    PALAU NATIONAL   CLIPPERTON MARINE ~   M.
                    MARINE SANCTUARY **Palau** PROTECTED AREA   A
                                                 France   SA
EQUATOR   GABON MARINE   Co
Gabon PROTECTED   **Galápagos Islands**
          AREA NETWORK   **Seychelles**   SOUTHERN LINE   Ecuador
Ascension   SEYCHELLES MARINE ISLANDS PROTECTED AREA **Southern**
U.K.   PROTECTED AREA   **Line Islands**
SOUTH   Kiribati
ATLANTIC   INDIAN   **New Caledonia**   **Niue**   MOTU MOTIRO HIVA   NA
OCEAN   OCEAN   AUSTRALIA France   N.Z.   MARINE PARK   DE
           Southern   **Rapa Iti**   MA
           Mozambique NIUE MARINE   France
                          PROTECTED AREA   De
                                          PITCAIRN ISLANDS   Isl
Tristan da Cunha   MARINE RESERVE   **Juan**
U.K.   **Pitcairn Islands** **Fernández** JUAN
                                          U.K.   **Islands** MARI
                                                              Chile
                                            SOUTH PACIFIC   Cape
                                               OCEAN   Chile

                          ROSS SEA   **Isla Salas y Gómez**
                          MARINE   Chile
                          PROTECTED AREA   DIEGO RAMÍREZ
ANTARCTICA   MARINE PARK
                          Ross Sea

● Completed expeditions   ● Protected areas

A WORD FROM

A Spiritual Experience We go to the pristine places in the ocean to try
to understand the ecosystems, to try to measure or count fish and
sharks and see how these places are different from the places we know.
But the best feeling is this biophilia that E. O. Wilson talks about, where
humans have this sense of awe and wonder in front of untamed nature
... If it were not for these places that show hope, I don't think I could continue doing this job.

—**ENRIC SALA,** *founder of Pristine Seas and National Geographic Explorer-in-Residence*

RISING
SEA LEVEL

FLOODING REACHES BEYOND FLOODPLAINS

Even in the absence of a hurricane, coastal cities face a twofold threat: Rising oceans will gradually inundate low-lying areas, and higher seas will extend the reach of storm surges. By the end of the century, a hundred-year storm surge like Hurricane Harvey's might occur every 10 years or even more often. Experts predict that sea level will rise at least 20 inches by 2070, putting 150 million people in the world's large port cities at risk from flooding and causing $35 trillion in property damage—equal to 9 percent of the global GDP.

IN 2012, **DURING** HURRICANE SANDY, STORM SURGE MET HIGH TIDE. WAVES GREW TO 32.5 FEET 15 MILES OFFSHORE, AND FLOODWATERS CLIMBED TO NEARLY 10 FEET ALONG THE NEW JERSEY COASTLINE.

In Manhattan, Hurricane Sandy's surging tide knocked out a Con Ed substation, darkening the city below Midtown.

Climate Change Risks
BY WORLD REGION

■ **AFRICA**
Shifts in biome distribution, loss of coral reefs, reduced crop productivity, adverse effects on livestock, vector- and water-borne diseases, undernutrition, and migration

■ **EUROPE**
Changes in habitats and species of flora and fauna—both terrestrial and marine—with local extinctions and continental-scale shifts in species distributions

■ **ASIA**
Reductions in food production and security; increases in mortality and morbidity from diarrheal diseases, dengue fever, and malaria with heavy rain and rising temperatures

■ **AUSTRALASIA**
Declines in coral reefs and montane eco-systems; reductions in water resources and agricultural production; increased frequency of deadly heat waves, floods, and wildfires

■ **NORTH AMERICA**
Stresses on ecosystems and water sources, declines in food production, and growing vulnerability to extreme weather events

■ **CENTRAL AND SOUTH AMERICA**
Increases in forest and farmland degrada-tion, biodiversity and ecosystem losses (including coastal and marine areas), extreme weather events, and food insecurity

■ **SMALL ISLANDS**
Threats from sea level rise, tropical and extratropical cyclones, increasing air and sea surface temperatures (causing ecosystem degradation), and changing rainfall patterns

■ **POLAR REGIONS**
Shifts in marine species' ranges and in timing and magnitude of seasonal biomass production; disruptions in food webs and survival of dependent species and in vulnerable settlements and economies

WINTER SKY

FINDING ORION

The winter sky hosts some of the brightest stars in the night sky, including the recognizable and popular constellation of Orion.

Orion: Hunter, Shepherd, Farmer

In the Northern Hemisphere, Orion is lord of the winter sky, his distinctive shape filled with bright stars and other astronomical sights. The constellation is named for a famed hunter of Greek mythology, but it is not the only story associated with this star pattern. Other cultures have seen the constellation as representing a shepherd or a harvesting scythe, because it first appears in the northern sky during harvest times.

Orion features two of the brightest stars in the sky. To the north, at the hunter's shoulder, is Betelgeuse, the ninth brightest star, with a diameter larger than the orbit of Earth and a mass of 20 suns. To the south Rigel, the sixth brightest, is also quite large (17 solar masses) and, thanks to its proximity to the Equator, was one of the "nautical stars" that sailors would use to locate themselves on the ocean. But the real action, astronomically speaking, is in Orion's belt and the "sword" that hangs from it. There you will find the Orion Nebula, one of the few easily seen with the naked eye.

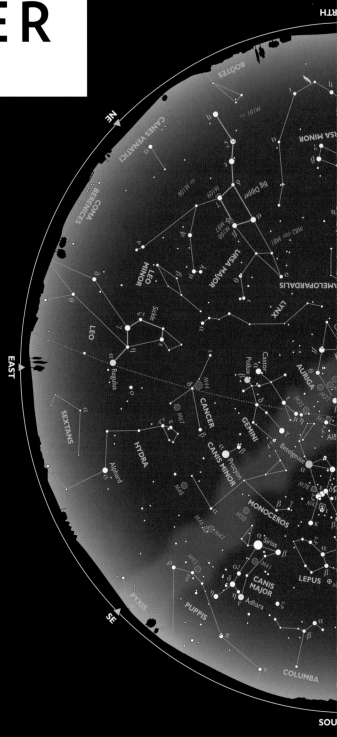

STELLAR MAGNITUDES

- −0.5 and brighter
- −0.4 to 0.0
- 0.1 to 0.5
- 0.6 to 1.0
- 1.1 to 1.5
- 1.6 to 2.0
- 2.1 to 2.5
- 2.6 to 3.0
- 3.1 to 3.5
- 3.6 to 4.0
- 4.1 to 4.5
- 4.6 to 5.0
- Variable star

DEEP SKY OBJECTS

- Open star cluster
- Globular star cluster
- Bright nebula
- Planetary nebula
- Galaxy

A WORD FROM

Stars Being Born Dangling below Orion's belt, there is a line of fainter stars just visible to the naked eye. This special "gleam" in the sword is a colossal stellar nursery more than 1,200 light-years distant called the Great Orion Nebula . . . a glowing cloud in the shape of a blooming flower made of dust and gas, mostly hydrogen. It's amazing to think that you see it glowing from the light of dozens of newborn stars inside.

—**ANDREW FAZEKAS,** *"The Night Sky Guy"*

SUMMER SKY

WARM WEATHER SKIES

When you're outside enjoying a pleasant summer evening, see how easy it is to find the Summer Triangle overhead.

The Bright Summer Triangle
Just because all of the officially recognized constellations were in place by the 18th century doesn't mean that people aren't finding new pictures and patterns in the sky. The Summer Triangle—an asterism (or group of stars) featuring three bright stars in three separate constellations—is an example of this: Although the asterism itself was first noted in the 19th century, the name Summer Triangle was not popularized until the 1950s, when British broadcaster and astronomer Sir Patrick Moore used it and astronomer H. A. Rey (creator of Curious George) included it in his guidebook, *Find the Constellations*.

The stars that create the Summer Triangle are three of the brightest in the northern sky: Vega, in Lyra, is the second brightest star in the summer sky and the first (apart from the sun) to be photographed. Deneb, in Cygnus, is estimated to be 60,000 times more luminous than the sun. Altair, in Aquila, is just 16.7 light-years away. The grouping is visible to most in the Northern Hemisphere.

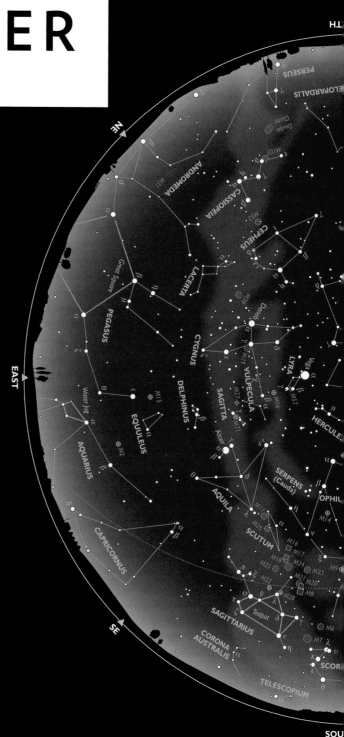

> **" THE STARS AWAKEN A CERTAIN REVERENCE, THOUGH ALWAYS PRESENT, THEY ARE INACC**
>
> —SARAH WILLIAMS, POET

STELLAR MAGNITUDES

- −0.5 and brighter
- −0.4 to 0.0
- 0.1 to 0.5
- 0.6 to 1.0
- 1.1 to 1.5
- 1.6 to 2.0
- 2.1 to 2.5
- 2.6 to 3.0
- 3.1 to 3.5
- 3.6 to 4.0
- 4.1 to 4.5
- 4.6 to 5.0
- Variable star

DEEP SKY OBJECTS

- Open star cluster
- Globular star cluster
- Bright nebula
- Planetary nebula
- Galaxy

GOING GREEN

For Bette
LIGHT

More than 80 perce
areas—and 99 perc
of the United States
under skies so blot
light that the Milky
virtually invisible.

SHAPES IN THE STARS

Connecting the Dots Humans have an urge to order the heavens—whether for tracking seasons, navigating travel, or conveying history and myth. Here are 16 easily distinguished constellations in the Northern Hemisphere.

ANDROMEDA, the Chained Maiden
View in Oct.–Nov.;
contains galaxy visible to naked eye

AQUARIUS, the Water Bearer
Large constellation visible
in the SW U.S. during autumn

CANIS MAJOR, the Dog
Just southeast of Orion; contains
Sirius, brightest star in the night sky

CAPRICORNUS, the Sea Goat
Distinctive triangle of 12 faint stars;
visible in southern sky in late summer

CASSIOPEIA, the Queen
W-shape visible year-round
near North Pole

CYGNUS, the Swan
Shaped as if a bird, wings out, flying
south; also called the Northern Cross

DRACO, the Dragon
A long tail visible year-round
between Ursa Major and Ursa Minor

GEMINI, the Twins
From the twins originate
December's Geminid meteor showers

HYDRA, the Sea Serpent
Largest constellation of all; a serpentine
series of 17 stars visible in spring

ORION, the Hunter
Huge stars; famous Orion Nebula
easy to spot under belt

PERSEUS, the Hero
Double star cluster atop head; source
of August's Perseid meteor shower

SAGITTARIUS, the Archer
Prominent in midsummer; contains
eight high-magnitude stars

SCORPIO, the Scorpion
Bright star Antares known to the
Romans as the "heart of the scorpion"

URSA MAJOR, the Great Bear
Includes the well-known Big Dipper;
points to the North Star

URSA MINOR, the Little Bear
Also called the Little Dipper;
includes Polaris, the North Star

VIRGO, the Virgin
Second largest constellation in the
sky; visible in the SE in late spring

> " THE COSMOS IS ALSO WITHIN US. WE ARE MADE OF STAR STUFF. WE ARE A WAY FOR THE COSMOS TO KNOW ITSELF."
>
> —CARL SAGAN, AUTHOR AND COSMOLOGIST

A meteor streaks the sky during the Geminids shower.

A YEAR OF THREE SUPERMOONS

A so-called supermoon occurs when two lunar events collide. First, the moon is full: This happens when the moon is opposite the sun in relation to Earth, hence the sun brightens the entire side of the moon that faces us. Second, the moon is close: This happens when the moon's orbit, which is not perfectly circular, brings it closest to Earth. Full moon plus close proximity equals supermoon, at least from our earthbound perspective. A supermoon can appear 14 percent larger and 30 percent brighter than a full moon in other months.

Skywatching Events
IN 2019

1 **TOTAL SOLAR ECLIPSE, JULY 2** Visible from central Chile, central Argentina, and the South Pacific

2 **TOTAL LUNAR ECLIPSE, JANUARY 21** Visible from most of North and South America, extreme western Europe, and Africa

3 **SUPERMOONS** Full moons on January 21, February 19, March 21

4 **MERCURY TRANSITS THE SUN, NOVEMBER 11** Rare opportunity to see Mercury cross the sun, won't happen again until 2039

5 **CONJUNCTION OF VENUS AND JUPITER, JANUARY 22 AND NOVEMBER 24** Two bright planets in eastern early morning sky

6 **MERCURY SIGHTINGS, JUNE 23 AND OCTOBER 20** On these dates Mercury will be at its highest above the horizon in evening sky.

7 **JUPITER SIGHTING, JUNE 10** Jupiter will be closest, hence brightest. Four moons may be visible with binoculars.

8 **SATURN SIGHTING, JULY 9** Saturn will be closest, hence brightest, and visible all night long.

9 **GEMINIDS METEOR SHOWER, DECEMBER 7 TO 17** A nearly full moon may diminish the number of meteors seen this year.

10 **PERSEIDS METEOR SHOWER, JULY 17 TO AUGUST 24** One of the most abundant of the annual meteor showers, with dozens of meteors an hour at peak

SPACE SCIENCE
TIME LINE

14 BYA to 1 BC	AD 1 to 1600	1600 to 1700	1700 to 1800

14 BYA to 1 BC

■ **13.8 bya***
The universe forms in the big bang.

■ **13.2 bya**
Our home galaxy, the Milky Way, forms.

■ **4.6 bya**
Our solar system starts to emerge around the sun.

■ **4.6 bya**
Planet Earth forms.

■ **4.5 bya**
Earth's moon forms from debris.

■ **240 BC**
Chinese astronomers make the first record of what becomes known as Halley's comet.

* *billion years ago*

AD 1 to 1600

■ **46**
Roman emperor Julius Caesar introduces the Julian calendar.

■ **ca 150**
Ptolemy writes the *Almagest*, a standard guide to astronomy for over a thousand years.

■ **310**
Chinese astronomers produce a comprehensive star map.

■ **1150**
Astronomer Solomon Jarchus compiles the first celestial almanac.

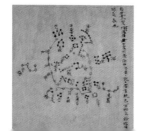

1600 to 1700

■ **1610**
Galileo observes four of Jupiter's moons.

■ **1645**
Flemish cartographer Michael Langrenus publishes the first map of the moon.

■ **1655**
Dutch scientist Christiaan Huygens confirms that Saturn has rings.

■ **1664**
English scientist Robert Hooke describes Jupiter's red spot.

■ **1676**
Danish astronomer Ole Rømer makes the first quantitative measure of the speed of light.

1700 to 1800

■ **1725**
Catalog of over 3,000 stars compiled by England's first Astronomer Royal, Rev. John Flamsteed, is published.

■ **1731**
English astronomer John Bevis discovers the Crab Nebula.

■ **1771**
Charles Messier publishes catalog of astronomical objects including galaxies, star clusters, and nebulae.

■ **1781**
British astronomer William Herschel discovers the planet Uranus.

■ **1783**
English physicist John Michell predicts the existence of black holes.

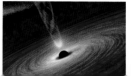

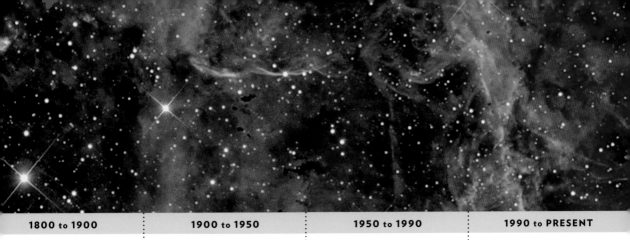

| **1800 to 1900** | **1900 to 1950** | **1950 to 1990** | **1990 to PRESENT** |

1838
Friedrich Bessel uses stellar parallax to estimate the distance to the star 61 Cygni.

1846
German astronomer Johann Galle is first to observe Neptune.

1872
American astronomer Henry Draper first photographs the spectrum of a star (Vega).

1877
Two moons of Mars, Phobos and Deimos, discovered by American astronomer Asaph Hall.

1889
American astronomer Edward Barnard takes first pictures of the Milky Way.

1915
Scottish astronomer Robert Innes locates Proxima Centauri, the nearest star to the sun.

1916
Albert Einstein publishes his paper on the general theory of relativity.

1927
Georges Lemaître proposes the big bang theory.

1930
Clyde Tombaugh discovers Pluto.

1957
USSR launches Sputnik 1, first man-made satellite to orbit Earth.

1961
Russian astronaut Yuri Gagarin becomes first man in space.

1966
U.S.S.R. lands Luna 9, unmanned vehicle, on moon.

1969
U.S. Apollo 11 mission puts first men on moon.

1981
U.S. space shuttle *Columbia* completes maiden flight.

1990
Hubble Space Telescope launched into orbit.

2000
Two Russians and one American become the first crew to occupy the International Space Station.

2004
NASA lands two rovers, Spirit and Opportunity, on Mars.

2012
Mars Science Lab and Curiosity rover land on Mars.

2012
NASA's Voyager 1, launched in 1977, leaves the solar system and enters interstellar space.

2012
NASA's New Horizons probe passes close to Pluto and continues on to the Kuiper belt.

OUR
NEIGHBORHOOD

ONCE UPON A TIME

Many of us grew up with the idea of a static solar system, with well-behaved planets in their reliable orbits. But a more dramatic view has arisen among some scientists. Not only did the solar system go through a dramatic birth, but it also experienced a raucous adolescence: Hundreds of millions of years after they formed, the biggest planets were swept into new orbits, casting large rocks and comets every which way. The scarred surface of the moon is lingering testimony to a period of epic mayhem and gravitational instability.

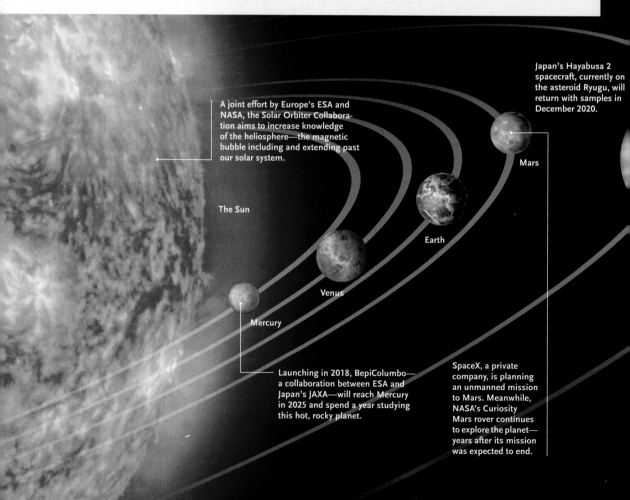

A joint effort by Europe's ESA and NASA, the Solar Orbiter Collaboration aims to increase knowledge of the heliosphere—the magnetic bubble including and extending past our solar system.

Japan's Hayabusa 2 spacecraft, currently on the asteroid Ryugu, will return with samples in December 2020.

Mars

The Sun

Earth

Venus

Mercury

Launching in 2018, BepiColumbo—a collaboration between ESA and Japan's JAXA—will reach Mercury in 2025 and spend a year studying this hot, rocky planet.

SpaceX, a private company, is planning an unmanned mission to Mars. Meanwhile, NASA's Curiosity Mars rover continues to explore the planet—years after its mission was expected to end.

A current theory is that our planets grew to full size by absorbing planetesimals, like rocky asteroids, icy comets, and larger objects.

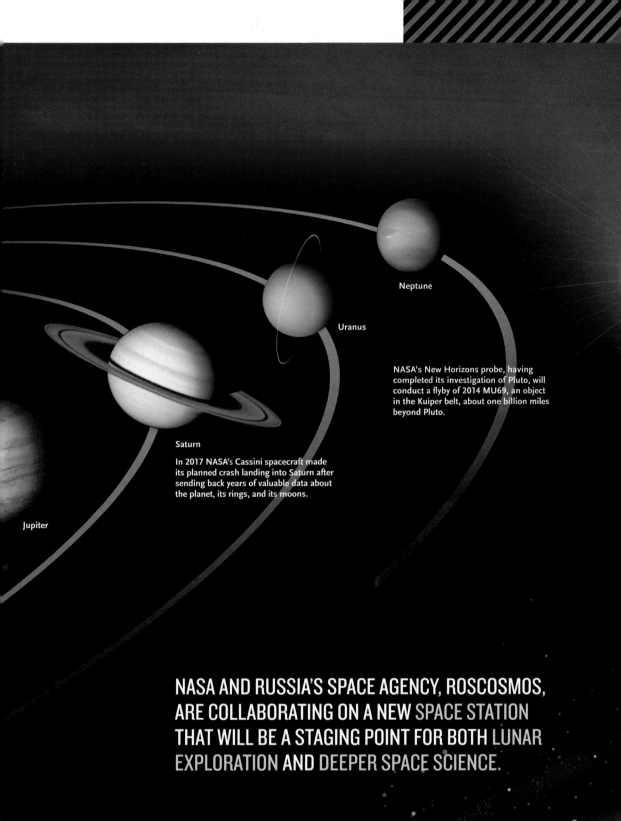

Neptune

Uranus

NASA's New Horizons probe, having
completed its investigation of Pluto, will
conduct a flyby of 2014 MU69, an object
in the Kuiper belt, about one billion miles
beyond Pluto.

Saturn

In 2017 NASA's Cassini spacecraft made
its planned crash landing into Saturn after
sending back years of valuable data about
the planet, its rings, and its moons.

Jupiter

NASA AND RUSSIA'S SPACE AGENCY, ROSCOSMOS,
ARE COLLABORATING ON A NEW SPACE STATION
THAT WILL BE A STAGING POINT FOR BOTH LUNAR
EXPLORATION AND DEEPER SPACE SCIENCE.

50 YEARS OF MOON EXPLORATION

Earthrise, as seen from the moon by Apollo 8 astronauts

GOING TO THE MOON

July 20, 2019, is the 50th anniversary of the first moonwalk, broadcast live to 600 million viewers across the globe. Neil Armstrong's monumental steps on the moon's surface came just a decade after fairly primitive instruments accomplished their the first forays, progress made possible by rapidly developing technology.

FLYBYS AND UNMANNED LANDINGS
In January 1959 Luna 1, a small Soviet sphere bristling with antennas, flew by the moon at a distance of some 3,725 miles. Later in 1959, Luna 2 became the first spacecraft to land on the moon's surface. In 1962 NASA placed its first spacecraft on the moon—Ranger 4. The Ranger missions were engineered to streak straight toward the moon and capture as many images as possible before crashing onto its surface. In 1966 the Luna 9 became the first

vehicle to soft-land safely on the surface. In 1966 and 1967 NASA launched lunar orbiters designed to circle the moon and chart its surface for future manned landings.

ONE GIANT LEAP
On July 20, 1969, Neil Armstrong and Edwin "Buzz" Aldrin became the first people to reach the moon when their Apollo 11 lunar lander touched down in the Sea of Tranquility. Later missions carried a lunar rover and saw astronauts spend as long as three days on the moon. Before the Apollo project ended in 1972, five other missions and a dozen men had visited the moon. NASA is again looking to the moon—this time as a staging point for human flight to Mars and beyond. Other countries, as well as international collaborations and private companies, consider the moon our next important stopping point in space.

Neil Armstrong's footprint remains undisturbed by weather or development.

FUTURE PLANS

If the race to put a man on the moon was the equivalent of building one of those giant, room-size, prodigiously expensive mainframe computers in the early days of high technology, today's race is analogous to a different era of computing: the race to put an affordable computer on everyone's desktop or telephone. Today computers are so tiny—and their batteries so compact—that we can reach the moon with increasingly smaller and decreasingly expensive devices. The next generation of machines exploring, mapping, and even mining the lunar landscape may well be the size of a child's Tonka truck. And they may have scaled-down costs as well.

KEY FACTS

Current and Future
MOON MISSIONS

BLUE ORIGIN
The self-funded commercial and space tourism enterprise of Amazon's Jeff Bezos may ship cargo to the lunar surface.

CHINA (CNSA)
Chang'e 5 will retrieve and return loose rock; Chang'e 4 will explore the moon's far side.

GOOGLE LUNAR XPRIZE (GLXP)
Teams continue to develop moon crafts initially designed for this competition, which none won.

INDIA (ISRO)
Chandrayaan-2, comprising an orbiter, lander, and rover, will study minerals and elements.

JAPAN (JAXA)
JAXA's SLIM (Smart Lander for Investigating Moon) is designed for complicated landings.

SPACEX
Founder Elon Musk's Dragon spacecraft aims to fly two private citizens around the moon as early as late 2018.

UNITED STATES (NASA)
NASA's Orion spacecraft will conduct unmanned and manned lunar missions.

VIRGIN GALACTIC
Richard Branson's spaceliner plans to operate brief suborbital space tours and other luxury tourist trips.

EARTH'S MOON

MAGNIFICENT DESOLATION

The topography of the moon is varied. Collisions with meteors over its 4.5-billion-year life have created a surface of pulverized rock, called regolith. Craters are as wide as 1,600 miles across, with mountainous walls as high as 4.8 miles. Its distinctive "seas" are actually areas given a smooth sheen by molten lava brought to the surface after major impacts that occurred around 3.8 to 3.9 billion years ago.

OCEANUS PROCELLARUM
This large, dark "ocean of storms," easily visible from Earth, is probably rift valleys formed by emerging magma. Apollo 12 landed here in 1969.

MONTES APENNINUS
Apollo 15 landed at the base of this mountain range in 1971. Formed by the impact of an asteroid, comet, or other object almost 4 billion years ago, it includes the tallest lunar mountain, Mons Huygens.

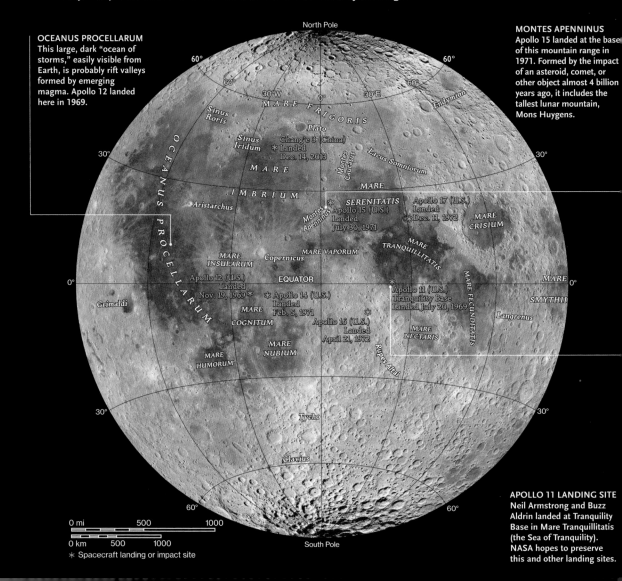

North Pole

South Pole

OCEANUS PROCELLARUM

MARE FRIGORIS

Sinus Roris

Sinus Iridum

Plato

Chang'e 3 (China)
* Landed
Dec. 14, 2013

Montes Caucasus

Lacus Somniorum

Endymion

MARE IMBRIUM

Aristarchus

Montes Apenninus

MARE SERENITATIS

Apollo 15 (U.S.)
Landed
July 30, 1971

Apollo 17 (U.S.)
Landed
Dec. 11, 1972

MARE CRISIUM

MARE VAPORUM

MARE TRANQUILLITATIS

MARE INSULARUM

Copernicus

EQUATOR

MARE FECUNDITATIS

MARE SMYTHII

Apollo 12 (U.S.)
Landed
Nov. 19, 1969 *

* Apollo 14 (U.S.)
Landed
Feb. 5, 1971

Apollo 11 (U.S.)
Tranquility Base
Landed July 20, 1969

Langrenus

Grimaldi

MARE COGNITUM

Apollo 16 (U.S.)
Landed
April 21, 1972

MARE NECTARIS

MARE NUBIUM

Rupes Altai

MARE HUMORUM

Tycho

Clavius

0 mi   500   1000

0 km   500   1000

* Spacecraft landing or impact site

APOLLO 11 LANDING SITE
Neil Armstrong and Buzz Aldrin landed at Tranquility Base in Mare Tranquillitatis (the Sea of Tranquility). NASA hopes to preserve this and other landing sites.

THE FAR SIDE OF THE MOON HAS PHASES JUST LIKE THE SIDE FACING EARTH. IT WAS FIRST MAPPED BY THE SOVIET LUNA 3 SPACECRAFT, WHICH IS REFLECTED IN MANY OF THE NAMES FOUND THERE.

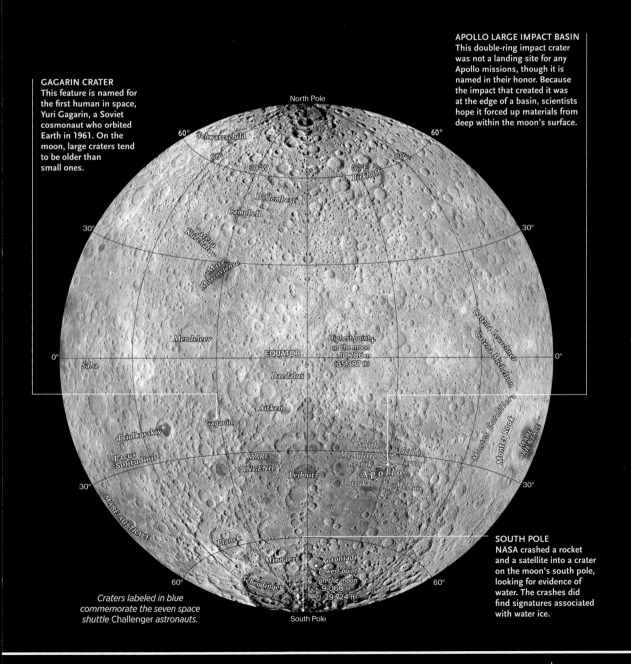

GAGARIN CRATER
This feature is named for the first human in space, Yuri Gagarin, a Soviet cosmonaut who orbited Earth in 1961. On the moon, large craters tend to be older than small ones.

APOLLO LARGE IMPACT BASIN
This double-ring impact crater was not a landing site for any Apollo missions, though it is named in their honor. Because the impact that created it was at the edge of a basin, scientists hope it forced up materials from deep within the moon's surface.

SOUTH POLE
NASA crashed a rocket and a satellite into a crater on the moon's south pole, looking for evidence of water. The crashes did find signatures associated with water ice.

Craters labeled in blue commemorate the seven space shuttle Challenger astronauts.

Labels on map:
North Pole
60° · 60°
Schwarzschild
60° · 60°
30°W · 0° · 30°E
Birkhoff
D'Alembert
Campbell
30° · 30°
Cordova Karsalatov
Mare Moscoviense
Mendeleev
EQUATOR
Highest point on the moon 10,786 m (35,387 ft)
0° · 0°
Saha
Daedalus
Cordova Leuschner
Cordova Michelson
Aitken
Gagarin
Tsiolkovskiy
Lacus Solitudinis
MARE INGENII
Leibnitz
Smith
McAuliffe Resnik
Scobie Jarvis
Apollo
Onizuka McNair
Montes Cordillera
Montes Rook
MARE ORIENTALE
30° · 30°
MARE AUSTRALE
Planck
Minnaert
Antoniadi Lowest point on the moon 9,060 m (-29,724 ft)
Schrödinger
60° · 60°
South Pole

ON TO MARS

WATER ON THE FOURTH PLANET

Astronomers using some of the world's most powerful telescopes have determined that an ocean at least a mile deep covered a significant fraction of the Martian surface four billion years ago. The research reinforces earlier evidence that water once existed on the surface of the red planet, leaving traces such as stream pebbles, ancient shorelines, river deltas, minerals that must have formed in a watery environment, and more.

CHRYSE PLANITIA
Scientists debate the origin of this plain—the landing site for both the Viking 1 lander, the first American spacecraft to reach the planet's surface, and the Mars Pathfinder probe. Was it formed by lava or by large bodies of water?

OLYMPUS MONS
This enormous shield volcano is nearly three times as high as Mount Everest and, at its base, as wide as Arizona.

North Pole

60° 60°

VASTITAS BOREALIS

Scandia Colles
Extent of seasonal frost
ACIDALIA PLANITIA

ARCADIA PLANITIA
Phoenix (U.S.) Landed May 25, 2008

30° Alba Mons
Ascuris
TEMPE TERRA
CHRYSE Cydonia Mensae 30°

Erebus Montes
Uranius Mons
Planum
PLANITIA
Mars Pathfinder (U.S.) Landed July 4, 1997

AMAZONIS
Lycus Sulci
Olympus Mons Highest point on Mars 69,715 ft 21,249 m
Jovis Tholus
Ceraunius Tholus
Viking 1 (U.S.) Sacra Landed Mensa July 20, 1976
330°

PLANITIA 210°
240°
Ascraeus Mons
270°
Tharsis Tholus
300°
ExoMars Schiaparelli (ESA) Crashed Oct. 19, 2016

Ulysses Tholus
Echus Montes
XANTHE

Biblis Tholus
Amazonis Mensae
Pavonis Mons
EQUATOR
TERRA
Meridiani

0° 0°
Arsia Mons
Ophir Planum
Planum

Syria Planum
Sinai Planum
Thaumasia Planum
Mars Exploration Rover-B, Opportunity (U.S.) Landed Jan. 25, 2004

DAEDALIA PLANUM
SOLIS PLANUM
Mars 6 (U.S.S.R.) Crashed Mar. 12, 1974

Mars 3 (U.S.S.R.) Landed, contact lost Dec. 2, 1971

30° Icaria Planum
Extent of seasonal frost
Bosporos Planum
Nereidum Montes
30°

AONIA
Aonia Planum
ARGYRE PLANITIA
Charitum Montes

ARGENTEA PLANUM

0 mi 750 1500 60° 60°
0 km 750 1500
Parva Planum

✱ Spacecraft landing or impact site
South Pole

VALLES MARINERIS
Largest known canyon in the solar system—almost 4 times longer, 20 times wider, and 4 times deeper than our Grand Canyon—this may have formed as the planet cooled.

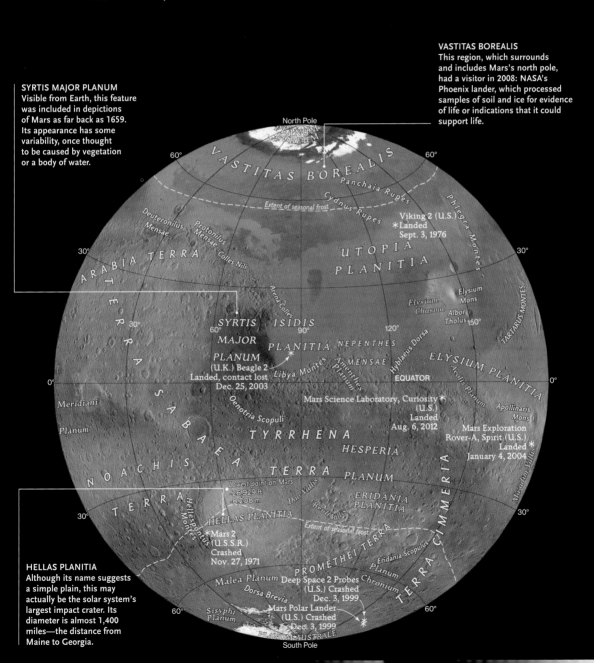

> **"** I'M CONVINCED THAT WE SHOULD DEVELOP A COLONY ON MARS, A PERMANENT SETTLEMENT, AND NOT JUST A LANDING AREA. PERMANENCE IS THE KEY, RIGHT FROM THE GET-GO. **"**
>
> —BUZZ ALDRIN, APOLLO 11 ASTRONAUT

VASTITAS BOREALIS
This region, which surrounds and includes Mars's north pole, had a visitor in 2008: NASA's Phoenix lander, which processed samples of soil and ice for evidence of life or indications that it could support life.

SYRTIS MAJOR PLANUM
Visible from Earth, this feature was included in depictions of Mars as far back as 1659. Its appearance has some variability, once thought to be caused by vegetation or a body of water.

HELLAS PLANITIA
Although its name suggests a simple plain, this may actually be the solar system's largest impact crater. Its diameter is almost 1,400 miles—the distance from Maine to Georgia.

North Pole
PLANUM BOREUM

VASTITAS BOREALIS

Panchaia Rupes

Cydnus Rupes

Extent of seasonal frost

Deuteronilus Mensae

Protonilus Mensae

Colles Nili

Phlegra Montes

Viking 2 (U.S.)
✳Landed
Sept. 3, 1976

ARABIA TERRA

UTOPIA PLANITIA

Arena Colles

Elysium Chasma

Elysium Mons

Albor Tholus

TARTARUS MONTES

TERRA

SYRTIS MAJOR PLANUM

ISIDIS PLANITIA

NEPENTHES MENSAE

Hyblaeus Dorsa

ELYSIUM PLANITIA

(U.K.) Beagle 2
Landed, contact lost
Dec. 25, 2003

Libya Montes

Arenthes Planum

EQUATOR

Aeolis Planum

Apollinaris Mons

Meridiani Planum

Oenotria Scopuli

SABAEA

Mars Science Laboratory, Curiosity ✳
(U.S.)
Landed
Aug. 6, 2012

Mars Exploration Rover-A, Spirit (U.S.)
Landed ✳
January 4, 2004

TYRRHENA

HESPERIA

TERRA

Medusae Fossae

NOACHIS

TERRA

Lowest point on Mars
-26,929 ft
-8,208 m

Dao Vallis

Reull Vallis

PLANUM

ERIDANIA PLANITIA

TERRA CIMMERIA

Hellespontus Montes

HELLAS PLANITIA

Extent of seasonal frost

Mars 2
(U.S.S.R.)
Crashed
Nov. 27, 1971

Eridania Scopulus

PROMETHEI TERRA

Malea Planum

Deep Space 2 Probes
(U.S.) Crashed
Dec. 3, 1999

Planum Chronium

Dorsa Brevia

Mars Polar Lander
(U.S.) Crashed
Dec. 3, 1999 ✳

Sisyphi Planum

PLANUM AUSTRALE

South Pole

SATISFYING OUR CURIOSITY

CONFIRMING THAT MARS IS HOSPITABLE TO LIFE

For the first time ever, we can say that another planet could have sustained life! Mars's overall red color indicates the presence of acidic iron compounds, which can destroy traces of organics. But Curiosity—exploring the planet Mars since 2012—has detected large concentrations of a gray clay (smectite) and, as project scientist John Grotzinger put it, "A gray Mars suggests habitability."

NOT A PHONE CAMERA
The most prominent of the rover's 17 cameras is the Mastcam, which takes color images and video footage. It sits atop the ChemCam, which fires a laser and then analyzes the vaporized materials with its spectrograph.

CURIOSITY CALLING
The rover uses this antenna to send messages to the Mars Reconnaissance Orbiter, which then relays them to Earth.

INDEPENDENT WHEELS
A traction-control algorithm adjusts each wheel's speed by using real-time data to reduce pressure from the rocks.

The Curiosity rover, which weighs about 2,000 pounds, is the size of a car.

> "OUR ROBOT IS NO ANSEL ADAMS, AND GALE CRATER IS NOT THE NEXT NATIONAL PARK, BUT ITS STRIKINGLY EARTH-LIKE APPEARANCE IN CURIOSITY'S POSTCARDS HAS DELIGHTED THE PUBLIC."

—JOHN GROTZINGER, CHIEF SCIENTIST CURIOSITY MISSION

DUAL-ACTION DRILL
Used more than a dozen times already, the drill has both a hammering action and a rotating-bit action to penetrate and collect samples.

What Curiosity Teaches Us
ABOUT MARS

▪ **A HABITABLE ENVIRONMENT**
The rover found evidence that an intermittent lake was once present at Yellowknife Bay, with freshwater and other chemical ingredients that life requires—the first time this claim has been made about another celestial body.

▪ **LOW METHANE LEVELS**
Curiosity tracks changes in methane—a gas that can be a result of present-day biological activity—which fluctuates by up to a factor of 10 for unknown reasons in the Martian atmosphere.

▪ **HIGH RADIATION EXPOSURE**
It measured elevated levels of cosmic and solar radiation on its journey from Earth to Mars and keeps tabs on radiation exposure on the red planet—important for planning manned travel and exploration.

▪ **DIVERSE GEOLOGIC HISTORY**
The rover has found various types of rocks, from volcanic to mudstones to rocks bearing cracks filled with mineral veins, each telling the story of a different environment; for example, it found a rock called a conglomerate, which forms on Earth when water flows about knee deep.

▪ **PRESENCE OF ORGANICS**
It detected simple organics, though these may be ones brought inadvertently by the rover—a risk all future missions will face.

▪ **CARBON AVAILABLE**
Carbon in the form of carbon dioxide was found in a drill sample, and it likely coincided with the period of habitability on Earth, some 3.8 billion years ago.

▪ **LOTS MORE TO EXPLORE**
Curiosity has been so successful that NASA is planning to send another rover in 2020, with the possibility of identifying and storing some rocks for a future sample return to Earth.

JUPITER & ITS MOONS

LEARNING FROM JUNO'S OBSERVATIONS

According to NASA, Jupiter is "a physics lab of sorts," and one of the phenomena under study is the Jovian magnetosphere, using data and images collected by the Juno spacecraft, which spent a few years in orbit around our largest planet. For example, scientists are working to understand Jupiter's radiation belts, in part because protecting spacecraft and astronauts from radiation is a constant concern. And unlike auroras in our atmosphere (triggered by extraplanetary particles), Jupiter's most intense auroras are the result of an as-yet unknown acceleration process.

POP!

TOP 10 SPACE FLICKS

- *Metropolis* (1927)
- *Star Wars, Episode IV: A New Hope* (1977)
- *Alien* (1979)
- *E.T. The Extra-Terrestrial* (1982)
- *Aliens* (1986)
- *WALL-E* (2008)
- *Star Trek* (2009)
- *Gravity* (2013)
- *Star Wars, Episode VII: The Force Awakens* (2015)
- *Arrival* (2016)

Jupiter's Great Red Spot is 1.3 times as wide as Earth.

> ## " I LOVE EUROPA, WHO DOESN'T? IT HAS TWICE AS MUCH SEAWATER AS THE EARTH. LET'S GO!"
>
> — BILL NYE, THE SCIENCE GUY

Europa, one of Jupiter's 69 moons

OTHER MOON LANDINGS

For obvious reasons, investigating a gas giant needs to be done from some distance, but we may be able to get a vessel on or near Jupiter's four Galilean moons—the largest among its 69—instead. Here's why Europa seems to be the most likely destination.

Great Amenities and Quite a View

Although this moon has an outer crust of solid ice, cracks in its surface indicate that the crust sits on top of liquid water. Because little warmth from the sun reaches Europa, it's likely that its ocean is kept from freezing by hydrothermal vents. Hubble telescope images from 2013 show plumes of liquid water at Europa's south pole, too. All of this—water! heat! nutrients!—makes Europa a compelling candidate for life.

Because it will be years before a spacecraft (already being referred to as the Europa Clipper) reaches Europa, scientists are investigating life found in Earth's extreme environments to feed their imagination of what life on other planets might look like.

KEY DATES

Getting to Know JUPITER

■ 1610: GALILEO SEES THE MOONS, ROCKS THE WORLD
When astronomer Galileo Galilei observed four satellites orbiting Jupiter through his improved telescope, he also identified the key to Copernicus's sun-centered model, displacing the Earth-centered Ptolemaic system.

■ 1676: PATIENT DATA COLLECTION FINDS THE SPEED OF LIGHT
Danish astronomer Ole Rømer was devoted to Io, Jupiter's volcanic moon—so much so that his careful measurements of its daily appearance over many years led to the measurement of the speed at which light travels.

■ 1831: RED SPOT SPOTTED
Although several stargazers had noted Jupiter's spotted appearance, Samuel Heinrich Schwabe, a German amateur astronomer studying sunspots, first described the planet's distinctive Great Red Spot (a cyclone).

■ 1955: JUPITER SPEAKS TO US
While collecting radio signals to map the spring sky, astronomers Bernard Burke and Kenneth Franklin captured interference eventually revealed as coming from Jupiter—and that helped find the planet's rotation speed.

■ 1979: PUT A COUPLE RINGS ON IT
Saturn's always been the one with flashy rings, but Jupiter's dusty, beautiful rings were photographed by the paparazzi known as Voyager 1 and 2 (and, later, Galileo).

■ 1995: AN EXTENDED STAY
When the Galileo spacecraft arrived in Jupiter's neighborhood for a four-year visit to the planet and its moons, it brought along a probe that entered the planet's atmosphere.

■ 2016: JUNO CALLING
Data from the Juno orbiter will be analyzed by pros and citizen scientists studying structure, composition, and magnetic and gravitational fields. Highlights include the stunning, mysterious auroras at the north pole.

BEST OF @NATGEO

OUR FAVORITE PHOTOS OF THE NIGHT SKY

@donnyfallgatter | DONNY FALLGATTER
The Milky Way rises over the photographer's grandmother's property in North Dakota.

@irablockphoto | IRA BLOCK
Photographers attempt to capture the cosmic spectacle of the northern lights at Jökulsárlón, a glacial lagoon in Iceland.

@babaktafreshi | BABAK TAFRESHI
Atop Maui's Haleakalā summit, the moon shines bright while a towering cloud billows up from below.

@diegorizzophoto | DIEGO RIZZO
Guatemala's Volcán de Fuego ("volcano of fire") erupts near the city of Antigua.

> **"ALL HUMAN CULTURES NO MATTER HOW PRIMITIVE HAVE FELT IT IMPORTANT TO TELL STORIES ABOUT THE STARS."**
>
> —TIMOTHY FERRIS, AUTHOR OF BOOKS ON ASTRONOMY AND COSMOLOGY

@pedromcbride | PETE MCBRIDE
A supermoon rises over Manhattan, the brightest moon in decades.

@abhishek_deopurkar | ABHISHEK DEOPURKAR
A long exposure reveals the stars' paths over a campsite in India.

@paulnicklen | PAUL NICKLEN
Aurora borealis lights up the winter sky over Whitehorse, Yukon Territory.

GRANT COLLINS
SpaceX's Falcon 9 spacecraft carves a bright arc across an early morning sky in Florida.

BIRTH OF THE UNIVERSE

A HISTORY SHAPED BY DARK FORCES

Cosmologists have determined that the universe was born 13.8 billion years ago. But they've also concluded that what we see in the sky makes up only 5 percent of the observable universe. The invisible majority consists of 27 percent dark matter and 68 percent dark energy.

What's Dark Matter?

We can't see dark matter, but we can see the effects of its gravity. And dark matter can't just be inconspicuous

normal matter—in no plausible scenario would it add up to five times the mass of the bright stuff—hence scientists think it must be made of more exotic materials.

What's Dark Energy?

Dark energy, even more mysterious, refers to whatever is accelerating the rate at which the cosmos expands. It has been called a "general label for what we do not know about the large-scale properties of our universe."

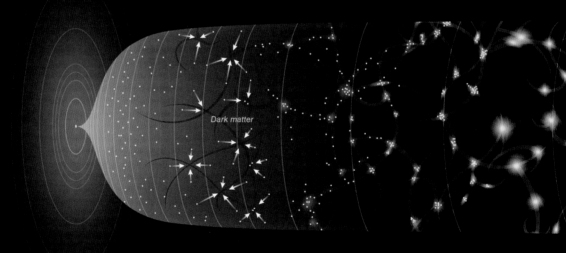

Dark matter

The big bang
13.8 billion years ago

Our universe blossoms from a hot, dense state smaller than an atom. Within milliseconds it inflates enormously.

Dark matter forms
First seconds of the universe

Dark matter also emerges in the first second. Interacting with particles of normal matter only through gravity, it begins to pull them together.

Stars light up
100 million years after the big bang

Clouds of hydrogen assembled by the gravity of dark matter collapse to form the first scattered stars. Nuclear fusion inside them creates heavier elements—and lights space.

Composition of the universe

Dark energy <1%

Dark matter <1%

Matter <1%   Radiation 99%*

86%

<1%   <1%

13%

A BELGIAN PRIEST NAMED GEORGES LEMAÎTRE FIRST
SUGGESTED THE BIG BANG THEORY IN THE 1920S WHEN
HE THEORIZED THAT THE UNIVERSE BEGAN FROM
A SINGLE PRIMORDIAL ATOM.

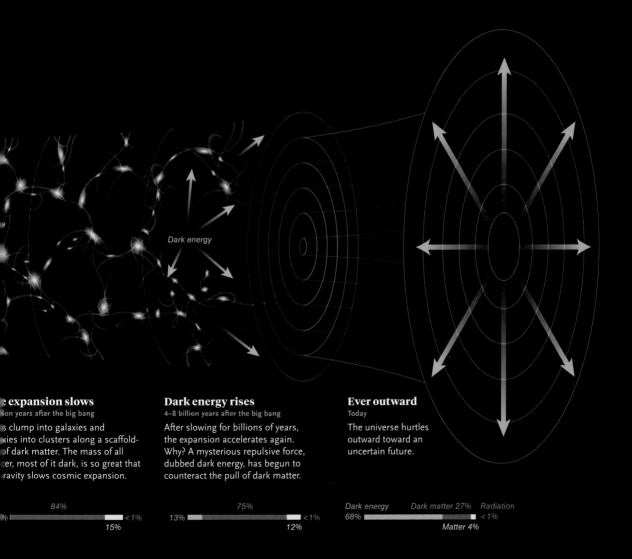

Dark energy

expansion slows
ion years after the big bang

s clump into galaxies and
xies into clusters along a scaffold-
of dark matter. The mass of all
er, most of it dark, is so great that
ravity slows cosmic expansion.

84%

% |▬▬▬▬▬▬▬▬▬▬▬▬▬| <1%
15%

Dark energy rises
4–8 billion years after the big bang

After slowing for billions of years,
the expansion accelerates again.
Why? A mysterious repulsive force,
dubbed dark energy, has begun to
counteract the pull of dark matter.

75%

13% |▬▬▬▬▬▬▬▬▬▬| <1%
12%

Ever outward
Today

The universe hurtles
outward toward an
uncertain future.

Dark energy   Dark matter 27%   Radiation
68% |▬▬▬▬▬▬▬▬▬▬▬▬▬| <1%
                   Matter 4%

*Percentages do not add up to 100 due to rounding.

VERA RUBIN
ASTRONOMER

A LIFELONG FASCINATION

Born July 23, 1928, Vera Rubin was fascinated with astronomy when she was growing up in Washington, D.C. There, she would watch the stars from a window and marvel at the precise paths they followed across the sky. It's an epic bit of foreshadowing, because nearly five decades later, her most spectacular contribution to astronomy would also be based on the motions of stars.

The Curiosity Mars rover spent time investigating an area that NASA has dubbed the "Vera Rubin Ridge."

After her application for graduate studies at Princeton University was rejected—the program didn't admit women until 1975—Vera Rubin went instead to Cornell University. She left with a master's degree and returned to Washington, to complete her Ph.D. at Georgetown University.

YET SHE PERSISTED

Her 1954 doctoral thesis revealed that galaxies tended to clump together in space rather than being haphazardly sprinkled throughout the universe—a structure acknowledged by astronomers today. But Rubin's observations of this structure were mostly ignored for the better part of two decades.

HARD EVIDENCE OF UNSEEN MASS

In 1978, Rubin was studying the rotation rates of stars whirling around the Andromeda galaxy's cosmic spiral with colleague Kent Ford, expecting to find that, as Isaac Newton had predicted, the stars nearest the galactic core would be moving more quickly than those on the fringe. But in fact, the stars at the galaxy's edge were zooming around so fast that all calculations suggested they should be flying off into space.

Then Rubin remembered the similar observations of Fritz Zwicky, who in 1933 had concluded that some type of massive, unobservable substance was lending gravitational heft to the cluster and helping to keep the thing intact. Rubin's observations also pointed to the existence of this cosmic glue. By the time of her death in 2016, Vera Rubin was recognized as a pioneering astrophysicist—the president of the Carnegie Institution called her "a national treasure"—whose work was essential to our growing understanding of dark matter.

Rubin was an ardent advocate for women in the sciences.

KEY DATES

Observing
THE INVISIBLE

■ 1933
Zwicky realized the revolution speed of a galaxy cluster was not proportional to the mass of its visible light and proposed that missing mass came from dark matter.

■ 1978
Rubin and Ford found objects at a galaxy's edges that should have escaped the center's gravity were held in place—a finding consistent with Zwicky's theory.

■ 2006
Astronomers discovered that dark and normal matter were wrenched apart by a tremendous collision of two large clusters of galaxies 3.4 billion light-years away.

■ 2014
Scientists observed that our galaxy's center produces more high-energy gamma rays than can be explained apart from the presence of dark matter.

WHEN A STAR EXPLODES

THE LIFE CYCLE OF A STAR

Every star begins as a collapsing cloud of interstellar dust. Stars stabilize when the temperature in the core is hot enough to begin nuclear fusion: turning hydrogen into helium. From there, a star grows and changes, using the hydrogen at its core as fuel along the way. Eventually, there's nothing left to burn, and some of the star's mass flows into its core. Once the core reaches critical mass— becoming too heavy to withstand its own gravitational force—the star collapses in on itself, producing massive shock waves and the giant explosion of a supernova.

A WORD FROM

Recipe for Life The atoms that comprise life on Earth, the atoms that make up the human body, are traceable to the crucibles that cooked light elements into heavy elements in their core, under extreme temperatures and pressures. These stars, the high mass ones among them, went unstable in their later years, collapsed and then exploded, scattering their enriched guts, across the galaxy … These ingredients become part of gas clouds that condense, collapse, form the next generation of solar systems, stars with orbiting planets and those planets now have ingredients for life itself.

—NEIL DEGRASSE TYSON, *astrophysicist*

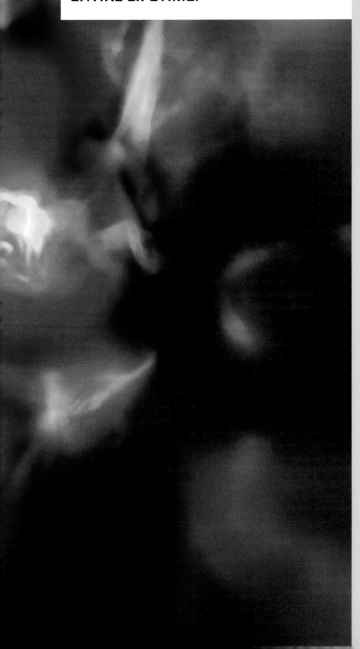

IN THE SPACE OF JUST A FEW YEARS, A SUPERNOVA, A SPECIAL KIND OF EXPLODED STAR, RADIATES MORE ENERGY THAN OUR SUN DOES IN ITS ENTIRE LIFETIME.

KEY DISTANCES

Distances Out Into
THE UNIVERSE

ASTEROID: 26,000 MILES
A tiny asteroid, just 50–100 feet long and known as 2012 TC4, flew very close to Earth on Oct. 12, 2017, just above the orbit of communications satellites.

COMET: 1.4 MILLION MILES
Appearing about four times as large as a full moon to the naked eye in July 1770, comet Lexell (aka D/1770 L1) was six times as far away as the moon.

NEXT STAR: 4.25 LIGHT-YEARS (LY)
Proxima Centauri, our second nearest star (the sun is closer, obviously), is in the constellation of Centaurus. It is part of a three-star system with Alpha Centauri A and B.

HABITABLE EXOPLANET: 4.25 LY
Our nearest star has in its orbit an exoplanet (Proxima Centauri B) that could, based on its size and location, have liquid water.

SUPERNOVA CANDIDATE: 150 LY
The most likely star to become a supernova is the smaller partner in a binary system known as IK Pegasi at a not insignificant distance from Earth—but by the time it explodes, millions of years from now, the distance will be much greater.

PLANETARY NEBULA: 650 LY
Not actually home to planets, this celestial object is the glowing remnants of a sunlike star. The Helix Nebula, in the constellation of Aquarius, is likely the closest to us.

GALAXY: 25,000 LY
The Canis Major dwarf galaxy, closest to us and to the center of the Milky Way (42,000 ly), is being unraveled by our galaxy's gravity.

BLACK HOLE: 3,000 LY
Almost every galaxy has a supermassive black hole in its center. Ours is 27,000 ly from Earth. A stellar-mass black hole, V616 Monocerotis, is about 3,000 ly away.

GALAXIES

SHOCK AND AWE

Even on the starriest of nights, the human eye sees just a tiny fraction of the cosmos. How many more phenomena, then, must exist out of view?

Do You See What I See?

That thought led astronomer Natasha Hurley-Walker deep into the outback of Western Australia and to the Murchison Widefield Array, a radio telescope comprising thousands of antennas that see through celestial dust and detect "radio light"—revealing colors and objects in a spectrum not visible to humans.

Hurley-Walker and a team of researchers stitched together more than 40,000 images taken by the telescope, creating a groundbreaking portrait of the entire southern sky. It exposes hundreds of thousands of galaxies millions of light-years away. And it shows in unobscured, blazing color the radio glow of the Milky Way

The Murchison Widefield Array antennas stretch across nearly four square miles of Australian desert.

JEDIDAH ISLER
ASTROPHYSICIST

BLACK HOLES AND BLAZARS

Jedidah Isler studies celestial objects that are hard to even imagine, much less explore: supermassive, hyperactive black holes that produce jets of charged particles at unimaginable speeds. "If we can push on our understanding of physical laws," she says, "we can find out some fundamental processes of the universe."

Isler uses astrophysics to probe (as the saying goes) space: the final frontier.

ONE IN FIVE SUNLIKE STARS **HARBORS AN** EARTH-SIZE WORLD **THAT ORBITS IN A "HABITABLE ZONE" FRIENDLY TO OCEANS AND PERHAPS LIFE.**

Earth   Kepler-62e   Kepler-62f

IN SEARCH OF EARTHS

For nearly four years NASA's Kepler spacecraft stared from its perch in space toward a patch of sky studded with 156,000 stars. Its goal? To find the frequency of Earthlike planets in the habitable zones of stars. The spacecraft did this by watching for the periodic blips in starlight produced when a planet passed between its star and Kepler's unblinking eye. Some of the most intriguing planets are relatively nearby, which makes them obvious targets in the search for life.

EXOPLANETS
IS THERE LIFE?

IN SEARCH OF GOLDILOCKS

When astronomers discuss planets that might support life, they refer to Goldilocks: Conditions have to be just right for life to happen. Once an exoplanet (a planet outside our solar system) is identified, astronomers assess its distance from the star it orbits and determine whether it is too close or too far to keep surface water in a liquid state. Size also matters: A planet that's too small cannot maintain an atmosphere; one that's too large will have a crushing atmosphere. "Goldilocks" planets have the right atmospheric pressure and the right temperature.

POP!

PLANETARY PLAYLIST

- "Aquarius (Let the Sunshine In)," The 5th Dimension
- "Fly Me to the Moon," Frank Sinatra
- "From Here to the Moon and Back," Dolly Parton
- "Gagarin," Public Service Broadcasting
- "Here Comes the Sun," George Harrison
- "Kuiper Belt," Sufjan Stevens, Bryce Dessner, Nico Muhly & James McAlister
- "Man on the Moon," R.E.M.
- "Pluto," Clare & the Reasons
- "Rocket Man," Elton John
- "Space Oddity," David Bowie
- "Stars Align," Lindsey Stirling
- "Supermassive Black Hole," Muse
- "We Are All Made of Stars," Moby

Imagine a planet with two nearby moons, visible day and night.

"THE UNIVERSE IS STRANGE, WONDERFUL, AND VAST—ACTUALLY, TOO VAST TO BE EXPLORED BY A SPACESHIP."

—NATASHA HURLEY-WALKER, ASTROPHYSICIST

Celestial Objects
YOU CAN SEE

1 **MOON** Even modest binoculars give you a good look at features on the moon, especially during full moons and supermoons.

2 **PLANETS** Venus is bright and early. Use star calendars to find others, including reddish Mars and even Jupiter's moons.

3 **MULTIPLE STAR SYSTEM** The Big Dipper's handle pivots at a double star, bright Mizar and dimmer Alcor.

4 **BRIGHTEST STARS** Sirius, in Canis Major, is three times brighter than the next brightest, Arcturus, seen in the Northern Hemisphere in spring.

5 **ORION NEBULA** Orion's sword, just below his belt, includes a stellar nursery 2,000 times more massive than the sun.

6 **ANDROMEDA GALAXY** Home to a trillion stars, this wonder appears between Cassiopeia's W and Pegasus's square.

7 **GLOBULAR STAR CLUSTERS** Look for M13 (the Hercules cluster) with binoculars or M5 (below Virgo) with a telescope.

8 **THE NORTH STAR** Sailors in the past and even hikers today use Polaris to mark north.

9 **SHOOTING STARS** The naked eye is best for scanning the skies for meteors; the Perseids peak annually in August.

10 **SATELLITES AND THE INTERNATIONAL SPACE STATION** Use an app or website to learn when and where these will pass overhead.

An earthbound astronaut who explores with science, not spaceships, Isler has expertise in a cutting-edge area of astronomy: the physics of particle jets emanating from black holes at the centers of distant galaxies. This area of study makes her a pioneer in another aspect, too, for after earning a B.A., an M.A., and an M.S. in physics, she became, in 2014, the first African-American woman to earn a Ph.D. in astrophysics from Yale.

A IS FOR ASTRONOMY

When she was in middle school, Isler decided to do some career research. One of the first options she came across—since the book she chose presented disciplines in alphabetical order—was astronomy. Already curious about the night sky, she chose then to become an astrophysicist. She eventually narrowed her focus to blazing quasars, or blazars: black holes, found at the center of very active galaxies, with plasma jets that emit light from all over the spectrum—jets that accelerate particles to 99.99 percent of the speed of light and are pointed toward Earth.

ALWAYS ROOM FOR MORE

Even as she ponders the universe's wonders, Isler advocates for inclusive STEM (science, technology, engineering, and math) programs at all levels of education, emphasizing the need for all contributions and perspectives—including those of people from underrepresented backgrounds—in the pursuit of scientific knowledge. To this end, she gives public lectures and media interviews and founded Vanguard: Conversations with Women of Color in STEM, a web-based program fostering community and mentorship.

> **" I WANT TO SEE THE BEST POSSIBLE SCIENCE DONE. THE ONLY WAY TO DO THAT IS TO MAKE SURE THAT EVERYONE WHO HAS AN INTEREST IN IT IS ALLOWED A SEAT AT THE TABLE."**

A galaxy's black hole ejects particle jets at nearly the speed of light.

KEY DATES

Learning About BLACK HOLES

1916
Black holes predicted by Albert Einstein's general theory of relativity

1971
A binary black hole (Cygnus X-1/HDE 226868) identified by x-ray emissions

1974
Theoretical physics posits that black holes emit so-called Hawking radiation

2002
Evidence that center of our galaxy is a supermassive black hole (Sagittarius A*)

2012
First photo evidence of black hole, shows black hole consuming and ejecting a star

2016
Detection of gravitational waves from two black holes colliding and merging

FURTHER

LOOKING BACK IN TIME

NASA's James Webb Space Telescope, a joint project with Canadian and European space agencies, will elucidate the early universe over the coming years as it investigates small sections of the Hubble Ultra-Deep Field and the Great Observatories Origins Deep Survey—dense sections that include approximately 10,000 galaxies. The older the galaxy, the more its light is shifted into the near- and mid-infrared parts of the electromagnetic spectrum, which the Webb telescope is especially designed to see. We'll soon be cooing over the universe's baby pictures.

This Hubble Ultra-Deep Field image captures thousands of galaxies in parts of the sky that look empty to us, revealing objec

THE WEBB TELESCOPE WILL FOCUS ON A SLIVER OF SKY—
ABOUT AS BIG AS YOU'D SEE PEEKING THROUGH A SODA STRAW—
AND MAKE VISIBLE TO US THOUSANDS OF GALAXIES THAT ARE
ABOUT A BILLION TIMES FAINTER THAN OUR EYES CAN SEE.

LIFE ON EARTH

ALL LIVING THINGS | OF THE EARTH

An emperor penguin grazes the water's surface of Antarctica's Ross Sea.

QUIZ
MASTER

Know Your Biosphere? Ever wonder what's the meaning of life? Start here for answers by exploring the many forms of life, from microbes to megafauna, from rarely seen life-forms to the plants and animals we know and love.

—CARA SANTA MARIA, *Our Favorite Nerd*

NAME ONE OF THE TWO NICKNAMES **GIVEN TO THE** ANIMALS CALLED TARDIGRADES.

p212

IN WHAT DECADE WERE PLASTICS INTRODUCED TO THE WORLD?

NAME OUR LARGEST LIVING PRIMATE RELATIVE.

p164

p207

THE FIRST **EARTH DAY** WAS CELEBRATED IN WHAT YEAR: 1950, 1960, 1970, **OR** 1980?

p181

WAS THE SPINOSAURUS DINOSAUR AN HERBIVORE, CARNIVORE, OR OMNIVORE?

WHAT WAS THE NAME OF THE LAST PASSENGER PIGEON TO SURVIVE BEFORE THE SPECIES WENT EXTINCT?

p162

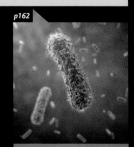

NAME THE THREE DOMAINS OF LIFE.

p166

THE OLDEST CORAL FOSSILS DATE BACK HOW FAR—5, 15, 50, OR 500 **MILLION YEARS AGO?**

p168

p188

HOW MUCH DOES THE SMALLEST HUMMINGBIRD **SPECIES WEIGH?**

p198

WHICH IS THE WORLD'S LARGEST PREDATORY FISH— MAKO SHARK, OCEANIC WHITETIP **SHARK,** GREAT WHITE SHARK, OR TIGER SHARK?

TRUE OR FALSE: THE NUMBER OF MANATEES **ALIVE IN THE WORLD IS** RAPIDLY **DECREASING.**

p191

WHAT IS THE **NAME OF THE FUNGUS** THREATENING THE WORLD'S **FROG** SPECIES?

p189

WHAT ANIMAL IS CONSIDERED THE GARBAGE CAN OF THE **SEA?**

NAME THE SHIP ON WHICH **CHARLES DARWIN** JOURNEYED TO **THE GALÁPAGOS,** PERFORMING STUDIES THAT LED TO HIS **THEORY OF EVOLUTION.**

p176

p161

LIFE SCIENCE
TIME LINE

900 to 1 BC	AD 1 to 1100	1100 to 1600	1600 to 1800

900 to 1 BC

ca 900 BC
Neolithic farmers use fertilizer and irrigation.

ca 800 BC
Egyptians use artificially heated incubators to hatch eggs.

ca 400 BC
Hippocrates of Kos describes human anatomy.

ca 350 BC
Aristotle draws up a classification scheme for plants and animals.

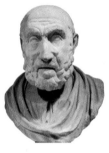

300 BC
Diocles of Carystus is credited with writing the first text on anatomy.

AD 1 to 1100

77
Roman scholar Pliny the Elder summarizes natural history as known to the Romans in his *Naturalis Historia*.

752
Chinese physician Wang Tao describes ailments including diabetes and malaria, along with remedies.

ca 900
Arab physician Rhazes distinguishes between measles and smallpox.

ca 1075
Female physician Trotula of Salerno writes about hygiene and women's disorders.

1100 to 1600

ca 1260
Arab physician Ibn al-Nafis describes the pulmonary circulation of the blood.

1276
Giles of Rome discusses the role of both parents in procreation in his work, *De Formatione Corporis*.

1410
Italian physician Benedetto Rinio catalogs more than 500 medicinal plants.

1517
Girolamo Fracastoro proposes that fossils are the petrified remains of once living organisms.

1583
Italian botanist Andrea Cesalpino devises a system of classifying plants by their structure.

1600 to 1800

1658
Dutch naturalist Jan Swammerdam describes red blood cells.

1665
Robert Hooke coins the word "cell" to describe individual units in plant tissues.

1677
Dutch scientist Antonie van Leeuwenhoek reports on his observations of bacteria.

1735
Swedish naturalist Carolus Linnaeus introduces the binomial naming system.

1796
Georges Cuvier identifies "elephant" remains from Siberia as a separate and extinct species: "mammoth."

1800 to 1900

■ 1822
Englishwoman Mary Ann Mantell discovers teeth from one of the first fossils to be recognized as a dinosaur.

■ 1831–1836
Darwin completes a five-year voyage on the H.M.S. *Beagle,* during which he conducted studies that lead to his theory of evolution.

■ 1860
The first fossil of *Archaeopteryx,* a birdlike prehistoric flying reptile, is found.

■ 1865
Gregor Mendel presents his ideas on inheritance.

■ 1876
Mitosis, the process of cell replication, is first described by Eduard Strasburger.

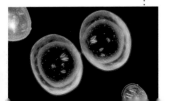

1900 to 1925

■ 1900
Cuban-American physiologist Aristides Agramonte y Simoni discovers that yellow fever is transmitted through mosquitoes.

■ 1901
Russian scientist Élie Metchnikoff determines the role of white blood cells in fighting infection.

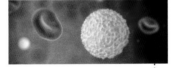

■ 1913
Alfred Sturtevant introduces the technique of chromosome mapping to record positions of genes.

■ 1919
Karl von Frisch describes the "bee's dance," the way in which honeybees communicate.

■ 1924
Fossils of human ancestor *Australopithecus* are discovered, helping establish Africa as the site of humankind's origins.

1925 to 1960

■ 1926
Walter Cannon introduces the concept of homeostasis, in which the body's systems work together to maintain balance.

■ 1944
Oswald Avery shows that nearly all organisms have DNA as their hereditary material.

■ 1953
Francis Crick, James Watson, and Rosalind Franklin determine the double-helix structure of DNA.

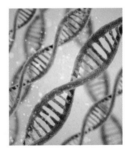

■ 1960
Jane Goodall begins her studies of chimpanzees in Gombe, Tanzania.

1960 to PRESENT

■ 1969
The first human eggs are fertilized using in vitro fertilization.

■ 1996
Scottish scientists clone a sheep named Dolly.

■ 2000
The Human Genome Project produces a rough draft of the human genome sequence.

■ 2006
Analysis of a 375-million-year-old fossil shows it to be a "missing link" between fish and four-legged vertebrates.

■ 2010
Genetic evidence shows that interbreeding between humans and Neanderthals took place and that some modern humans have Neanderthal genes.

DOMAINS OF LIFE

AN INVISIBLE WORLD

We share this planet with more than eight million other species, and each of them falls into one of only three types: Archaea, the ancient line; bacteria, the microbial line; and Eukarya, which includes plants, animals, fungus, and others.

ARCHAEA

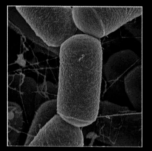

METHANOSARCINA SP.
A type of archaea
that produces methane

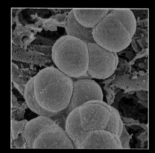

METHANOBREVIBACTER SP.
One of the archaea found
in the human gut

SULFOLOBUS SP.
Thrives in hot springs
>176°F (80°C)

ARCHAEA & BACTERIA

BACTERIA

MILLIONS OF MICROORGANISMS

Archaea are so difficult to detect that they were unknown until the 1970s. They resemble bacteria in their simple shape and lack of complex cellular organs, but they are as genetically distinct from bacteria as humans are. Their ancient genetic markers suggest that life may have started in the hydrothermal vents of the deep ocean.

Despite their microscopic size, bacteria make up most of the mass of life on Earth. There are as many bacteria on your skin and inside your body as there are human cells making it up. Although the battle against bacterial infection has been common for centuries, this microbial world represents an ecosystem scientists are only starting to approach cohesively.

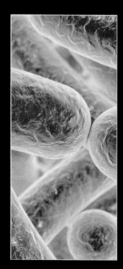

MYCOBACTERIUM SP.
This bacterium
causes tuberculosis.

SALMONELLA SP.
Infected food causes
gastric disease.

FUNGI

POLYPORUS SP.
Shelf fungus, grows
on dead or dying trees

COOKEINA SP.
Tropical toadstool,
grows on trees

PLANTS

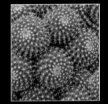

MAMMILLARIA SP.
Twin-spined cactus,
from Mexico

COSMOS
Annual seed-
bearing flower

POACEAE SP.
One of 8,000 species
of grasses

QUERCUS SP.
Southern live oak,
North America

EUKARYA

FROM FUNGI TO PRIMATES

Eukarya, which contain every complex multicellular organism on the planet, are divided into four taxonomic kingdoms: Plants, Animals, Fungi, and Protoctista. Despite their seeming diversity, Eukarya share a single set of characteristics: multicellular organisms with clearly defined cellular structures, such as a nucleus, mitochondria, and other organelles.

ANIMALS

TANGARA SP.
Golden-hooded tanager,
from Costa Rica

CHAETODON SP.
Masked butterfly fish,
from Asia

ELEPHANT
Two species,
Indian and African

CHIMPANZEE
In African rain forests,
woods, and grasslands

KEY DATES

Dates in the Evolution of
LIFE ON EARTH

■ **CA 4 BILLION YEARS AGO**
Life begins on planet Earth.

■ **CA 2.4 BILLION YEARS AGO**
Great oxidation event occurs, giving Earth its oxygen.

■ **1.5 BILLION YEARS AGO**
Plants, animals, and fungus separate into distinct types.

■ **500 MILLION YEARS AGO**
Life moves onto land.

■ **65 MILLION YEARS AGO**
The Cretaceous–Tertiary extinction wipes out the dinosaurs.

■ **7 TO 8 MILLION YEARS AGO**
Hominids share last common ancestor with bonobos and chimpanzees.

TARDIGRADES

MASTERS OF SURVIVAL

Meet the toughest creatures on the planet. These millimeter-long "moss piglets" have been frozen, boiled, and exposed to both lethal radiation and crushing pressure. In 2007, tardigrades endured exposure in the cold vacuum of space for 10 days and not only survived, but also reproduced on their return to Earth. Not all 1,250 species of tardigrades are equally resilient. For some of these "water bears," though, even world-changing events like asteroid impacts or nearby supernova explosions wouldn't be fatal.

MOUTH
Tardigrades need a thin layer of water around their bodies to breathe, eat, mate, and move around.

A WORD FROM

Finding New Life-Forms We mounted an expedition to look for missing heat in the ocean. We went along this mountain range, in an area along Galápagos Rift, and did we find the missing heat! It was amazing. These giant chimneys, huge giant chimneys. We went up to them with our submersible. We wanted to get a temperature probe—it pegged off scale. The pilot made this great observation: "That's hot." We discovered a profusion of life, in a world where it should not exist. We found these incredible clam beds sitting on the barren rock. And when we cut them open, they didn't have the anatomy of a clam. Their bodies had been taken over by another organism, a bacterium, that had figured out how to replicate photosynthesis in the dark, through a process we now call chemosynthesis. We did not know about this life system … We stumbled on it, looking for some missing heat.

—**ROBERT BALLARD,** *oceanographer*

These eight-legged invertebrates can survive for years without food or water.

IN 1948, AN ITALIAN SCIENTIST REANIMATED A TARDIGRADE THAT HAD BEEN DRIED UP IN A MUSEUM FOR 120 YEARS.

BODY
Tardigrades survive through cryptobiosis, a process where the animal loses 97 percent of the water in its body and curls up into a ball known as a tun.

LEGS
The clawed legs that give these water bears their name are mostly used for swimming, not climbing.

SPINOSAURUS

RIVER MONSTER OF THE CRETACEOUS

About 97 million years ago, *Spinosaurus* was the largest carnivore in Africa—even larger than *Tyrannosaurus rex*—but it didn't hunt on land. *Spinosaurus* was a river hunter, using its long jaws to snatch massive sawfish, lungfish, and coelacanth. It spent up to 80 percent of its life swimming through the waters like an ancient crocodile. Its six-foot sail rose out of the water like a shark fin. Before this point, dinosaurs had only ruled the land. *Spinosaurus* was the first to rule the rivers.

LOCATION
SIZE

Spinosaurus
Northern Africa
50 ft., 6–7 tons

Giganotosaurus
South America
42 ft., 8 tons

T. rex
North America
41 ft., 8 tons

200 million years ago   145   95   65   Today

MESOZOIC ERA   CENOZOIC ERA

A WORD FROM

More to Discover   We CT scanned all the bones and built a digital *Spinosaurus* skeleton. And we realized that this was a dinosaur like none other . . . a river monster, a predatory dinosaur bigger than *T. rex,* the ruler of this ancient river of giants. And some people told me, "Wow, this is a once-in-a-lifetime discovery. There are not many things left to discover in the world." I think nothing could be further from the truth . . . When people tell me there are no places left to explore, I like to quote a famous dinosaur hunter, Roy Chapman Andrews, who said, "Always, there has been an adventure just around the corner—and the world is still full of corners." It is still true today.

—NIZAR IBRAHIM, *paleontologist*

Spinosaurus's barrel-shaped torso recalls dolphins and whales, and its high-set nostrils would allow it to breathe with much of its head submerged.

FOSSILS
PAST LIVES

LASTING IMPRESSIONS Fossils are the preserved remains or imprints of ancient living things. They offer clues about past life-forms and environments and are keys to understanding the evolution of life on Earth.

> ## "NO FOSSIL IS BURIED WITH ITS BIRTH CERTIFICATE."
> —HENRY GEE, PALEONTOLOGIST

POP!

MOVIES STARRING DINOSAURS

- *The Lost World* (1925)
- *When Dinosaurs Ruled the Earth* (1970)
- *The Land Before Time* (1988)
- *Jurassic Park* (1993)
- *Walking with Dinosaurs* (1999)
- *Dinotopia* (2002)
- *King Kong* (2005)
- *Land of the Lost* (2009)
- *Jurassic World* (2015)

PLANT PARTS
Leaves, spores, pollen from as far back as 450 mya

PETRIFIED WOOD
Preserved when minerals fill pores in organic material

GRAPTOLITES
Wormlike marine animals from 500–315 mya

BRYOZOANS
Aquatic colonies in shallow limestone formations

CORALS
Main component of reefs; some date to 500 mya

TRILOBITES
Extinct animals that once dominated Earth's oceans

BRACHIOPODS
Tens of thousands of species of these once flourished.

BIVALVES
Ancestors of today's clams, mussels, oysters, and scallops

GASTROPODS
Remains of ancient snails and sea slugs

AMMONITES
Spiral-shelled creatures once prolific, extinct about 65 mya

ECHINODERMS
Five-point symmetry, like sand dollars of today

CRINOIDS
Marine animals: flexible stalk, head of waving filaments

FISH
First vertebrates in fossil record, starting 500 mya

SHARK TEETH
One ancient species left behind teeth 7 inches long.

INSECTS
Amber, fossilized tree resin, has preserved whole bodies.

These impressive footprints, nearly six feet in length, belong to a long-necked sauropod.

DINO TRACKS

GIANT FOOTSTEPS 120 MILLION YEARS AGO

A remarkable 16-mile stretch of land in Western Australia has yielded the world's most varied collection of dinosaur tracks, including some measuring nearly six feet long—among the world's largest. The Goolarabooloo, a local indigenous group, feared a planned natural-gas plant could damage the tracks, which they had known about for generations and which are important to their cultural history. The group asked researchers to join them in surveying the sites on foot and by drone, yielding a report that identified tracks from 21 different dinosaur species and a convincing reason to relocate the gas plant.

> "THE TRACKS PROVIDE A SNAPSHOT— A CENSUS, IF YOU WILL—OF AN EXTREMELY DIVERSE DINOSAUR FAUNA."
>
> —STEVE SALISBURY, PALEONTOLOGIST

DE-EXTINCTION
REANIMATING THE PAST

THE DEAD LIVE AGAIN

Might we one day view a landscape, not a museum display, with mammoths and saber-toothed tigers?

BRINGING THEM BACK

Extinction is forever. It is the complete elimination of the last of a species on the planet—or is it? Scientists may be on the edge of reversing extinction. By combining cloning techniques with DNA from preserved specimens, we may be able to resurrect extinct species. Whether this expensive procedure is the right moral choice remains hotly debated, and some scientists fear resurrecting creatures into ecosystems they've never known.

Others are working to protect endangered species before they go extinct by breeding threatened species in captivity and reintroducing their offspring back into the wild. Those include the Vancouver Island marmot and the Puerto Rican crested toad.

WOOLLY MAMMOTH

A group of Siberian scientists is hoping to resurrect the iconic woolly mammoth as part of a "Pleistocene Park," which could prevent a devastating release of carbon now under the frozen tundra. Their current experiment has shown that introducing Pleistocene-era animals can lower the temperature of the permafrost by as much as 15°F.

TASMANIAN TIGER

Wolf-size thylacines, also called Tasmanian tigers, went extinct in the 1980s due to human interference. But the predatory marsupial's genes have already been sequenced, and scientists hope cloning can help bring it back.

> **" IF WE VIEW** FOREST ECOLOGY **AS A DANCE, THE ONLY ANIMAL THAT CAN KEEP STEP WITH THE TREES IS THE PASSENGER PIGEON. IT'S THE** DANCE PARTNER **OF THE FOREST."**
>
> —BEN J. NOVAK, LEAD RESEARCHER, REVIVE & RESTORE'S GREAT PASSENGER PIGEON COMEBACK

GREAT AUK

The last of these penguin-like creatures was seen in 1852, but they once roamed the North Atlantic coasts like their close genetic relatives, the razorbill and puffin, did. Scientists believe they can re-create the auks using a genetic relative as the starting point.

PASSENGER PIGEON

Passenger pigeons once darkened North American skies by the billions, but hunters devastated the species. In 1914, the last one, known as Martha, died in the Cincinnati Zoo. Now scientists are trying to re-create the once ubiquitous bird.

Researchers have sequenced the thylacine's entire genome.

Auk fat, eggs, and feathers were sold as commercial goods.

A project in Australia seeks to edit rock pigeon DNA to bring passenger pigeons back.

BEST OF @NATGEO

OUR FAVORITE PHOTOS OF LIFE ON LAND

@timlaman | TIM LAMAN
A Bornean orangutan climbs a tree in the rain forest of Gunung Palung National Park.

@paulnicklen | PAUL NICKLEN
A curious female polar bear noses into the photographer's cabin in Svalbard, Norway.

@stefanounterthiner | STEFANO UNTERTHINER
Two European bison—a species threatened but gaining in number in recent years—butt heads in Białowieża, Poland.

@stevewinterphoto | STEVE WINTER
A mother tiger rests with her young cub in Bandhavgarh National Park in India.

> ## " TAKING PICTURES IS SAVORING LIFE INTENSELY, EVERY HUNDREDTH OF A SECOND."
>
> —MARC RIBOUD, PHOTOJOURNALIST

@christianziegler | CHRISTIAN ZIEGLER
A four-year-old bonobo in the Democratic Republic of the Congo.

@franslanting | FRANS LANTING
An elephant and a herd of kudus gather at a water hole in Botswana's Okavango Delta.

@peteressick | PETER ESSICK
Fleischmann's glass frog, a small species from South America, is struggling to survive in a warming climate.

@arni_coraldo | COREY ARNOLD
A red fox walks on the side of a snowy road in Alaska, hoping for a snack from a passing car.

TELLTALE TRACKS

Who Goes There? There is a hidden world all around you: Animals you do not see may still leave traces of their lives behind. By studying animal tracks, scientists and guides can estimate population size, ages, and even what the animal was doing as it left the marks.

VIRGINIA OPOSSUM
North America's only marsupial

BLACK-TAILED PRAIRIE DOG
Complex tunnel town dwellers

NORTHERN FLYING SQUIRREL
Can glide up to 300 feet

EASTERN GRAY SQUIRREL
Tail serves as umbrella or wrap.

EASTERN CHIPMUNK
Caches food underground for winter

AMERICAN BEAVER
Incisors fell trees to build dams.

NORTH AMERICAN PORCUPINE
Sharp quills fend off predators.

MUSKRAT
Still trapped for fur

NORTH AMERICAN DEER MOUSE
Huddles together in cold weather

HOUSE MOUSE
Can have up to 14 litters a year

NORWAY RAT
Prefers to live near humans

ANTELOPE JACKRABBIT
Huge ears help cool off.

EASTERN COTTONTAIL
Named for its powder-puff tail

NORTHERN SHORT-TAILED SHREW
Preys with poisonous bite

EASTERN MOLE
Flat, clawed forefeet dig tunnels

BOBCAT
Most widespread cat in North America

MOUNTAIN LION
Solitary unless mating

COYOTE
So adaptable, now in cities

RED FOX
Imported from Europe for sport

AMERICAN BLACK BEAR
Males weigh up to 900 pounds.

NORTH AMERICAN RIVER OTTER
Playful swimmer

BLACK FOOTED FERRET
Nearly extinct; takes over prairie dog dens

STRIPED SKUNK
Spray can be smelled half mile away.

RACCOON
Handy thanks to dexterous fingers

Scientists studying wolf vocalizations found 21 different dialects.

WOLF-RELATED TOURISM IN YELLOWSTONE NATIONAL PARK HAS GENERATED AN ADDITIONAL $5 MILLION ANNUALLY.

WOLVES

THE POWER OF PREDATORS

Wolves were driven out of Yellowstone National Park in 1926, many caught and killed for a U.S. government bounty. Without wolves, the ecosystem shifted. Elk populations exploded and started overgrazing the river habitat where wolves once hunted. Coyotes took over as the top predator, reducing the amount of small prey, including rabbits and beavers. Scavengers like eagles, ravens, and badgers went hungry without wolf kills.

After wolves were reintroduced, the changes were dramatic. Elk retreated from exposed riverside, leaving plants like aspen and willow time to recover. Coyote populations declined, and small animals rebounded. The ecosystem's balance was restored.

A WORD FROM

A Wolf's Devotion You can see a lot of your dog in the wolf and a lot of the wolf in your dog. They're both social animals, and just like elephants, gorillas, and whales, they educate their young, take care of their injured, and live in family groups. In a wolf pack, each wolf devotes itself completely to the pups that are born to the alpha pair, making sure that the pups grow up to be strong and beneficial additions to the pack. Only a deeply social and family-oriented animal would demonstrate such devotion to another's offspring.

— JIM AND JAMIE DUTCHER, *wolf conservationists*

ENDANGERED FROGS

THE ENVIRONMENTALISTS' CANARY IN A COAL MINE

The Panamanian golden frog survives only in human care.

A KEY INDICATOR

ABOUT TO CROAK?

Amphibians around the world are in peril. Of the world's roughly 6,000 amphibian species, nearly a third have been deemed threatened or extinct. Climate change and habitat loss are major drivers, because frogs cannot easily respond or adapt to changes. A fast-spreading type of fungus, known as chytrid, is also responsible. The fungus latches onto a frog's skin and begins to spread. Since frogs use their skin for hydration and respiration, the animals suffocate inside their own skin. Frogs are an indicator species: Because they absorb chemicals through their skin, they are the first to show signs of environmental stress. The indications now bode ill not just for frogs, but for the whole ecosystem.

STOPGAP MEASURES

AN ARK FOR AMPHIBIANS

To save these vital species, scientists from around the world have unveiled a massive global conservation program: the Amphibian Ark. These conservationists and scientists believe it may not be possible to protect the frogs if they are left in the ecosystem they are in at present, so they hope to step in and save them directly. Begun in 2007, the Amphibian Ark program is trying to create breeding programs of 500 frogs at zoos around the world. The zoos could then keep the animals safe and protected until they can be released again into the wild. It's an ambitious endeavor, but one that, if successful, could save hundreds, even thousands of species worldwide.

This endangered San Lucas marsupial frog is endemic to Ecuador.

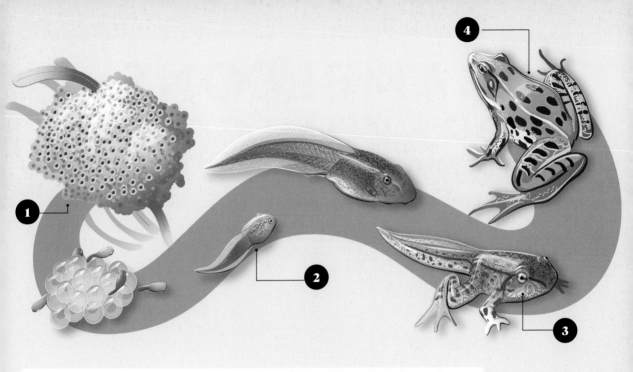

Because frog eggs are permeable and laid in water, they are especially susceptible to pollutants in the environment.

A FROG'S LIFE

[1] EGG

Frogs can lay anywhere from two to 10,000 eggs. These eggs cluster to form large floating blobs known as egg masses.

[2] TADPOLE

Tadpoles are primarily both vegetarian and aquatic, with no hind or front legs and a dominant tail. They will live off algae and other plants.

[3] FROGLET

As the tadpole transforms, every organ begins to change. The legs and feet develop, the gills recede, and the lungs enlarge to adapt to life on land.

[4] FROG

As the frog reaches full maturity, the tongue muscles strengthen, the skull fully forms, and the intestines shrink to adapt to a carnivorous diet. It is now a true frog and will be fully mature in three years.

GOING GREEN

Ways You Can Help
THE FROGS

Caring for the water in your landscape is one way you can do your part to help save the frogs. You will be protecting local wetlands when you avoid applying chemicals on your lawn or rinsing them down the drain in your house. Don't flush medicine down the drain, because it can enter the water table, where it might be absorbed into a frog's sensitive skin. Finally, avoid wasting water. The less water we use, the more is left for the frogs. You can also take active measures, like participating in local bio-blitz efforts or belonging to conservation groups that support national and international efforts to save frog species and their habitats.

CHAMELEONS SPEAK IN COLOR

COATS OF MANY COLORS

Chameleons mostly live in the rain forests and deserts of Africa.

AN ANIMAL OF ODDITIES

Chameleons are strange creatures. Their eyes are domed telescopes, capable of moving independently. Their feet form naturally textured mittens with a grip that lets them climb sheer vertical surfaces. Their tongues, which are twice the length of their entire body, reach speeds faster than actual rockets. But their most iconic ability is the ability to change colors.

CRYSTAL CLEAR COMMUNICATORS

Beneath a chameleon's skin are nanoscale crystals that the chameleon controls. By altering the spacing of these crystals, chameleons can alter the color they reveal. It was thought that this ability was for camouflage. Recent science, however, suggests chameleons aren't hiding their colors; they're flaunting them. These animals are using colorful language to threaten rivals, seduce romantic partners, and reflect environmental stress.

FIGHTING WITH COLOR

The most dramatic displays are used when two males are fighting. The chameleons will puff up their size and begin to fight not with teeth, but colors, showing off their speed and palette at a distance. Color is so important: Most conflict is resolved through this color duel. The loser slinks off in dull browns.

Color Coding

Chameleons can quickly change their appearance in response to temperature, environment, and mood. Scientists recently identified a key factor in their ability to do this: The lizards can "tune" the distances between nanoscale crystals in their skin that reflect light, creating a spectrum of colors.

Color changes take 30 seconds to two minutes.

Panther chameleon
Furcifer pardalis

Under Its Skin

SUBMISSIVE
A chameleon turns darker when it needs to demonstrate that it's not a threat—such as after losing a fight—by dispersing melanin, a dark pigment, into its upper skin layers.

NEUTRAL
At rest, it's typically green or brown to match its environment. Blue and green wavelengths reflect off tightly packed crystals; red and yellow pass through.

EXCITED
Vibrant colors can signal aggression or a desire to mate. Crystals move wider apart, reflecting yellow, orange, and red wavelengths.

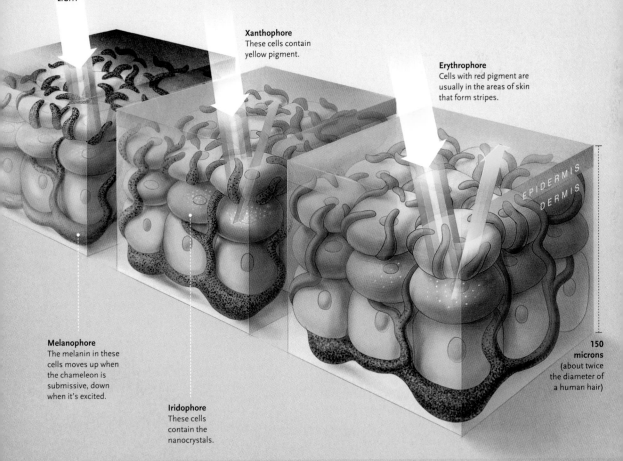

LIGHT

Xanthophore
These cells contain yellow pigment.

Erythrophore
Cells with red pigment are usually in the areas of skin that form stripes.

EPIDERMIS
DERMIS

Melanophore
The melanin in these cells moves up when the chameleon is submissive, down when it's excited.

Iridophore
These cells contain the nanocrystals.

150 microns
(about twice the diameter of a human hair)

PRIMATE FAMILY TREE

OUR DISTANT COUSINS

Humans have many characteristics that make each of us unique, but biologically, we're not a class unto ourselves. Among the more than 500 different species of primate, we humans are just one. And these days, our family could use some help: Most of our cousins live in the shrinking tropical rain forest, and two-thirds of us are at risk of extinction.

SPECTRAL TARSIER

One of the smallest primates in the world is a scant three and a half inches in length. Although they may look adorable, tarsiers are the only truly carnivorous primates, grabbing beetles, bats, and even snakes— often in midair—before devouring them.

GOLDEN LION TAMARIN

These iconic creatures live in the forests of Brazil. Tamarin juveniles, which are raised by the entire community, are sometimes twins—rare among primates. Once on the edge of extinction, tamarins have been saved by intensive conservation efforts.

HAMADRYAS BABOON

These amazingly social creatures can often be seen in troops numbering in the hundreds. Though found across northeast Africa and the Arabian Peninsula, they are locally extinct in Egypt, where they were once revered as favorites of Thoth, the ancient Egyptian god of learning.

ORANGUTAN

Orangutans are the only great apes found outside of Africa: They live in the forests of Borneo and Sumatra, where they spend almost all of their time aloft. Like many primates, they have been seen creating and using simple tools when hunting and are chimpanzees' closest genetic relatives.

GORILLA

The largest of the primates, gorillas may look intimidating, but these herbivorous apes are more Curious George than King Kong. They spend most of their day wandering about, eating plants, and building new nests every night. A group of gorillas, called a "troop," can be as large as 30 individuals.

CHIMPANZEE

One of our closest genetic relatives, chimps live in tightly bonded families, use tools, and even eat medicinal plants when injured. Generally fruit and plant eaters, they also consume insects, eggs, and meat, including carrion. With such a varied diet, they can habituate themselves to African rain forests, woodlands, and grasslands. They are known to make weapon commit murder, and even coordinate attacks on other tribes.

> ❝ WE ARE, INDEED, UNIQUE PRIMATES, WE HUMANS, BUT WE'RE SIMPLY NOT AS DIFFERENT FROM THE REST OF THE ANIMAL KINGDOM AS WE USED TO THINK.❞
>
> —JANE GOODALL, PRIMATOLOGIST

A WORD FROM

Models of Good Behavior
I study chimpanzees because I think they can give us insight into our own species … You see a level of social cohesion in these savanna chimps that has affected their sharing and cooperation. That's something I think is overlooked because we tend to focus on how aggressive chimps can be. But sharing and cooperation are key to our own species, and I think these savanna chimps show how it might have developed.

—**JILL PRUETZ,** *anthropologist*

ROSALIND FRANKLIN
BIOPHYSICIST

DNA DETECTIVE

In the 1950s, scientists raced to uncover the secret to life. Scientists from several countries and colleges sought out the best minds they could find to help them crack the code. Rosalind Franklin was one of the brightest. Having graduated with a Ph.D. from Cambridge University in 1945, Franklin was working in Paris as an expert in x-ray crystallography, using x-rays to photograph the structure of atomic-scale objects. When she was offered the chance to return to England and do DNA research at King's College of London, she took it.

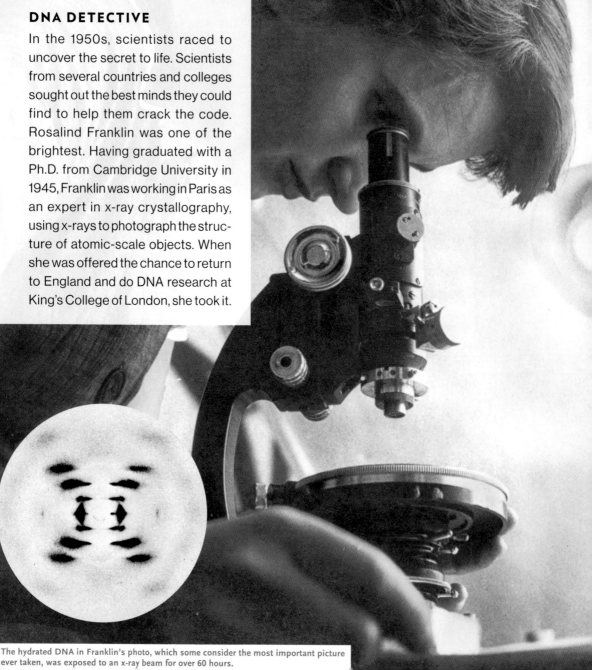

The hydrated DNA in Franklin's photo, which some consider the most important picture ever taken, was exposed to an x-ray beam for over 60 hours.

When Rosalind Franklin began her work in London, she understood herself to be working independently on DNA research, trying to establish its makeup and structure. Her colleague Maurice Wilkins, however, assumed she would be his assistant, since they were both using photographic and chemical approaches—unlike scientists James Watson and Francis Crick who were trying to build DNA chemically.

The breakthrough was an x-ray crystallography image taken in Franklin's lab. This image, known as B 51, unlocked a vital secret of DNA: its helical structure. Wilkins, without Franklin's permission, shared some of her early data, including B 51, with Crick and Watson. The photo helped reshape their own work and led to their discovery of DNA's double-helix structure. When the paper describing their findings was published in 1953, Watson and Crick received widespread praise and fame. Franklin went uncelebrated, even though she had a paper published in that same journal issue.

LIFE AFTER DNA

Franklin left King's College in 1953 for Birkbeck College, where she would spend the next, and last, five years of her life. She focused on the x-ray crystallography of viruses and uncovered the structure of the tobacco mosaic virus and the polio virus. She died of ovarian cancer in 1958 at just 37 years old. Her life, one professor said, "was a perfect example of single-minded devotion to research." In 1962, Wilkins, Watson, and Crick won the Nobel Prize for their work on DNA. Franklin, by then deceased, was ineligible.

> " SCIENCE, FOR ME, GIVES A PARTIAL EXPLANATION OF LIFE. IN SO FAR AS IT GOES, IT IS BASED ON FACT, EXPERIENCE, AND EXPERIMENT."

Barely 30 when she made her discovery, Franklin died before its significance was recognized.

KEY DATES

The History of DNA

■ **1859**
Charles Darwin publishes *On the Origin of Species.*

■ **1865**
Austrian monk Gregor Mendel presents the principles of genetics.

■ **1944**
Avery, MacLeod, and McCarty's experiment shows DNA is hereditary.

■ **1952**
Rosalind Franklin photographs DNA fibers, revealing double-helical structure.

■ **1953**
James Watson and Francis Crick publish on structure of DNA.

■ **2003**
After 13 years, the Human Genome Project completes its work.

■ **2012**
CRISPR enables simpler genetic editing using viruses.

BEST OF @NATGEO

OUR FAVORITE PHOTOS OF SEA LIFE

@joelsartore | JOEL SARTORE
A giant Pacific octopus waves its many tentacles at the Dallas World Aquarium.

@paulnicklen | PAUL NICKLEN
A friendly female leopard seal approaches the photographer in Antarctic waters.

@ladzinski | KEITH LADZINSKI
A diverse ecosystem thrives in the cold waters of Olympic National Park in Washington State.

@cristinamittermeier | CRISTINA MITTERMEIER
In the waters of Galicia, Spain, mussels grow on ropes until they reach commercial size.

> ❝ THE SEA, ONCE IT CASTS ITS SPELL, HOLDS ONE IN ITS NET OF WONDER FOREVER.❞
>
> —JACQUES-YVES COUSTEAU, OCEAN EXPLORER AND FILMMAKER

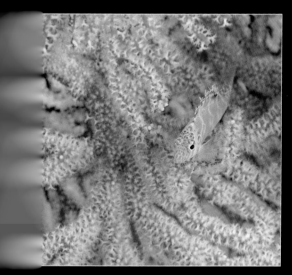

@timlaman | TIM LAMAN
A threadfin hawkfish is perfectly camouflaged in the delicate fronds of a gorgonian sea fan.

@DavidDoubilet | DAVID DOUBILET
A clownfish peers out from the tentacles of its host anemone in Kimbe Bay, Papua New Guinea.

@jenniferhayesig | JENNIFER HAYES
Seeking shelter from the wind, a harp seal pup hides behind a piece of ice in Canada's Gulf of St. Lawrence.

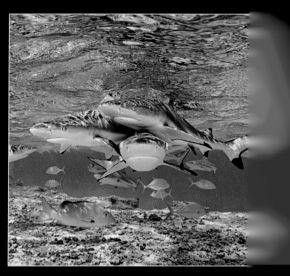

@BrianSkerry | BRIAN SKERRY
Blacktip reef sharks mingle with twinspot snappers and blue trevallies at Millennium Atoll, a pristine Pacific reef.

CORAL REEFS

PARADISE ALMOST LOST

Coral reefs may seem like an explosion of color, but coral themselves are translucent. Reefs get their radiant hues by hosting billions of colorful algae, which they use for food. Unfortunately, when waters warm, reefs expel these algae, leaving the reefs bleached and damaged. Back-to-back bleaching events in 2016 and 2017 damaged or destroyed over half of the Great Barrier Reef. A quarter of all marine species live on the reefs and rely on these algae. Without them, the whole ecosystem crumbles.

A marine scientist explores a garden of stony corals.

OVER 2,000 **NEW** MARINE SPECIES **ARE DISCOVERED EVERY YEAR. BUT FOR THE COUNTLESS DIVERSE SPECIES LIVING IN CORAL REEFS, AS MANY AS** 8 MILLION **MORE REMAIN** UNDISCOVERED.

PAPUA NEW GUINEA

SOLOMON SEA

Great Barrier Reef in Peril

A new aerial survey shows that portions of the reef are more damaged than previously thought.

NORTHERN SECTOR

Cape York Peninsula

0 mi   140
0 km   140

Port Douglas
Cairns

GREAT BARRIER REEF

MARINE PARK

CENTRAL SECTOR

AUSTRALIA

Townsville

ASIA
PACIFIC OCEAN

INDIAN OCEAN

AREA ENLARGED

AUSTRALIA

Mackay

CORAL SEA

SOUTHERN SECTOR

TROPIC OF CAPRICORN

SOURCE: ARC CENTRE OF EXCELLENCE FOR CORAL REEF STUDIES

NORTHERN SECTOR
Severely bleached **81%**   Not bleached **<1%**

CENTRAL SECTOR
Severely bleached **33%**   Not bleached **10%**

SOUTHERN SECTOR
Severely bleached **1%**   Not bleached **25%**

GOING GREEN

Protecting Our
REEFS

Diving a coral reef can be the experience of a lifetime, but it can also be a threat to the ecosystem you're observing. Keep the corals safe by only using eco-conscious operators, never touching the reef with any part of a body or boat, and wearing sun-protective clothes instead of applying sunscreen, which has harsh chemicals that can promote coral bleaching.

TOOTHY SPLENDOR

MAGNIFICENT CREATURES KEY TO KEEPING OCEAN LIFE IN BALANCE

Great whites can sense the tiny electromagnetic fields generated by prey.

GREAT WHITE SHARK

APEX PREDATOR

Great whites are the largest predatory fish on Earth, growing up to 20 feet long and weighing up to 2.5 tons. Their keen sense of smell can detect a single drop of blood in 25 gallons of water. Once on the hunt, they can use their powerful tails to launch themselves fully out of the water, breaching the surface like a rocket, before grabbing onto prey with 300 razor-sharp serrated teeth. They are carnivorous perfection, but humans are not on the menu.

Like dogs, great whites explore with their mouths, so most attacks of swimmers and surfers aren't fatal by design. These attacks are "sample bites" to see whether we taste good. When we don't—and we don't—they usually spit out the bite and swim away in search of other food.

MAKO SHARK

SPEED DEMON

Mako sharks are one of the fastest fish on the planet, with speeds of over 35 miles an hour, and they are able to swim up to 60 miles a day—capable of outrunning the speediest tuna and the sleekest dolphin. They've developed keen eyesight for hunting at high speeds and can launch 20 feet out of the water. Such amazing feats require heat and energy, so makos, like great whites, can warm up their blood, allowing them to swim longer and faster than colder, slower prey. Unfortunately, they cannot outswim powerboats: Makos are a profitable catch—both their meat and their fins are prized in Asia. But because they don't reproduce quickly, they are vulnerable to overfishing.

Makos venture into depths and regions too cold for most other shark species.

Whitetips spend their days resting in reef caves, sometimes in groups.

WHITETIP SHARK

MOST DANGEROUS

This open-ocean shark patrols every major ocean, swimming at greater depths and for longer distances than most other sharks. Whitetips are one of the most common large fish in the ocean, often seen wandering the depths with remora and other scavenger fish in tow. They are brazen, even fearless, in investigating their waters and, while usually alone, can come together in a "feeding frenzy" if food is available. Although rarely encountered from shore, whitetips may be responsible for more deaths than any other shark. Sharks presumed to be whitetips swarmed the sinking U.S.S. *Indianapolis* during World War II. Hundreds died, as many as 150 eaten by sharks. This and other incidents led Jacques Cousteau to consider them, not great whites, the most dangerous sharks of all.

A WORD FROM

Shark Grace For the artist within me, sharks represent an endless well of inspiration, a blend of grace and power that lures me into the sea time after time in hopes of producing a new rendering that truly captures their essence. As a journalist, I'm driven by a sense of responsibility and a sense of the urgent need to broadcast that sharks are in trouble and need our help.

—BRIAN SKERRY, *photographer*

SHARKS USE SPECIALIZED ORGANS THAT SENSE ELECTRICAL FIELDS AROUND THEM TO AVOID PREDATORS OR TARGET PREY.

Tiger sharks are ambush predators and prefer murky waters.

TIGER SHARK

VORACIOUS EATERS

Tiger sharks get their name from the distinctive stripes along their sides. These are most visible on juveniles and fade to mere shadows on mature sharks. Don't let the name fool you, though: These animals are more scavenger than predator. Nicknamed "the garbage cans of the sea," they are voracious eaters, and they're not picky about what they eat. Tiger sharks have been found with hubcaps, license plates, pets, and even a whole suit of armor in their stomachs. But because they have an almost completely undiscerning palate, they are not likely to swim away after biting a human, as great whites frequently do. Unlike many other sharks, tiger sharks do well in warmer waters and can easily adapt their diet to changing conditions. As the climate warms, the garbage eaters could become kings of the sea.

SEA SHELLS

A Home in the Sea Creatures started building shells around 500 million years ago. Since then, they have evolved spirals, spines, and ridges, but the purpose is still the same: to protect the delicate animal living inside it.

FLORIDA FIGHTING CONCH
Spurred foot for defense, burrowing

FRILLED DOGWINKLE
Preys with tongue and poison

KNOBBED WHELK
Like conch, can be made into a horn

LETTERED OLIVE
Used by Native Americans for jewelry

ATLANTIC PLATE LIMPET
Attaches to rocks by suction

ATLANTIC SLIPPER SHELL
Shells stack for reproduction

BAY SCALLOP
Senses predators with 18 pairs of eyes

PACIFIC LITTLENECK CLAM
Abundant in U.S. West Coast shallows

EASTERN OYSTER
Must attach to hard surface to mature

PACIFIC RAZOR CLAM
Meaty edible bivalve

ATLANTIC JACKKNIFE CLAM
Digs itself down into sand or mud

ATLANTIC AUGER
Stuns prey with poisonous barb

PACIFIC GEODUCK
Can age to more than 150 years

NORTHERN QUAHOG
Harvested for clam chowder

MARINE MUSSEL
One of many edible mussel species

BLACK TURBAN SNAIL
Feeds on algae, has many predators

COMMON MARSH SNAIL
Breathes air, feeds on marsh grasses

COMMON PERIWINKLE
Two antennae, one foot

RED ABALONE
Long valued for pearlescent colors

VIOLET SEA SNAIL
Churns bubbles and floats to survive

> ❝ **NATURE IS THE MOST BEAUTIFUL ENGINEER AND IT ALWAYS HAS A REASON FOR CHOOSING ANY SHAPE.** ❞
>
> —DR. CHANDRA TIWARY, INDIAN INSTITUTE OF SCIENCE

Populations of this endangered marine mammal are increasing, so it may be reclassified as threatened.

MANATEES

PROTECTING AQUATIC CELEBRITIES

Hidden in the wetlands of coastal Florida are a pack of one-ton con-servation success stories: the manatees. Manatees move slowly, floating just below the surface looking for plants or warmth. Boat strikes once put the lumbering "sea cows" at risk of extinction, and many still have pink scars across their thick skin from propellers or boat hulls. New speed limits and education efforts have reduced the injuries. Absent the boat strikes, manatee populations rebounded: There are now 6,000 in Florida alone.

DOLPHIN
BRAINS

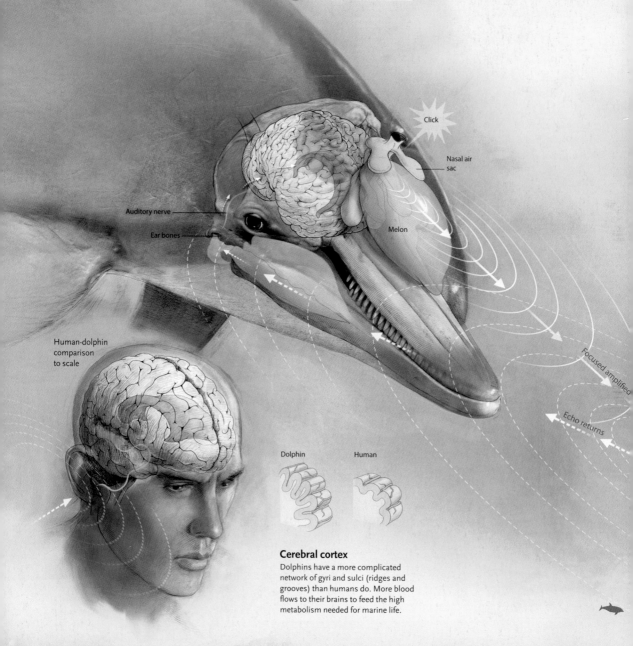

Click

Nasal air sac

Auditory nerve

Ear bones

Melon

Human-dolphin comparison to scale

Focused amplified

Echo returns

Dolphin   Human

Cerebral cortex

Dolphins have a more complicated network of gyri and sulci (ridges and grooves) than humans do. More blood flows to their brains to feed the high metabolism needed for marine life.

Seeing With Sound

Dolphins have evolved a sensory system to detect objects underwater using the echoes created by sounds. Sound travels four times as fast in the water as in the air.

Dolphin Behaviors

Using tools
In Australia some dolphins put marine basket sponges on their rostra, or beaks, to protect against abrasion while they probe the seafloor for prey.

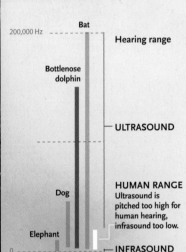

200,000 Hz — — — — — **Bat**

Hearing range

Bottlenose dolphin

— ULTRASOUND

HUMAN RANGE
Ultrasound is pitched too high for human hearing, infrasound too low.

Dog

Elephant

0 — — — — — — — INFRASOUND

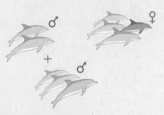

Teaming up
Two small groups of males sometimes work together to herd a female away from her companions. If they succeed, one of the groups gets to mate with her.

Strand feeding
Some dolphins will charge toward shore, making waves that force fish onto land. The dolphins then beach themselves to feast.

The beam of clicks bounces off the target and returns to the echolocating dolphin. Clicks can be overheard by neighboring dolphins.

Remembering each other
Dolphins can recognize the signature whistles of other dolphins, perhaps even if the animals haven't encountered each other for as long as 20 years.

Echolocating dolphins can identify targets as far away as half a mile.

A Mind of Their Own

Since the ancestors of dolphins left their fellow mammals behind and entered the water more than 50 million years ago, humans and dolphins have evolved radically different bodies adapted to wholly separate environments. But we share one notable piece of anatomy—a large, complicated brain. Among the challenges to our own big brains: penetrating the mystery of how dolphins use theirs.

> **❝ THE QUESTION IS NOT HOW SMART ARE DOLPHINS, BUT HOW ARE DOLPHINS SMART?"**
>
> **—STAN KUCZAJ,**
> **COMPARATIVE PSYCHOLOGIST**

BEST OF @NATGEO

OUR FAVORITE PHOTOS OF LIFE ON THE WING

@timlaman | **TIM LAMAN**
On Batanta Island in Indonesia, a red bird of paradise displays its plumage.

@anandavarma | **ANAND VARMA**
A new honeybee emerges from a brood cell, in a digital composition of 23 merged photos.

@peteressick | **PETER ESSICK**
Monarch butterflies gather in Mexico's El Rosario Preserve, a stop on their epic annual migration.

@paulnicklen | **PAUL NICKLEN**
A bounty of little auks, also known as dovekies, fill the sky in Svalbard, Norway.

> ❝ PHOTOGRAPHY IMPLIES THE RECOGNITION OF A RHYTHM IN THE WORLD OF REAL THINGS. ❞
>
> —HENRI CARTIER-BRESSON, PIONEERING PHOTOGRAPHER

@ladzinski | KEITH LADZINSKI
A bright green color around the beak only appears on great white egrets during the mating season.

@kirstenluce | KIRSTEN LUCE
Fireflies at dusk at the Santuario de las Luciernagas in Tlaxcala, Mexico

@ronan_donovan | RONAN DONOVAN
A spotted owl in California's Yosemite National Park, where it finds the old-growth forest it needs to survive

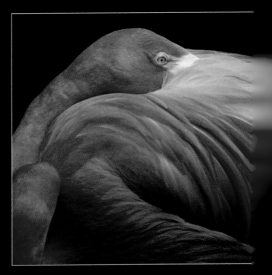

@robertclarkphoto | ROBERT CLARK
The greater flamingo's distinctive pink color is a result of its diet, which is rich in beta-carotene.

BACKYARD BIRDS

Flights of Fascination Birds wing their way through everyone's landscape, on every continent, whether hot or cold, rural or urban. Birding is about more than checking lists: Birders turn their love of these avians into real science.

AMERICAN GOLDFINCH
One of the few vegan birds

HOUSE FINCH
Males have rose-colored breast.

BALTIMORE ORIOLE
Weaves hanging nest of fibers

AMERICAN ROBIN
Traditional sign of spring

BLACK-CAPPED CHICKADEE
Chirps its own name

WESTERN BLUEBIRD
Nests in knotholes or birdhouses

EASTERN BLUEBIRD
Eats primarily insects and grubs

SONG SPARROW
May raise two or more broods a year

TUFTED TITMOUSE
Hoards food for winter

WARBLING VIREO
Melodious, recognizable song

NORTHERN CARDINAL
Males bright red, females olive

HOUSE SPARROW
Prefers to live near to humans

NORTHERN FLICKER
Digs in soil for ants and beetles

HOUSE WREN
Wide range, Canada through S. America

RED-WINGED BLACKBIRD
Winter flocks in the millions

RUBY-THROATED HUMMINGBIRD
Sips from red and orange flowers

GREAT HORNED OWL
Head swivels to look in all directions.

EASTERN PHOEBE
Perching, tail wags up and down

EUROPEAN STARLING
Mimics calls of other birds

CLIFF SWALLOW
Creates gourd-shaped nest of mud

AMERICAN CROW
Crafts tools to get at food

PURPLE MARTIN
Will move into erected nesting boxes

NORTHERN MOCKINGBIRD
May learn 200 different songs

WHITE-BREASTED NUTHATCH
Creeps along tree trunks, often head down

BLUE JAY
Throat pouch can hold 2–3 acorns.

Gardens can bloom with flower varieties chosen to attract birds.

TUNING IN

Humankind has always loved its birds. In Papua New Guinea, feathers are essential ceremonial attire; Native Americans developed sacred ceremonies around the eagle; the Chinese associated cranes with immortality; and ravens still walk the Tower of London. Today, over 45 million Americans identify as bird-watchers.

CITIZEN SCIENCE

Events like the Great Backyard Bird Count, Journey North, and HawkWatch are letting these enthusiastic amateurs generate real scientific data. A technological revolution in birding is powering the hobby by making it easier to find, track, and identify birds using apps on smartphones and tablets. Birders can get text messages in real time about rare birds in the area and where to find them, for instance, and keeping each other informed contributes to a stronger sense of community among birders. The Cornell Lab of Ornithology set up eBird, a database that allows scientists to access and analyze these data for patterns and to track changes in population, migration patterns, feeding habits, and distribution in ways that were never thought possible. By becoming citizen scientists, backyard birders help scientists understand birds better than ever.

> " IF YOU TAKE CARE OF THE BIRDS, YOU TAKE CARE OF MOST OF THE BIG ENVIRONMENTAL PROBLEMS IN THE WORLD."
>
> —THOMAS E. LOVEJOY,
> CONSERVATION BIOLOGIST

PARTS OF A BIRD

To identify songbirds, such as this wood thrush, look for characteristic parts.

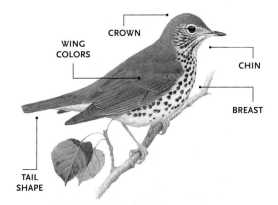

CROWN

WING COLORS

CHIN

BREAST

TAIL SHAPE

HUMMINGBIRDS
WINGED WONDERS

FIREWORKS IN FLIGHT

Hummingbirds fly like magical fairies and shimmer like jewels in the sky, but scientists have never fully understood these glorious birds. The hummingbird can fly backward, hover, and even fly sideways—all at incredible speed. But how? The answer comes in unique biological adaptations only recently discovered: larger brains to process information, symmetrical wing strokes, and longer "hands" for greater flexibility and movement. Despite their diminutive size—the smallest of 340 species weighs less than two grams—their brain represents 4.2 percent of their body weight, making it proportionally one of the largest in the animal kingdom.

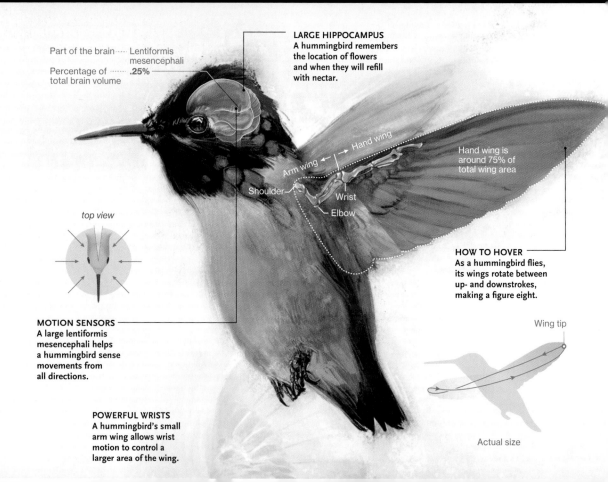

Part of the brain···· Lentiformis mesencephali

Percentage of ······· .25%
total brain volume

LARGE HIPPOCAMPUS
A hummingbird remembers the location of flowers and when they will refill with nectar.

Hand wing

Arm wing

Shoulder

Wrist

Elbow

Hand wing is around 75% of total wing area

top view

MOTION SENSORS
A large lentiformis mesencephali helps a hummingbird sense movements from all directions.

POWERFUL WRISTS
A hummingbird's small arm wing allows wrist motion to control a larger area of the wing.

HOW TO HOVER
As a hummingbird flies, its wings rotate between up- and downstrokes, making a figure eight.

Wing tip

Actual size

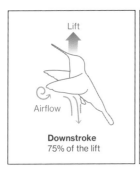

Lift

Airflow

Downstroke
75% of the lift

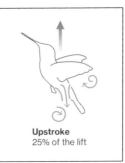

Upstroke
25% of the lift

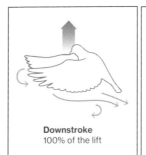

Downstroke
100% of the lift

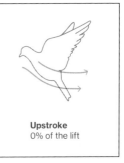

Upstroke
0% of the lift

DOWNSTROKE
Hummingbirds produce
lift with both upward and
downward wing strokes.

UPSTROKE
They can beat
their wings up to
100 times a second.

PROPULSION
In larger birds,
all the propulsion comes
from downward wing strokes.

FORWARD
Larger birds
tend to fly forward
rather than hovering.

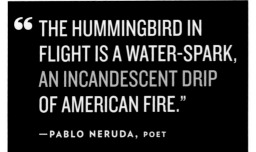

" THE HUMMINGBIRD IN FLIGHT IS A WATER-SPARK, AN INCANDESCENT DRIP OF AMERICAN FIRE."

—PABLO NERUDA, POET

SEEING EVERY MOVE

FLIGHT OF HANDS

By using super-high-speed cameras to slow down time, scientists are finally unlocking the secrets of the world's smallest bird. Hummingbirds have, proportionally, the longest hands and shortest arms of any bird. Arm wings are often used for gliding, while hand wings provide the lift. With a larger hand wing, hummingbirds can rotate the shape of their wing on every stroke, generating precise and constant lift, at the cost of constant flapping. Moving at this speed and control takes massive brainpower. Here too, the hummingbird is unique, having proportionally the second largest brain in the animal kingdom. Speed, smarts, and control are vital for the birds to access the nectar they so desperately need.

TOP FIVE

Best Flowers for
HUMMINGBIRDS

1 SCARLET BEE BALM
Hummingbirds love this hardy perennial. Its red, pink, or lavender petals catch a wandering bird's eye.

2 CARDINAL FLOWER This 48-inch-tall flower is loaded with long-lasting deep-red blossoms providing nectar and height to any garden.

3 TRUMPET VINE The bright orange flowers on this creeping vine delight hummingbirds and other avians but can take over small areas.

4 LUPINE This early blooming flower attracts the first hummingbirds of the season.

5 BUTTERFLY BUSH True to its name, the thick clusters of flowers on this bountiful bush attract insects as well as hummingbirds.

NOAH STRYCKER
BIRDER

TAKING BIRD-WATCHING TO EXTREMES

Noah Strycker had a simple plan: see more birds in one calendar year than anyone else on the planet. Doing it would require traveling nonstop over 100,000 miles across 41 countries on seven continents—and, of course, identifying at least 12 distinct species of bird every single day for 365 days.

Strycker encountered armed conflicts and other obstacles on his 2015 trip, but he still strives to travel without reference to borders, just as birds do.

Noah Strycker is a self-identified bird nerd who first started categorizing birds and tracking sightings at the age of 10. Over time, one goal became clear: the "Big Year," a quest to spot the most birds in 365 days. The global record of 4,341 birds, set by a British couple, had been unchallenged for almost a decade. Strycker decided to smash it in 2015.

THE BIG YEAR

Technology has brought about a revolution in birding. Birders around the world can instantly share sighting lists and track finds on apps. It has created a global community of birders, giving Strycker the ability to research locations and species before ever setting foot in a country. He tapped into that community to find local guides and assistants.

The planning and hard work paid off. In Ecuador, Strycker added 625 species to his list in just 12 days, while in Brazil, he witnessed a harpy eagle bringing food to his nesting family. In the Philippines, he found the critically endangered spoon-billed sandpiper, and in New Britain, he observed the golden masked owl, a bird recently thought to be extinct. Strycker blew past the record with a month to spare, eventually seeing or hearing over 6,042 birds on his journey around the world.

A YEAR OF CHANGE

Like so many animals, birds are starting to suffer the effects of climate change, as Strycker saw on his journey. Yet he found reason to be hopeful: "I discovered a thriving, friendly, sharp, and helpful world-wide community of birders," he said. "We all share the language of delight in birds."

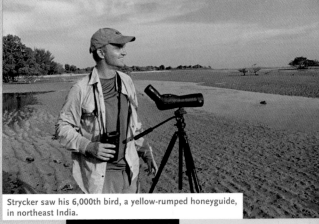

Strycker saw his 6,000th bird, a yellow-rumped honeyguide, in northeast India.

KEY MOMENTS

High Points in Noah's BIG YEAR

■ **ANTARCTICA IN JANUARY**
Coldest place visited: just below freezing; sees petrels, albatrosses, and penguins

■ **PERU IN FEBRUARY**
Wettest place visited: drenched in the Amazon; sees Junín grebe, one of world's most endangered birds

■ **ECUADOR IN MARCH**
Sees most species in shortest time: 625 in 12 days!

■ **UGANDA IN AUGUST**
Sees second most species in shortest time: 517 in 11 days

■ **INDIA IN SEPTEMBER**
Passes standing world record; Sri Lanka frogmouth is 4,342nd species seen

■ **THAILAND IN NOVEMBER**
Sees near-extinct spoon-billed sandpiper

■ **AUSTRALIA IN DECEMBER**
Hottest place visited: Melbourne at 110°F (43°C); sees 215 species in Queensland

WHOSE CATERPILLAR?

MIRACULOUS TRANSFORMATION

The famous transformation from caterpillar to butterfly looks a little different to scientists studying the creatures than to poets writing about them. To change their structure so completely, caterpillars almost completely dissolve themselves into a stem cell soup inside the cocoon. They rebuild themselves from scratch using pockets of specialized imaginal cells before emerging in their new form.

GREAT PURPLE HAIRSTREAK
Seeks mistletoe, eats leaves and male flowers

PIPEVINE SWALLOWTAIL
Eats leaves of pipevine

WESTERN TIGER SWALLOWTAIL
Spins silk for shelter

BLACK SWALLOWTAIL
When threatened, forked gland spews odor

CABBAGE WHITE
Hatches from eggs laid on garden greens

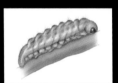

GRAY HAIRSTREAK
Tended and defended by ants

GULF FRITILLARY
Eats only passionflower plants

MOURNING CLOAK
Eats leaves of hardwood trees and shrubs

RED ADMIRAL
Eats tender inside stem of nettles

AMERICAN LADY
Seeks sunflowers to eat

COMMON BUCKEYE
Metallic-blue branching spines

MONARCH
Turns distasteful to predators by eating milkweed

VICEROY
Mottled body resembles bird dropping

REGAL MOTH
Called hickory-horned devils, but harmless

IO MOTH
Prickly green spines that can sting

LUNA MOTH
Spins papery brown cocoon

BUTTERFLIES SIP WATER, NECTAR, AND EVEN ANIMAL BLOOD USING A LONG, THIN PROBOSCIS. ALTHOUGH IT LOOKS LIKE A STRAW, BUTTERFLIES DO NOT SUCK THROUGH IT. INSTEAD, THE ORGAN SOAKS UP FLUID BY CAPILLARY ACTION, AS IF IT WERE A TUBE MADE OUT OF PAPER TOWEL.

GREAT PURPLE HAIRSTREAK
Brilliant blue on upper wing

PIPEVINE SWALLOWTAIL
Poisons from pipevine deter predators.

WESTERN TIGER SWALLOWTAIL
Clusters in mud puddles

BLACK SWALLOWTAIL
Courting pairs flutter before landing.

CABBAGE WHITE
One of spring's first butterflies

GRAY HAIRSTREAK
3–4 generations a year in the southern U.S.

GULF FRITILLARY
Migrates south to escape cold

MOURNING CLOAK
Long life span of 11–12 months

RED ADMIRAL
Prefers dung and carrion to nectar

AMERICAN LADY
Males are territorial.

COMMON BUCKEYE
Wing eyespots may scare predators.

MONARCH
State insect or butterfly in seven U.S. states

VICEROY
Mirrors bitter-tasting monarch as defense

REGAL MOTH
Adults do not eat at all.

IO MOTH
When disturbed, spreads wings to show eyespots

LUNA MOTH
Wing tails distract bats from preying on body.

MONARCHS

MULTIGENERATIONAL MIGRATORS

Each fall, millions of monarch butterflies leave their summer breeding grounds in the northeastern United States and Canada and travel upward of 3,000 miles to reach overwintering grounds in southwestern Mexico. It will take four to five generations for them to return. Each new generation slowly advances north until one supergeneration is born, living twice as long as all others combined, and returns to Mexico. This multigenerational migration spreads plant pollen up and down the North American continent.

Monarchs roost on Chincua Mountain, one of their five winter destinations in Mexico.

MONARCH BUTTERFLIES HAVE BEEN FOUND RIDING THERMAL CURRENTS OVER A MILE INTO THE AIR ALONG THEIR MIGRATION PATH.

GOING GREEN

How to Welcome Them
ALONG THE WAY

Monarch butterflies need two things along their migration: places to rest and nectar to eat. Although milkweed is their primary food source, any nectar-producing plant may attract their attention. Pollinator gardens along their route can host hundreds or even thousands of monarchs during migration.

CONSERVATION
TIME LINE

8000 to 1 BC	AD 1 to 1850	1850 to 1900	1900 to 1950

8000 BC
Organized agriculture begins: cultivated plants and herded animals.

6000 BC
Animal manure is used as fertilizer.

6000 BC
Maize is domesticated in the Americas.

ca 1500 BC
Aztecs build chinampas, floating gardens, on edges of Mexican lakes.

1661
London's Vauxhall Gardens open to the public.

1701–1731
Jethro Tull invents seed drill, improves plow, and makes other farming innovations.

1730
British statesman-farmer Charles Townshend develops four-year crop rotation.

1789
Englischer Garten opens in Munich, Germany.

1849
The U.S. Department of Interior is established.

1854
Henry David Thoreau's *Walden* is published.

1858
Construction of New York City's Central Park, the first major urban park in the U.S., is under way.

1863
Britain's Alkali Act curbs acid gas emissions.

1872
Yellowstone National Park, the first legislated national park, is established.

1892
The Sierra Club is founded, with John Muir as its first president.

1913
German People's Park Association (Deutscher Volksparkbund) is founded in Germany.

1916
U.S. and Canada sign Migratory Birds Treaty, first international conservation effort.

1916
The U.S. National Park Service is established.

1918
Fritz Haber receives Nobel Prize for synthesizing ammonia, used for fertilizer.

1940s
High-yield wheat is introduced in Mexico, starting "green revolution."

1950 to 1970

1962
Rachel Carson's *Silent Spring* is published.

1964
U.S. legislates Wilderness Act, protecting lands from development.

1968
Apollo 8 astronauts create "Earthrise" photo.

1968
First edition of the *Whole Earth Catalog* is published.

1968
Paul R. Ehrlich's *The Population Bomb* is published.

1970 to 1980

1970
About 20 million participate in first Earth Day, April 22.

1970
The U.S. Environmental Protection Agency is established.

1970
Monsanto develops glyphosate herbicide, soon known as Roundup.

1971
Greenpeace begins as protest against nuclear testing in Alaska.

1972
Apollo 17 astronauts create "Blue Marble" photo.

1973
U.S. Congress approves Endangered Species Act.

1979
An accident occurs at Three Mile Island nuclear power plant.

1980 to 2000

1980
Green Party is established in West Germany.

1987
Montreal Protocol, which reduces emissions that deplete the ozone layer, is signed by 140 nations.

1988
First GMO crops, Roundup-resistant soybeans, developed.

1992
United Nations convenes Earth Summit in Rio de Janeiro, Brazil.

2000 to PRESENT

2000
In U.S., Green Party presidential candidate Ralph Nader receives 2.7% of vote.

2008
Svalbard Global Seed Vault is established in Norwegian Arctic.

2011
The population of humans on Earth reaches 7 billion, according to estimates from the United Nations.

2016
Paris Agreement is ratified, joining nations in combating climate change.

PHOTO ARK

USING HIS ART TO SAVE ENDANGERED SPECIES

The number of animals going extinct is growing exponentially, warn the experts. Witnessing the problem firsthand, photographer Joel Sartore wanted to make a difference. Now he and his team are creating the National Geographic Photo Ark, collecting portraits of every animal species under human care—he figures the total is about 12,000, and in 2016 he reached the halfway point by photographing an endangered proboscis monkey at the Singapore Zoo.

A reticulate Gila monster *(Heloderma suspectum suspectum)* does its best to smile for Joel Sartore's camera.

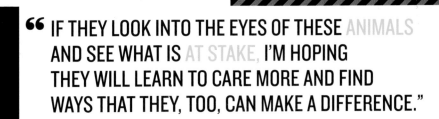

Joel Sartore warily eyes the Gila monster at the Lincoln (Nebraska) Children's Zoo.

KEY NUMBERS

Species and Subspecies
PHOTOGRAPHED

■ **AMPHIBIANS**
639 species

■ **BIRDS**
2,205 species

■ **FISH**
1,128 species

■ **INVERTEBRATES**
(TERRESTRIAL AND AQUATIC)
1,893 species

■ **MAMMALS**
1,077 species

■ **REPTILES**
1,486 species

■ **TOTAL**
8,428 species and subspecies
photographed as of June 2018

THREATENED & NEEDING HELP

OUR MOST BELOVED CREATURES ARE UNDER SIEGE

About half of all living tigers are Bengal tigers.

TIGER

A REASON FOR HOPE

Just over 100 years ago, there were 100,000 tigers in the wild. Poaching and habitat destruction have killed 96 percent of them, and they are still killed for their exotic fur and meat. Just 4,000 tigers are left in the wild. Three subspecies have already gone extinct. Their once vast range has been reduced to just 7 percent of what it once was. For example, rain forest habitat in Sumatra is being replaced by palm oil plantations as demand for this widely consumed vegetable oil increases. The good news? Tiger populations are starting to increase, and conservation and education efforts around the world are having an impact.

RHINOCEROS

EDGE OF EXTINCTION

A century ago rhinoceroses flourished in Africa and Asia, half a million strong. But these days, the only ones remaining live on national parks, where they are under the near constant supervision of antipoaching patrols. Rhino horn is valued for many traditional medicines—rhino horn is often ground to a powder and ingested as a treatment for everything from cancer to sea snake bites and hangovers—and is used in ceremonial dagger handles. Two Asian species cling to existence, with just a few dozen animals remaining. In Africa, southern white rhinos have come back from the brink, but the last surviving male northern white rhinoceros died in March 2018 at the age of 45.

Horn of the white rhino sells for up to $3,000 a pound.

About 27,000 elephants in Africa are slaughtered annually.

BY 2100, HUMAN ACTIVITIES MAY DRIVE MORE THAN HALF OF TODAY'S MARINE AND LAND SPECIES TO EXTINCTION.

There are over 16,000 species today—ones from every continent—at risk of extinction.

ELEPHANT

AN ENDANGERED ICON

The African elephant wanders through 37 countries on the continent, and Asian elephants range from Syria to Borneo. Not surprisingly, Earth's largest land animal takes a lot of habitat space, and that means a lot of interaction with humans. Elephants can inadvertently damage property or crops, and in retaliation, or simply out of fear, be hurt or killed themselves. Poachers, who still hunt them for their ivory tusks, remain a threat as well. In 2011 alone, 100,000 African elephants were killed for their tusks. Hopefully, China's recent ivory ban, which closed all government-licensed carving factories and ivory retailers, will deter future catastrophes. An international ivory trade ban has been in effect since 1990, but before 2018, China had not observed it.

A WORD FROM

A Ranger's Responsibility We teach our ranger foot patrols how to defend themselves in case they meet with poachers or other threats while they work. We have to defend ourselves. It's a risk. But it's our choice. We chose this job, to defend nature. We can't accept that people come inside the forest and kill animals or cut down trees. Without nature, there is no life. We have to defend the wildlife.

—**INNOCENT MBURANUMWE,** *park ranger, Virunga National Park, Democratic Republic of the Congo*

GORILLA

A COUSIN IN DANGER

The largest of the great apes shares a lot with humanity, including our diseases. In 2003 the world's gorilla population was decimated by the Ebola virus, which was transferred from human to ape; scabies, tuberculosis, and other diseases have also made the leap. Disease is far from the only threat apes face. Poachers hunt the animals for their meat, hands, and skins. Because only 17 percent of gorillas live in protected areas, few criminals are caught. In the mountains of Rwanda, where primatologist Dian Fossey famously studied gorillas, fees paid by tourists—more than 30,000 hiked into the park in 2016—ensure the government's commitment to protecting the species.

PLASTIC IN OUR WORLD

AN ENDURING THREAT

Since it was first mass-produced in the 1940s, plastic has made its way into every corner of life, from soda bottles and IV bags, to car parts and insulation, and even soaps and shampoos. It has revolutionized our society—but at a cost. Plastic takes more than 400 years to degrade, so most of it still exists in some form. Only 12 percent has been incinerated, and only 9 percent has been recycled. Of the 8.3 billion metric tons produced to date, 6.3 billion has become plastic waste.

The vast majority of plastic waste—79 percent—is accumulating in landfills or sloughing off in the natural environment as litter.

THE SOUTH PACIFIC HAS A ZONE OF PLASTIC POLLUTION UPWARD OF A MILLION SQUARE MILES IN SIZE, MAKING IT LARGER THAN MEXICO.

Do Your Part to Minimize
POLLUTION

When it comes to pollution, simple acts can make a difference—especially when finding alternatives to single-use plastics. One million shopping bags are used every minute, but each one lasts 1,000 years—so bring reusable bags to the store. Reuse glass containers for spices or bulk goods instead of tossing your empties. And decline plastic straws, which are uniquely dangerous to marine life and among the most common items found on beaches.

KIKE CALVO
CONSERVATIONIST

TAKING AN AERIAL VIEW

Kike Calvo has photographed remote communities around the world, as well as whales in the ocean and polar bears in the Arctic. You could say he goes above and beyond to get a shot—but in this case, *above* is not a figure of speech: Calvo is also one of the pioneers of drone photography for conservation.

Calvo lends his expertise in drone photography to conservation efforts.

Kike Calvo isn't your typical photographer. Born in Spain, he originally wanted to be an economist. After his father died of cancer, photography became an escape from grief. When he returned to school, media—rather than money—was on his mind. Opportunities soon followed in the Galápagos, at the United Nations, and in 95 countries around the world. The revolution of drone photography opened up new avenues in his work, and he literally wrote the books on how to use drones in conservation and mapping.

INDIGENOUS PEOPLE, INDIGENOUS STORIES

Calvo is happy to teach others, especially on National Geographic Expeditions around the world and in indigenous communities. Calvo works to bring stories from different cultures to the rest of the world, whether he is among Buddhist monks in Cambodia, the indigenous Emberá tribe in Colombia, or dancers in Latin America. Providing these small, unmanned aerial systems to groups lets them tell their own stories and help solve the problems they face. For example, Calvo traveled to Nepal after the April 2015 earthquake to teach students how to use drones for mapping their country, because maps are crucial in disaster preparedness and response and in construction and engineering projects.

Calvo takes the same fresh storytelling approach to commercial and editorial work. When photographing dancers all over the world, he brings them outside—on sidewalks, in fountains, near landmarks, along trails, atop a bus—so they can communicate new expressions of a traditional art.

> " I BELIEVE IT'S OUR JOB AS PHOTOGRAPHERS TO TAKE VIEWERS ON A CREATIVE AND EMOTIONAL JOURNEY—TO BRING THEM TO THE CENTER OF THE ACTION."

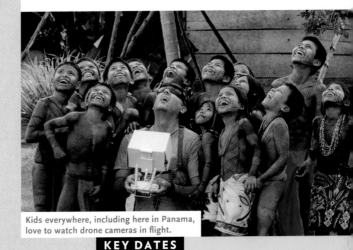

Kids everywhere, including here in Panama, love to watch drone cameras in flight.

KEY DATES

History of Aerial PHOTOGRAPHY

■ **1858**
The first aerial photograph is taken from hot air balloon in France.

■ **1906**
Great San Francisco quake damage is photographed from kites.

■ **1903–1909**
Bavarian Pigeon Corps explores animal-mounted cameras.

■ **1909**
Wilbur Wright takes first photograph from a plane.

■ **1916**
World War I replaces standard maps with aerial photographs of front line.

■ **1972**
Aerial photography enters a new phase as cameras map the moon.

CONSERVATION
IN YOUR BACKYARD

EVERYDAY ACTIONS MAKE A DIFFERENCE

Cities are competing for the title of "most bikeable."

TRANSPORTATION

MAKE A MOVE

Transportation is one of the biggest drivers of climate change, creating 15 percent of all carbon pollution. Scaling back on transportation can make a real difference. Canceling a work-related long-distance flight and holding a conference call instead can keep tons of carbon pollution from going into the atmosphere. Changing to an electric vehicle reduces emissions, too. Even better, find ways to use public transportation, to share rides, or to cycle or walk to your destination—good for you and the planet.

Young people are driving less than teens did a generation ago, and they are delaying getting driver's licenses. Their new attitudes toward mobility already are beginning to curb the trajectory of energy use in the industrialized world.

RECYCLING

REDUCE, REUSE, REPAIR, RETHINK

Recycling has been dramatically increasing, as cities across the country and around the world implement curbside recycling and limit collection of trash destined for the landfill. Just over a third of all the solid waste in the country last year was recycled. But recycling programs are struggling. Dirty bottles and plastic grocery bags can contaminate a whole load of recycling, sending it into the trash instead. Help by keeping your recycling sorted, clean, and dry, and by only recycling appropriate materials. Reusing glass jars, paper bags, and other materials before tossing them into the recycling bin can be a great way to shrink your footprint.

Reusing shopping bags, even plastic ones, reduces waste.

A plant-based diet is good for more than the waistline.

FOOD CHOICES

PLANT-BASED AND EARTH-FRIENDLY

Over 30 percent of the landmass of the planet goes to creating meat, eggs, and dairy for public consumption, and that figure is growing. These animals are taking up ever more agricultural space and resources, and the waste they generate at factory-scale facilities can pollute waterways.

If each American replaced chicken with a plant-based food at just one meal a week, the carbon dioxide savings would be the same as taking more than half a million cars off the road. Switching to a plant-based diet is one of the best ways we can lower our carbon footprint, because it removes hundreds of thousands of pounds of carbon from the atmosphere. Seek out recipes in which meat adds flavor instead of being a main dish.

A WORD FROM

Connecting With Trees I asked how I could bring my message to people who might not already be convinced of the importance of trees . . . I took a clue from the fact that trees have a peculiar structure. Each twig is connected to another twig, each branch to another branch—and I realized that I could explore the connection of the ecological value of trees to societal values that already exist: recreational values, aesthetic values, spiritual values, and social justice values.

—**NALINI NADKARNI,** *rain forest ecologist*

We need water—and so does all life on the planet.

WATER

AWARENESS LEADS TO CONSERVATION

Water is life on planet Earth. But our blue planet is running out of freshwater. Every drop of water that we use has to be removed from the environment, keeping it from sustaining wetlands downstream.

By planting sustainable lawns and agriculture and by minimizing freshwater use in our daily lives, we can make a difference. Inside the house, when you reduce water consumption by running full loads of laundry and dishes, turning off the faucet when not actively in use, and fixing leaky faucets and toilets, you are helping keep rivers flowing freely. With even basic conservation measures in place, the average household could save 44,000 gallons a year. If you're more ambitious than that, start collecting and using rainwater.

FURTHER

TO SAVE A FUTURE FOR ELEPHANTS

A recent census put the African elephant population at just over 350,000, suggesting an 8 percent annual loss currently. Global efforts to save the species from extinction now focus on controlling the ivory trade, considered responsible for the slaughter of tens of thousands of elephants each year. Countries around the world have enacted bans on the sale of ivory objects, yet the illegal trade goes on. One shipment alone, discovered in 2017 in Hong Kong, contained nearly eight tons of ivory valued at nine million dollars. Around the world, officials are staging dramatic ivory burns and crushes as a way to send a message.

Elephants graze in Kenya's Amboseli National Park.

" BY ANY MEASURE, TIME IS SHORT. IN THE 19TH CENTURY, AFRICA BOASTED AN ESTIMATED 12 MILLION ELEPHANTS. **TODAY, THAT POPULATION HAS BEEN REDUCED** 97 PERCENT **AND IS DROPPING FASTER THAN EVER."**

—PAUL G. ALLEN, PHILANTHROPIST AND SPONSOR OF GREAT ELEPHANT CENSUS

THE SCIENCE OF US

ORIGINS | MANY VOICES

From this tiny beginning, a world unfolds.

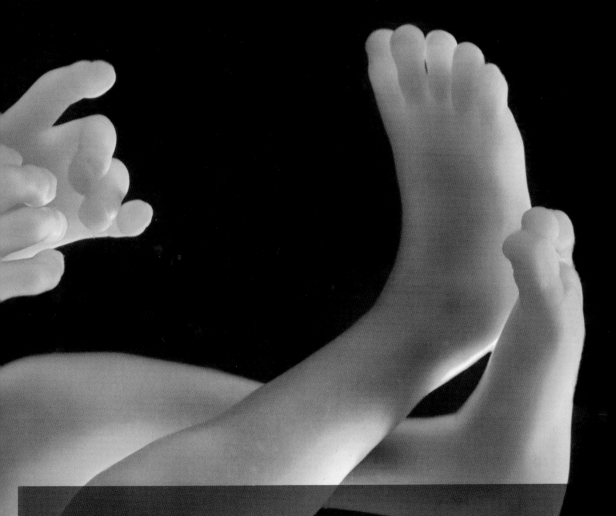

BODY & BRAIN | HEALTH & MEDICINE

QUIZ MASTER

Expert on You and Me? There's a lot to know about the world of us humans, from our earliest ancestors to our cities today, from the microbes in our gut to the neurons in our brain. And you don't have to leave home to do the exploring!

—CARA SANTA MARIA, *Our Favorite Nerd*

WHAT WORLD RELIGION HAS THE MOST FOLLOWERS?

p250

p230

IS MITOCHONDRIAL DNA PASSED DOWN THROUGH THE PATERNAL OR THE MATERNAL GENETIC LINE?

IN WHAT CONTINENT DID HORSES ORIGINATE?

p237

p262

ROUGHLY HOW MANY MICROBES LIVE IN THE HUMAN BODY: 30 MILLION, BILLION, OR TRILLION?

IN WHAT CENTURY DID LOUIS BRAILLE DEVELOP A WRITING SYSTEM FOR THE BLIND?

p260

p247

WHAT WILL BE THE WORLD'S BIGGEST CITY IN 2030?

IN WHAT EUROPEAN COUNTRY WERE THE FIRST FOSSILS OF NEANDERTHAL MAN DISCOVERED?

p225

DO WE HAVE AN EFFECTIVE VACCINE AGAINST THE RHINOVIRUS?

p278

WHAT IS THE GENUS AND SPECIES NAME OF THE ANCIENT HUMAN ANCESTOR COMMONLY KNOWN AS LUCY?

p226

IN WHAT COUNTRY DID PALEOANTHROPOLOGIST LEE BERGER AND HIS TEAM DISCOVER THE NEW SPECIES CALLED HOMO NALEDI?

p229

WHAT SUB-SAHARAN CITY IS EXPECTED TO BECOME ONE OF THE WORLD'S TOP TEN LARGEST CITIES BY 2030?

p247

WHAT FAMILIAR HERB IS ALSO AN ANCIENT CURE FOR INDIGESTION?

p276

IN WHAT YEAR DID THE PROPORTION OF THE WORLD'S PEOPLE LIVING IN URBAN AS OPPOSED TO RURAL SETTINGS TIP PAST 50 PERCENT?

p246

WHAT PROPORTION OF THE CALORIES REPRESENTED BY CROPS GROWN AROUND THE WORLD TODAY GOES TO FEEDING LIVESTOCK—8%, 24%, OR 36%?

p255

HUMAN EVOLUTION
TIME LINE

4 MYA to 80,000 YA	80,000 YA to 8000 BC	8000 to 1500 BC	1500 to 1 BC

■ 3.5 mya*
Upright bipedalism—walking on two legs—evolves.

■ ca 1.75 mya
Homo erectus, an early ancestor of modern humans, uses stone tools.

■ ca 400,000 ya**
Neanderthals use fire as a tool in some areas.

■ ca 160,000 ya
Homo sapiens, the modern human race, first appears.

■ ca 120,000 ya
Neanderthals live in modern-day Europe.

■ ca 80,000 ya
Early humans begin moving out of Africa onto other continents.

* *million years ago*
** *years ago*

■ ca 80,000 ya
Modern humans move into Europe and live alongside Neanderthals.

■ ca 65,000 ya
Modern humans reach the Australian continent.

■ ca 40,000 ya
Neanderthals die out.

■ ca 25,000 ya
A small figurine called the Venus of Willendorf is crafted. It is the oldest known art in Europe.

■ ca 15,000 ya
The first human settlements appear in North America.

■ ca 11,000 ya
Agricultural systems begin to emerge in the Middle East, as humans cultivate plants and domesticate animals.

■ ca 6500 BC
Farming begins in the Indus Valley in modern-day Pakistan and western India.

■ ca 5000 BC
Rice is cultivated as a crop in central and eastern China.

■ ca 3500 BC
First wheels appear in Mesopotamia, used for pottery and later for vehicular use.

■ 2630 BC
The Egyptians begin building pyramids.

■ ca 2300 BC
The earliest known maps are produced in Mesopotamia.

■ ca 2000 BC
Austronesians settle on islands in the South Pacific.

■ ca 1550 BC
The Mesopotamian empire begins to grow from the city of Mittani.

■ ca 1050 BC
Ironworking is introduced to Greece.

■ 1000 BC
The Phoenicians develop an alphabet.

■ ca 600 BC
The Maya use cacao to make a chocolate drink.

■ ca 400 BC
Hippocrates of Kos describes human anatomy and various diseases.

■ ca 300 BC
The Maya build pyramids in modern-day Mexico.

| AD 1 to 1850 | 1850 to 1900 | 1900 to 1975 | 1975 to PRESENT |

1677

Dutch scientist Antonie van Leeuwenhoek observes and describes both bacteria and human sperm cells.

1691

John Ray suggests that fossils are the remains of creatures from the distant past.

1735

Swedish naturalist Carolus Linnaeus introduces the binomial naming system.

1836

English naturalist Charles Darwin completes his five-year voyage on the H.M.S. *Beagle*.

1856

Workmen digging in the valley of the Neander River near Düsseldorf, Germany, discover remains of Neanderthal man.

1859

Charles Darwin publishes *On the Origin of Species*, the book in which he puts forward his theory of evolution.

1865

Austrian monk Gregor Mendel presents his research on inheritance.

1868

French paleontologist Louis Lartet excavates fossils of Cro-Magnon man in southwestern France.

1891

Dutch anthropologist Eugene Dubois discovers fossils of the human ancestor "Java man," now known as *Homo erectus*.

1924

Raymond Dart discovers the first fossils of human ancestor *Australopithecus* in Africa.

1933

Anthropologists discover a 92,000-year-old fossil of *Homo sapiens* in Israel.

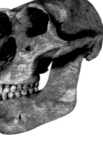

1948

English anthropologist Mary Leakey discovers fossils of possible ape ancestor *Proconsul africanus* in Africa.

1960

Anthropologist Jonathan Leakey discovers the remains of *Homo habilis* in Tanzania.

1972

Anthropologist Richard Leakey finds an intact skull of *Homo habilis*.

1974

Donald Johanson unearths "Lucy," a fossil of *Australopithecus afarensis*, in Ethiopia.

1993

Anthropologists from Berkeley discover remains of oldest known hominoid, *Ardipithecus ramidus*.

2004

An 80,000-year-old skeleton of a small humanoid called *Homo floresiensis* is found in Indonesia.

2008

Fossil of a new hominid, *Australopithecus sediba*, is discovered by Lee Berger in South Africa.

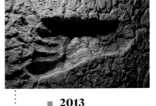

2013

Multiple remains of a newly discovered species, *Homo naledi*, are found in a cave in South Africa.

MEET OUR HUMAN ANCESTORS

HOW WE GOT TO WHERE WE ARE NOW

Scientists no longer use a family tree to depict relationships among early humans. It is now understood that several lines of early humans evolved at the same time. We also know that chimpanzees (or other apes) didn't evolve into humans. Instead, both lineages descended from a common ancestor and went their separate ways.

ARDIPITHECUS RAMIDUS (4.4 MYA)

Found in northeastern Ethiopia in 1992–1994, the partial skeleton of a female *Ar. ramidus* (nicknamed "Ardi") is more like a human— and less like a chimpanzee—than was expected in the human- ape record. For example, some believe foot and pelvis character- istics indicate that *Ar. ramidus* walked upright when on the ground. It is not clear yet whether it is an ancestor of *H. sapiens*.

AUSTRALOPITHECUS AFARENSIS (3.85–2.95 MYA)

"Lucy" *(Au. afarensis),* the most famous of our fossilized ancestors, was discovered in 1974 in eastern Africa. Scientists have concluded that *Au. afarensis* climbed trees, though it was mostly bipedal. Despite having a brain about one-third of modern humans', this tenacious species lived for over 900,000 years.

PARANTHROPUS BOISEI (2.3–1.2 MYA)

P. boisei, discovered in 1955, was immediately distinctive, because of its large jaw. This indicates a diet that required heavy chewing, though other evidence that it consumed hard substances (like nuts) is lacking. A recent report identified another exceptional characteristic: It may have carried HSV2, the virus causing genital herpes.

HOMO HABILIS (2.4–1.4 MYA)

H. habilis (aka "handy man") was discovered in 1960 at Tanzania's Olduvai Gorge at the same site and by the same team that found *P. boisei*. Its appearance reoriented the search for human origins from Asia, where *H. erectus* had been found, to Africa. A prominent researcher recently argued that it is different enough from other *Australopithecus* and *Homo* specimens to merit its own genus.

HOMO ERECTUS (1.89 MYA–143,000 YA)

H. erectus has proportions similar to modern humans', including shorter arms and longer legs in relation to the torso. Tools such as hand axes have been found near to and in the same sediment layers as *H. erectus,* marking an important moment in evolution. *H. erectus* was also migratory. In fact, it was first discovered in Indonesia in 1891.

HOMO SAPIENS IS NOW THE ONLY SPECIES OF HUMAN ON EARTH. BUT THAT'S BEEN TRUE FOR LESS THAN 30,000 YEARS.

POP!

PREHISTORIC FICTIONS

- *One Million Years B.C.* (1966)
- *The Land That Time Forgot* (1974)
- *At the Earth's Core* (1976)
- *Quest for Fire* (1981)
- *Iceman* (1984)
- *The Clan of the Cave Bear* (1986)
- *Encino Man* (1992)
- *10,000 B.C.* (2008)
- *The Croods* (2013)
- *Early Man* (2018)

SHARED TIME ON EARTH?

These hand bones are among thousands recently found by paleoanthropologist Lee Berger and his team in South Africa. They belong to an all-new hominid species, *Homo naledi*, which likely lived alongside *Homo sapiens* less than 500,000 years ago.

MARINA ELLIOTT
PALEOANTHROPOLOGIST

FOR THE LOVE OF BONES

Marina Elliott actually dissected roadkill as a girl, so it's not surprising that her first career was as a veterinary nurse, working with small and exotic animals. She shifted to biological anthropology, though, after taking a human origins class during her first year of college. These seemingly disparate interests came together in the field of paleoanthropology.

Marina Elliott is one of the six paleoanthropologists selected to explore this site in tandem with dozens of scientists aboveground.

Marina Elliott was finishing her Ph.D. in biological anthropology when, in 2013, she made the fateful decision to answer paleoanthropologist Lee Berger's call for help in excavating a cave called Rising Star, northwest of Johannesburg in South Africa. The work would involve squeezing through very small cracks, not more than 10 inches high—including a 40-foot chute filled with what Elliott calls "shark-teeth protrusions" and spending hours in cramped, dark spaces, sifting through the dirt for fossil bones.

Not only had Elliott's undergraduate education in archaeology included fieldwork in the harsh environments of Siberia and Alaska, but she was also a recreational caver: the perfect candidate. She ended up leading Berger's team of six uniquely qualified "underground astronauts"—all women.

FINDING NEW ANCESTORS

The team's objective was to excavate what Berger calls "the largest assemblage of fossil human relatives ever discovered in Africa." One of the greatest fossil discoveries of the past half century, this find introduced us to a new species of human ancestor, *Homo naledi*. Lab tests suggest that the Rising Star fossils are between 236,000 and 335,000 years old—which means *Homo naledi* may have lived side by side with our own ancestors.

"In some areas of the cave I have to excavate lying on my chest or in the fetal position, with both my shoulders pinned in by rock on either side," Elliott explains. Combining courage, skill, knowledge, and physical endurance, she and the others on Berger's team are reshaping human history.

" IT'S JUST EXCITING TO REALIZE THAT THE GREAT AGE OF EXPLORATION ISN'T OVER WITH, THAT THERE ARE PLACES TO EXPLORE AND THERE ARE THINGS TO FIND."

Marina Elliott and teammate Steven Tucker maneuver through the intricate Rising Star cave system.

COOL STUFF

Print Your Own
3-D FOSSILS

Taking an open-access approach to the *Homo naledi* discoveries, researchers at Rising Star scanned more than 150 specimens and made them available through MorphoSource at no cost to create on a 3-D printer. Whether you're an educator or just the curious type, re-create some of these fossils to learn firsthand about your prehistoric ancestors and the excavations identifying them.

OUR DEEP ANCESTRY

STAGES OF HUMAN MIGRATION

The character of a person's mitochondrial DNA (passed down intact from mother to child) and, in each male, of the Y chromosome (passed intact from father to son) are only two threads in the vast tapestry of genetic information in any individual's genome. Studies like the years-long National Geographic Genographic Project now allow us to map human migration over tens of thousands of years by comparing the mtDNA and Y chromosomes of people from various populations.

What Stories Do Our Genes Tell?
Between 70,000 and 50,000 years ago, a small group of *Homo sapiens*—perhaps as few as 1,000, to whom all modern non-Africans are related—emigrated from Africa. One group continued along the coast to southern Asia, reaching a super-continent made up of Tasmania, Australia, and New Guinea. Recent DNA research confirms that Aboriginal civilization is one of the longest continuous human occupations outside Africa.

EARLY HUMAN MIGRATIONS

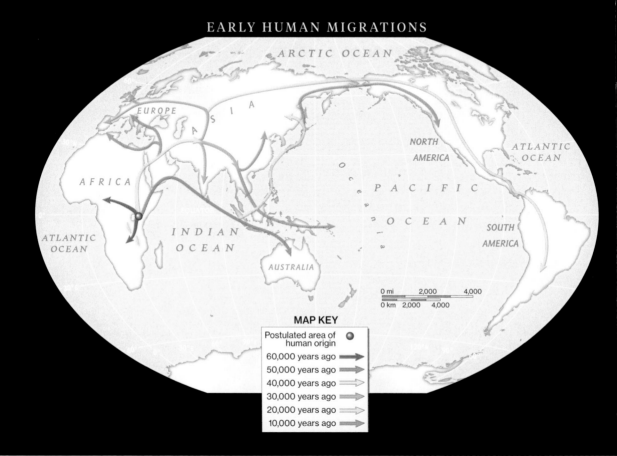

MAP KEY

Postulated area of human origin
60,000 years ago
50,000 years ago
40,000 years ago
30,000 years ago
20,000 years ago
10,000 years ago

FINDING YOUR ROOTS

TRACKING THE HUMAN JOURNEY

These days it's possible to learn more about your own deep ancestry through projects like National Geographic Genographic Project or commercial offerings from companies like Ancestry.com or 23andMe. A swab of cells from inside your cheek provides enough to learn what your genetic makeup tells about the path your long-ago ancestors took in the massive human migrations over tens of thousands of years. You may find your ancestors coming from one of several directions.

AFRICA

The diversity of genetic markers is greatest in the African continent, the earliest home of modern humans. "The genetic makeup of the rest of the world is a subset of what's in Africa," says Yale geneticist Kenneth Kidd.

ASIA

As some modern humans pushed into Central Asia, others traveled through Southeast Asia and China, eventually reaching Japan and Siberia. Humans in northern Asia eventually migrated to the Americas.

EUROPE

Genetic data show that the DNA of today's western Eurasians resembles that of people in India. It's possible that an inland migration from Asia seeded Europe between 40,000 and 30,000 years ago.

THE AMERICAS

When sea levels were low and the first humans crossed the land bridge between Siberia and Alaska, ice sheets covered the interior of North America, forcing the new arrivals to travel down the west coast.

> " WE CAN APPRECIATE THE DIVERSITY OF THE HUMAN WORLD, WHILE UNDERSTANDING THAT WE ALL SHARE DEEPER SIMILARITIES THAT TIE US TOGETHER IN A HUMAN FAMILY."
>
> —SPENCER WELLS, FOUNDING DIRECTOR, NATIONAL GEOGRAPHIC GENOGRAPHIC PROJECT

Paul Salopek is re-creating humanity's migration.

KEY DATES

Salopek's Out of Eden
MOMENTS

JANUARY 21, 2013
Began his walk in Ethiopia

AUGUST 24, 2014
Reached Cyprus

OCTOBER 31, 2016
Crossed through Uzbekistan

NOVEMBER 27, 2017
Joined the Silk Road in Pakistan

CA 2023
Projected to complete the 21,000-mile journey

NEANDERTHALS
JOIN THE FAMILY

NOT-SO-DISTANT RELATIVES

When our ancestors emerged from Africa into Eurasia around 45,000 years ago, they found the landscape already inhabited. Neanderthals were 99.5 percent genetically identical to modern humans *(Homo sapiens)* but had evolved distinctive anatomy—such as wide bodies to conserve heat—during hundreds of thousands of years in the cold Eurasian climate.

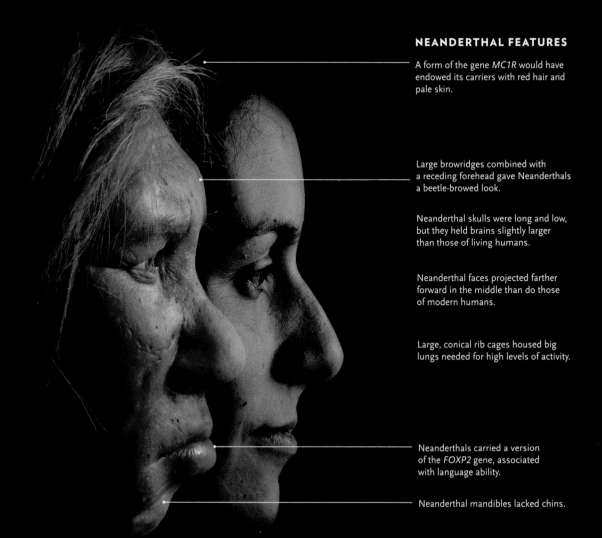

NEANDERTHAL FEATURES

A form of the gene *MC1R* would have endowed its carriers with red hair and pale skin.

Large browridges combined with a receding forehead gave Neanderthals a beetle-browed look.

Neanderthal skulls were long and low, but they held brains slightly larger than those of living humans.

Neanderthal faces projected farther forward in the middle than do those of modern humans.

Large, conical rib cages housed big lungs needed for high levels of activity.

Neanderthals carried a version of the *FOXP2* gene, associated with language ability.

Neanderthal mandibles lacked chins.

DIVERGENT LINES REUNITE

Neanderthals, our closest prehistoric relatives, dominated Eurasia for the better part of 200,000 years. During that time, they poked their famously large and protruding noses into every corner of Europe and beyond. But climate swings and competition with newcomers may have combined to push Neanderthals into a few outposts before they went extinct, mysteriously dying out about 30,000 years ago.

Friend or Foe?

Scientists posit that the lineages of Neanderthals and their European successors diverged long before modern humans migrated out of Africa, as far back as 370,000 years ago. But until recently, questions lingered: Did modern humans replace Neanderthals, or did they interbreed with them?

Then, in 2010, scientists uncovered the first solid genetic evidence that "modern" humans interbred with their Neanderthal neighbors. Today, we know that genomes of people currently living outside Africa are composed of 1.8 to 2.6 percent Neanderthal DNA. Some parts of non-African genomes are totally devoid of Neanderthal DNA, but other regions abound with it, including those containing genes that affect our skin and hair. This hints that those Neanderthal gene versions conferred some benefit and were retained during evolution. Other genes, however, match segments now closely associated with various health concerns, including blood cholesterol levels and rheumatoid arthritis.

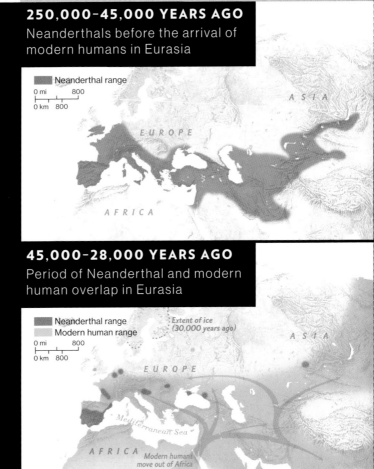

250,000–45,000 YEARS AGO
Neanderthals before the arrival of modern humans in Eurasia

Neanderthal range
0 mi 800
0 km 800

ASIA
EUROPE
AFRICA

45,000–28,000 YEARS AGO
Period of Neanderthal and modern human overlap in Eurasia

Neanderthal range
Modern human range
Extent of ice (30,000 years ago)
0 mi 800
0 km 800

ASIA
EUROPE
Mediterranean Sea
AFRICA
Modern humans move out of Africa

DIGGING DEEPER

At-Home
DNA TESTING

Today it is possible to collect a DNA sample, send it in, and have it analyzed for ancestry markers. Some organizations will link you up with other contemporary individuals who are a match and have a good probability of being related to you. National Geographic's Genographic Project, which has more than 800,000 participants, probes further, providing regional and deep ancestry going back hundreds of generations—even identifying two hominin species, Neanderthals and Denisovans. The project has found that most non-Africans are about 2 percent Neanderthal and slightly less than 2 percent Denisovan.

INTANGIBLE CULTURE

MORE THAN MONUMENTS AND ARTIFACTS

Communities worldwide are working to identify and preserve practices, events, skills, and knowledge—"intangibles"—passed down by ancestors.

Clowning for the camera during Carnival in Recife, Brazil

PERFORMING ARTS

FREVO MUSIC AND DANCE, BRAZIL

Dancers leap and music throbs as the city of Recife celebrates its colorful carnival each year. Frevo is a distinctive hybrid of dance and music, combining marching band beats, the tango and the polka, and the loud sounds of brass horns, steel drums, and boisterous partygoers.

TSIATTISTA POETIC DUELING, CYPRUS

In the tradition of Tsiattista, a pair of quick-witted poet-singers joust in the Greek Cypriot dialect, wielding improvised rhyming couplets before crowds at weddings and other celebrations. "Tsiattistaes" are usually men of average income and education, though talented women have been performing recently too.

CULTURAL PRACTICES

OBSERVATION OF 24 SOLAR TERMS, CHINA

Ancient Chinese astronomers marked 24 terms in the sun's annual path. For centuries, these culturally important observations informed politics through astrology and agriculture through astronomy. References to them can still be found in farming practices, community festivals, and nursery rhymes.

THE WHISTLED LANGUAGE OF SILBO GOMERO, CANARY ISLANDS (SPAIN)

This language re-creates Castilian Spanish by replacing spoken sounds with whistling sounds of varying pitch and duration—useful over long distances and in La Gomera's rugged hills and valleys. To avoid its extinction, it is now taught in the island's schools.

Expert whistler in France's Ossau Valley

Ethiopian Christians gather for the Meskel ceremony.

CELEBRATIONS

FESTIVAL OF MESKEL, ETHIOPIA
Beginning with a conical pyre in the capital, this 1,600-year-old national celebration marks the finding of Christ's True Holy Cross, now believed to be at an Ethiopian monastery. Christians prepare for the festival by seeking reconciliation and resolving quarrels.

NAN PA'CH CEREMONY, GUATEMALA
In gratitude for successful crops, especially corn, residents of Sacatepéquez perform traditional rituals and say prayers in a Maya language. Led by farmers and elders in the community, participants honor the connection between humans and nature.

GOING GREEN

Indigenous Wisdom of PLANTS

Ethnobotanists are trying to preserve the indigenous knowledge about medicinal plants that is disappearing along with plant species and habitats. They interview practitioners to learn their treatments for everything from infections and heart disease to mental illness and cancer.

Delicate painting on a wooden bowl in Ukraine

ARTS & CRAFTS

PETRYKIVKA PAINTING, UKRAINE
In the small city that gives its name to this craft, homes, household items, and musical instruments are decorated with a distinctive ornamental floral painting style. At least one person in each family is able to participate in this meaningful folk art tradition, which is taught in local schools.

CRAFT OF MAKING BRASS AND COPPER UTENSILS, PUNJAB, INDIA
The Thatheras are a small group of Hindu artisans known for creating brass and copper vessels and utensils by hand. The practice, which involves flattening and hammering metal over small stoves, is taught within families. This craft and livelihood provides structure and values to families and the community.

BEST OF @NATGEO

OUR FAVORITE PHOTOS OF TRADITIONS AROUND THE WORLD

@argonautphoto | **AARON HUEY**
A Dogon funeral dance takes place atop the Bandiagara
cliffs in Mali.

@yamashitaphoto | **MICHAEL YAMASHITA**
Monks stand in line to receive gifts of rice and other offerings
from Buddhists in Bagan, Myanmar.

@chancellordavid | **DAVID CHANCELLOR**
In South Africa, boys gather for Umkhwetha, a Xhosa
initiation into manhood.

@michaelchristopherbrown | **MICHAEL CHRISTOPHER BROWN**
A Lakota dancer prepares for competition during an annual
powwow on the Pine Ridge Indian Reservation.

BEST OF @NATGEO

OUR FAVORITE PHOTOS OF TRADITIONS AROUND THE WORLD

@argonautphoto | **AARON HUEY**
A Dogon funeral dance takes place atop the Bandiagara cliffs in Mali.

@yamashitaphoto | **MICHAEL YAMASHITA**
Monks stand in line to receive gifts of rice and other offerings from Buddhists in Bagan, Myanmar.

@chancellordavid | **DAVID CHANCELLOR**
In South Africa, boys gather for Umkhwetha, a Xhosa initiation into manhood.

@michaelchristopherbrown | **MICHAEL CHRISTOPHER BROWN**
A Lakota dancer prepares for competition during an annual powwow on the Pine Ridge Indian Reservation.

Elaborate horse masks, improbable in battle, are used for parades.

Crow horse mask, circa 1860, Montana

Blackfeet horse mask, 2008, Montana

RETURN OF A NATIVE

The horse originated in North America two million years ago and spread to Eurasia over the Bering land bridge. Then, about 10,000 BC, horses vanished from the New World, possibly killed for food by humans who had come to the continent from Eurasia. When the horse returned with European conquistadors and colonists, it transformed the culture of many Native American tribes. In turn, Native Americans and settlers changed the horse, developing new breeds from Old World stock. For Native Americans today, horses endure as an emblem of tradition and a source of pride, pageantry, and healing.

Nez Perce horse mask, 1875–1900, Idaho or Washington

Lakota horse mask, circa 1860, North or South Dakota

1493–1500s

COLONIAL SPANISH
Expeditions carried a variety of Iberian breeds to the Caribbean. As the herds grew, Spaniards seeking gold and glory took horses to mainland North America. The first to do so: Hernán Cortés in 1519.

ATLANTIC OCEAN

Spain

Spain

Caribbean Sea

1514

1509

PANAMA

COLOMBIA

Old World stock

Sorraia

Barb

Spanish jennet

For people of the Wanapum and Nez Perce tribes (above and below), horses express pride in tradition.

THE HORSE IN NORTH AMERICA

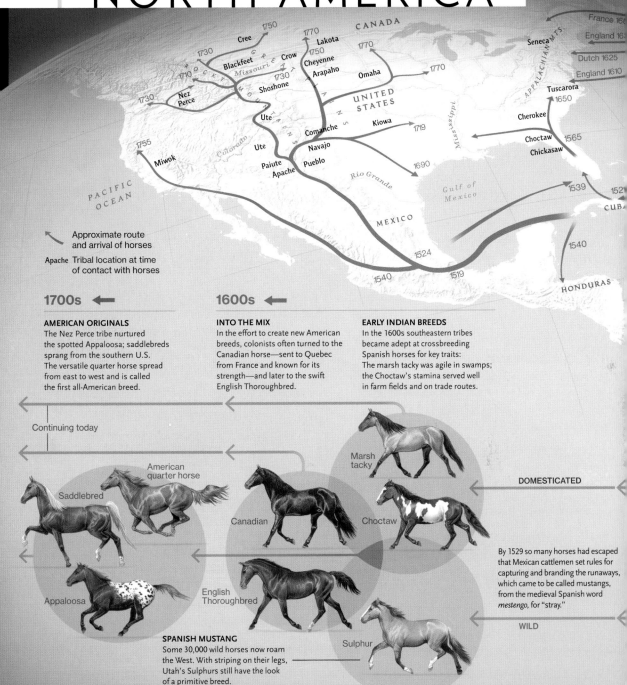

France 16[...]
England 16[...]
Seneca MTS.
Dutch 1625
England 1610
Tuscarora 1650
Cherokee
Choctaw 1565
Chickasaw
1539 1521
CUBA
1540
HONDURAS

CANADA
Cree 1750 1770 Lakota 1770
1730 Blackfeet Crow 1750 Cheyenne 1770
1710 Missouri 1730 Arapaho Omaha 1770
Nez Perce Shoshone UNITED STATES
1730
Ute Comanche Kiowa 1719
Ute Navajo 1690
1755 Paiute Pueblo
Miwok Apache Rio Grande
Colorado
PACIFIC OCEAN Gulf of Mexico
MEXICO
1524
1540 1519

↖ Approximate route
and arrival of horses

Apache Tribal location at time
of contact with horses

1700s ←

AMERICAN ORIGINALS
The Nez Perce tribe nurtured the spotted Appaloosa; saddlebreds sprang from the southern U.S. The versatile quarter horse spread from east to west and is called the first all-American breed.

1600s ←

INTO THE MIX
In the effort to create new American breeds, colonists often turned to the Canadian horse—sent to Quebec from France and known for its strength—and later to the swift English Thoroughbred.

EARLY INDIAN BREEDS
In the 1600s southeastern tribes became adept at crossbreeding Spanish horses for key traits: The marsh tacky was agile in swamps; the Choctaw's stamina served well in farm fields and on trade routes.

Continuing today

American quarter horse

Saddlebred

Marsh tacky

DOMESTICATED

Canadian

Choctaw

Appaloosa

English Thoroughbred

By 1529 so many horses had escaped that Mexican cattlemen set rules for capturing and branding the runaways, which came to be called mustangs, from the medieval Spanish word *mestengo,* for "stray."

WILD

SPANISH MUSTANG
Some 30,000 wild horses now roam the West. With striping on their legs, Utah's Sulphurs still have the look of a primitive breed.

Sulphur

Ethiopian Christians gather for the Meskel ceremony.

TO SAFEGUARD THE WORLD'S INTANGIBLE HERITAGE, UNESCO NOW RECOGNIZES 470 EXPRESSIONS FROM 117 COUNTRIES.

Delicate painting on a wooden bowl in Ukraine

CELEBRATIONS

FESTIVAL OF MESKEL, ETHIOPIA

Beginning with a conical pyre in the capital, this 1,600-year-old national celebration marks the finding of Christ's True Holy Cross, now believed to be at an Ethiopian monastery. Christians prepare for the festival by seeking reconciliation and resolving quarrels.

NAN PA'CH CEREMONY, GUATEMALA

In gratitude for successful crops, especially corn, residents of Sacatepéquez perform traditional rituals and say prayers in a Maya language. Led by farmers and elders in the community, participants honor the connection between humans and nature.

ARTS & CRAFTS

PETRYKIVKA PAINTING, UKRAINE

In the small city that gives its name to this craft, homes, household items, and musical instruments are decorated with a distinctive ornamental floral painting style. At least one person in each family is able to participate in this meaningful folk art tradition, which is taught in local schools.

CRAFT OF MAKING BRASS AND COPPER UTENSILS, PUNJAB, INDIA

The Thatheras are a small group of Hindu artisans known for creating brass and copper vessels and utensils by hand. The practice, which involves flattening and hammering metal over small stoves, is taught within families. This craft and livelihood provides structure and values to families and the community.

GOING GREEN

Indigenous Wisdom of PLANTS

Ethnobotanists are trying to preserve the indigenous knowledge about medicinal plants that is disappearing along with plant species and habitats. They interview practitioners to learn their treatments for everything from infections and heart disease to mental illness and cancer.

@stephsinclairpix | STEPHANIE SINCLAIR
Dangol, a nine-year-old girl from Nepal, is a living goddess among the Newar people.

@melissafarlow | MELISSA FARLOW
A diminutive cowboy, son of a wild horse trainer, on a ranch near Prineville, Oregon

@edkashi | ED KASHI
A Kurdish family poses for a photo near their home in Diyarbakir, Turkey.

@chamiltonjames | CHARLIE HAMILTON JAMES
A young Awá boy with his monkey in the eastern Amazon rain forest in Brazil

DISAPPEARING
LANGUAGES

WE MAY LOSE OVER HALF OF OUR 7,000 LANGUAGES BY 2100

Language defines a culture, through the people who speak it and what it allows speakers to say. Words that describe a particular cultural practice or idea may not translate precisely into another language. To lose those words is to lose those treasures.

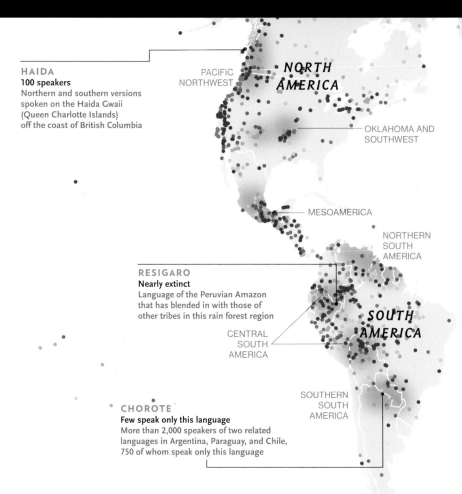

HAIDA
100 speakers
Northern and southern versions spoken on the Haida Gwaii (Queen Charlotte Islands) off the coast of British Columbia

PACIFIC NORTHWEST

NORTH AMERICA

OKLAHOMA AND SOUTHWEST

MESOAMERICA

NORTHERN SOUTH AMERICA

RESIGARO
Nearly extinct
Language of the Peruvian Amazon that has blended in with those of other tribes in this rain forest region

CENTRAL SOUTH AMERICA

SOUTH AMERICA

WESTER AFRIC

CHOROTE
Few speak only this language
More than 2,000 speakers of two related languages in Argentina, Paraguay, and Chile, 750 of whom speak only this language

SOUTHERN SOUTH AMERICA

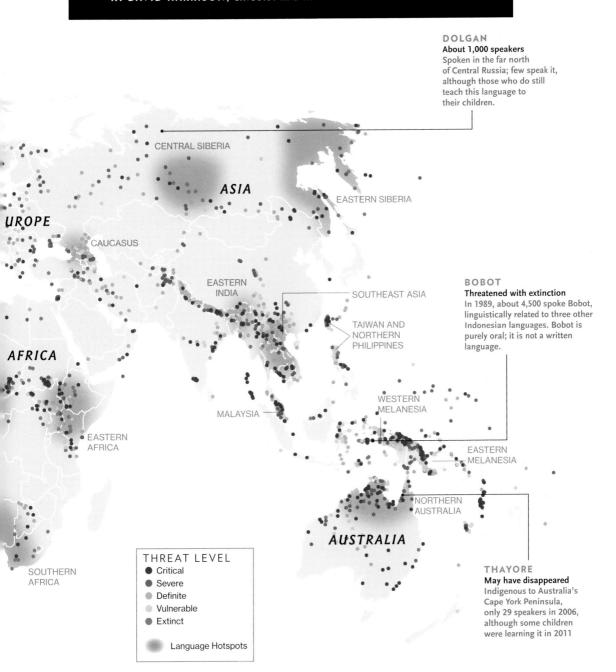

> ## " EVERY TIME A LANGUAGE DIES, WE LOSE PART OF THE PICTURE OF WHAT OUR BRAINS CAN DO."
>
> —K. DAVID HARRISON, LINGUIST AND ANTHROPOLOGIST

DOLGAN
About 1,000 speakers
Spoken in the far north of Central Russia; few speak it, although those who do still teach this language to their children.

CENTRAL SIBERIA

ASIA

EASTERN SIBERIA

UROPE

CAUCASUS

EASTERN INDIA

SOUTHEAST ASIA

TAIWAN AND NORTHERN PHILIPPINES

BOBOT
Threatened with extinction
In 1989, about 4,500 spoke Bobot, linguistically related to three other Indonesian languages. Bobot is purely oral; it is not a written language.

AFRICA

WESTERN MELANESIA

MALAYSIA

EASTERN AFRICA

EASTERN MELANESIA

NORTHERN AUSTRALIA

AUSTRALIA

SOUTHERN AFRICA

THREAT LEVEL
- Critical
- Severe
- Definite
- Vulnerable
- Extinct

Language Hotspots

THAYORE
May have disappeared
Indigenous to Australia's Cape York Peninsula, only 29 speakers in 2006, although some children were learning it in 2011

JOHN MCWHORTER
LINGUIST

WATCH ENGLISH EVOLVE

While some are alarmed to hear abbreviations associated with texting—such as LOL (pronounced LAWL, for "laugh out loud") and IRL (pronounced EYE-ARE-ELL, for "in real life")—sneaking into everyday speech as words in their own right, linguist John McWhorter is excited to witness a language evolve over years instead of decades or centuries.

In addition to writing and speaking, McWhorter teaches at Columbia University and hosts the *Lexicon Valley* podcast.

Professor and linguist John McWhorter is known for his thought-provoking ideas on language changes as well as issues of race. His main area of study is the history and evolution of languages, such as when adults are acquiring a second language. For example, he has investigated the development of various creole languages, concluding (somewhat controversially) that as creole emerges, speakers instinctively simplify the older languages' structures and discard their random, quirky features.

EMBRACING THIS NEW LANGUAGE

So unlike academics and parents who fret over the state of contemporary writing and speech—consider the ubiquitous "like," which McWhorter says "is not just a tic of heedless, underconfident youth"—he takes the long view, fascinated by how languages are always changing. In a 2013 TED Talk, he argues that texting is neither a spoken language nor a written language; it is a new "fingered speech" with "a kind of emergent complexity."

For instance, in his TED Talk, McWhorter discusses LOL (laughing out loud), which arose in humorous text conversations. However, he explains, now we find "LOL is being used in a very particular way. It's a marker of empathy. It's a marker of accommodation." He adds that teens from 25 years ago would probably find it difficult to decipher a text message written by a teen today, "because a whole new language has developed among our young people doing something as mundane as what it looks like to us when they're batting around on their little devices."

Language is political, as McWhorter's talks and articles often show.

FIRST WORDS

Mommy and Daddy
AROUND THE WORLD

- **FRENCH** maman and papa
- **ITALIAN** mamma and babbo
- **NORWEGIAN** mamma and papa
- **WELSH** mam and tad
- **SWAHILI** mama and baba
- **TAGALOG** nanay and tatay
- **FIJIAN** nana and tata
- **CHECHEN** naana and daa
- **INUIT** anaana and ataata
- **PIPIL** naan and tatah

1st

There's a First Time for Everything In fact, we are so inundated by "firsts" that it's easy to lose sight of when the milestones took place. Some firsts happened earlier than you might think: The first successful cesarean in the United States was performed in 1794—by the patient's husband. Other "firsts" occurred in an order that seems unexpected: The moon was mapped centuries before the ocean floor.

Renaissance 1350–1650

Printing press
1439

This technology revolutionizes the manufacture of books.

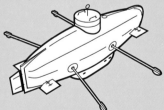

Chocolate to Europe
1519

The Aztec introduce chocolate to Hernán Cortés, who later takes cacao pods back to Europe.

Submersible
1620

Dutch engineer Cornelis Drebbel reportedly waterproofs the craft with greased leather.

Air pump
1650

Otto von Guericke invents the air pump, which he uses to study light and sound in a vacuum.

Enlightenment 1650–1800

Scientific map of the moon
1679

Giovanni Cassini publishes drawings of lunar landscapes seen through a telescope.

Piano
circa 1700

Bartolomeo Cristofori allegedly creates the modern piano.

Sextant
mid-1700s

A tool is designed to find longitude by measuring the angular distance between the moon and a nearby star.

Industrial Revolution 1760–1900

A   B   C

Sign language
1770s

Abbé Charles Michel de l'Épée invents the first widely used sign language for the deaf.

Human flight
1783

Non-tethered human flight takes place in a hot-air balloon that rises 500 feet above Paris.

Photograph
circa 1826

Taken in France, the first photo is titled "View From the Window at Le Gras."

Skyscraper
1885

Chicago's steel-frame Home Insurance Building is built, reaching 10 stories high.

War & Postwar
1914–1950

Space Age
1957–1980

Information Age
1971–Present

Adhesive bandage
1920

Earle Dickson, a cotton buyer, invents this for his accident-prone wife.

Satellite in space
1957

The Soviet Union launches the beach ball–size Sputnik 1, the first artificial satellite to orbit Earth.

Email
1971

Programmer Ray Tomlinson sends this message: QWERTYUIOP.

Human in space
1961

Cosmonaut Yuri Gagarin orbits Earth, a 108-minute mission.

Smartphone
1994

IBM's Simon—the first cellular phone to have "personal digital assistant" features such as email—goes on sale.

Penicillin
1928

Alexander Fleming accidentally discovers the antibiotic in a petri dish.

Oral contraceptive
1951

Chemist Carl Djerassi creates the pill by synthesizing hormones from yams.

Man on the moon
1969

American Neil Armstrong's words as he becomes the first person to walk on the moon: "That's one small step for a man, one giant leap for mankind."

Cloned mammal
1996

Dolly the sheep is cloned from a mammary cell and named for Dolly Parton.

Organ transplant
1954

The first successful procedure moves a kidney from one twin to another.

Internet
1969

Data are sent between California universities, setting the stage for the Internet's development.

Voyager 1
2012

The spacecraft is the first human-made object to venture into interstellar space.

URBANIZATION

TODAY, 3.5 BILLION URBANITES—DOUBLE BY 2050?

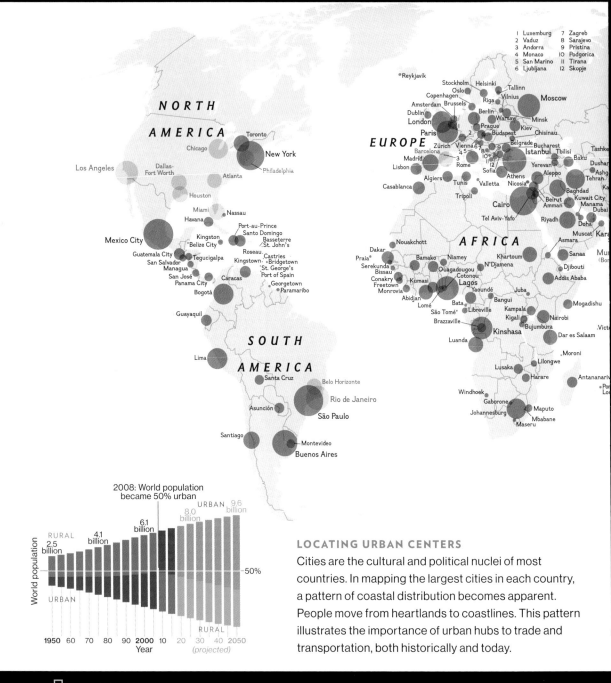

1	Luxemburg	7	Zagreb
2	Vaduz	8	Sarajevo
3	Andorra	9	Pristina
4	Monaco	10	Podgorica
5	San Marino	11	Tirana
6	Ljubljana	12	Skopje

2008: World population became 50% urban

LOCATING URBAN CENTERS

Cities are the cultural and political nuclei of most countries. In mapping the largest cities in each country, a pattern of coastal distribution becomes apparent. People move from heartlands to coastlines. This pattern illustrates the importance of urban hubs to trade and transportation, both historically and today.

MANY MEGACITIES' POPULATIONS AND ECONOMIES ARE LARGER THAN THOSE OF SOME INDIVIDUAL NATIONS.

A

Ulaanbaatar
Almaty
kek
Harbin
Shenyang
Pyongyang
Beijing
Tianjin
Seoul
Tokyo
Nagoya
Nanjing
Xian
Suzhou
ahore
Delhi
Chengdu
Chongqing
Kathmandu
Thimphu
Osaka-Kobe
Kitakyushu-Fukuoka
Wuhan
Shanghai
Hangzhou
Ahmadabad
Dhaka
Dongguan
Taipei
Kolkata
(Calcutta)
Yangon
Guangzhou
Foshan
Shenzhen
Hong Kong
a
aluru
alore)
Hyderabad
Chennai
(Madras)
Vientiane
Bangkok
Manila
Phnom
Penh
Ho Chi Minh City
Koror
Palikir
Majuro
Colombo
Male
Kuala Lumpur
Bandar Seri Begawan
Tarawa
Yaren
Singapore
Jakarta
Dili
Port Moresby
Honiara
Apia
Port Vila
Suva
Nuku'alofa

AUSTRALIA

Sydney
Auckland

URBAN AGGLOMERATIONS

LARGEST CITY IN COUNTRY   OTHER CITIES ABOVE 5 MILLION

Paris   Beijing   Urban agglomeration with more than 10 million people (megacity)

Madrid   Miami   Urban agglomeration with more than 5 million people

Bangui   Largest urban agglomeration per country

Dots are scaled proportionally based on city population sizes

Changes in Rankings BY 2030

1   **TOKYO, JAPAN** Though the population will drop from 38 to 37 million, it will still be ranked as the world's biggest city.

2   **DELHI, INDIA** Projected to grow by almost 10 million people, reaching 36 million, it will keep its second-place spot.

3   **SHANGHAI, CHINA** China's biggest city will stay in third place by adding 6 million people to its current 24 million.

4   **MUMBAI, INDIA** The last of the cities to maintain its current ranking, it will go from a population of 21 to 27 million.

5   **BEIJING, CHINA** Expanding to 27 million from 21 million, it moves up to fifth, displacing São Paulo, Brazil, to 11th.

6   **DHAKA, BANGLADESH** Finally reaching the top 10, it will comprise 27 million people, adding 9 million to its present total.

7   **KARACHI, PAKISTAN** Previously at 12th, when it hosted one in 10 Pakistanis, it will go from 17 to almost 25 million.

8   **CAIRO, EGYPT** The only city in the Middle East to reach the top 40, it will go from 19 to 24 million—and climb from ninth to eighth.

9   **LAGOS, NIGERIA** Jumping from 17th to ninth—and from 13 to 24 million people—it is the second African city in the top 10.

10   **MEXICO CITY, MEXICO** Despite growing from 21 to 23 million people, it will slip three spots from seventh to 10th.

Greening Our Cities

More than half the world's population lives in urban areas. By 2050 cities will likely be bursting with two-thirds of the people on the planet. Because urban areas already account for an estimated 76 percent of CO_2 emissions from energy use—and many are especially vulnerable to flooding and higher temperatures—it makes sense that city officials are taking on climate change. After all, doing so also gives them a shot at reducing pollution, improving aging infrastructure, and making their cities more attractive to residents and businesses.

SMART STREETS

Chicago has built what city officials call the "greenest street in America"—a two-mile stretch in the industrial neighborhood of Pilsen. Bike and parking lanes are paved with smog-eating concrete; sidewalks are made from recycled materials. Wind and sun power streetlights. Bioswales, thick with drought-tolerant plants, divert storm water from overburdened sewers. The spruced-up streetscape uses 42 percent less energy than it used to—and costs 21 percent less than a traditional road project.

"Mayors don't have to wait for national governments or a new global climate agreement to act. They can take action today—and increasingly, they are."

Michael Bloomberg
former mayor of New York City, May 27, 2014

Shade trees and other vegetation can reduce city temperatures and energy use.

"Adaptive" LED streetlights use less energy by responding to traffic and weather conditions.

Car travel decreases in cities where development centers around transit stations.

Protected bike lanes encourage people to commute by bicycle rather than by car.

Roads paved with photocatalytic concrete can neutralize harmful pollutants before they contaminate the environment.

London has installed more than 700 electric-car chargers throughout the city.

Georgetown, Texas, population 50,000, has been powered entirely by renewable energy since 2017.

In Amsterdam more than a quarter of all trips in the city are made by bicycle.

GREEN BUILDINGS

Buildings are responsible for approximately one-third of all greenhouse gas emissions, a figure likely to shrink as more cities require municipal buildings to be energy efficient. Increasingly, government office buildings will have solar panels and even gardens on roofs, sensors to douse lights in empty rooms, windows lined with heat-trapping film, and energy-efficient HVAC systems.

SUSTAINABLE WATER MANAGEMENT

Despite its reputation as a water guzzler, Los Angeles is pioneering ways to capture every drop that falls from the sky. On a flood-prone block of Elmer Avenue in the east San Fernando Valley, storm water used to be funneled into drains and out to the ocean. A $2.7 million project has transformed the block into a sponge, capable of collecting enough water yearly to supply 30 families.

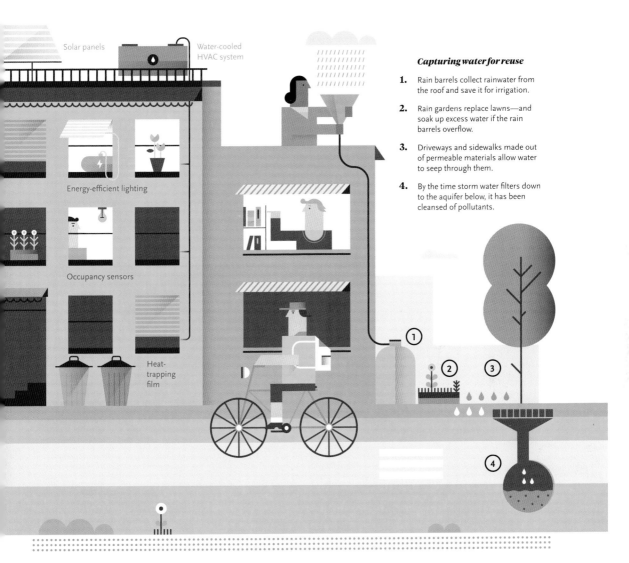

Solar panels

Water-cooled HVAC system

Energy-efficient lighting

Occupancy sensors

Heat-trapping film

Capturing water for reuse

1. Rain barrels collect rainwater from the roof and save it for irrigation.

2. Rain gardens replace lawns—and soak up excess water if the rain barrels overflow.

3. Driveways and sidewalks made out of permeable materials allow water to seep through them.

4. By the time storm water filters down to the aquifer below, it has been cleansed of pollutants.

 In 2014 U.S. mayors rated energy-efficient lighting as the most promising technology for reducing urban energy use and carbon emissions.

 The public heating system in Drammen, Norway, extracts heat from a local fjord.

 Most Hong Kong residents live near mass transit; 43 percent within 1,640 feet; 75 percent within two-thirds of a mile.

RELIGION
AROUND THE WORLD

CULTURE AND MEANING

Religion's great power comes from its ability to speak to the heart and longings of individuals and societies. In time, an untold number of local religious practices yielded to just a few widespread traditions.

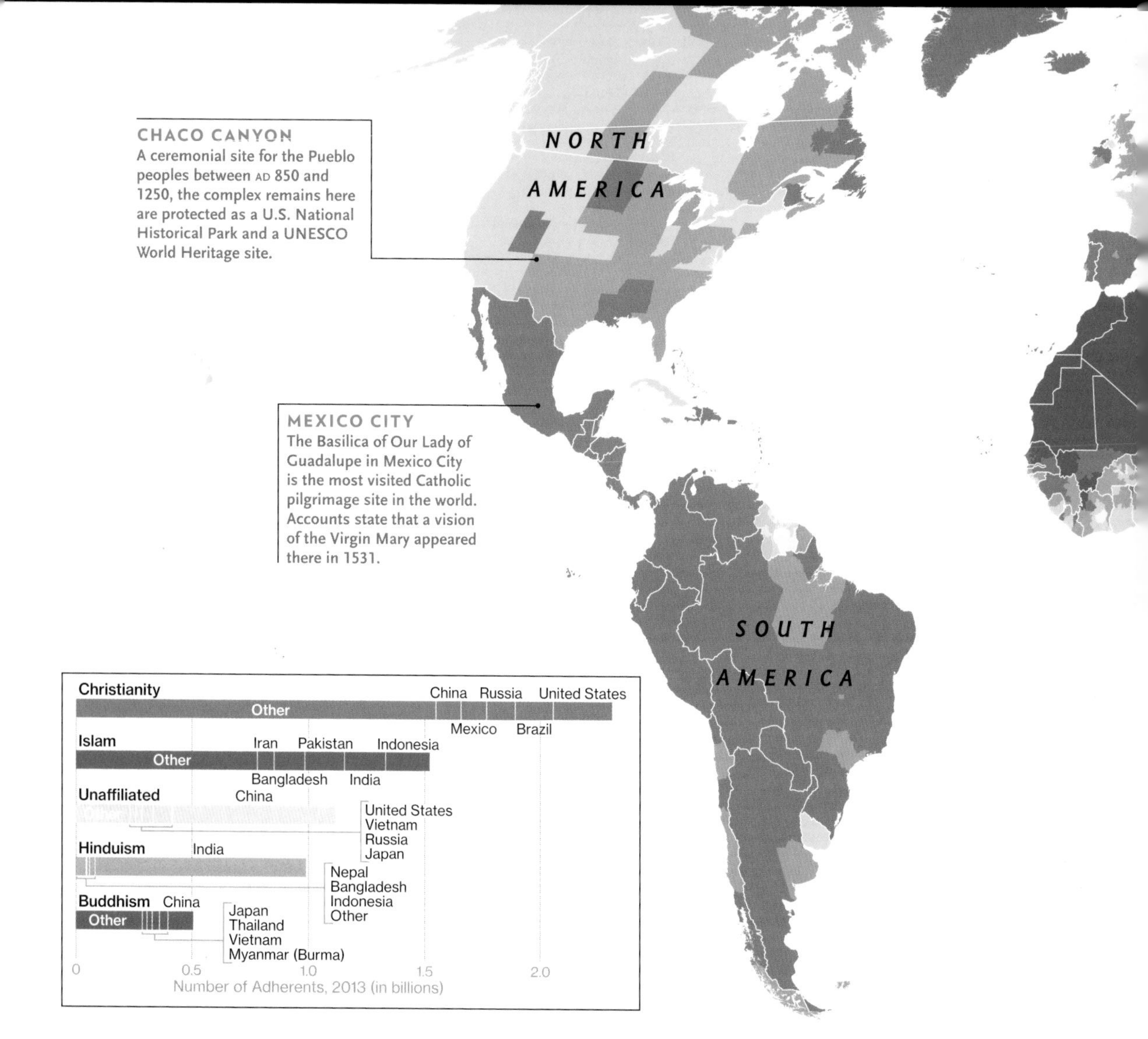

CHACO CANYON
A ceremonial site for the Pueblo peoples between AD 850 and 1250, the complex remains here are protected as a U.S. National Historical Park and a UNESCO World Heritage site.

NORTH AMERICA

MEXICO CITY
The Basilica of Our Lady of Guadalupe in Mexico City is the most visited Catholic pilgrimage site in the world. Accounts state that a vision of the Virgin Mary appeared there in 1531.

SOUTH AMERICA

Christianity
Other
China Russia United States
Mexico Brazil

Islam
Other
Iran Pakistan Indonesia
Bangladesh India
China

Unaffiliated
United States
Vietnam
Russia
Japan

Hinduism
India
Nepal
Bangladesh
Indonesia
Other

Buddhism China
Other
Japan
Thailand
Vietnam
Myanmar (Burma)

0   0.5   1.0   1.5   2.0
Number of Adherents, 2013 (in billions)

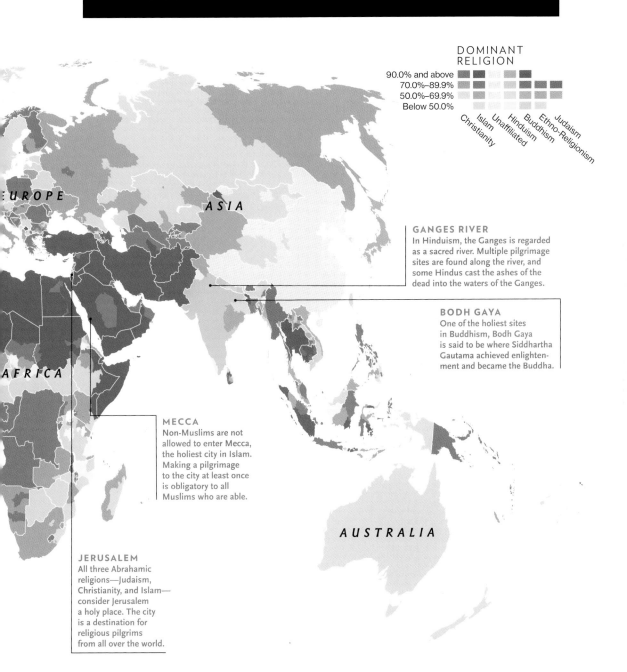

" THERE ARE WAYS IN WHICH WE CAN CONSCIOUSLY WORK TO DEVELOP FEELINGS OF LOVE AND KINDNESS. FOR SOME OF US, THE MOST EFFECTIVE WAY TO DO SO IS THROUGH RELIGIOUS PRACTICE." —THE 14TH DALAI LAMA

DOMINANT RELIGION

90.0% and above
70.0%–89.9%
50.0%–69.9%
Below 50.0%

Christianity
Islam
Unaffiliated
Hinduism
Buddhism
Ethno-Religionism
Judaism

GANGES RIVER
In Hinduism, the Ganges is regarded as a sacred river. Multiple pilgrimage sites are found along the river, and some Hindus cast the ashes of the dead into the waters of the Ganges.

BODH GAYA
One of the holiest sites in Buddhism, Bodh Gaya is said to be where Siddhartha Gautama achieved enlightenment and became the Buddha.

MECCA
Non-Muslims are not allowed to enter Mecca, the holiest city in Islam. Making a pilgrimage to the city at least once is obligatory to all Muslims who are able.

JERUSALEM
All three Abrahamic religions—Judaism, Christianity, and Islam—consider Jerusalem a holy place. The city is a destination for religious pilgrims from all over the world.

BEST OF @NATGEO

OUR FAVORITE PHOTOS OF PEOPLE AROUND THE WORLD

@stephsinclairpix | **STEPHANIE SINCLAIR**
Eight-year-old Yemeni brides prepare a family meal outside Hajjah, Yemen.

@paleyphoto | **MATTHIEU PALEY**
A bride prepares for the arrival of her husband in a remote village in Pakistan.

@gerdludwig | **GERD LUDWIG**
A young couple act out a cosplay (costume play) performance in their apartment near Moscow.

@marcogrob | **MARCO GROB**
The land mines peppering South Sudan pose great risk to the nomadic Mundari and their livestock.

@stevemccurryofficial | STEVE MCCURRY
Buddhist monks at Shaolin Monastery in China find serenity in physical strength and dexterity.

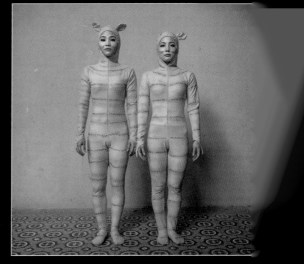

@christian_foto | CHRISTIAN RODRÍGUEZ
Performers from the Vietnam Circus Federation pose backstage before a performance in Hanoi.

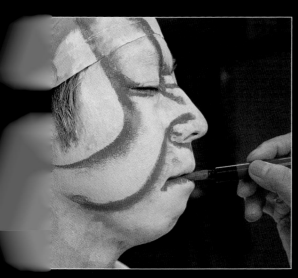

@yamashitaphoto | MICHAEL YAMASHITA
A young amateur actor prepares to perform Kabuki, traditional Japanese theater.

@salvarezphoto | STEPHEN ALVAREZ
Life in the Arctic Circle is full of challenges—it was -36°F (-37°C) when this portrait of a Finnish man was taken.

FEEDING
THE WORLD

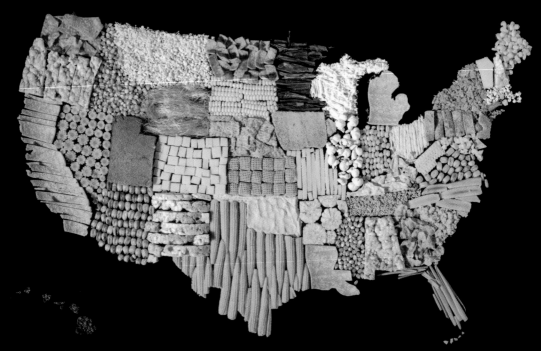

UNITED STATES OF CORN

Photographer Henry Hargreaves and artist Caitlin Levin created a "food map" series—a collection of country and continent maps made using ingredients synonymous with those regions. Think India rendered in spices, New Zealand in kiwifruit, South America in citrus. In some cases, the foods commonly associated with a place aren't actually native to that spot. Tomatoes, for example, come from South America, yet today they're an integral part of Italian cuisine. For their map of the United States, the artists chose as their medium an assemblage of corn varieties and corn-derived products. No other country produces more of the crop, which came north from Mexico and is now grown throughout the United States, in every state—from New Hampshire to Hawaii.

ENOUGH FOR EVERYONE?

The population of the planet, which already exceeds seven billion, will grow to nine billion by 2050. To provide everyone with a diet like that available in developed countries by mid-century, food production will need to double. Yet food insecurity is already an urgent concern at current population levels. For although the Food and Agriculture Organization of the United Nations reports that 100 million fewer people are chronically undernourished today than a decade ago, over 800 million people (one in nine) still do not have access to the daily recommended minimum of 2,000 to 2,500 calories per person. The majority of the undernourished live in developing countries; of greatest concern are communities in sub-Saharan Africa and southern Asia. In striking contrast, patterns of consumption in developed countries reveal that changing diets—which incorporate more fat, sugar, and salt—are leading to both undernourishment and widespread obesity. And because land use related to food production alters our environment, we need to consider what we're eating and how we're growing.

5-Step Plan to
FEED THE WORLD

1 **FREEZE AGRICULTURE'S FOOTPRINT** Whole ecosystems around the globe have been lost to crops and livestock.

2 **GROW MORE ON FARMS WE'VE GOT** We need to turn our attention to increasing yields on less-productive farmlands.

3 **USE RESOURCES MORE EFFICIENTLY** We can achieve high yields while also reducing the environmental impacts of conventional farming.

4 **SHIFT DIETS** Eating less meat and finding more efficient ways to grow meat will free up substantial amounts of food.

5 **REDUCE WASTE** About 25 percent of the world's food calories and up to 50 percent of total food weight are lost or wasted.

Terraced fields in Vietnam grow rice, a staple in many diets around the world.

TODAY ONLY 55% OF THE WORLD'S CROP CALORIES FEED PEOPLE DIRECTLY. THE REST ARE FED TO LIVESTOCK (ABOUT 36%) OR TURNED INTO BIOFUELS AND INDUSTRIAL PRODUCTS (9%).

Eating Insects

As incomes rise in developing countries, so too does the demand for meat. But raising livestock uses a lot of resources. Eating insects—already common in many tropical countries—could be an alternative. Beetles and crickets, for example, are packed with nutrients and provide protein at a low environmental cost.

Palatability poses a problem. "People have an emotional response to bugs—it's the yuck factor," says Arnold van Huis of Wageningen University in the Netherlands. To disguise their form, insects can be processed into powders or pastes. What's next? Protein-rich "bug flours" that are part flour and part ground insect are starting to appear on the market.

ON THE MENU

2 billion

MORE THAN A FOURTH OF THE WORLD'S PEOPLE EAT INSECTS.
The popularity of Western diets is reducing insect consumption in developing countries.

2,000

NUMBER OF KNOWN EDIBLE SPECIES

EFFICIENT PROTEIN

Edible insects provide a sustainable alternative to meat. They are a healthy food source with a high protein and fat content, but their nutritional value varies by species.

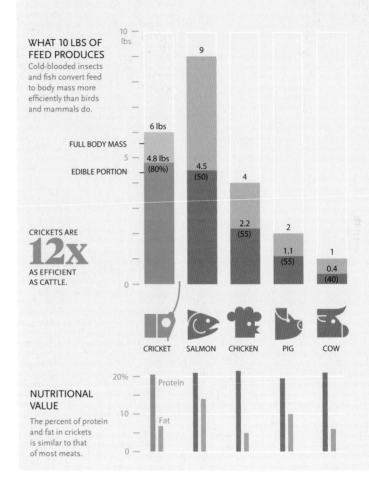

WHAT 10 LBS OF FEED PRODUCES
Cold-blooded insects and fish convert feed to body mass more efficiently than birds and mammals do.

FULL BODY MASS
EDIBLE PORTION

CRICKETS ARE

12x

AS EFFICIENT AS CATTLE.

CRICKET · SALMON · CHICKEN · PIG · COW

6 lbs / 4.8 lbs (80%) — CRICKET
9 / 4.5 (50) — SALMON
4 / 2.2 (55) — CHICKEN
2 / 1.1 (55) — PIG
1 / 0.4 (40) — COW

NUTRITIONAL VALUE
The percent of protein and fat in crickets is similar to that of most meats.

Protein
Fat

MOST COMMONLY CONSUMED
Beetles are the most consumed species; mealworms are beetle larvae.

BEETLES	CATERPILLARS			OTHER
31%	18%	15%	13%	23%
		ANTS, BEES, WASPS	CRICKETS, GRASS-HOPPERS, LOCUSTS	DRAGONFLIES, FLIES, TERMITES

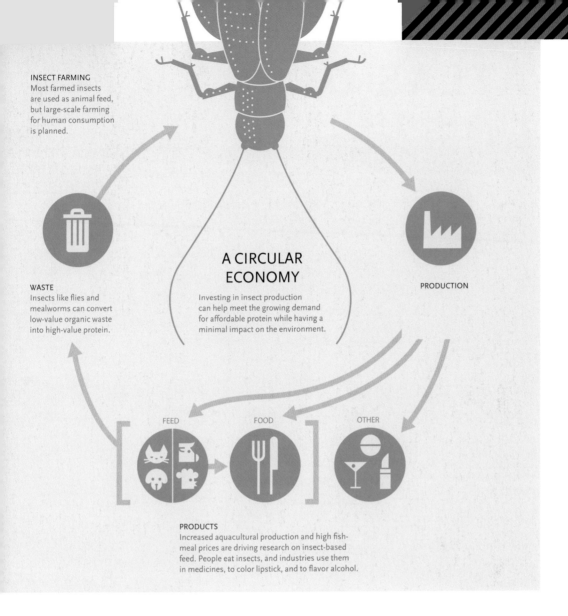

INSECT FARMING
Most farmed insects are used as animal feed, but large-scale farming for human consumption is planned.

WASTE
Insects like flies and mealworms can convert low-value organic waste into high-value protein.

A CIRCULAR ECONOMY

Investing in insect production can help meet the growing demand for affordable protein while having a minimal impact on the environment.

PRODUCTION

FEED

FOOD

OTHER

PRODUCTS
Increased aquacultural production and high fish-meal prices are driving research on insect-based feed. People eat insects, and industries use them in medicines, to color lipstick, and to flavor alcohol.

ENVIRONMENTAL IMPACT

Insects emit fewer greenhouse gases and require less land to produce than livestock such as pigs and cattle.

GREENHOUSE GAS PRODUCTION
Pounds of CO_2-eq* generated from producing a pound of protein

14
MEALWORM

38
PIG

LAND USE
Square feet needed to produce a pound of protein

88
MEALWORM

269
PIG

A DELICACY

IN UGANDA A POUND OF GRASSHOPPERS COSTS

40%

MORE THAN
A POUND OF BEEF

*CO_2-equivalents: the sum of carbon dioxide, methane, and nitrous oxide emissions

ATLAS OF HAPPINESS

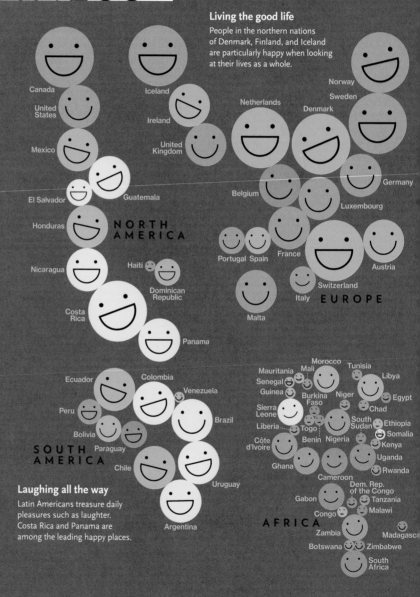

Living the good life
People in the northern nations of Denmark, Finland, and Iceland are particularly happy when looking at their lives as a whole.

NORTH AMERICA

Canada
United States
Mexico
El Salvador
Guatemala
Honduras
Nicaragua
Haiti
Dominican Republic
Costa Rica
Panama

Iceland
Ireland
United Kingdom

EUROPE

Norway
Sweden
Netherlands
Denmark
Belgium
Germany
Luxembourg
Portugal Spain
France
Austria
Italy
Switzerland
Malta

Laughing all the way
Latin Americans treasure daily pleasures such as laughter. Costa Rica and Panama are among the leading happy places.

SOUTH AMERICA

Ecuador
Colombia
Venezuela
Peru
Brazil
Bolivia
Paraguay
Chile
Uruguay
Argentina

AFRICA

Morocco
Mauritania Mali Tunisia
Senegal Libya
Guinea Burkina Niger
Faso Egypt
Sierra Chad
Leone South
Liberia Togo Sudan Ethiopia
Côte Benin Nigeria Somalia
d'Ivoire Kenya
Ghana Uganda
Rwanda
Cameroon
Dem. Rep.
of the Congo
Gabon Tanzania
Congo Malawi
Zambia Madagascar
Botswana Zimbabwe
South Africa

What does it take to be happy? Every year the Gallup World Poll tries to figure that out using dozens of questions to measure happiness in over 140 countries. Three of its themes are the focus here: how people see their lives as a whole, their daily happiness, and their physical health. One thing is clear: Different cultures have different ideas about what it means to thrive.

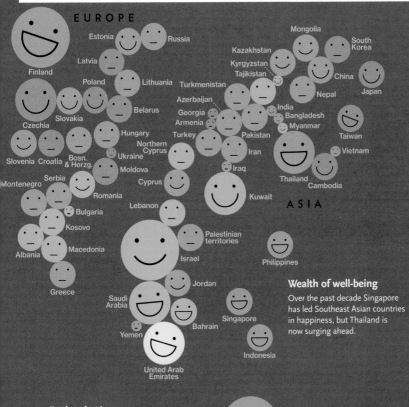

> ## " YOU CAN'T MEASURE HAPPINESS. IT'S REALLY A COMPOSITE OF THINGS: HEALTH, EMOTIONS, THE WAY YOU EVALUATE YOUR LIFE, AND THE EXTENT TO WHICH YOU'RE LIVING OUT YOUR VALUES. "
>
> —DAN BUETTNER, *THE BLUE ZONES OF HAPPINESS*

EUROPE

Finland
Estonia
Latvia
Russia
Poland
Lithuania
Turkmenistan
Belarus
Slovakia
Czechia
Azerbaijan
Georgia
Armenia
Hungary
Northern Cyprus
Turkey
Slovenia Croatia Bosn. & Herzg. Ukraine
Moldova
Montenegro Serbia
Romania Cyprus
Bulgaria
Kosovo
Lebanon
Albania Macedonia
Israel
Greece
Jordan
Saudi Arabia
Yemen Bahrain
United Arab Emirates

Mongolia
Kazakhstan
Kyrgyzstan
Tajikistan
South Korea
China
Japan
Nepal
India
Bangladesh
Myanmar
Pakistan
Taiwan
Iran
Vietnam
Iraq
Thailand Cambodia
Kuwait

ASIA

Palestinian territories
Philippines

Singapore
Indonesia

Wealth of well-being

Over the past decade Singapore has led Southeast Asian countries in happiness, but Thailand is now surging ahead.

Back to basics

North Africa's better infrastructure—paved roads, piped water, and cell phone coverage—helps raise happiness levels compared with the south.

Australia

New Zealand

OCEANIA

More than 55%
35-55%
15-34%
Less than 15%

PERCENTAGE CONSIDERED THRIVING

Life as a whole

People reflect on their lives and rate them from zero to 10. Those who respond seven or above are considered to be thriving.

Less than 65 65-69 70-75 More than 75

DAILY HAPPINESS IS SCORED 0 TO 100, BY COUNTRY.

Daily happiness

People are asked five questions to determine if they're happy in the moment. For example: Does their day include laughter?

18% 27% 36%

PERCENTAGE CONSIDERED THRIVING

Physical well-being

People are queried on their health. Data are converted into a scale from "suffering" to "thriving."

MEDICINE TIME LINE

6500 to 1 BC

■ ca 6500 BC
The first known surgery is completed.

■ ca 3000 BC
The Ayurveda, a Hindu medical treatise, establishes a holistic medical system still in use today.

■ ca 2500 BC
Chinese doctors use acupuncture to heal ailments.

■ ca 2000 BC
In Syria and Babylon, medicine becomes an important practice; recipes for ointments and poultices are recorded on clay tablets.

■ ca 1550 BC
Egyptians have about 700 drugs and medications in use.

■ 440 BC
The Hippocratic Corpus, a collection of medical treatises from ancient Greece, is compiled.

AD 1 to 1500

■ ca 30
Roman doctors use splints and bandages stiffened with starch to set broken bones.

■ 77
Pedanius Dioscorides writes a guide to medicinal herbs and drugs that remains authoritative until the 15th century.

■ 1012
Persian physician Ibn Sina publishes an influential medical text, *The Canon of Medicine*.

■ ca 1286
Eyeglasses are invented in Italy.

■ 1347–1351
The Black Death spreads across Europe and Asia in one of the most devastating pandemics in history.

1500 to 1850

■ 1628
English physician William Harvey explains the circulation of blood in the body.

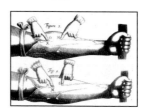

■ 1796
English physician Edward Jenner introduces the smallpox vaccination in Europe.

■ 1805
Japanese physician Hanaoka Seishu performs the first surgery on a patient using general anesthesia.

■ 1824
Louis Braille invents the Braille alphabet to aid blind people in reading and writing.

■ 1840
Jakob Henle proposes the germ theory of disease.

1850 to 1900

■ 1854
English physician John Snow connects cholera and contaminated water.

■ 1863
Louis Pasteur invents a sterilization process now known as pasteurization.

■ 1867
Joseph Lister publishes a paper on the use of antiseptic surgical methods.

■ 1885
Sigmund Freud begins developing his theories of psychoanalysis.

■ 1893
Surgeon Daniel Hale Williams performs the first heart surgery.

■ 1895
German physicist Wilhelm Röntgen takes the first x-ray.

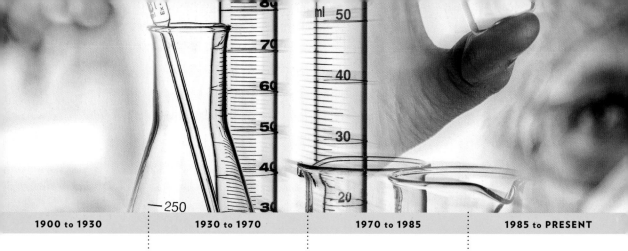

| 1900 to 1930 | 1930 to 1970 | 1970 to 1985 | 1985 to PRESENT |

■ 1917

Margaret Sanger opens a birth control clinic in the United States.

■ 1921

Psychiatrist Hermann Rorschach introduces his inkblot test for studying personality.

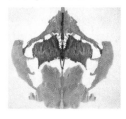

■ 1922

Vitamins D and E are first discovered.

■ 1925

Biologist Ernest Just demonstrates that UV radiation can cause cancer.

■ 1928

Scottish bacteriologist Alexander Fleming discovers penicillin.

■ 1937

Italian scientist Daniel Bovet identifies the first antihistamine effective in treating allergies.

■ 1948

The World Health Organization is founded.

■ 1950

Link between smoking and lung cancer is shown.

■ 1952

Jonas Salk develops the first polio vaccine.

■ 1953

Francis Crick, James Watson, and Rosalind Franklin determine the double-helix structure of DNA.

■ 1967

South African surgeon Christiaan Barnard performs the first successful heart transplant.

■ 1973

American and English physicians begin to develop magnetic resonance imaging (MRI) scanning.

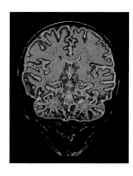

■ 1976

The Ebola virus is first identified after outbreaks in Africa.

■ 1978

The first "test tube" baby is born in England.

■ 1982

The first genetically engineered insulin is produced.

■ 1983

Luc Montagnier and Robert Gallo discover the human immuno-deficiency virus (HIV).

■ 1998

Researchers at Johns Hopkins University successfully grow human stem cells in a lab.

■ 2001

American researchers successfully clone a human embryo.

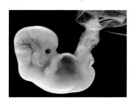

■ 2007

Geneticist J. Craig Venter publishes his entire genetic sequence—the first genome published of a single person.

■ 2010

World's first all-robotic surgery takes place in Canada.

■ 2013

Researchers develop a 3-D printed prosthetic hand that can be produced at a low cost.

MICROBIOME

MEET YOUR MICROBES

The human body contains as many microbes as it does cells—nearly 30 trillion of them. The human gut teems with bacteria, which help us digest food and absorb nutrients and protect our intestinal walls, and scientists suspect they help regulate weight and ward off autoimmune diseases. Several ecosystems are found on our skin too: Your forearm has the richest community, with an average of 44 species, while your nostril, ears, and inguinal crease (between leg and groin) are the most stable habitats. Our rarely scrubbed belly buttons are pristine microbial landscapes.

LACTOBACILLI **As infants, we acquire these bacteria—which create lactic acid from sugars—from breast milk. Throughout our lives, they help our bodies make key vitamins, such as B_{12} and K.**

FIBER **As bacteria consume the fiber we ingest, they release by-products that are beneficial to us. Edible fiber is found in plants, not in meat or dairy products, so one should aim for a plant-based diet.**

To illustrate the diverse contents of the human gut more vividly, a researcher colorized an actual microphotograph of human feces.

THE GUT MICROBIOME AMONG MOST WESTERNIZED, INDUSTRIALIZED POPULATIONS IS LESS DIVERSE AND DOMINATED BY DIFFERENT BACTERIAL SPECIES THAN THAT OF PEOPLE FROM RURAL, LESS DEVELOPED POPULATIONS.

STREPTOCOCCUS SALIVARIUS This bacterium is an ally, helping prevent tooth decay, gum disease, and throat infections. It is just one of almost 8,000 species residing on your tongue.

GOING GREEN

Best Ways to
FEED YOUR MICROBIOME

You'll find probiotic and prebiotic supplements on the shelves of natural foods stores, but the best way to foster a healthy microbiome is to eat prebiotic (which are consumed by bacteria in your gut) and fermented foods. Vegetables and grains with soluble fiber are ideal prebiotics: Unlike insoluble fiber, soluble fiber is available when it reaches the colon, where beneficial bacteria feed on it. Such foods also provide the complex sugars these bacteria need. Include fermented foods—from pickles to kombucha and soy sauce—in your diet too. Unpasteurized yogurt, which has living probiotics, is great for a healthy gut, especially yogurt without added sugars.

INSIDE YOUR BRAIN

ANATOMY OF A NERVE CELL

Cell body
The neuron's powerhouse, responsible for generating energy and synthesizing proteins

Dendrites
Branching projections that pick up signals from other neurons

An image a millimeter high—less than four-hundredths of an inch—shows nerve cells arranged in orderly layers and columns.

The 1-mm image is from different data set than the other images.

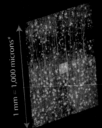

1 mm = 1,000 microns*

100 microns

— Blood vessels

10 microns

Deep Brain Dive

For the first time scientists can visualize how neurons actually connect with one another. The three blocks at right have been colorized but are not an artist's conception: They show, at increasing levels of magnification, real neurons in part of a mouse's brain receiving signals from the face. Technology may soon make possible a similar reconstruction of an entire mouse brain—and eventually of the vastly more complicated architecture of the human brain, opening the way for advances in understanding schizophrenia, depression, and other mental diseases.

A section a hundredth the size reveals blood vessels among pink cell bodies and a tangle of their axons and dendrites.

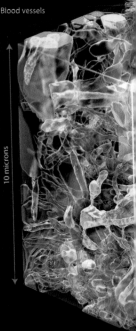

Magnified again by 100, this section more clearly shows axons (blue) and dendrites (yellow). Budlike dendritic spines receive information from other cells' axons across gaps called synapses.

HALF THE WORLD'S HARD DRIVES
Visualizing neurons at the level of detail shown in these images requires unprecedented computing power. Producing an image of an entire human brain at the same resolution would consume nearly half the world's digital storage capacity.

Storage capacity needed to produce mouse brain image
450,000 terabytes

Storage capacity needed to produce human brain image
1.3 billion terabytes

Global digital storage, 2012:
2.7 billion terabytes

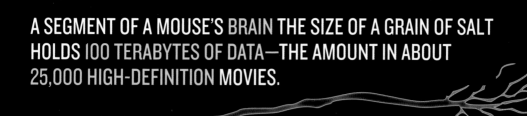

A SEGMENT OF A MOUSE'S BRAIN THE SIZE OF A GRAIN OF SALT HOLDS 100 TERABYTES OF DATA—THE AMOUNT IN ABOUT 25,000 HIGH-DEFINITION MOVIES.

Axon
A long nerve fiber that conducts information from the cell body in the form of an electrical impulse

Axonal terminal
End point of an axon's branches, where electrical impulses are discharged; releases neurotransmitters that carry chemical messages to other cells' dendrites

Glial cells
The glue of the nervous system, supporting, feeding, and protecting neurons

3 microns

1 micron

Magnified yet again, this sect
synaptic vesicles (yellow grai
neurotransmitters, which ca
messages across synapses,
receiving nerve cell to fire or

SANTIAGO RAMÓN Y CAJAL
NEUROANATOMIST

FINDING THE ART IN SCIENCE

Born in a Spanish village in May 1852, Santiago Ramón y Cajal went on to revolutionize the field of neurology—drawing comparisons to Einstein and his head-spinning reconception of physics. In addition to Cajal's contributions to medicine, his artistic work has enduring fascination.

Early neuroscientist Ramón y Cajal helped us see how the brain works.

O ver a century ago, Spanish scientist Santiago Ramón y Cajal, one of the founders of modern neuroscience, became the first person to get a clear look at the neural network that houses our thoughts, revealed by neurons stained with a silver chromate salt. Cajal depicted these and other emerging wonders with exquisite detail and anatomical precision.

SLIDES AND SKETCHES

As a child, Cajal wanted to pursue a career as an artist, but he eventually gave in to his father's wishes that he study medicine. After serving as an army medical officer in Cuba, which was a Spanish colony, he took a position as a professor of anatomy. He purchased a microscope with his military pay and began studying the body's secrets—his life's pursuit.

A turning point came in 1887 when, as Cajal later recounted, a psychiatrist friend showed him "those famous sections of the brain impregnated by the silver method of the Savant of Pavia." This savant was Camillo Golgi, with whom Cajal would later share the 1906 Nobel Prize for Physiology or Medicine.

Cajal went on to create extraordinary sketches of what he saw on microscope slides. But he also changed the basic understanding of the nervous system by identifying individual cells, or neurons, connected by synapses; previously, scientists thought the nervous system was a web-like continuous system. Cajal published his findings and his beautiful illustrations, some of which are still included in neuroscience texts today.

" IN SOME WAY OR OTHER, THE SIMPLE ADMIRATION OF THE CELLULAR FORM WAS ONE OF MY GREATEST DELIGHTS."

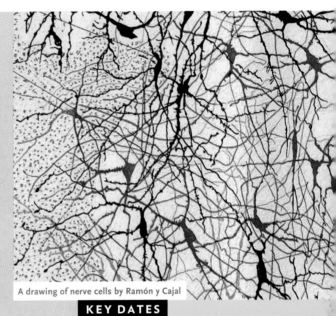

A drawing of nerve cells by Ramón y Cajal

KEY DATES

Observing
THE INVISIBLE

■ 1877
Received M.D. degree, Madrid, Spain

■ 1887
Appointed professor of histology and pathological anatomy, Barcelona

■ 1890
Published *Manual of General Pathological Anatomy*

■ 1892
Became professor of histology and pathological anatomy, Madrid

■ 1897–1899
Published *Texture of the Nervous System of Man and the Vertebrates*

■ 1906
With Camillo Golgi, won Nobel Prize for work on structure of nervous system

ADDICTION

PATHWAYS TO CRAVING

Desire is triggered when dopamine, which originates near the top of the brain stem, travels through neural pathways to act on the brain. Drugs increase the flow of dopamine.

Dorsal striatum
Neurons here help form habits by identifying enjoyable patterns, such as the anticipation of buying drugs.

Ventral tegmental area (VTA)
Dopamine is produced here and flows outward along neurons distributed throughout the brain's reward system.

Prefrontal cortex
The amino acid glutamate, produced here, interacts with dopamine to spark visualizations that cue cravings.

DOPAMINE

Amygdala
Neurons here are stimulated by learned emotional responses, such as memories of cravings and pleasure.

Brain stem
Basic visceral sensations and reactions to pleasure, such as smiling, originate from this hot spot.

Orbitofrontal cortex
This hot spot gives a sense of gratification but is also the first to shut down if a person has indulged too much.

Ventral pallidum
Animal experiments show that damaging this hot spot can turn something that once gave pleasure into a source of disgust.

Nucleus accumbens
A hot spot within this key part of the craving circuitry amplifies the response to pleasure.

PLEASURE HOT SPOTS

A system of small hedonic hot spots, unrelated to dopamine, provides temporary sensations of pleasure and forms a feedback loop with the reward system that controls desire.

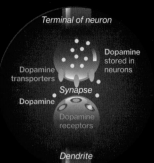

Terminal of neuron

Dopamine
transporters

Dopamine
stored in
neurons

Synapse

Dopamine

Dopamine
receptors

Dendrite

THE REWARD SYSTEM, A PRIMITIVE PART OF THE BRAIN, EXISTS TO ENSURE WE SEEK WHAT WE NEED. BUT THE SYSTEM CAN TRIP US UP IN A WORLD WITH 24/7 OPPORTUNITIES TO FULFILL OUR DESIRES.

NEURON ACTIVITY

In a normal state
Neurotransmitters carry
nerve impulses across
synapses between cells
to excite or inhibit activity.

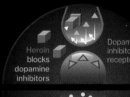

Dopamine
temporarily
floods
synapse

Dopamine
transporters
remove excess
dopamine from
synapse

In an excited state
Dopamine temporarily floods
a synapse when a pleasurable
activity, such as gambling, sex,
shopping, or gaming, is
anticipated or experienced.

A NATURAL HIGH

Our brains evolved a dopamine-based
reward system to encourage behaviors
that help us survive, such as eating,
procreating, and interacting socially.

Heroin
blocks
dopamine
inhibitors

Dopamine
inhibitor
receptors

Dopamine
floods
synapse

On heroin
Synapses flood
with dopamine when
heroin blocks dopamine
inhibitors in the VTA.

A CHEMICAL RUSH

Different drugs interact with the reward
system in unique ways to keep synapses
artificially flooded with dopamine.
That dopamine rush can rewire your brain
to want more drugs, leading to addiction.

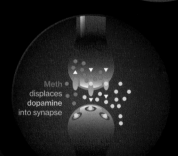

Meth
displaces
dopamine
into synapse

On methamphetamine
The drug reverses the natural,
controlled flow of dopamine
into neurons, forcing dopamine
to rush into synapses instead.

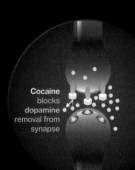

Cocaine
blocks
dopamine
removal from
synapse

On cocaine
By interfering with dopamine
transport, cocaine prevents
removal of excess dopamine
from synapses.

Antibiotic Resistance

THE POULTRY CASE STUDY

Americans today eat three times as much poultry as they did in 1960. Since most U.S. chickens are raised in large, crowded facilities, farmers feed them antibiotics to prevent disease as well as speed their growth.

Decades of Antibiotics

Since the 1950s, farmers have fed antibiotic growth promoters (AGPs) to livestock. Overusing these substances can create superbugs, pathogens that are resistant to multiple drugs and could be passed along to humans. Mindful of that, companies such as Perdue Farms have stopped using the drugs to make chickens gain weight faster. Since Denmark banned AGPs in the 1990s, the major pork exporter says it's producing more pigs— and the animals get fewer diseases. Says Centers for Disease Control and Prevention epidemiologist Tom Chiller, "Antibiotics are miracle drugs that should only be used to treat diseases."

MEAT CONSUMPTION IN THE U.S.

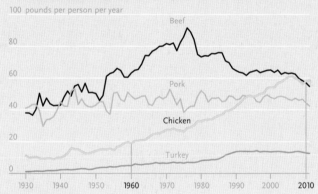

100 pounds per person per year

Antibiotics as Growth Promoters

They help chickens grow bigger faster, making the meat . . .

. . . cheaper for the consumer.

In 1960 it took 63 days to grow a 3.4-pound broiler.

\$3.24* a pound

In 2011 it took 47 days to grow a 5.4-pound one.

\$1.29 a pound

* 2011 dollars, adjusted for inflation

AS OF 2015, ANTIBIOTICS GIVEN TO MEAT ANIMALS AROUND THE WORLD TOTALED 126 MILLION POUNDS.

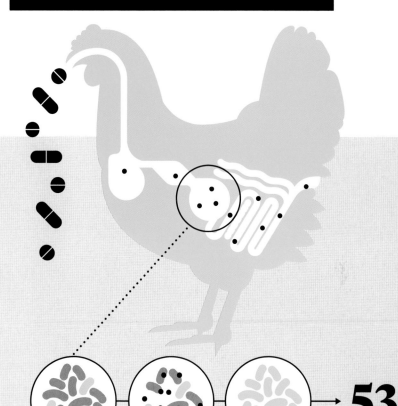

How Resistance Develops and Spreads

1.

Antibiotics can be given to livestock in their feed or sprayed on them, to be ingested when the animals groom themselves.

2.

The bacteria causing an infection are usually not resistant to drugs.

But some of them can be naturally drug resistant.

When antibiotics kill the nonresistant bacteria . . .

. . . the resistant ones, the superbugs, can flourish.

53%

of grocery store chicken sampled in a 2013 study had resistant *E. coli*.

3.

Superbugs can be passed to humans in many ways.

Farmworkers often have direct contact with animals.

Drug-resistant bacteria can linger on improperly cooked meat.

Fertilizer or water containing animal feces can spread superbugs to food crops.

VENOM AS MEDICINE

DEFANGING TOXINS

Venom, nature's most efficient killer, is made of toxins that often target the same molecules that need to be controlled to treat diseases. For example, in the 1970s, ACE inhibitors—a very popular class of drugs used to treat high blood pressure—were developed from a synthetic version of the Brazilian pit viper's venom, which causes a precipitous drop in blood pressure and then a loss of consciousness in its victims.

A WORD FROM

Screening Toxins   We have 20 different medicines coming from animal venom—for high blood pressure, for cardiac failure, for cancer and HIV pain, and for diabetes. But still in nature we have 20 million toxins left unstudied, in spiders, scorpions—it's not only snakes. It's sea animals and amphibians. Even some primates have toxic secretions. We collect all these venomous creatures from all over the world and create toxin libraries, and we screen out which is the best match for a target in the human body, because that can be a potential future medication.

—**ZOLTAN TAKACS,** *herpetologist and toxinologist*

The deadly poisonous Jameson's mamba, native to central Africa, may hold clues for the development of effective antitoxins.

THE MALE DUCK-BILLED PLATYPUS, **WHICH** CARRIES VENOM **INSIDE ITS ANKLE SPURS, IS ONE OF THE FEW VENOMOUS MAMMALS.**

THE PRODUCTS OF VENOM

10–15 diagnostics
Snake venom toxins act on the molecules that control blood clotting and muscle contraction.

RUSSELL'S VIPER
dRVVT

TEST: Measures blood-clotting time, which is longer in people with the lupus anticoagulant

VENOM: Disrupts clotting and attacks kidneys, muscles, and nerves; often fatal in humans

10–20 medicines
These treat pain, diabetes, and major cardiovascular diseases. Most come from snakes.

GILA MONSTER
Exenatide

DRUG: Treats type 2 diabetes by stimulating the pancreas to secrete insulin

VENOM: Causes severe pain, swelling, nausea, hypotension, and shock in humans

1 cosmetic
A wrinkle treatment— a snake's answer to Botox— is the only one of its kind.

TEMPLE PIT VIPER
Syn-Ake

CREAM: Sold to smooth wrinkles by blocking nerve signals that cause muscles to contract

VENOM: Contains unique toxins that target receptors responsible for muscle contraction

YOUR BRAIN ON NATURE

PATHWAY TO CALM, CONCENTRATION, AND WELL-BEING

Science is proving the value of a walk in the woods.

NATURE'S BEST BUTTON

Constantly multitasking and dodging countless distractions can erode mental acuity. Our brains are easily fatigued. What is the antidote? Nature. When we stop the busywork and take in beautiful natural surroundings, not only do we feel restored, but our mental performance also improves.

Large-scale public health problems such as obesity, depression, and even nearsightedness are clearly associated with time spent indoors. This pattern has motivated scientists

to look with renewed interest at how nature affects us. Measurements of everything from stress hormones to heart rate to brain waves to protein markers indicate that when we spend time in green space, our prefrontal cortex, the brain's command center, can dial down and rest, like an overused muscle.

Dutch researchers found a lower incidence of 15 diseases—including depression, anxiety, heart disease, diabetes, asthma, and migraines—in people who lived within a half mile of green space.

RESEARCHERS FIND THAT TREES AND PLANTS EXUDE OILS THAT BOOST THE BRAIN'S OWN PRODUCTION OF CALMING CHEMICALS.

LOOK OUT THE WINDOW

English researchers found that people living near more green space reported less mental distress, even after adjusting for income, education, and employment.

GREEN SPACE: PRICELESS

Studies show that short doses of nature, or even pictures of the natural world, can calm people down and sharpen their performance. Compared with people who have obstructed window views, those who can see trees and grass have been shown to recover faster in hospitals, perform better in school, and even display less violent behavior. In one Korean study, looking at urban scenes increased blood flow in the amygdala, which processes fear and anxiety. In contrast, natural scenes lit up the anterior cingulate and the insula—areas associated with empathy and altruism.

The science is clear: Immersing yourself in nature has restorative effects.

Ways to Bring Nature
INTO YOUR LIFE

1 MAKE IT A PRIORITY Schedule time on the calendar for outdoor adventures, even if you only have time for a short hike.

2 OBSERVE WILDLIFE Grab a field guide to local birds and keep track of your finds on a "life list." Having a pair of binoculars helps.

3 WATCH PATIENTLY Select a tree near your home and follow its life over the course of a year, documenting with photos and notes.

4 FIND A WAY TO EAT "OUT" Pack a picnic or a thermos of hot chocolate and head out to the back-yard or the park—in any season.

5 RELOCATE A HABIT Do you usually sort mail or read magazines at the dining table? Step onto your patio or deck instead.

6 MAKE NEW FRIENDS Join a local group that cleans up river-banks, rakes leaves for seniors, or plants trees to stop erosion.

7 LOOK UP Even if you can't see many stars from your yard, follow the phases of the moon or the planets' movements.

8 MEET THE NEIGHBORS Plan a block party, a neighborhood bar-becue, or a mini-Olympics for the kids and start socializing outside.

9 PLAN TO BE SPONTANEOUS Put outdoor shoes, bug spray, and sunscreen in the car so you can take advantage of any opportunity.

10 GRAB A BIKE OR A BALL While 70 percent of mothers in the U.S. recall playing outdoors every day, only 26 percent say their kids do.

HERBS & SPICES
FOR HEALTH

BASIL
Fragrant annual
native to India

BAY
Aromatic shrub leaf
flavors soups.

CHERVIL
Delicate relative
of parsley

CHIVES
Tender stalks
in onion family

CILANTRO
Leaves of plant whose
seeds are coriander

DILL
Ancient cure
for indigestion

FENNEL
Seeds, leaves, stalks,
bulbs all tasty

LEMONGRASS
Southeast Asian native,
citrus flavor

MARJORAM
Sweet herb, makes
a calming tea

OREGANO
Classic herb in
Mediterranean cuisines

PARSLEY
Edible garnish high
in antioxidants

PEPPERMINT
Tea is a favorite
stomach soother.

ROSEMARY
Research affirms
tradition as pain reliever.

SAGE
Honeybees love
sage flowers.

TARRAGON
Fragile flavor best captured
in vinegar

THYME
Good in cooking;
tea also calms a cough.

ALLSPICE
Ground from dried berries, Caribbean native

BLACK PEPPER
Native to India, spurred spice trade in 1600s

CARDAMOM
Ancient Egyptians chewed it for clean breath.

CAYENNE
Powdered hot peppers, rich in vitamins and minerals

CINNAMON
Inner bark of tropical tree, lowers blood sugar

CLOVES
Ground tree buds, antioxidant and mildly anesthetic

CORIANDER
Seed of cilantro plant, often used in curries

CUMIN
Aromatic seed essential to Mexican and Indian cuisines

GINGER
Ground root, traditional remedy for seasickness

MACE
Outer covering of nutmeg; both appetite stimulants

PAPRIKA
Bright red, made of dried peppers, typical in Hungary

TURMERIC
Related to ginger, provides many health benefits

ANCIENT WISDOM

Herbs and spices add flavor, aroma, color, texture, and nutrients to food—and many improve health as well. Herbs are leaves or stems of plants from temperate zones, used fresh or dried. Spices come from many parts of tropical plants—dried seeds, flowers, fruit, bark, or roots—and are used either whole or ground fine. Most of these provide vitamins and minerals, and many have healing properties.

A WORD FROM

Learning From Plants If you reduce these plants to merely their constituents, synthesize them, reproduce them, and use them as drugs, you've not changed anything. Dietary supplements and botanicals are a multibillion-dollar industry. But instead of really getting to the root problems of our health and promoting wellness, we're looking for things inside of a pill—and that's not what the plants are here for. Plants are seeds, they grow, and they teach us about the cycles of life and death. If you took some of those children on Ritalin and put them in a garden and got them planting seeds and tending the soil, and working on their own inner landscape, you might find that they would be just fine without their medication.

—**TIERAONA LOW DOG, M.D.,** *integrative physician*

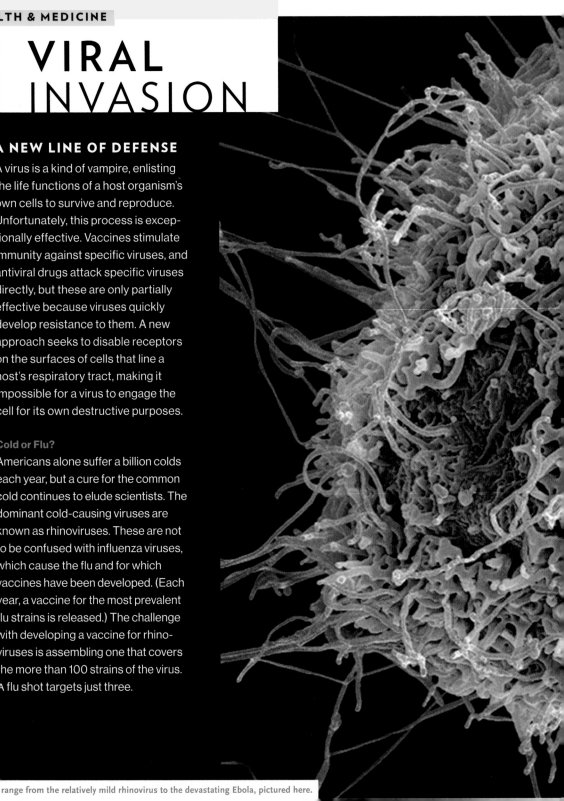

VIRAL INVASION

A NEW LINE OF DEFENSE

A virus is a kind of vampire, enlisting the life functions of a host organism's own cells to survive and reproduce. Unfortunately, this process is exceptionally effective. Vaccines stimulate immunity against specific viruses, and antiviral drugs attack specific viruses directly, but these are only partially effective because viruses quickly develop resistance to them. A new approach seeks to disable receptors on the surfaces of cells that line a host's respiratory tract, making it impossible for a virus to engage the cell for its own destructive purposes.

Cold or Flu?

Americans alone suffer a billion colds each year, but a cure for the common cold continues to elude scientists. The dominant cold-causing viruses are known as rhinoviruses. These are not to be confused with influenza viruses, which cause the flu and for which vaccines have been developed. (Each year, a vaccine for the most prevalent flu strains is released.) The challenge with developing a vaccine for rhinoviruses is assembling one that covers the more than 100 strains of the virus. A flu shot targets just three.

range from the relatively mild rhinovirus to the devastating Ebola, pictured here.

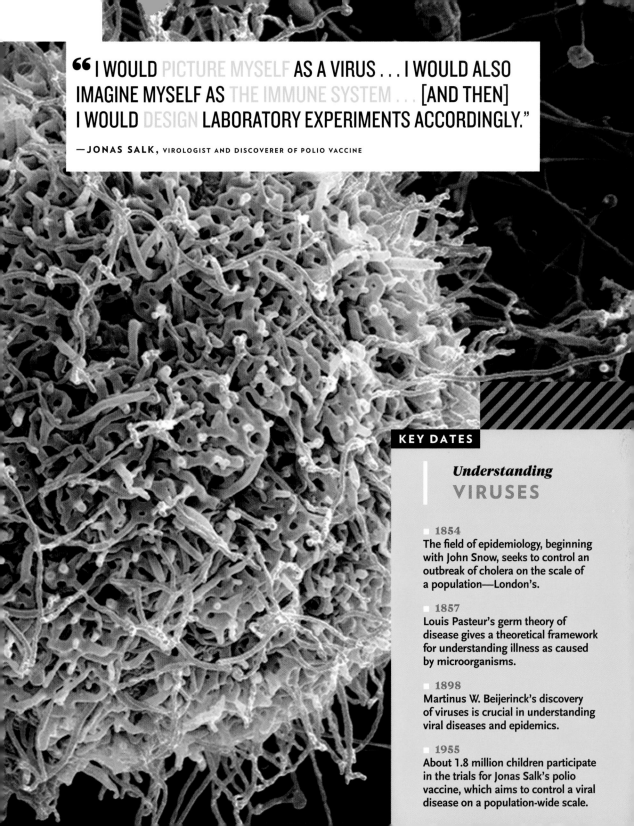

> **" I WOULD** PICTURE MYSELF **AS A VIRUS . . . I WOULD ALSO IMAGINE MYSELF AS** THE IMMUNE SYSTEM **. . . [AND THEN] I WOULD** DESIGN **LABORATORY EXPERIMENTS ACCORDINGLY."**
>
> **—JONAS SALK,** VIROLOGIST AND DISCOVERER OF POLIO VACCINE

KEY DATES

Understanding VIRUSES

■ **1854**
The field of epidemiology, beginning with John Snow, seeks to control an outbreak of cholera on the scale of a population—London's.

■ **1857**
Louis Pasteur's germ theory of disease gives a theoretical framework for understanding illness as caused by microorganisms.

■ **1898**
Martinus W. Beijerinck's discovery of viruses is crucial in understanding viral diseases and epidemics.

■ **1955**
About 1.8 million children participate in the trials for Jonas Salk's polio vaccine, which aims to control a viral disease on a population-wide scale.

FURTHER

LIGHTING THE SKY WITH GOOD WISHES

Spirits soar and wishes float up to the heavens each year in northern Thailand during the Yi Peng Lantern Festival. The sky is already bright, since the festival occurs on the full moon of the 12th lunar month each year (November 13 in 2019). Celebrants add illumination by releasing candlelit lanterns into the night sky. The brightest celebration—the mass lantern release—takes place at Maejo University, outside the city of Chiang Mai. A Buddhist tradition, the Yi Peng Festival commands respect: modest clothing, deference for the monks conducting the ceremony. As people release their lanterns, they resolve best behavior and visualize good fortune in the year to come.

Flame heat lifts lanterns sky-high during Thailand's Lantern Festival.

TRADITION PROMISES THAT IF YOUR LANTERN'S FLAME STAYS LIT UNTIL IT DISAPPEARS FROM SIGHT, YOUR WISH WILL BE GRANTED.

YESTERDAY TO TOMORROW

Cleaning a tooth from *Homo naledi*, recently discovered prehuman ancestor

WORLD HISTORY | U.S. HISTORY

Looking Back For some, the definition of nerdy is being able to recite little-known facts about history. Truth is, understanding our past helps us shape our future. Here's a chapter that looks out over millennia and dives deep into a few special stories.

—**CARA SANTA MARIA**, *Our Favorite Nerd*

p313

IN WHAT CONTINENT IS THE ANCIENT CITY OF TIMBUKTU?

p 302

WHAT AMERICAN FIRST LADY BECAME A U.S. DELEGATE TO THE UNITED NATIONS?

p293

WHAT MATERIAL DID THE 1856 GUANO ISLANDS ACT GIVE CONGRESS THE RIGHT TO MINE?

p322

TULIPS HAVE BEEN CULTIVATED FOR HOW LONG: 1,000 YEARS, 500 YEARS, OR 150 YEARS?

WHAT IS THE ONLY U.S. STATE TO HAVE A FLAG THAT IS NOT RECTANGULAR?

p320

p304

WHAT TWO ENGLISH FAMILIES FOUGHT IN THE WAR OF THE ROSES?

WHAT YEAR DID SOUTH KOREA DECLARE ITS INDEPENDENCE?

p30

HOW MANY YEARS DID **SOUTH AFRICAN LEADER NELSON MANDELA** SPEND IN PRISON?

FOR WHAT SOCIAL CAUSE DID **ELIZABETH CADY** STANTON MAKE HER DECLARATION OF **SENTIMENTS** PUBLIC IN SENECA FALLS, **NEW YORK?**

WHAT ANCIENT CULTURE USED CONCRETE TO BUILD AQUEDUCTS?

NAME THE LAST TERRITORIES TO BECOME **STATES** AND WHEN.

WHAT WAS THE FIRST STATE TO RATIFY THE U.S. CONSTITUTION?

WHAT IS ALFRED **NOBEL** FAMOUS FOR INVENTING?

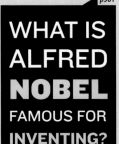

WHICH AMERICAN FIRST LADY WAS RESPONSIBLE FOR **RAISING FUNDS** TO SUPPORT THE LEWIS & CLARK EXPEDITION WESTWARD?

PREHISTORY TO 1600
TIME LINE

PREHISTORY	3000 to 1000 BC	1000 to 500 BC	500 to 1 BC

PREHISTORY

ca 100,000 ya*
Early humans migrate from Africa to other continents.

ca 80,000 ya
Neanderthals and modern humans live alongside each other in Europe.

ca 14,500 ya
Human populations are present in North and South America.

ca 10,000 ya
Agriculture develops in the Yellow River Valley and other places in China.

ca 3200 BC
Sumer, the first known civilization, emerges in modern-day Iraq.

*years ago

3000 to 1000 BC

ca 2575 BC
Ancient Egypt's Old Kingdom begins.

ca 2500–1900 BC
The Indus civilization thrives in modern-day Pakistan and northwest India.

ca 1766–1122 BC
The Shang dynasty rules in ancient China.

ca 1500 BC
Olmec culture develops in modern-day Mexico.

ca 1200 BC
Proto-Celtic people of Indo-European origin settle in central Europe.

1000 to 500 BC

753 BC
Rome is founded by Romulus and Remus, according to legend.

ca 700 BC
Athens and other Greek city-states become centers of learning and maritime trade.

ca 560 BC
Siddhartha Gautama is born in the Himalayan foothills; he is later known as the Buddha.

509 BC
The Roman Republic is established.

500 to 1 BC

ca 500 BC
Iron tool technology spreads across Africa.

334 BC
Alexander the Great invades Persia and carves out an empire stretching from Greece to northwestern India.

ca 100 BC
Buddhism spreads into Central Asia along the Silk Road.

27 BC
Augustus becomes the first emperor of Rome.

| AD 1 to 500 | 500 to 1090 | 1090 to 1400 | 1400 to 1600 |

■ 79
Mount Vesuvius erupts, destroying Pompeii and Herculaneum.

■ ca 300
Maya in South America develop a script and a calendar.

■ 312
Constantine I becomes the emperor of Rome and expands legal rights for religions.

■ 441
Attila the Hun launches a massive attack on the Eastern Roman Empire.

■ ca 500
The empire of Ghana gains prominence in West Africa.

■ 570
Muhammad, the Prophet and future messenger of Islam, is born in Mecca.

■ 800
Charlemagne is crowned the Holy Roman Emperor.

■ 960
The Song dynasty reunifies China and ushers in economic, social, and cultural change.

■ ca 1000
Leif Eriksson sails to North America.

■ 1054
The schism between the Roman and Eastern Christian churches becomes permanent.

■ 1095
The First Crusade begins, inaugurating a series of religious wars that would last for hundreds of years.

■ 1206
Genghis Khan becomes leader of the Mongol confederation.

■ 1337
The Hundred Years' War begins between England and France.

■ 1368
Zhu Yuanzhang founds the Ming dynasty in China.

■ 1440
Moctezuma I becomes ruler of the Aztec.

■ 1478
The Spanish Inquisition begins.

■ 1517
Martin Luther instigates the Protestant Reformation.

■ 1519–1521
Spain conquers the Aztec Empire, beginning a century-long colonial period.

■ 1560s
The transatlantic slave trade grows in West Africa.

■ 1577–1580
English explorer Sir Francis Drake circumnavigates the globe.

VIKINGS

THE REALM OF THE VIKINGS

Norway, Denmark, and Sweden hosted a rich seafaring tradition ruled by competing regional kings and chiefs. Swedish traders dominated eighth-century eastward expansion and became leaders of the Rus, who traded with the Arab and Byzantine worlds.

SCANDINAVIAN
HIGH-STATUS
WARRIOR

SCANDINAVIAN
HIGH-STATUS
WOMAN

Bronze oval brooches, often with beads strung between them, fastened apron straps. Fashions varied by region.

Metal helmets denoted high status. Only one complete Viking metal helmet has ever been discovered.

Chain mail armor was worn by Viking elites.

Women hung tools like knives, needle cases, and shears from their brooches or belts.

Swords, often double-edged with richly decorated hilts, could be more than three feet long.

Women's clothing could include several layers, with an apron and a shawl.

The underdress was made of linen.

FROM THE 8TH TO THE 11TH CENTURIES, VIKING SHIPS JOURNEYED TO LANDS AS FAR-FLUNG AS TODAY'S AFGHANISTAN AND CANADA, INTERACTING AND TRADING WITH MORE THAN 50 OTHER CULTURES.

RUS MAN

HIGH-STATUS
RUS WOMAN

Hats could be made of exotic fabrics, with fur trim and a silver tassel.

Married Viking women may have covered their hair.

Caftans were often made of wool, with silk decorations and trim.

The Rus adopted Christianity from the Byzantine Empire.

Trade with the Arab world included vast amounts of silver, often used for jewelry.

Baggy, Eastern-style pants worn by Rus men became fashionable across Scandinavia.

1600 TO RECENT PAST
TIME LINE

| 1600 to 1700 | 1700 to 1800 | 1800 to 1860 | 1860 to 1900 |

■ 1600s

European powers expand their colonization around the world.

■ ca 1600

Algonquin tribes unite to form the Powhatan Confederacy in North America.

■ 1633

For his theory that Earth circles the sun, Galileo goes on trial for heresy.

■ 1649

Civil war in England results in the execution of King Charles I.

■ 1661

Swedish banknotes become the first paper currency in use in Europe.

■ 1701

The Asante kingdom expands in West Africa under the reign of Osei Tutu.

■ 1762

Catherine II proclaims herself empress of Russia.

■ 1770

Aboard the *Endeavour*, James Cook claims Australia for Britain.

■ 1776

Americans post their Declaration of Independence.

■ 1789

A mob storms the Bastille, marking the beginning of the French Revolution.

■ 1801

A slave rebellion succeeds, leading to Haiti's independence from France three years later.

■ 1815

Simón Bolívar writes his "Letter from Jamaica," outlining his vision of South America freed of colonial rule.

■ 1833

Slavery is abolished throughout the British Empire.

■ 1837

Queen Victoria begins her 63-year reign.

■ 1845–1851

Irish potato famine causes poverty and mass starvation; millions emigrate to North America.

■ 1861

Tsar Alexander II frees serfs in Russia.

■ 1863

Abraham Lincoln issues the Emancipation Proclamation, freeing slaves in 10 states.

FREEDOM TO SLAVES!

■ 1867

Provinces in Canada unite into a single country.

■ 1884–1885

The Berlin Conference divides Africa among various European powers.

■ 1897

First Zionist Congress convenes in Basel, Switzerland.

| 1900 to 1925 | 1925 to 1950 | 1950 to 1975 | 1975 to 2000 |

1900 to 1925

■ 1914
The Panama Canal opens, enabling faster transoceanic shipping.

■ 1914
Assassination of Archduke Ferdinand sparks years-long World War I.

■ 1917
Lenin and the Bolsheviks overthrow the tsar in Russian Revolution.

■ 1920
Mohandas Gandhi becomes India's leader in its struggle for independence.

1925 to 1950

■ 1929
Wall Street stock market crashes, beginning the Great Depression.

■ 1933
Adolf Hitler is appointed chancellor of Germany.

■ 1939–1945
In World War II, Allied powers (including U.K., U.S., Soviet Union, France, and China) battle Axis powers (Germany, Italy, and Japan).

■ 1945
United Nations is founded.

■ 1949
Marxist leader Mao Zedong transforms China into Communist People's Republic of China.

1950 to 1975

■ 1955
Rosa Parks's arrest in Alabama sets the American civil rights movement in motion.

■ 1957
European Economic Community, precursor to the European Union, is established.

■ 1959
Fidel Castro takes over Cuba after leading a Marxist revolution.

■ 1973
Organization of Petroleum-Exporting Countries (OPEC) embargoes oil supplies, causing a worldwide energy crisis.

1975 to 2000

■ 1979
Muslim cleric Ayatollah Ruhollah Khomeini seizes power in Iran.

■ 1986
Disastrous accident at Chernobyl nuclear power plant in Ukraine forces massive resettlement.

■ 1989
Thousands of students occupy Beijing's Tian'anmen Square, advocating democracy in China.

■ 1989
Built in 1961 to encircle Germany's West Berlin, the Berlin Wall falls, a sign of the end of the Cold War.

■ 1990
Nelson Mandela is released after 27 years in prison, signifying end of apartheid in South Africa.

TULIPS
PRECIOUS AS GOLD

FANTASTIC FLORAL FRENZY

The unassuming tulip grew naturally across Asia Minor. Its arrival in Europe around 1550 is attributed to Ferdinand I's ambassador to Turkey. By the early 1600s, tulip mania had taken over Holland. Demand so exceeded supply that by 1610 houses and businesses were being mortgaged to purchase a coveted flower. But when demand waned in 1637, the tulip market crashed almost overnight, causing many to blame the flower for nearly bankrupting traders. Although the tulip may never again generate such fervor, the Dutch continue to grow exquisite varieties.

The tulip was originally called *dulband*—Persian for "turban"—and later *tuliband* by the Ottomans.

THE REIGN OF OTTOMAN SULTAN AHMED III (1703–1730) IS KNOWN AS THE TULIP AGE FOR HIS OBSESSION WITH THE FLOWER AND ITS UBIQUITOUS APPEARANCE IN TEXTILES, ARCHITECTURE, AND GARDENS.

KEY DATES

Cultivation and Travels of
TULIPS

■ **1000**
Ottoman Turks begin cultivating tulips.

■ **1573**
Carolus Clusius, court gardener, receives seed and plants first tulips in Vienna.

■ **1593**
Moving to Holland, Clusius starts first ornamental garden.

■ **1633**
Tulip craze sends European prices soaring.

■ **1637**
Tulip markets crash.

■ **1845**
Tulip export to America begins.

■ **1928**
Virus that causes color breaks is isolated, allowing new variegated tulips to be hybridized.

ART & IDEAS
TIME LINE

2000 to 750 BC

■ **ca 2000 BC**
The Akkadian *Epic of Gilgamesh,* oldest surviving heroic epic, combines history, myth, and poetry.

■ **ca 1792 BC**
Babylonian Code of Hammurabi, inscribed on a standing slab of basalt, articulates many civil and moral rules.

■ **ca 1500–1200 BC**
The Vedas—ancient scriptures written in Sanskrit and fundamental to Hinduism—are composed.

■ **ca 750 BC**
Homer composes the *Iliad* and *Odyssey* as oral poetry in ancient Greece.

750 BC to AD 1000

■ **444 BC**
Compiling six centuries of history, Judaism's sacred book, the Torah, is canonized.

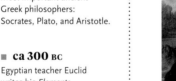

■ **367 BC**
Aristotle enters Plato's Academy, linking the three most important ancient Greek philosophers: Socrates, Plato, and Aristotle.

■ **ca 300 BC**
Egyptian teacher Euclid writes his *Elements,* consolidating knowledge in logic and mathematics, especially geometry.

■ **AD 300**
A decimal system, expressing any number using just 10 digits including zero, is now being used for counting and calculating in India.

■ **AD 825**
Musa al-Khwarizmi, Baghdadi scholar, publishes work introducing algebra.

1000 to 1575

■ **1215**
King John of England signs the Magna Carta.

■ **ca 1506**
Leonardo da Vinci paints the *Mona Lisa.*

■ **1541**
Michelangelo completes the Sistine Chapel in Rome's Vatican Palace.

■ **1543**
Copernicus publishes work proposing a heliocentric model of the known universe.

■ **1572**
Tycho Brahe carefully observes and records a supernova explosion.

1575 to 1750

■ **ca 1600**
Kabuki theater becomes a popular art form in Japan.

■ **1623**
English Parliament passes a statute banning monopolies and enstating protection of patents.

■ **1677**
Antonie van Leeuwenhoek reports on observing microscopic forms of life.

■ **1687**
Isaac Newton publishes *Principia Mathematica.*

■ **1742**
Handel's *Messiah* is first performed in Dublin.

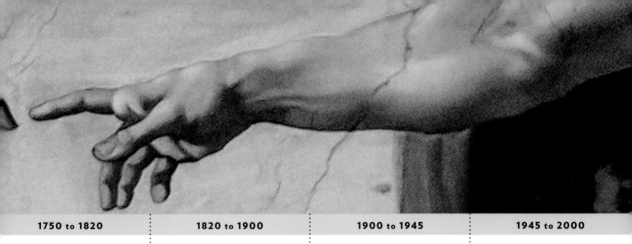

| **1750 to 1820** | **1820 to 1900** | **1900 to 1945** | **1945 to 2000** |

1750 to 1820

■ **1762**
French author Jean-Jacques Rousseau publishes *The Social Contract,* inspiring revolutions in America, France, and elsewhere.

■ **1792**
Mary Wollstonecraft publishes *A Vindication of the Rights of Woman,* considered the first feminist tract.

■ **1798**
English economist Thomas Malthus predicts overpopulation.

■ **1812**
Jacob and Wilhelm Grimm publish the first volume of fairy tales.

■ **1818**
Mary Shelley's *Frankenstein,* considered the first science fiction novel, is published in London.

1820 to 1900

■ **1839**
Louis Daguerre patents a process for capturing and printing images.

■ **1848**
Elizabeth Cady Stanton addresses convention on women's rights in Seneca Falls, New York.

■ **1848**
Karl Marx and Friedrich Engels publish the *Communist Manifesto.*

■ **1869**
Dmitry Mendeleev organizes chemical elements based on atomic weights and creates the periodic table.

■ **1874**
French painters including Cezanne, Degas, Monet, and Renoir exhibit paintings and are soon dubbed Impressionists.

1900 to 1945

■ **1900**
Sigmund Freud publishes *The Interpretation of Dreams.*

■ **1905**
Albert Einstein overturns Newtonian physics with his paper on special relativity.

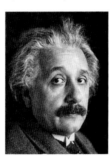

■ **1907–1914**
Pablo Picasso and Georges Braque pioneer the Cubist movement.

■ **1927**
The first film with a full sound track, Al Jolson's *The Jazz Singer,* debuts.

1945 to 2000

■ **1948**
Nightly TV news begins with Douglas Edwards on CBS.

■ **1956**
Elvis Presley makes his first television appearance on *The Ed Sullivan Show,* singing "Hound Dog" and "Don't Be Cruel."

■ **1964**
The Beatles hit #1 on the U.S. pop charts with "I Want to Hold Your Hand."

■ **1964**
U.S. President Lyndon B. Johnson signs historic Civil Rights Act, banning discrimination and guaranteeing voting rights.

■ **1996**
Google, the Internet search engine, becomes operational.

SARAH PARCAK
ARCHAEOLOGIST

LOOKING WITH NEW EYES

Egyptologist and archaeologist Sarah Parcak is often described as a hybrid of Indiana Jones and Google Earth. A pioneer in the field of space archaeology, she blends old-fashioned digging, her expertise with advanced computer programs, and satellite-imagery analysis to reveal thousands of new sites that might be too remote to survey or are otherwise obscured by modern development and debris or by forests and various natural coverings, such as soil. She has demonstrated that, remarkably, images taken from 400 miles above us can reveal what's under our feet.

At a dig site in Point Rosee, Newfoundland, Parcak and her team have uncovered evidence of possible Viking settlements.

S arah Parcak used to study aerial photographs of forested areas with her grandfather, a forestry professor, so she was curious enough in college to take a class in remote sensing—gathering information about things from a distance. Now a world-renowned National Geographic Explorer and "space archaeologist," she has an ambitious plan to use technology and crowdsourcing to protect remnants of the ancient world.

NEW TECHNOLOGY, OLD SITES

When Parcak, an archaeological evangelist, won the million-dollar 2016 TED Talk Prize, she set out to democratize archaeological discoveries and to quickly identify sites threatened by development or looting. She did this by creating GlobalXplorer, a digital platform that crowdsources the detection and protection of ancient sites using satellite imagery. Parcak's first GlobalXplorer project focused on Peru's Machu Picchu and geoglyphs known as the Nasca Lines. It was set up as a game using images that covered some hundred thousand square miles of farms, towns, and countryside. In just a few months, more than 45,000 volunteer virtual sleuths viewed 10 million images and identified thousands of architectural features.

For another study, Parcak and her team reviewed satellite images that had been taken of 267 archaeological sites in Egypt between 2002 and 2013, looking for evidence of pillage and destruction. The images revealed roughly 200,000 individual looting pits, as well as a staggering increase in looting across Egypt. Parcak estimates that as many as 10,000 artifacts may be on the black market each day.

> **" WE'RE ALL BORN** EXPLORERS, **CURIOUS AND INTRINSICALLY INTERESTED IN OTHER HUMANS. WE WANT TO** FIND OUT MORE **ABOUT OTHER PEOPLE, AND ABOUT OURSELVES AND OUR PAST."**

Parcak found evidence of 200,000 looting pits at 267 sites in Egypt.

KEY DATES

Revealing What Has Been HIDDEN

■ **2007**
Founds the Laboratory for Global Observation at the University of Alabama at Birmingham

■ **2009**
Publishes *Satellite Remote Sensing for Archaeology*, first textbook on the field

■ **2011**
Announces discovery of Egypt's "lost city" of Tanis—touted in ancient hieroglyphs—with 17 potential buried pyramids, 3,000 settlements, and 1,000 tombs

■ **2015**
Identifies and breaks ground at a potential Viking site in Newfoundland, Canada

■ **2016**
Publishes article identifying a structure in Petra using satellite imagery, drone photography, and ground surveys

BEST OF @NATGEO

OUR FAVORITE PHOTOS OF HISTORIC PLACES

@simonnorfolkstudio | SIMON NORFOLK
The remains of Persepolis, the ceremonial capital of the ancient Achaemenid Empire in modern-day Iran

@yamashitaphoto | MICHAEL YAMASHITA
Kimono-clad tourists walk through the famous tunnel of 10,000 torii at Fushimi Inari Shrine.

@jimrichardsonng | JIM RICHARDSON
Llamas overlook the ruins of Machu Picchu, a 15th-century Inca citadel in Peru.

@mmuheisen | MUHAMMED MUHEISEN
Visitors enjoy the ice-skating rink outside the Rijksmuseum, a collection of Dutch art and history, in Amsterdam.

TIMBUKTU
MYTHICAL CITY

THRIVING CENTER OF ISLAMIC SCHOLARSHIP

A death in a prominent family draws a crowd of mourners.

ISLAM IN AFRICA

CENTER OF TRADE AND LEARNING

Early in the second century AD, Timbuktu emerged at the intersection of two critical trade arteries—the Saharan caravan routes and the Niger River—in what is now the West African country of Mali. Merchants brought cloth, spices, and salt from places as far afield as Granada, Cairo, and Mecca to trade for gold, ivory, and slaves from the African interior. As its wealth grew, the city erected grand mosques, attracting scholars who formed academies and imported books from throughout the Islamic world. As a result, fragments of the *Arabian Nights,* Moorish love poetry, and Koranic commentaries from Mecca mingled with narratives of court intrigues and military adventures of mighty African kingdoms. As new books arrived, armies of scribes copied elaborate facsimiles for the private libraries of local teachers and their wealthy patrons.

ARMIES OF SCRIBES

MANUSCRIPT COLLECTIONS

Timbuktu's 25,000-student university and its other madrassas served as wellsprings for the spread of Islam throughout Africa from the 13th to 16th centuries. Sacred Muslim texts, in bound editions, were carried great distances to Timbuktu—soon synonymous with the uttermost end of the Earth—to be used by eminent resident scholars from Cairo, Baghdad, Persia, and elsewhere who were in residence in the city. The great teachings of Islam, from astronomy and mathematics to medicine and law, were collected and produced here in several hundred thousand manuscripts. Many of them remain, though they are in precarious condition, to form a priceless written record of African history.

This gold-adorned ancient manuscript is kept in a government library.

1600 to 1800	1800 to 1900	1900 to 1950	1950 to PRESENT

1600 to 1800

■ **1609–1610**
Galileo first observes Earth's moon and four moons of Jupiter with a telescope.

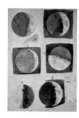

■ **1626**
St. Peter's Basilica is completed in Rome after 120 years of construction.

■ **1716**
The first lighthouse in North America is built, in Boston Harbor.

■ **1752**
After demonstrating the electrical nature of lightning, Benjamin Franklin invents the lightning rod.

■ **1775**
Inventor Alexander Cummings patents the first flushing toilet.

1800 to 1900

■ **1843**
Ada Lovelace and Charles Babbage collaborate on the world's first computer.

■ **1844**
Samuel Morse sends the first telegraph message in the United States.

■ **1867**
Alfred Nobel patents dynamite in Britain.

■ **1876**
Alexander Graham Bell invents the telephone and makes the first long-distance call.

■ **1898**
German chemist Hans von Pechmann synthesizes polyethylene, the world's first plastic.

1900 to 1950

■ **1901**
Italian scientist Guglielmo Marconi makes the first transatlantic radio broadcast.

■ **1904**
German engineer Christian Hülsmeyer patents the first radar system, used to prevent collisions among shipping vessels.

■ **1931**
The Empire State Building in New York City becomes the world's tallest building.

■ **1943**
Jacques Cousteau begins using the Aqua-Lung, which he designed with engineer Émile Gagnan, for underwater diving.

■ **1945**
Americans manufacture, test, and deploy the atom bomb.

1950 to PRESENT

■ **1954**
The first solar cells, converting sunlight to electricity, are developed.

■ **1959**
Unimate #001, the first industrial robot, is deployed in a General Motors engine plant.

■ **1959**
The microchip, key component of computers, is invented.

■ **1989**
The World Wide Web is initiated by British computer scientist Tim Berners-Lee.

■ **2000**
The International Space Station begins operating with a crew.

INNOVATIONS
TIME LINE

6000 to 1500 BC	1500 to 1 BC	AD 1 to 1000	1000 to 1600

■ ca 6000 BC
The world's first known city, Çatalhöyük, is built in Anatolia.

■ ca 3500 BC
Wheeled vehicles are in use in the Middle East.

■ ca 3000 BC
Egyptians have developed a process for making paper from the papyrus plant.

■ ca 2500 BC
The Great Pyramids and the Sphinx are completed in Egypt.

■ ca 2500 BC
Peruvians use a canal system to irrigate crops.

■ ca 1525 BC
Stonehenge is completed in England.

■ ca 1400 BC
Iron weapons are in use by the Hittites of modern-day Turkey.

■ ca 500 BC
The abacus, earliest calculating tool, is in use in China.

■ ca 300 BC
The Maya begin constructing their monumental pyramids in Mexico and Central America.

■ 214 BC
The main section of the Great Wall of China is completed.

■ ca 120 BC
Romans use concrete to create paved streets, aqueducts, and bridges.

■ ca 200
Porcelain is being produced in Han dynasty China.

■ 350
Antioch, in today's Turkey, becomes the first city to have a system of street lighting.

■ ca 600
Chatrang, an early version of chess, is popular in parts of Central Asia.

■ 607
Japan's Horyuji Temple, the world's oldest wooden building, is completed.

■ ca 800
Islamic scientists use the astrolabe for celestial observation.

■ ca 1000
Fireworks, made of a bamboo tube filled with gunpowder, are invented in China.

■ ca 1040
Chinese explorers use magnetic compasses to navigate.

■ ca 1286
In Italy, the first known eyeglasses are manufactured to correct vision.

■ ca 1450
The Inca construct a 20,000-mile-long roadway to unite their empire.

■ 1455
Johannes Gutenberg prints the Bible on a movable type press.

@stevewinterphoto | STEVE WINTER
The Eiffel Tower shines in Paris, France. It was built as the entrance to the 1889 World's Fair.

@coryrichards | CORY RICHARDS
The sun illuminates a misty landscape as it rises over a Buddhist temple in Bagan, Myanmar.

@jimrichardsonng | JIM RICHARDSON
Sheep graze among the Stones of Stenness, a folk stone circle even older than Stonehenge.

@johnstanmeyer | JOHN STANMEYER
The Sher-Dor Madrasah, a 17th-century building in Samarkand, Uzbekistan

Sidi Yahya, a 15th-century mosque assaulted by jihadists in 2012, was repaired and reopened in 2016.

BY MODERN CALCULATIONS, EMPEROR MANSA MUSA WAS WORTH A STAGGERING US$400 BILLION, AFTER ADJUSTING FOR INFLATION.

THE CITY'S FUTURE

PRESERVATION AND RESTORATION

Today, most of Timbuktu's priceless manuscripts are in private hands, where they've been hidden for many years. Thanks to donations from governments and private institutions, three new state-of-the-art libraries have been constructed to collect, restore, and digitize Timbuktu's manuscripts. Three restored mud mosques, among West Africa's oldest, were placed on the UN's World Heritage List, though regional political unrest earned an "under threat" designation.

In West Africa, salt and gold were almost equal in value.

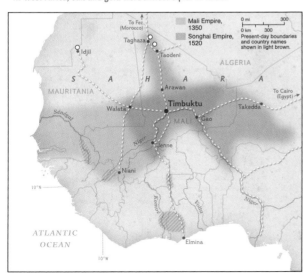

KEY DATES

The History of
TIMBUKTU

■ **CA 1100**
Founded by Tuareg herders as a seasonal camp

■ **1200–1600**
Serves as wellspring for the spread of Islam throughout Africa

■ **1327**
Emperor Mansa Musa returns from Mecca and orders new mosque in Timbuktu.

■ **1495**
Emperor of Songhai has pyramidal Tomb of Askia built.

■ **1593**
Moroccans invade and deport scholars.

■ **1828**
French explorer visits and describes "ill-looking houses" and "profound silence."

■ **1894–1960**
Under French colonial rule

■ **1988**
Added to the UN World Heritage List

■ **1990–2005**
Placed on the List of World Heritage in Danger until major improvements made to preserve three ancient mosques

■ **2012–PRESENT**
Again placed on the List of World Heritage in Danger because of regional armed conflict

MILITARY HISTORY
TIME LINE

1200 to 1 BC

ca 1200 BC
Craftsmen in Mesopotamia perfect iron tools and weapons.

1279–1213 BC
Ramses II rules Egypt, expanding the kingdom through conquest.

ca 800 BC
The Greek city-state of Sparta develops a highly trained military force.

721–705 BC
Under Sargon II, Assyrians conquer new territories and form empire.

480 BC
Xerxes, king of Persia, prepares a massive military force to invade the Greek mainland.

330 BC
Alexander the Great declares himself emperor of Persia.

AD 1 to 1200

66–70
A Jewish rebellion against Roman rule in Judea is the first in a series of clashes lasting decades.

410
Visigoth forces under Alaric sack Rome, leading to fall of Roman Empire.

750
Teotihuacan, the capital of the Maya empire, is abandoned.

ca 1000
The Chinese use explosives in warfare.

1095
Pope Urban II launches the First Crusade, beginning centuries of religious warfare.

1200 to 1500

1211
Genghis Khan leads an army of 50,000 across the Gobi to conquer China.

ca 1428
The Aztec reach the height of their power in Mesoamerica.

1453
Turkish forces led by Mehmed II seize Constantinople and rename it Istanbul, capital of Ottoman Empire.

1455
The War of the Roses begins in England between the Lancasters and the Yorks.

1487–1505
Under the Hongzhi emperor, much of the Ming-era Great Wall of China is constructed.

1500 to 1800

1588
The Spanish Armada attempts to invade England but is defeated.

1618–1648
The Thirty Years' War rages in central Europe, primarily in Germany.

1683
The Ottomans lose a last siege against Vienna and begin withdrawing from Europe.

1754
The French and Indian War breaks out in North America between Britain and France.

1775
The American Revolution begins.

JOIN, or DIE.

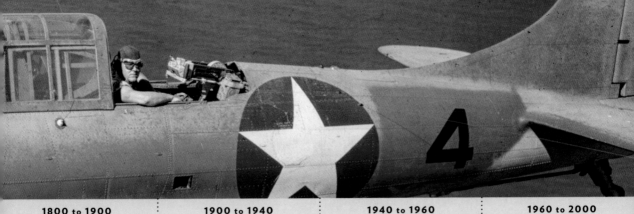

| **1800 to 1900** | **1900 to 1940** | **1940 to 1960** | **1960 to 2000** |

1800 to 1900

■ **1813–1890**
Warfare perpetuates between Native Americans and U.S. military troops in the American West.

■ **1815**
Britain's Duke of Wellington defeats Napoleon at the Battle of Waterloo, ending the Napoleonic Wars between France and Britain.

■ **1821**
Greece declares independence from the Ottoman Empire.

■ **1898**
The United States wins the Spanish-American War, ending Spanish colonial rule in North America.

■ **1899**
The Boer War breaks out between Afrikaners and the British in South Africa.

1900 to 1940

■ **1914**
World War I begins after Archduke Franz Ferdinand of Austria is assassinated.

■ **1918**
World War I ends when an armistice is signed between the Allies and Germany.

■ **1923**
The Pan-American treaty is signed to prevent conflicts between nations.

■ **1926**
Emperor Hirohito takes over the Japanese throne.

■ **1939**
Germany invades Poland; Britain and France declare war on Germany, beginning World War II.

1940 to 1960

■ **1941**
Japan bombs Pearl Harbor, and the United States joins the Allies in World War II.

■ **1944**
On June 6, D-Day, Allied troops land on France's Normandy beach, invading Europe.

■ **1945**
World War II ends after first Germany and then Japan both surrender.

■ **1950**
North Korea invades South Korea, initiating the Korean War.

■ **1954**
Defeat by North Vietnam at Dien Bien Phu marks the end of France's rule in Indochina.

1960 to 2000

■ **1961–1975**
U.S. involvement in Vietnam escalates, troop presence peaking in 1969.

■ **1967**
In the Six-Day War, Israel fights Arab forces and takes possession of the Gaza Strip, West Bank, Golan Heights, and Sinai Peninsula.

■ **1980**
Iraq's Saddam Hussein declares war on Iran, beginning an eight-year-long war.

■ **1991**
U.S.-led Operation Desert Storm initiates the Persian Gulf War, responding to Iraq's occupation of Kuwait.

■ **1994**
Tribal conflict in Rwanda results in mass killing of hundreds of thousands of Tutsis and flight of millions of refugees, primarily Hutus.

WAR IN OUR
TIMES

THE EVOLUTION OF WEAPONS OF WAR

Strategies of war often pivot on newly available technologies, such as chemical weapons amid trenches in WWI and coordinated ground, naval, and air attacks in both theaters of WWII. By the late 20th century, the U.S. military was deploying surveillance drones (remotely piloted aerial systems). Unmanned weaponized drones soon followed and have been key in efforts against non-state actors such as al Qaeda and ISIS, which often embed militants among civilians in cities. Future conflicts will use multiple stealth vehicles, weapons systems, and cyberweapons.

AT PRESENT, OVER 65 MILLION PEOPLE HAVE HAD TO FLEE THEIR HOMES BECAUSE OF CONFLICTS—15 MILLION MORE THAN WERE DISPLACED AT THE CONCLUSION OF WORLD WAR II.

Since civil war broke out in 2011, hundreds of thousands of Syrians have been killed.

KEEPING THE PEACE

Since its founding in 1948, the United Nations has operated 71 peacekeeping missions—almost two-thirds of those in the last 30 years. Today, over 110,000 peacekeepers are part of more than a dozen ongoing missions.

MAY 1948, MIDDLE EAST

The UN's first and longest-running peacekeeping mission continues to promote stability to the Middle East.

JANUARY 1949, INDIA AND PAKISTAN

This mission has been in place for decades to observe the cease-fire in the disputed region of Kashmir.

MARCH 1964, CYPRUS

With no political settlement between the Greek and Turkish communities, this mission maintains buffer zones, among other responsibilities.

MAY 1974, SYRIA

Originally in place to maintain the cease-fire between Israeli and Syrian forces, peacekeepers seek to de-escalate armed conflicts in the area.

MARCH 1978, LEBANON

Started to confirm Israel's withdrawal from Lebanon, the mission continues to monitor hostilities and ensure humanitarian access to civilians.

APRIL 1991, WESTERN SAHARA

This mission aims to help the people of Western Sahara choose independence or integration with Morocco.

JUNE 1999, KOSOVO

Having helped this republic (claimed by Serbia) gain autonomy, the mission now provides security and stability.

JULY 2007, DARFUR

Along with the African Union, this mission is in place to protect civilians, facilitate humanitarian aid, and help the political process.

JULY 2010, DEMOCRATIC REPUBLIC OF THE CONGO

Armed peacekeepers are deployed to protect civilians under imminent threat of physical violence and to support stabilization efforts.

JUNE 2011, ABYEI

The armed mission in this volatile region, claimed by Sudan and South Sudan, monitors the border, facilitates delivery of aid, and protects civilians.

JULY 2011, SOUTH SUDAN

In South Sudan, the world's newest country, peacekeepers work to protect civilians, reduce hostilities, and deliver humanitarian assistance.

APRIL 2013, MALI

Alongside Mali's transitional authorities, this mission focuses on civilian security and the reestablishment of government after regional conflicts.

APRIL 2014, CENTRAL AFRICAN REPUBLIC

Created amid political crisis, this mission is tasked with protecting civilians and supporting transition processes.

OCTOBER 2017, HAITI

This nonmilitary mission, which follows successful elections, helps develop the National Police, strengthen justice institutions, and protect human rights.

An estimated 2.5 million people lost their lives during the Korean War.

KEY DATES

Events and Politics in
NORTH KOREA

■ **1945**
After Japanese occupation, U.S. holds the south and Soviets hold the north.

■ **1948**
Kim Il Sung establishes dictatorship of Democratic People's Republic of Korea.

■ **1950**
War begins, two years after South declares independence.

■ **1985**
North Korea joins the nuclear Non-proliferation Treaty, which leads to 1992 no-nukes agreement with South Korea.

■ **1994**
Kim Jong Il assumes duties after father's death, agrees not to create weapons-grade plutonium.

■ **1996**
Famine spreads after extensive flooding; Jong Il stops honoring 1953 armistice.

■ **2002**
Admits to developing nuclear weapons

■ **2011**
Kim Jong Un assumes duties after father's death.

■ **2018**
North and South Korean leaders hold a summit.

UNITED STATES
TIME LINE

1500 to 1650	1650 to 1770	1770 to 1800	1800 to 1850

1587

English colonists settle briefly at Roanoke Island.

1607

Capt. John Smith founds the Jamestown settlement on behalf of England.

1619

The Virginia Assembly, the oldest governing body in the modern United States, first meets.

1620

The *Mayflower* lands in modern-day Massachusetts.

1625–1643

The colonies of New Hampshire, Massachusetts, Rhode Island, Connecticut, Maryland, and Delaware are established.

1636

Harvard College is founded.

1692

The Salem witch trials occur in Massachusetts.

1720s–1740s

A religious revival, the Great Awakening, sweeps through the British colonies.

1754

The French and Indian War breaks out between Britain and France.

1763

Chief Pontiac leads a Native American rebellion against British settlers near Detroit.

1763–1767

Surveyors Charles Mason and Jeremiah Dixon lay out the boundary between Pennsylvania, Maryland, and Delaware.

1775

Fighting at Lexington and Concord begins the American Revolution; the next year, the Continental Congress adopts the Declaration of Independence.

1781

At the Battle of Yorktown, American and French forces defeat the British Army.

1783

By the Treaty of Paris, Britain accepts American independence.

1789

George Washington becomes the first president of the United States of America.

1800

Washington, D.C., becomes the seat of the U.S. government.

1803

Napoleon sells the lands between the Mississippi River and the Rocky Mountains to the U.S. for $15 million in the Louisiana Purchase.

1812–1814

The War of 1812 is fought between the U.S. and the British; British forces burn down the White House.

1825

The Erie Canal opens, allowing boats to travel from the Great Lakes to the Atlantic.

1830s

The Cherokee, Chickasaw, Choctaw, Creek, and Seminole tribes are forced west on the Trail of Tears.

1841

The first wagon trains to cross the Rocky Mountains arrive in California.

1850 to 1900

■ 1850
Harriet Tubman returns to Maryland after escaping from slavery.

■ 1857
The Dred Scott decision makes the Missouri Compromise unconstitutional, increasing tension over slavery between the North and the South.

■ 1861
The American Civil War begins when Confederates fire on Fort Sumter.

■ 1863
President Abraham Lincoln signs the Emancipation Proclamation, freeing slaves in the Confederate states.

■ 1865
Robert E. Lee surrenders at Appomattox Court House, ending the Civil War.

1900 to 1940

■ 1903
Orville and Wilbur Wright fly a powered airplane at Kitty Hawk, North Carolina.

■ 1908
Teddy Roosevelt undertakes the first inventories of public lands and their resources in the United States.

■ 1917
The U.S. enters World War I.

■ 1920
The 19th Amendment gives women the right to vote.

■ 1929
The Wall Street stock market crash signals the beginning of the Great Depression.

1940 to 1970

■ 1941
Japanese planes bomb the American base at Pearl Harbor; the following day the U.S. joins the Allies in World War II.

■ 1945
The U.S. drops atomic bombs on Hiroshima and Nagasaki; World War II ends soon after.

■ 1963
President John F. Kennedy is assassinated in Dallas, Texas.

■ 1968
Martin Luther King, Jr., is assassinated in Memphis, Tennessee.

■ 1969
Apollo 11 lands the first men on the moon.

1970 to PRESENT

■ 1973
The U.S. and South Vietnam sign a cease-fire agreement with North Vietnam and the last U.S. troops are withdrawn.

■ 1974
The Watergate scandal forces Richard Nixon to resign.

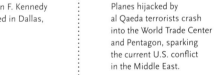

■ 2001
Planes hijacked by al Qaeda terrorists crash into the World Trade Center and Pentagon, sparking the current U.S. conflict in the Middle East.

■ 2008
Barack Obama is the first African American to be elected president of the United States.

JAMESTOWN
THIS LAND IS WHOSE LAND?

UNSETTLING THE LANDSCAPE

The colonists' arrival at Jamestown over 400 years ago unleashed changes that profoundly transformed the environment, shaping the American landscape as we know it. Within 60 years of their first landing in 1607, English settlers pushed the Indians off the most fertile land. By then, only about 2,000 of the approximately 15,000 Indians who were present in the region when settlers arrived still remained.

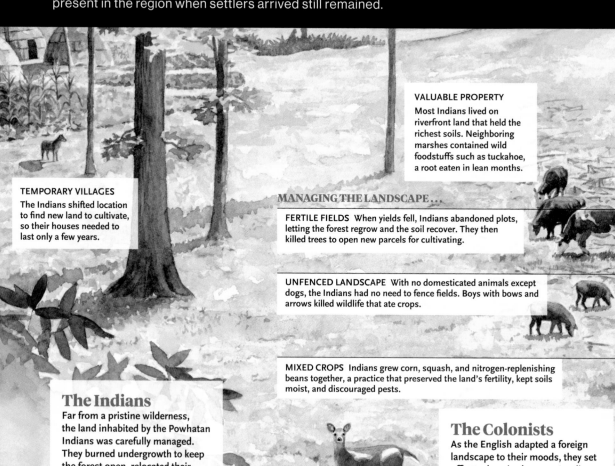

VALUABLE PROPERTY
Most Indians lived on riverfront land that held the richest soils. Neighboring marshes contained wild foodstuffs such as tuckahoe, a root eaten in lean months.

TEMPORARY VILLAGES
The Indians shifted location to find new land to cultivate, so their houses needed to last only a few years.

MANAGING THE LANDSCAPE . . .

FERTILE FIELDS When yields fell, Indians abandoned plots, letting the forest regrow and the soil recover. They then killed trees to open new parcels for cultivating.

UNFENCED LANDSCAPE With no domesticated animals except dogs, the Indians had no need to fence fields. Boys with bows and arrows killed wildlife that ate crops.

MIXED CROPS Indians grew corn, squash, and nitrogen-replenishing beans together, a practice that preserved the land's fertility, kept soils moist, and discouraged pests.

The Indians
Far from a pristine wilderness, the land inhabited by the Powhatan Indians was carefully managed. They burned undergrowth to keep the forest open, relocated their villages when crops depleted soils, and ranged widely to fish, hunt, and gather all they needed, moving with the seasons.

The Colonists
As the English adapted a foreign landscape to their moods, they set off cataclysmic changes. An alien presence themselves, they brought in animals, insects, and plants that would literally change the ground beneath the Indians' feet.

TEXTBOOKS OFTEN IMPLY THAT COLONISTS SETTLED PREVIOUSLY UNINHABITED LAND. IN FACT, THE SHIPS LANDED IN A SMALL BUT RAPIDLY EXPANDING INDIAN EMPIRE CALLED TSENACOMOCO.

Map labels:
Kent Island
MARYLAND
St. Marys City
VIRGINIA
Potomac
Chesapeake Bay
The Falls
ATLANTIC OCEAN
Berkeley Hundred
Jamestown
James
Cape Charles
Cape Henry

• Indian village
■ European settlement
■ European-occupied area

0 mi 20
0 km 20

SMALLER, THICKER FOREST
With metal axes, colonists cleared larger areas of woods than the Indians could with stone tools. No longer burned regularly, the remaining forest quickly became overgrown.

STAKING CLAIMS
Indians believed they "owned" plots only as long as they tilled them, but settlers took permanent possession of land. With houses and fences, they re-created the English landscape.

...OR HARNESSING THE LAND

SPENT SOIL When tobacco exhausted the land, colonists planted corn for a few years. They then moved on to unfarmed areas but kept the spent land in use for grazing.

FENCED PLOTS Colonists fenced their fields rather than their livestock, leaving imported cattle and pigs free to trample fields and eat Indian crops and wild edibles.

A CASH CROP Once it proved profitable, tobacco was planted over huge stretches of land. The colonists also brought in nonnative fruit trees and grapevines.

FIRST LADIES

MAKING THE MOST OF THEIR TIME IN THE WHITE HOUSE

For more than 230 years, first ladies have had an unofficial title and an important yet undefined role—falling somewhere between dinner host and presidential adviser. It remains to be seen what title will be given to the spouse of the first woman president.

Madison held crowded White House socials called "squeezes."

DOLLEY MADISON

AN ORCHESTRATOR, NOT AN OBSERVER

The title of first lady was first bestowed on Dolley Payne Todd Madison (1768–1849), who was a young widow when she wed James Madison. Her husband sought her counsel on matters of importance, though she had little formal education, and she was admired and celebrated by Washington society, where she was a power broker, not simply a host. She is commonly known today for saving a portrait of George Washington from British troops in 1814, but her other accomplishments include raising funds for Meriwether Lewis and George Rogers Clark's expeditions. On returning to the city after her husband's death, she was given the rare standing invitation to observe congressional debate from a seat on the House floor.

CAROLINE HARRISON

THE FIRST TO SPEAK IN HER OWN VOICE

President Benjamin and Caroline Lavinia Scott Harrison (1832–1892) moved their family, spanning four generations, into the White House in 1889. A music teacher and amateur painter, the first lady lobbied, unsuccessfully, for renovations that would have included an art gallery. She did, however, preside over the installation of electricity and other necessary upgrades to the rodent-infested residence. She championed and raised funds for organizations such as the Johns Hopkins University Medical School, which pledged to accept women as students, and the newly founded National Society Daughters of the American Revolution, before which she delivered a speech she had written—the first for a sitting president's wife.

At 60, Harrison died, in the White House, of tuberculosis.

Roosevelt's daily syndicated newspaper column ran for 27 years.

ELEANOR ROOSEVELT, CALLED THE "FIRST LADY OF THE WORLD," TRAVELED OVER 40,000 MILES IN HER FIRST YEAR AS FIRST LADY.

ELEANOR ROOSEVELT

INTELLIGENCE, INTEGRITY, EMPATHY

Anna Eleanor Roosevelt (1884–1962) was a powerful public advocate for children, women, and African Americans. President Franklin Roosevelt was elected to four terms, making her the longest-serving first lady. But for decades before that, she worked tirelessly for social reform and was regarded as his "political helpmate," especially after his polio diagnosis in 1921. She elevated the gravitas of first ladies and leveraged media access with lectures, a column, and radio appearances. In 1945, she was named as a delegate to the United Nations by President Harry Truman; President John Kennedy reappointed her. As chair of the UN Human Rights Commission, she helped create the Universal Declaration of Human Rights.

POP!

FILMS WITH FIRST LADIES

- Blythe Danner as Martha Jefferson in *1776* (1972)
- Diana Scarwid as Bess Truman in *Truman* (1995)
- Laura Linney as Abigail Adams in *John Adams* (2008)
- Sally Field as Mary Todd Lincoln in *Lincoln* (2012)
- Jane Fonda as Nancy Reagan in *The Butler* (2013)

Obama is one of three first ladies to have a graduate degree.

MICHELLE OBAMA

SUPPORTING FAMILIES AND COMMUNITIES

The first African-American first lady, Michelle LaVaughn Robinson Obama (b. 1964), grew up in humble circumstances but went on to get an Ivy League education. After working in corporate law, where she met her husband, Barack Obama, she left for a career in public service and community engagement. While first lady, she emphasized her role as a mother: Her daughters were just 10 and 7 years old when they moved into the White House. Her policy priorities—poverty, healthy eating and fitness, public education, and military families— reflect a parent's concerns. As first lady, she sought to address the experience of Americans of color, noting that, "I wake up every morning in a house that was built by slaves."

THE U.S. CONSTITUTION

THE FOUNDATION OF DEMOCRACY HERE AND ABROAD

In May 1787, state delegates gathered to revise the Articles of Confederation, which had been drawn up shortly after securing independence from England. The remarkable document that emerged after months of debate shaped not only the United States, but also countries around the world. Many issues over which the founders wrestled—such as the right balance between federal power and states' rights—are still debated today, as is the question of how to interpret the Constitution in our present context.

JOHN RUTLEDGE, SOUTH CAROLINA

OLIVER ELLSWORTH, CONNECTICUT

ELBRIDGE GERRY, MASSACHUSETTS

GEORGE WASHINGTON, VIRGINIA

JAMES MADISON, VIRGINIA

BENJAMIN FRANKLIN, PENNSYLVANI

In this mural by Barry Faulkner, Alexander Hamilton is portrayed with a drawn sword and in military garb to signify the coming War of 1812.

> ## " WHAT WAS REVOLUTIONARY WHEN IT WAS WRITTEN, AND WHAT CONTINUES TO INSPIRE THE WORLD TODAY, IS THAT THE CONSTITUTION PUT GOVERNANCE IN THE HANDS OF THE PEOPLE."
>
> —SANDRA DAY O'CONNOR,
> RETIRED SUPREME COURT JUSTICE

We the People

Article 1

No other governing document is as short as the Constitution.

LUTHER MARTIN, MARYLAND

GOUVERNEUR MORRIS, PENNSYLVANIA

ABRAHAM BALDWIN, GEORGIA

WILLIAM PATERSON, NEW JERSEY

ALEXANDER HAMILTON, NEW YORK

GEORGE READ, DELAWARE

KEY DATES

The Steps to Crafting a
CONSTITUTION

■ **MAY 1787**
55 men from 12 states meet in Philadelphia to revise Articles of Confederation.

■ **SEPTEMBER 17, 1787**
39 delegates sign the Constitution and send it to the states for ratification.

■ **DECEMBER 7, 1787**
Delaware becomes the first state to ratify the Constitution, with unanimous vote.

■ **MARCH 4, 1789**
First Congress convenes in New York City.

■ **SEPTEMBER 25, 1789**
First Congress adopts Bill of Rights and sends it to the states for ratification.

■ **DECEMBER 15, 1791**
With Virginia's ratification, the Bill of Rights is added to the Constitution.

STARS AND STRIPES
THROUGH THE CENTURIES

NO COUNTRY HAS CHANGED ITS FLAG AS MUCH AS THE UNITED STATES

The Continental Colors (below, top left) represented the colonies during the early years of the American Revolution. Its British Union Jack, which signified loyalty to the crown, was replaced on June 14, 1777, by a flag designed by New Jersey Congressman Francis Hopkinson to include 13 stars for the 13 colonies, "representing a new constellation," as was said at the time. In 1817 Congressman Peter Wendover of New York wrote the current flag law, which retains 13 stripes permanently but adds stars as new states join the union. The original "Star-Spangled Banner," which inspired Francis Scott Key during the War of 1812 to write what became our national anthem, is elegantly preserved at the Smithsonian's National Museum of American History in Washington, D.C.

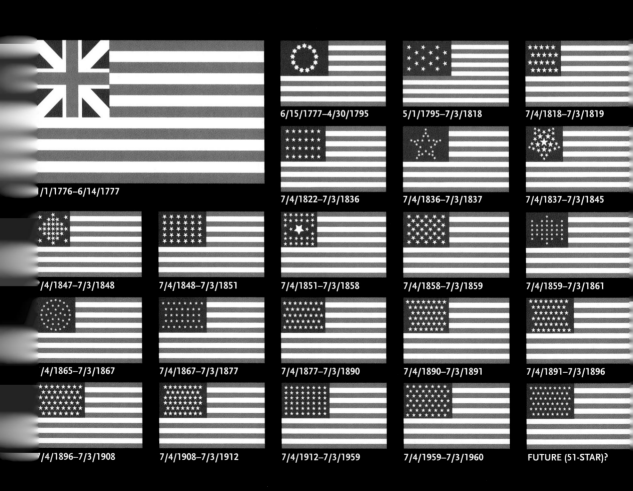

1/1/1776–6/14/1777

6/15/1777–4/30/1795

5/1/1795–7/3/1818

7/4/1818–7/3/1819

7/4/1822–7/3/1836

7/4/1836–7/3/1837

7/4/1837–7/3/1845

7/4/1847–7/3/1848

7/4/1848–7/3/1851

7/4/1851–7/3/1858

7/4/1858–7/3/1859

7/4/1859–7/3/1861

7/4/1865–7/3/1867

7/4/1867–7/3/1877

7/4/1877–7/3/1890

7/4/1890–7/3/1891

7/4/1891–7/3/1896

7/4/1896–7/3/1908

7/4/1908–7/3/1912

7/4/1912–7/3/1959

7/4/1959–7/3/1960

FUTURE (51-STAR)?

"THIS FLAG, WHICH WE HONOR AND UNDER WHICH WE SERVE, IS THE EMBLEM OF OUR UNITY, OUR POWER, OUR THOUGHT AND PURPOSE AS A NATION. IT HAS NO OTHER CHARACTER THAN THAT WHICH WE GIVE IT FROM GENERATION TO GENERATION."

—PRESIDENT WOODROW WILSON, 1917

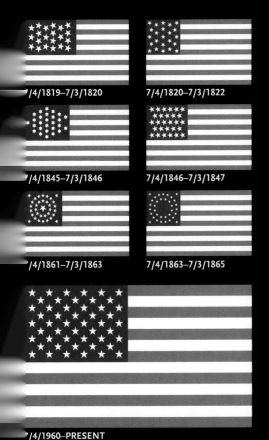

/4/1819–7/3/1820   7/4/1820–7/3/1822

/4/1845–7/3/1846   7/4/1846–7/3/1847

/4/1861–7/3/1863   7/4/1863–7/3/1865

/4/1960–PRESENT

The Evolution of the
U.S. FLAG

1776
The Grand Union Flag is replaced by the first true American flag, said to have been sewn by Betsy Ross.

1779
According to tradition, with stars now in rows, the Serapis flag or John Paul Jones flag flew through the War of 1812.

1821
Missouri joined the Union as the 24th state, and the 24-star flag lasted for 14 years and through three presidencies.

1837
Many versions of a Great Star Flag, with a star made of stars, flew in the 19th century.

1847
When Iowa joined the United States, it was time to design a 29-star flag. It lasted only one year.

1863
During the Civil War, the 34 stars were arranged in several designs: rows, circles, stars, even a flower.

1876
A centennial flag arranged 80 stars to spell out the numerals 1776 and 1876.

1892
The Pledge of Allegiance, written by Francis Bellamy, first appears in a magazine called *The Youth's Companion*.

1912
President Howard Taft signs an executive order specifying proportions and design of the U.S. flag.

1960
The addition of Alaska and Hawaii gives the U.S. flag the design we know today, with 50 stars for 50 states and 13 stripes for the 13 original colonies.

FLAGS OF THE
UNITED STATES

ALABAMA
Became a state in 1819
A simple design, crimson cross
on a field of white; until 1987 it could
be either square or rectangular.

ALASKA
Became a state in 1959
Against the blue of sea and sky,
the Big Dipper and Polaris,
signifying Alaska's northernmost position;
designed by a 13-year-old Alaskan.

ARIZONA
Became a state in 1912
A copper star, signifying Arizona's
industry, on a blue field in the fa
a setting sun with 13 rays
for the original colonies.

ARKANSAS
Became a state in 1836
Diamond signifies its status
as the sole diamond-producing state;
ring of 25 stars since it was
the 25th state to join the union.

CALIFORNIA
Became a state in 1850
Grizzly bear, also the state animal,
on red and white for bravery and purity;
first flown by settlers resisting
Mexican rule in 1846.

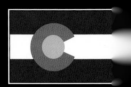

COLORADO
Became a state in 1876
White for snow-covered mountair
for sunshine, red for red soi
blue for clear blue skies,
and a C for the state's name

CONNECTICUT
Became a state in 1788
Three fruiting grapevines and
the state motto, "*Qui transtulit sustinet*
—He who transplanted still sustains."

DELAWARE
Became a state in 1787
Coat of arms with a ship, farmer,
militiaman, and ox; below, the date
when Delaware ratified the Constitution
and became the first state.

FLORIDA
Became a state in 1845
Red cross on white, in the cer
the state seal: Seminole wom
palmetto pine, and steambo
in nearby water.

GEORGIA
Became a state in 1788
Thick red and white stripes,
a blue square on which 13 stars
encircle the state seal; three pillars
represent three branches of government.

HAWAII
Became a state in 1959
Eight horizontal stripes representing
the eight major islands; a Union Jack
in the upper left, reflecting past
British rule.

IDAHO
Became a state in 1890
A robed woman represents lib
and justice; a miner holds a
and shovel; wheat sheaves and co
represent plentiful harvest

ILLINOIS
Became a state in 1818
State seal centered on white
[inc]ludes bald eagle holding banner
[w]ith motto, "State Sovereignty,
National Union."

INDIANA
Became a state in 1816
Torch of enlightenment circled
by stars: 13 for the first states,
five for the next, and a large one
for Indiana, 19th state.

IOWA
Became a state in 1846
An eagle flies amid red, whit[e]
and blue, carrying a banner
"Our liberties we prize an[d]
our rights we will maintain."

KANSAS
Became a state in 1861
[A] sunflower atop the state seal,
scenes of farming, a wagon train,
[Nati]ve Americans, buffalo, steamboat,
and the rising sun.

KENTUCKY
Became a state in 1792
A pioneer and a statesman
shake hands, surrounded
by the motto "United we stand,
divided we fall."

LOUISIANA
Became a state in 1812
White pelican nurtures her
nestling young with her own blo[od]
beneath them, the motto
"Union Justice Confidence."

MAINE
Became a state in 1820
[F]armer and sailor flank a crest
[w]ith an evergreen and a moose;
[abov]e, the North Star atop the motto
"Dirigo—I lead."

MARYLAND
Became a state in 1788
Checkerboard of two family arms:
Calvert, state founders, and Crossland,
mother of George Calvert,
the first Lord Baltimore.

MASSACHUSETTS
Became a state in 1788
Native American holds bow an[d]
arrow pointing down, symbolizing p[eace]
star at his shoulder means this w[as]
one of the first 13 states.

MICHIGAN
Became a state in 1837
[Mo]ose, elk, and bald eagle surround
[cre]st with explorer at water's edge,
[the] sun rising, topped with word
"Tuebor—I will defend."

MINNESOTA
Became a state in 1858
Native American and farmer,
tree stump for timber industry,
waterfall for wilderness.
"L'Etoile du Nord—the North Star State."

MISSISSIPPI
Became a state in 1817
In upper left, square canton
containing 13 stars for 13 colonie[s]
three broad stripes in red,
white, and blue.

MISSOURI

Became a state in 1821

...ars circle grizzlies clasping seal ...American eagle, crescent moon, and grizzly within; above, ...other 24 stars, since 24th state.

MONTANA

Became a state in 1889

Mountains, cliffs, trees, and river represent the landscape; tools represent farming and mining, as does motto: *"Oro y plata—gold and silver."*

NEBRASKA

Became a state in 1867

On blue, state seal with blacksmith in foreground, steam... and train in background, farm and homestead in betwee...

NEVADA

Became a state in 1864

...ht blue and in corner, silver star, ...of sagebrush, with banner reading ...attle Born," since state entered union during Civil War.

NEW HAMPSHIRE

Became a state in 1788

On blue field, seal portraying frigate *Raleigh*, one of the first American Revolutionary warships, built in Portsmouth.

NEW JERSEY

Became a state in 1787

On a buff background, seal inclu... plows for agriculture, helme... for courage, and figures of Libe... and Ceres, harvest goddess...

NEW MEXICO

Became a state in 1912

Red symbol for the sun, sacred to the Zia Indians, ...n a bright yellow background.

NEW YORK

Became a state in 1788

On blue, the seal portrays ships of commerce flanked by the figures of Liberty and Justice. Below, the motto *"Excelsior—ever upward."*

NORTH CAROLINA

Became a state in 1789

Broad stripes—top red, bottom wh... alongside a blue bar with "NC... a star, and two key dates as... the colony declared independen...

NORTH DAKOTA

Became a state in 1889

...ald eagle, wings spread, holds ...e branch and arrows in its talons; ...stars for 13 colonies spread out into sun rays.

OHIO

Became a state in 1803

Swallowtail burgee with red and white stripes, blue triangle with 17 stars, since the 17th state to join the Union.

OKLAHOMA

Became a state in 1907

An Osage warrior's rawhide shield hung with eagle feather... across which sit an olive branc... and a peace pipe.

OREGON

Became a state in 1859

...lue flag with yellow insignia. ...On front, state seal including ...on train, ships, and setting sun. ...back, the state animal: a beaver.

PENNSYLVANIA

Became a state in 1787

An eagle and two horses surround a crest with a ship, a plow, and wheat sheaves; below, the motto "Virtue Liberty and Independence."

RHODE ISLAND

Became a state in 1790

White flag bearing a golden anchor, circled by 13 gold sta... and beneath it a blue banne... with the simple motto "Hope...

SOUTH CAROLINA
Became a state in 1788
...escent, from local Revolutionary
...ar uniforms, and a palmetto
...ree—white designs against
deep blue.

SOUTH DAKOTA
Became a state in 1889
Farmer, livestock, factory,
and steamboat on the state seal,
circled by yellow sun rays
on a field of bright blue.

TENNESSEE
Became a state in 1796
A circle containing three white s...
representing East, Middle,
and West, all against red,
with blue and white edge.

TEXAS
Became a state in 1845
The famous "Lone Star"
...hite against a blue background
...ith broad horizontal panels
of white and red.

UTAH
Became a state in 1896
Beehive, symbol of industry,
surrounded by U.S. flags and a spread eagle.
Two dates: 1847, Mormons arrived,
and 1896, statehood.

VERMONT
Became a state in 1791
A field with sheaves, pine,
and cow stretches back to mount...
pine boughs on either side,
antlered buck atop.

VIRGINIA
Became a state in 1788
...nale Virtus (Virtue) stands over
...allen man, his crown toppled;
..., the motto *"Sic semper tyrannis—*
Thus always to tyrants."

WASHINGTON
Became a state in 1889
Portrait of George Washington
circled by yellow on a field of green—
the only U.S. flag with a
historical figure on it.

WEST VIRGINIA
Became a state in 1863
A farmer and a miner lean agai...
a rock inscribed with the dat...
of gaining statehood;
rhododendrons drape the sea...

WISCONSIN
Became a state in 1848
Against a bright blue background,
sailor and miner dominate the state seal,
topped by a badger
and the motto "Forward."

WYOMING
Became a state in 1890
State seal in blue against
the silhouette of a bison in white,
background blue with red,
and white borders top and bottom.

> **" I SALUTE THE FLAG OF THE STATE OF
> NEW MEXICO, THE ZIA SYMBOL OF PERFECT
> FRIENDSHIP AMONG UNITED CULTURES."**

—OFFICIAL PLEDGE TO NEW MEXICO'S FLAG

TERRITORIES OF THE UNITED STATES

AMERICAN SAMOA
Became a U.S. territory in 1900
Blue with red-edged white triangle;
bald eagle gripping native symbols of authority:
war club and coconut fiber whisk.

GUAM
Became a U.S. territory in 1898
Dark blue flag with red border; central emblem
shaped like native sling stone, encloses palm tr
outrigger canoe, and beach.

PUERTO RICO
Became a U.S. territory in 1898
Five bands of red and white; triangle of blue,
for sky and waters, with central white star,
which symbolizes Puerto Rico.

NORTHERN MARIANA ISLANDS
Became a U.S. territory in 1976
Blue flag containing gray foundation stones,
white star, and floral head wreath
representing native Chamorro culture.

U.S. INTEREST IN PACIFIC ISLANDS DATES BACK TO THE 1856 GUANO ISLANDS ACT, BY WHICH CONGRESS CLAIMED RIGHTS TO UNINHABITED ISLANDS IN ORDER TO MINE GUANO— BIRD DROPPINGS—FOR GUNPOWDER AND FERTILIZER.

U.S. VIRGIN ISLANDS
Became a U.S. territory in 1917
On field of white, yellow eagle holds olive
branch and arrows; modified U.S. coat of arm
in center, initials "V" and "I" on either side.

NOT QUITE STATES

BUT STILL PART OF THE U.S.

The U.S. Constitution gives Congress the power to incorporate new federal territories, organize them, and admit them as new states. The most recent territories to become states were Alaska and Hawaii, in 1959. Present-day U.S. territories range from uninhabited specks in the Pacific Ocean to the organized Caribbean island of Puerto Rico. Some of the small islands in the Pacific were once military bases, but many now function as wildlife refuges. American Samoa, Puerto Rico, and the Northern Mariana Islands all possess their own constitutions. The people living in these territories are U.S. citizens, but they are not allowed to vote in presidential elections.

DISTRICT OF COLUMBIA

NATION'S CAPITAL

"End Taxation Without Representation" reads the license plates of those who live in the District of Columbia, created in 1790 as a federal district for the new nation's capital city. Residents of the District have voted in presidential elections since 1964, but they do not have any representatives in Congress. Since the 1970s, many have been pushing for D.C. statehood.

The Other U.S.
TERRITORIES

■ **BAKER ISLAND**
A treeless atoll midway between Hawaii and Australia, this is a home to sea turtles and a migratory resting point for numerous bird species.

■ **HOWLAND ISLAND**
This is famous as the island toward which Amelia Earhart was flying when she disappeared.

■ **JARVIS ISLAND**
This national wildlife refuge, found just 22 miles south of the Equator, was expanded in 2009 to include about 430,000 submerged acres around it.

■ **JOHNSTON ATOLL**
Named a federal bird refuge in 1926, the atoll was later used as a nuclear test and chemical weapons storage site, prompting recent cleanup efforts.

■ **KINGMAN REEF**
Now a national wildlife refuge, this triangle of coral was once called Danger Reef, because it is treacherous for vessels.

■ **MIDWAY ISLANDS**
The position of these islands and an atoll fringe—equidistant from North America and Asia—made them a Pacific battleground during World War II.

■ **NAVASSA ISLAND**
Off the west coast of Haiti, this has hosted eight native species of reptile, although some may now be extinct.

■ **PALMYRA ATOLL**
A national wildlife refuge since 2001, its protection efforts are a partnership between U.S. and the Nature Conservancy.

■ **WAKE ISLAND**
Life-and-death battles were fought here during WWII, and its airfield is a refueling station.

FURTHER

NO LONGER FORBIDDEN

Past meets future in the heart of Beijing, where Gu Gong—the Forbidden City—stands, symbol of five centuries of imperial rule. In this palace lived the heavenly emperor, his quarters so private and protected that a wide moat and a 32-foot wall were built around them. Visitors enter the Forbidden City from Tian'anmen Square and can only begin to experience its 980 buildings and 9,999 rooms, filled with artifacts of the past. Just beyond, a 21st-century city, home to more than 20 million, reaches to the sky.

In Beijing, skyscrapers soar a short distance from the ancient imperial palace.

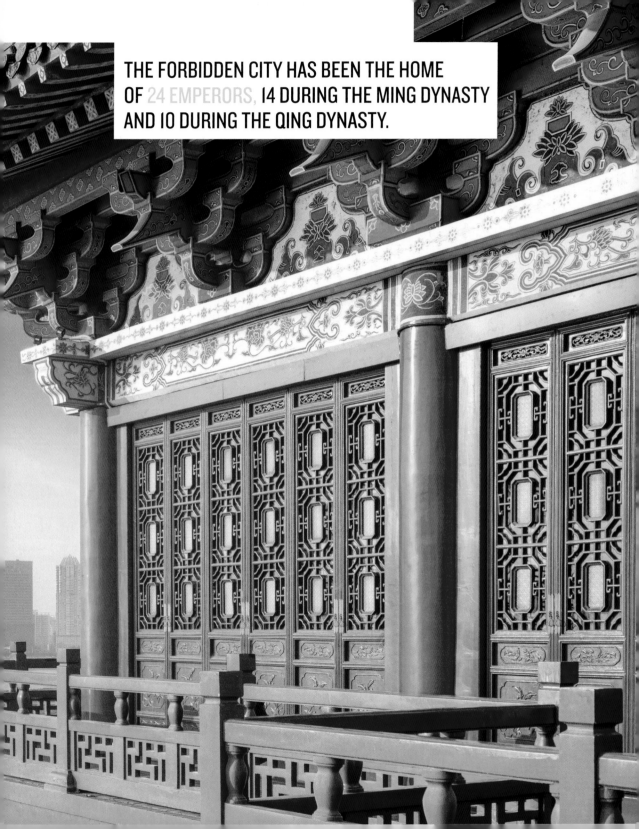

THE FORBIDDEN CITY HAS BEEN THE HOME OF 24 EMPERORS, 14 DURING THE MING DYNASTY AND 10 DURING THE QING DYNASTY.

OUR
WORLD

WORLD VIEWS | CONTINENTS & OCEANS

Clouds blanket the planet as seen from the International Space Station.

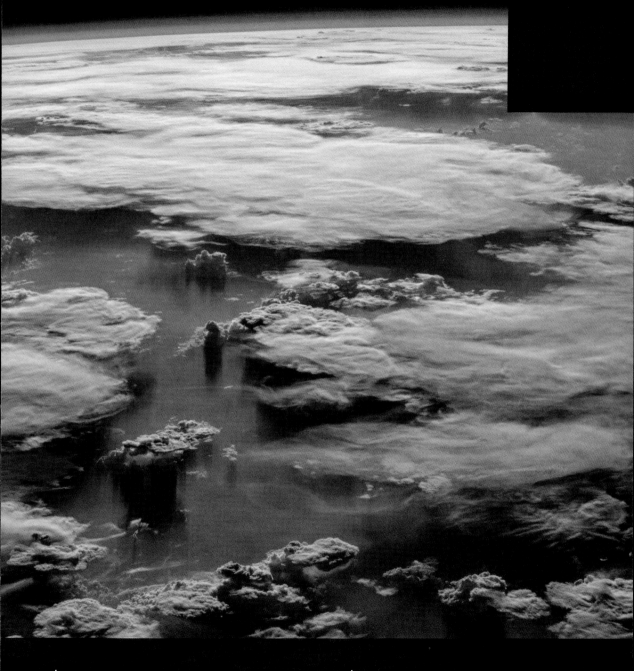

COUNTRIES OF THE WORLD | THE FUTURE

QUIZ
MASTER

Geographical Wizard? Places to know and forces to understand—geography sits at the heart of all knowledge. Here are maps galore, but they can only hint at the diversity of features that make Earth such a fascinating place to study.

—CARA SANTA MARIA, *Our Favorite Nerd*

WHAT BIRD **MIGRATES** BETWEEN THE **ARCTIC** AND THE **ANTARCTIC** EVERY YEAR?

p361

WHAT TWO **COUNTRIES** FORMED THE FIRST **WORLD PEACE** PARK ACROSS THEIR **SHARED BORDER?**

p338

WHICH CONTINENT CONTAINS THE **LARGEST** NUMBER OF **COUNTRIES?**

p347

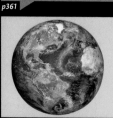

WHICH IS LONGER, THE UNDERWATER **MID-ATLANTIC RIDGE** OR SOUTH AMERICA'S ANDES **MOUNTAIN RANGE?**

p355

WHAT INDONESIAN **REPTILE** GROWS TO **TEN FEET** LONG AND CAN WEIGH AS MUCH AS 300 **POUNDS?**

p344

WHICH WARMS FASTER, LANDMASS OR **OCEAN** WATER?

p375

IN WHAT CENTURY WAS **BRASÍLIA,** THE CAPITAL OF **BRAZIL,** FOUNDED?

p340

WHICH COUNTRY HAS A **HIGHER PERCENTAGE** OF CITIZENS **BELOW THE AGE OF 20, JAPAN** OR **MALAWI?**

p378

p359

THE MASSIVE **2004 TSUNAMI OF SOUTHEASTERN ASIA** ORIGINATED AS AN EARTHQUAKE IN WHAT SEISMICALLY ACTIVE OCEAN **FLOOR FEATURE?**

AFTER WHAT **EXPLORER** IS THE PASSAGE **BETWEEN SOUTH AMERICA** AND **ANTARCTICA** NAMED?

p362

WHICH CONTINENT **IS** PREDICTED TO EXPERIENCE **THE GREATEST** INCREASE **IN** POPULATION IN THE NEXT **25 YEARS?**

p379

WHAT **ANTARCTIC** RESEARCH STATION **IS** CONSIDERED THE COLDEST PLACE ON **EARTH?**

p350

p343

WHICH IS THE SMALLEST COUNTRY IN **THE WORLD?**

IN WHAT AFRICAN COUNTRY WILL YOU FIND THE WORLD'S HIGHEST **MUD-BRICK MINARET, MORE THAN** 500 YEARS OLD, CALLED THE GRAND MOSQUE?

p346

OUR PHYSICAL
WORLD

PANAMA CANAL
East-west gateway
This 48-mile artificial waterway between the Atlantic and Pacific Oceans, the world's largest human-made structure, doubled in capacity with the 2016 opening of new locks.

GUYANA
Most forest
Of all countries, Guyana's terrain has the largest proportion of forested land. More than three-quarters is wooded, much of that as tropical rain forest.

ARCTIC

Queen Elizabeth Islands
Ellesmere Island
GREENLAND
Greenland Sea

Chukchi Sea
Beaufort Sea
Victoria Island
Baffin Bay
Baffin Island

SIBERIA
Brooks Ra.
Yukon
Great Bear Lake
ARCTIC CIRCLE
Iceland

Bering Sea
Denali (Mt. McKinley) 20,310 ft (6,190 m)
Great Slave Lake
Hudson Bay
Labrador Sea
British Isles

Aleutian Islands
NORTH
Lake Winnipeg
Canadian Shield
Ireland

Vancouver Island
ROCKY MOUNTAINS
Missouri
Great Lakes
AMERICA
Island of Newfoundland
Nova Scotia

Great Salt Lake
Great Plains
Appalachian Mountains
Azores

Death Valley -282 ft (-86 m)
Colorado
Mississippi
Madeira Islands

Hawaiian Islands
30°
TROPIC OF CANCER
Baja California
Rio Grande
Gulf of Mexico
West Indies
Canary Islands

Greater Antilles
Cape Verde Islands

CENTRAL AMERICA
Caribbean Sea
Lesser Antilles

POLYNESIA
Line Islands
150°
PACIFIC
120°
EQUATOR
90°
Galápagos Islands
Orinoco
Amazon
Amazon
ATLANTIC
30°

0°
OCEAN
Marquesas Islands
ANDES
Basin
SOUTH
OCEAN

Samoa Is.
Tuamotu Archipelago
Society Is.
Lake Titicaca
Brazilian Highlands
AMERICA

Tonga Is.
Cook Islands
Austral Is.
TROPIC OF CAPRICORN
Easter Island
Atacama Desert
Gran Chaco
Pampas
Paraná

Fiji Is.
30°
Cerro Aconcagua 22,831 ft (6,959 m)
ANDES

Isla Grande de Chiloé
Patagonia
Laguna del Carbón -344 ft (-105 m)

Falkland Is.
Tierra del Fuego
South Sandwich Islands

Strait of Magellan
60°
South Shetland Islands
ANTARCTIC CIRCLE

Bellingshausen Sea
Ellsworth Land
Antarctic Peninsula
Weddell Sea

Marie Byrd Land
Vinson Massif + 16,067 ft (4,897 m)
MOUNTAINS
TRANSANTARCTIC

EARTH'S **CIRCUMFERENCE** AT THE **EQUATOR** IS ABOUT 24,900 MILES. POLE TO POLE IT'S ABOUT 100 MILES LESS, MAKING EARTH NOT A SPHERE BUT AN **OBLATE SPHEROID.**

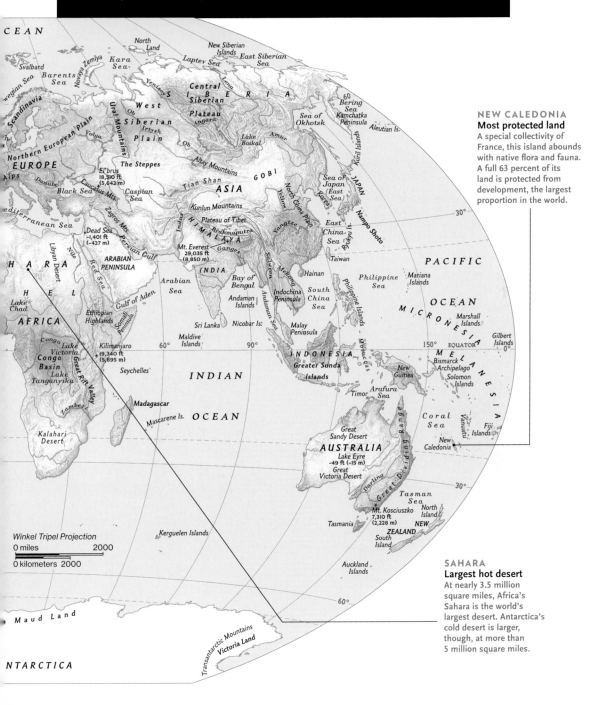

NEW CALEDONIA
Most protected land
A special collectivity of France, this island abounds with native flora and fauna. A full 63 percent of its land is protected from development, the largest proportion in the world.

SAHARA
Largest hot desert
At nearly 3.5 million square miles, Africa's Sahara is the world's largest desert. Antarctica's cold desert is larger, though, at more than 5 million square miles.

Winkel Tripel Projection
0 miles   2000
0 kilometers 2000

OUR POLITICAL
WORLD

HAITI
Successful slave rebellion
Haiti has been an independent Caribbean country since 1804, when a slave rebellion defeated the French colonialists. It was the first country founded by former slaves.

GALÁPAGOS
Population of newcomers
An archipelago of 20 islands with a population of roughly 25,000, Galápagos is a province of Ecuador. It is one of the few places in the world with no native inhabitants.

ARCTI

Chukchi
Sea

Beaufort
Sea

Queen Elizabeth Is.

Greenland
(Denmark)

RUSSIA

Baffin
Bay

60°

Alaska
(U.S.)

Great
Bear Lake

ARCTIC CI

Bering
Sea

Great
Slave Lake

ICELAND

Gulf of
Alaska

CANADA

Hudson
Bay

Labrador
Sea

UNI
KINGD

Lake
Winnipeg

IRELAND
(ÉIRE)

Great Lakes

FRA

UNITED STATES

ANDOR
PORTUGAL SP

30°

MOROCC

TROPIC OF CANCER

Gulf of
Mexico

BAHAMAS

Western
Sahara
(Morocco)

Hawai'i
(U.S.)

CUBA

DOMINICAN REP.

Puerto Rico (U.S.)

ST. KITTS & NEVIS
ANTIGUA & BARBUDA
Guadeloupe (France)
DOMINICA
Martinique (France)

CABO
VERDE

MAURITANIA

MEXICO

BELIZE

HAITI

JAMAICA

Caribbean Sea

SENEGAL

BU

GUATEMALA
EL SALVADOR

HONDURAS

ST. LUCIA

GAMBIA
GUINEA-
BISSAU

NICARAGUA

GRENADA

BARBADOS
ST. VINCENT & THE GRENADINES
TRINIDAD & TOBAGO

GUINEA

COSTA RICA

VENEZUELA

GUYANA

SIERRA
LEONE
LIBERIA

PACIFIC

PANAMA

COLOMBIA

French Guiana
(France)

SURINAME

CÔTE D'IVOIRE
(IVORY COAST)

EQUATOR

150°

120°

90°

Galápagos
Islands
(Ecuador)

ECUADOR

60°

30°

EQ. GUINEA

KIRIBATI

OCEAN

Marquesas
Islands
(France)

PERU

BRAZIL

SAO TO
A
PRINC

SAMOA

American
Samoa
(U.S.)

French Polynesia
(France)

BOLIVIA

ATLANTIC

TONGA

TROPIC OF CAPRICORN

PARAGUAY

OCEAN

URUGUAY

Chatham Is.
(N.Z.)

CHILE

ARGENTINA

30°

Falkland
Islands
(U.K.)

Drake Passage

ANTAR

60°

Weddell
Sea

Ross
Sea

A N

NATIONAL GEOGRAPHIC RECOGNIZES 195 DIFFERENT COUNTRIES IN THE WORLD TODAY.

BURKINA FASO
Name from two languages
Once called Upper Volta, this African country was renamed in 1984, using a word from each of two local languages: Burkina ("honest people" in Mossi) and Faso ("fatherland" in Dyula).

The People's Republic of China claims Taiwan as its 23rd province. Taiwan's government (Republic of China) maintains that there are two political entities.

INDONESIA
Thousands of islands
To clarify sovereignty, Indonesia is doing a recount of its islands, currently numbered at 14,752—and that is only the islands that have names.

Winkel Tripel Projection

0 miles   2000

0 kilometers   2000

BEST OF @NATGEO

OUR FAVORITE PHOTOS OF LANDSCAPES AROUND THE WORLD

@ladzinski | KEITH LADZINSKI
Sunlight slices through smoke blown in from neighboring fires in Glacier National Park.

@jimrichardsonng | JIM RICHARDSON
The Scottish moors along the River Dee awash in purple heather during autumn

@pedromcbride | PETE MCBRIDE
An aerial shot of dried-out drainage tendrils in Mexico's Colorado River Delta

@yamashitaphoto | MICHAEL YAMASHITA
Radiant green terraced fields above the clouds in Guizhou, China

> **"IN EVERY OUTTHRUST HEADLAND, IN EVERY CURVING BEACH, IN EVERY GRAIN OF SAND THERE IS THE STORY OF THE EARTH."** —RACHEL CARSON, AUTHOR AND CONSERVATIONIST

@pedromcbride | PETE MCBRIDE
Salar de Uyuni, the world's largest salt flat, is located on the site of prehistoric lakes in southwest Bolivia.

@jimmy_chin | JIMMY CHIN
Manhattan is a human-made landscape of brightly lit skyscrapers and city streets.

@stevewinterphoto | STEVE WINTER
Wind from an incoming storm blows through a wheat field in County Cork, Ireland.

@cookjenshel | DIANE COOK & LEN JENSHEL
Utah's Grand Staircase-Escalante National Monument is a cultural and geologic treasure.

THE CONTINENTS

LANDFORMS CHANGE SHAPE OVER MILLENNIA

With the unceasing movement of Earth's tectonic plates, continents "drift" over geologic time—breaking apart, reassembling, and again fragmenting to repeat the process. Three times during the past billion years, Earth's drifting landmasses have merged to form so-called supercontinents. Rodinia, the earliest known supercontinent, began breaking apart in the late Precambrian, about 750 million years ago (mya).

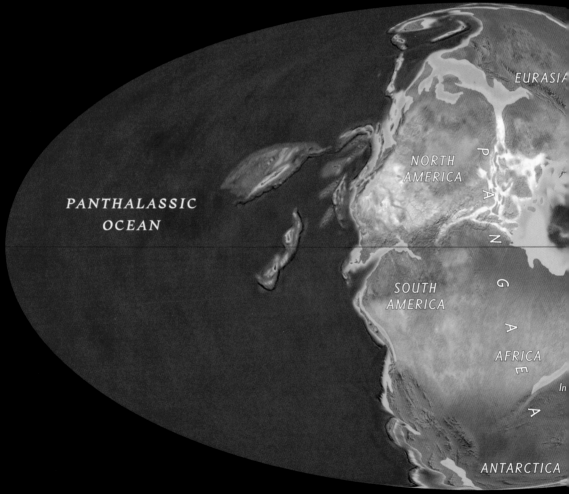

EURASIA

PANTHALASSIC
OCEAN

NORTH
AMERICA

P
A
N
G
A
E
A

SOUTH
AMERICA

AFRICA

In

ANTARCTICA

PANGAEA, 240 MILLION YEARS AGO
Even when most of Earth's landmass was a single continent, named Pangaea, surrounded by a single ocean, the Panthalassic (predecessor to the Pacific), configurations began taking shape that presaged the continents of today. The Tethys Ocean ultimately became the Mediterranean.

DINOSAURS ROAMED POLE TO POLE ON PANGAEA, BUT OVER TIME THE CONTINENTS SPLIT AND DISTINCT DINOSAUR SPECIES EVOLVED SEPARATELY IN DIFFERENT LOCATIONS.

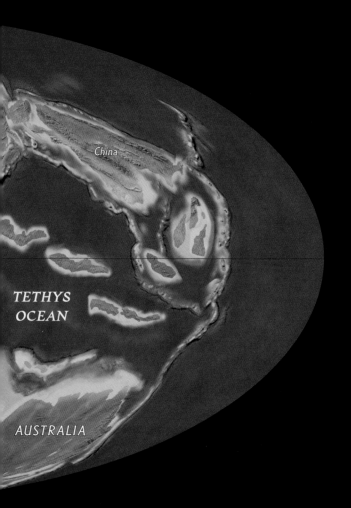

China

TETHYS OCEAN

AUSTRALIA

KEY DATES

Stages in Earth's EVOLUTION

■ **PRECAMBRIAN TIME (4,500–542 MYA)**
Archaean eon (ca 3,800–2,500 mya)
First life-forms appear on Earth.

Proterozoic eon (2,500–542 mya)
In latter part of this eon, continental fragments join into one: Pannotia.

■ **PHANEROZOIC EON (542 MYA–PRESENT)**
Paleozoic era (542–251 mya)
Includes Cambrian, 500 mya: Multicellular animals leave abundant fossil evidence.

Includes Devonian, 400 mya: Freshwater fish migrate freely; plants colonize land.

Mesozoic era (251–65.5 mya)
Includes Triassic, 240 mya: Geologic catastrophes caused massive extinctions; surviving lizards evolved into dinosaurs.

Cenozoic era (65.5 mya–present)
Includes K-T extinction event, 65 mya: Half the plant and animal species become extinct.

Includes last great ice age, 18,000 ya: North and south are locked in ice; continents as we know them begin to form, further defined by retreating glaciers.

NORTH AMERICA

Greenland
(Denmark)

ALASKA
U.S.

C A N A D A

WORLD'S FIRST PEACE PARK
In 1932 Canada and the United
States combined two national
parks to form Waterton-Glacier
International Peace Park,
a symbol of goodwill between
the two countries. Stretching
from prairie to mountains,
the park contains a rock
sequence that spans more
than 1,250 million years.

U N I T E D   S T A T E S

A CITY WITH A HISTORY
Santo Domingo, capital
of the Dominican Republic,
was the first permanent
establishment of the
New World and the site
of America's first cathedral,
hospital, customhouse,
and university.

BAHAMAS

WILDLIFE ABUNDANCE
Comprising 38 islands
and adjacent waters, Panama's
Coiba National Park is home
to 760 fish species, 33 shark
species, and several threatened
animal species including
the crested eagle and the
scarlet macaw.

MEXICO

CUBA

HAITI

DOM.REP.

JAMAICA

ANTIGUA &
BARBUDA

ST. KITTS
& NEVIS

DOMINICA

ST. LUCIA

BARBADOS

ST. VINCENT &
THE GRENADINES

GRENADA

TRINIDAD
& TOBAGO

BELIZE

GUATEMALA   HONDURAS

EL SALVADOR   NICARAGUA

COSTA RICA

PANAMA

Steam rises from a geyser basin in Yellowstone National Park.

SOUTH AMERICA

SAFEGUARDING SPECIES
The Central Suriname Nature Reserve, established in 1998, encompasses more than 10 percent of the country. Jaguars, giant armadillos, giant river otters, eight primate species, and 400 bird species including the harpy eagle live within these four million acres.

LINES IN THE ROCK
Their purpose a mystery, the Nasca Lines of southern Peru are geometrical figures etched into the surface of high desert land during the first century AD. Many are biomorphs: images of plants or animals, including a hummingbird and a monkey.

TOTALLY MODERN CITY
Brazil's capital, Brasilia, was established and built in the 1950s, hence its design and architecture is modernist, visionary, and symbolic of a new approach to urban living. Two axes define the city—public buildings run east to west, residences north to south.

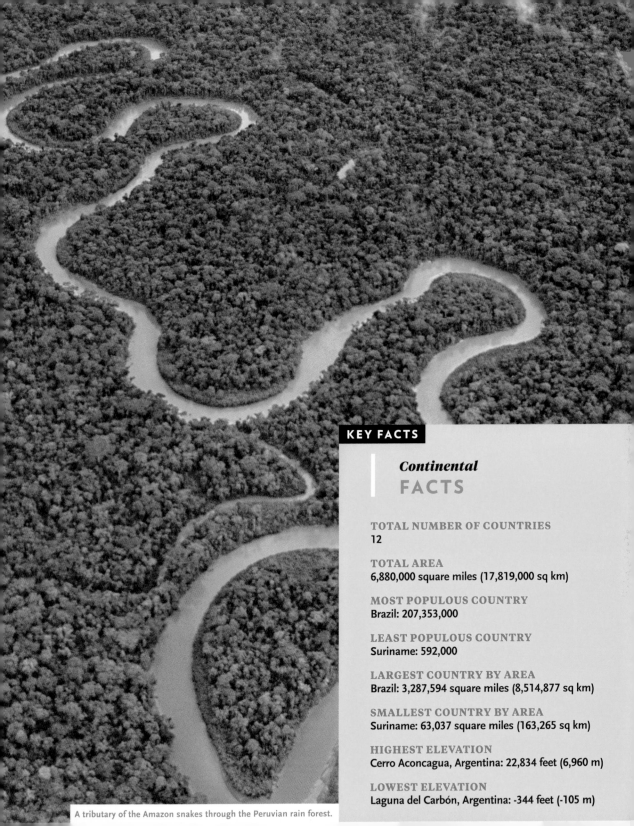

A tributary of the Amazon snakes through the Peruvian rain forest.

Continental
FACTS

TOTAL NUMBER OF COUNTRIES
12

TOTAL AREA
6,880,000 square miles (17,819,000 sq km)

MOST POPULOUS COUNTRY
Brazil: 207,353,000

LEAST POPULOUS COUNTRY
Suriname: 592,000

LARGEST COUNTRY BY AREA
Brazil: 3,287,594 square miles (8,514,877 sq km)

SMALLEST COUNTRY BY AREA
Suriname: 63,037 square miles (163,265 sq km)

HIGHEST ELEVATION
Cerro Aconcagua, Argentina: 22,834 feet (6,960 m)

LOWEST ELEVATION
Laguna del Carbón, Argentina: -344 feet (-105 m)

EUROPE

CITY OF HEALING WATERS
Thanks to many natural springs flowing into the Danube River, Budapest is a city of exquisite bathhouses where people "take the waters" for healing and pleasure. Occupied since the Paleolithic period, it was originally two settlements, Buda and Pest.

ULTIMATE FJORDLAND
Sognefjord, the deepest and longest of the Norwegian fjords, reaches more than 120 miles inland and plummets to depths of over 4,000 feet.

ICELAND

N O R W A Y

S W E D E N

FINLAND

ESTONIA

(ÉIRE) IRELAND

UNITED KINGDOM

DENMARK

LATVIA

LITHUANIA

RUSSIA

R U S S I A

BELARUS

KAZAKHSTAN

NETH.

BELG.

LUX.

GERMANY

POLAND

CZECHIA (CZECH REP.)

U K R A I N E

FRANCE

LIECH.

SWITZ.

AUSTRIA

SLOVAKIA

MOLD.

HUNGARY

SLOV.

CROATIA

ROMANIA

ANDORRA

MONACO

SAN MARINO

BOSN. & HERZG.

SERBIA

PORTUGAL

SPAIN

ITALY

VATICAN CITY

MONTEN.

KOS.

MACED.

BULGARIA

TURKEY

ALBANIA

GREECE

MALTA

THE MONASTERIES OF METEORA
Between the 14th and 16th centuries, devout monks built dwellings on nearly inaccessible sandstone cliffs above the town of Kalambaka in western Thessaly. Six of the 24 monasteries remain, testaments to a devoted life of the spirit.

The Eiffel Tower punctuates a Parisian sunset.

Continental FACTS

TOTAL NUMBER OF COUNTRIES
46

TOTAL AREA
3,841,000 square miles (9,947,000 sq km)

MOST POPULOUS COUNTRY
*Russia: 142,258,000

LEAST POPULOUS COUNTRY
Vatican City: 1,000

LARGEST COUNTRY BY AREA
*Russia: 6,601,631 square miles (17,098,242 sq km)

SMALLEST COUNTRY BY AREA
Vatican City: 0.2 square miles (0.4 sq km)

HIGHEST ELEVATION
El'brus, Russia: 18,510 feet (5,642 m)

LOWEST ELEVATION
Caspian Sea: minus 92 feet (-28 m)

*Area and population figures reflect
the total of Asian and European regions.

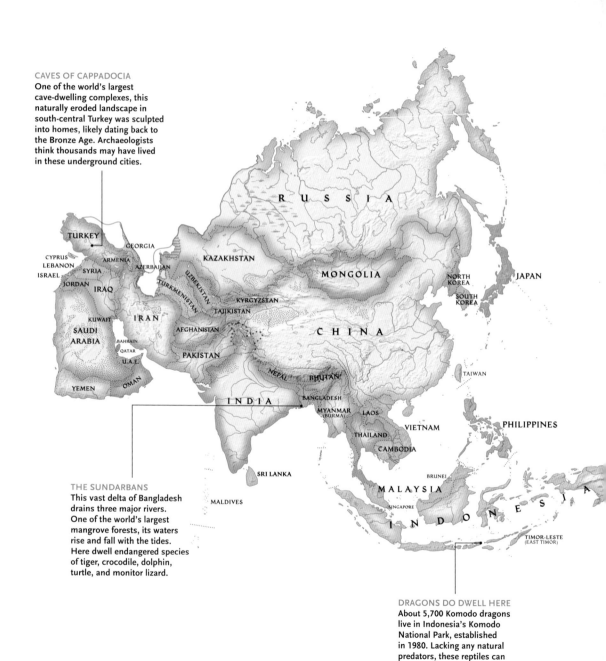

CAVES OF CAPPADOCIA
One of the world's largest cave-dwelling complexes, this naturally eroded landscape in south-central Turkey was sculpted into homes, likely dating back to the Bronze Age. Archaeologists think thousands may have lived in these underground cities.

THE SUNDARBANS
This vast delta of Bangladesh drains three major rivers. One of the world's largest mangrove forests, its waters rise and fall with the tides. Here dwell endangered species of tiger, crocodile, dolphin, turtle, and monitor lizard.

DRAGONS DO DWELL HERE
About 5,700 Komodo dragons live in Indonesia's Komodo National Park, established in 1980. Lacking any natural predators, these reptiles can grow up to 10 feet in length and can weigh more than 300 pounds.

RUSSIA

TURKEY
CYPRUS
LEBANON
ISRAEL
SYRIA
JORDAN
IRAQ
KUWAIT
SAUDI ARABIA
BAHRAIN
QATAR
U.A.E.
YEMEN
OMAN
GEORGIA
ARMENIA
AZERBAIJAN
IRAN
TURKMENISTAN
KAZAKHSTAN
UZBEKISTAN
KYRGYZSTAN
TAJIKISTAN
AFGHANISTAN
PAKISTAN
MONGOLIA
CHINA
NORTH KOREA
SOUTH KOREA
JAPAN
NEPAL
BHUTAN
INDIA
BANGLADESH
MYANMAR (BURMA)
LAOS
VIETNAM
THAILAND
CAMBODIA
TAIWAN
PHILIPPINES
SRI LANKA
MALDIVES
BRUNEI
MALAYSIA
SINGAPORE
INDONESIA
TIMOR-LESTE (EAST TIMOR)

Still reflection doubles the beauty of India's Taj Mahal.

Continental
FACTS

TOTAL NUMBER OF COUNTRIES
46

TOTAL AREA
17,209,000 square miles (44,570,000 sq km)

MOST POPULOUS COUNTRY
China: 1,379,303,000

LEAST POPULOUS COUNTRY
Maldives: 393,000

LARGEST COUNTRY BY AREA
*China: 3,705,407 square miles (9,596,960 sq km)

SMALLEST COUNTRY BY AREA
Maldives: 115 square miles (298 sq km)

HIGHEST ELEVATION
Mount Everest, China/Nepal: 29,035 feet (8,850 m)

LOWEST ELEVATION
Dead Sea, Israel/Jordan: -1,401 feet (-427 m)

*Russia straddles both Asia and
Europe and exceeds China in area.*

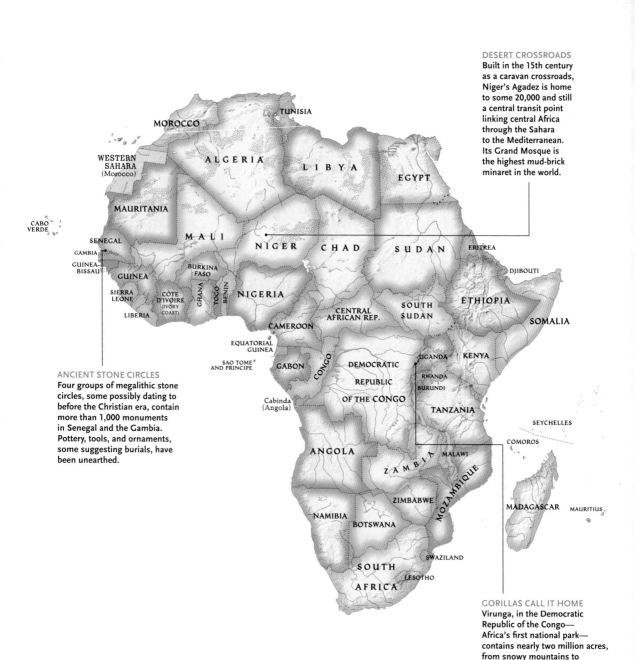

DESERT CROSSROADS
Built in the 15th century
as a caravan crossroads,
Niger's Agadez is home
to some 20,000 and still
a central transit point
linking central Africa
through the Sahara
to the Mediterranean.
Its Grand Mosque is
the highest mud-brick
minaret in the world.

ANCIENT STONE CIRCLES
Four groups of megalithic stone
circles, some possibly dating to
before the Christian era, contain
more than 1,000 monuments
in Senegal and the Gambia.
Pottery, tools, and ornaments,
some suggesting burials, have
been unearthed.

GORILLAS CALL IT HOME
Virunga, in the Democratic
Republic of the Congo—
Africa's first national park—
contains nearly two million acres,
from snowy mountains to
lowland forests and lava plains.
It is home to a quarter of the
world's critically endangered
mountain gorillas.

TUNISIA
MOROCCO
WESTERN
SAHARA
(Morocco)
ALGERIA
LIBYA
EGYPT
CABO
VERDE
MAURITANIA
MALI
NIGER
CHAD
SUDAN
ERITREA
SENEGAL
GAMBIA
GUINEA-
BISSAU
DJIBOUTI
GUINEA
BURKINA
FASO
SIERRA
LEONE
CÔTE
D'IVOIRE
(IVORY
COAST)
GHANA
TOGO
BENIN
NIGERIA
ETHIOPIA
LIBERIA
SOUTH
SUDAN
SOMALIA
CENTRAL
AFRICAN REP.
CAMEROON
EQUATORIAL
GUINEA
SAO TOME
AND PRINCIPE
GABON
CONGO
DEMOCRATIC
REPUBLIC
OF THE CONGO
UGANDA
KENYA
RWANDA
BURUNDI
Cabinda
(Angola)
TANZANIA
SEYCHELLES
COMOROS
ANGOLA
ZAMBIA
MALAWI
MOZAMBIQUE
MADAGASCAR
MAURITIUS
ZIMBABWE
NAMIBIA
BOTSWANA
SWAZILAND
SOUTH
AFRICA
LESOTHO

A dusky glow surrounds elephants in Botswana's Chobe National Park.

Continental FACTS

TOTAL NUMBER OF COUNTRIES
54

TOTAL AREA
11,608,000 square miles (30,065,000 sq km)

MOST POPULOUS COUNTRY
Nigeria: 190,632,000

LEAST POPULOUS COUNTRY
Seychelles: 94,000

LARGEST COUNTRY BY AREA
Algeria: 919,590 square miles (2,381,741 sq km)

SMALLEST COUNTRY BY AREA
Seychelles: 176 square miles (455 sq km)

HIGHEST ELEVATION
Kilimanjaro, Tanzania: 19,340 feet (5,895 m)

LOWEST ELEVATION
Lake Assal, Djibouti: -509 feet (-155 m)

AUSTRALIA & OCEANIA

MICRONESIAN DYNASTY

Built atop an offshore reef near Pohnpei Island, the city of Nan Madol contained palaces, temples, tombs, and residences—now all stone ruins. Archaeologists date them to about AD 1200, the same time that Paris's Notre Dame was built.

MARSHALL ISLANDS

PALAU

FEDERATED STATES OF MICRONESIA

K I R I B A T I

NAURU

SEA COWS AND STROMATOLITES

Encompassing more than 54 million acres, the Shark Bay region of Western Australia is home to dugongs (nicknamed "sea cows"), massive sea grass beds, and stromatolites—colonies of fossilized algae deposits, one of the oldest life-forms on Earth.

PAPUA NEW GUINEA

SOLOMON ISLANDS

TUVALU

SAMC

VANUATU

FIJI

TONGA

A U S T R A L I A

FRIGID NESTING PARADISE

Spreading nearly 200,000 acres, New Zealand's five subantarctic island groups abound with 126 bird species including 10 different types of penguin. As many as two million sooty shearwaters nest each season on the Snares, one of these island groups.

NEW ZEALAND

Continental
FACTS

TOTAL NUMBER OF COUNTRIES
14

TOTAL AREA
3,286,000 square miles (8,510,700 sq km)

MOST POPULOUS COUNTRY
Australia: 23,232,000

LEAST POPULOUS COUNTRY
Nauru: 11,400

LARGEST COUNTRY BY AREA
Australia: 2,969,906 square miles (7,692,024 sq km)

SMALLEST COUNTRY BY AREA
Nauru: 8 square miles (21 sq km)

HIGHEST ELEVATION
Mount Wilhelm, Papua New Guinea: 14,793 feet (4,509 m)

LOWEST ELEVATION
Lake Eyre, Australia: -52 feet (-16 m)

Coral profusion populates Australia's Great Barrier Reef.

ANTARCTICA

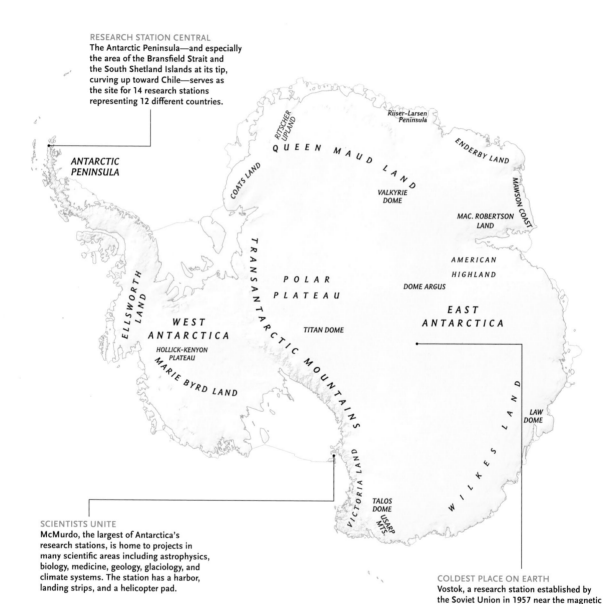

RESEARCH STATION CENTRAL
The Antarctic Peninsula—and especially
the area of the Bransfield Strait and
the South Shetland Islands at its tip,
curving up toward Chile—serves as
the site for 14 research stations
representing 12 different countries.

ANTARCTIC
PENINSULA

RITSCHER
UPLAND

Riiser-Larsen
Peninsula

QUEEN MAUD LAND

ENDERBY LAND

COATS LAND

MAWSON COAST

VALKYRIE
DOME

MAC. ROBERTSON
LAND

AMERICAN
HIGHLAND

DOME ARGUS

POLAR
PLATEAU

EAST
ANTARCTICA

TITAN DOME

ELLSWORTH
LAND

WEST
ANTARCTICA

HOLLICK-KENYON
PLATEAU

MARIE BYRD LAND

TRANSANTARCTIC MOUNTAINS

VICTORIA LAND

WILKES LAND

LAW
DOME

TALOS
DOME

USARP
MTS.

SCIENTISTS UNITE
McMurdo, the largest of Antarctica's
research stations, is home to projects in
many scientific areas including astrophysics,
biology, medicine, geology, glaciology, and
climate systems. The station has a harbor,
landing strips, and a helicopter pad.

COLDEST PLACE ON EARTH
Vostok, a research station established by
the Soviet Union in 1957 near the magnetic
South Pole, is traditionally called the coldest
place on Earth, with temperatures generally
ranging from minus 44°F (-42°C) to minus
85°F (-65°C).

Chinstrap penguins congregate on an Antarctic iceberg.

Continental FACTS

JURISDICTION
1959 treaty precludes sovereign control

NUMBER OF RESEARCH STATIONS
70 to 80

POPULATION
1,000 to 5,000 temporary residents, depending
on season

TOTAL AREA
5,100,000 square miles (13,209,000 sq m)

HIGHEST ELEVATION
Vinson Massif: 16,067 feet (4,897 m)

LOWEST ELEVATION
Byrd Glacier (Depression): -9,416 feet (-2,870 m)

OCEANS
OF THE WORLD

A BLUE PLANET

Earth's predominant physical feature is the vast, continuous body of water that accounts for more than two-thirds of its surface, totaling some 139 million square miles. The global ocean is a dominant climate factor, with currents carrying heat from the Equator toward the poles, and a vital resource providing food to much of the world's population and serving as a key transportation route between continents.

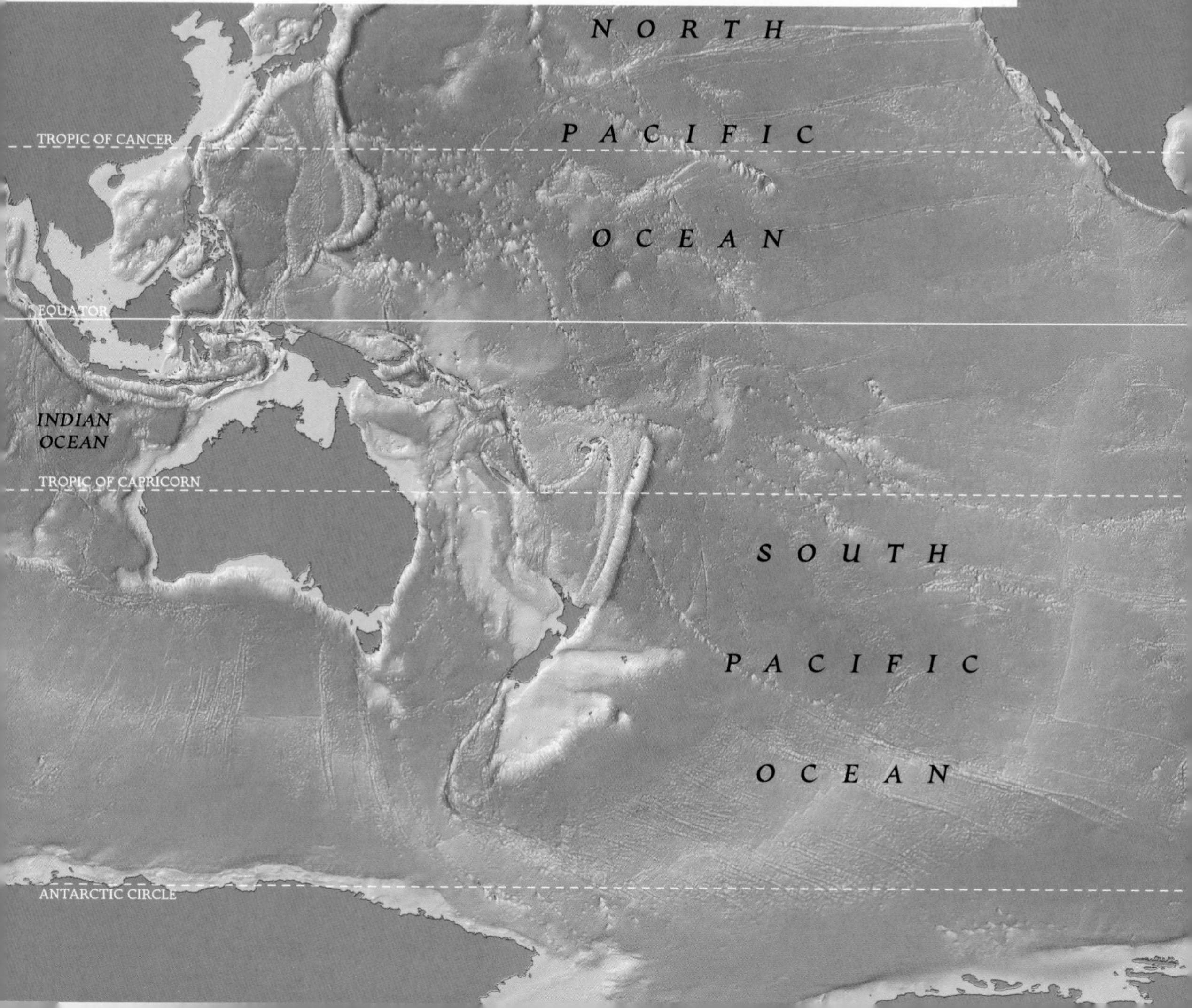

NORTH

TROPIC OF CANCER

PACIFIC

OCEAN

EQUATOR

INDIAN
OCEAN

TROPIC OF CAPRICORN

SOUTH

PACIFIC

OCEAN

ANTARCTIC CIRCLE

> **"EVEN IF YOU NEVER HAVE THE CHANCE TO SEE OR TOUCH THE OCEAN, THE OCEAN TOUCHES YOU WITH EVERY BREATH YOU TAKE, EVERY DROP OF WATER YOU DRINK, EVERY BITE YOU CONSUME."**
>
> **—SYLVIA EARLE,** OCEANOGRAPHER AND EXPLORER

N O R T H

A T L A N T I C

O C E A N

TROPIC OF CANCER

ARCTIC CIRCLE

EQUATOR

S O U T H

A T L A N T I C

O C E A N

INDIAN

OCEAN

TROPIC OF CAPRICORN

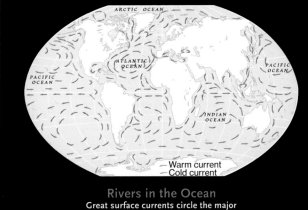

Rivers in the Ocean
Great surface currents circle the major
ocean basins, ferrying the heat of the tropical
sun north to warm and expand the temperate zones.

ANTARCTIC CIRCLE

ATLANTIC OCEAN

OCEAN TRENDS

Oceans are living things, with environments and processes that affect us all. They play huge roles in our lives as highways for travel and sources of food. Their vitality shapes the future of life on this planet. Here are a few indicators of ocean well-being today.

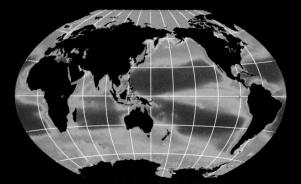

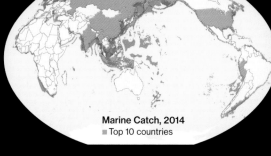

Marine Catch, 2014
■ Top 10 countries

Chlorophyll

Tiny phytoplankton are crucial to life inside and outside the oceans, and their blooming is tracked through the observation of chlorophyll concentrations. Nutrient-deficient areas are known as "deserts." Fluctuations and storms such as El Niño and Atlantic hurricanes can shift these patterns, causing some "deserts" to occasionally bloom.

Chlorophyll concentration (mg/m³), July 2002–Aug. 2013 average
>.01
1
20
■ No data

Fishing Activity

Roughly one billion people depend on fish as their main protein source. As demand for fish has risen, the global fishing industry has grown. Unfortunately, fishing is often practiced unsustainably, and current overfishing threatens ocean ecosystems. Crude fishing techniques can result in unintentional bycatch, which accounts for more than 40 percent of all marine catch globally.

Average annual marine catch metric tons per sq km/year
10
3
0.25

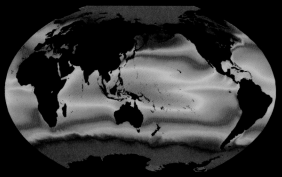

Sea Surface Temperatures

Sea surface temperature drives many of the oceans' most crucial systems. Destructive tropical storms are generated and sustained only in areas with high surface temperatures. So with ocean temperatures rising across the globe, the threat of more frequent and more destructive storms is increasing as well.

Sea surface temperature, July 2002–Aug. 2013 average
High
Low

KEY FACTS

About the ATLANTIC

TOTAL AREA
35,400,000 square miles (91,700,000 sq km)

AVERAGE DEPTH
10,925 feet (3,300 m)

DEEPEST POINT
Puerto Rico Trench: -28,232 feet (-8,605 m)

LARGEST ISLAND
Greenland

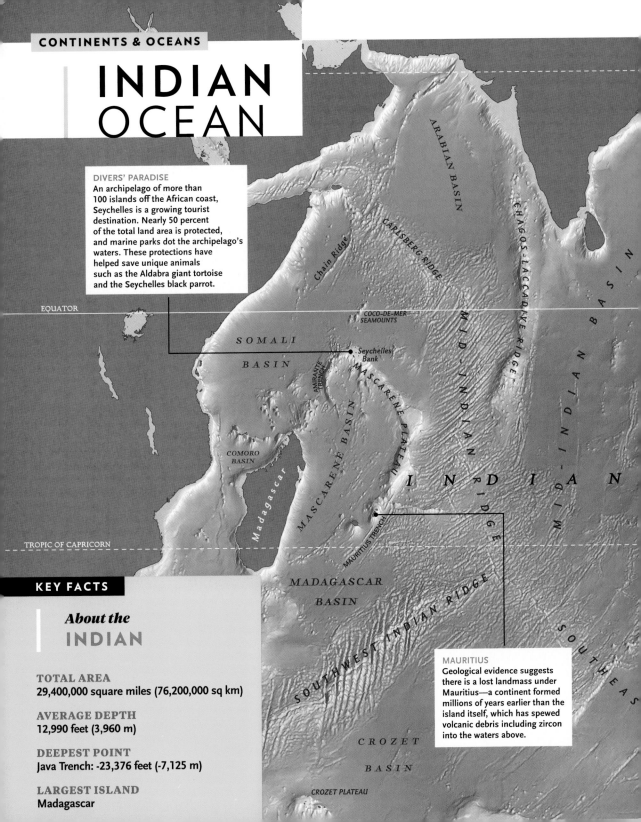

INDIAN OCEAN

DIVERS' PARADISE
An archipelago of more than 100 islands off the African coast, Seychelles is a growing tourist destination. Nearly 50 percent of the total land area is protected, and marine parks dot the archipelago's waters. These protections have helped save unique animals such as the Aldabra giant tortoise and the Seychelles black parrot.

EQUATOR

ARABIAN BASIN

CHAGOS-LACCADIVE RIDGE

CARLSBERG RIDGE

Chain Ridge

COCO-DE-MER SEAMOUNTS

SOMALI BASIN

Seychelles Bank

AMIRANTE TRENCH

MASCARENE PLATEAU

MID-INDIAN BASIN

MID-INDIAN RIDGE

COMORO BASIN

MASCARENE BASIN

Madagascar

I N D I A N

MAURITIUS TRENCH

MADAGASCAR BASIN

SOUTHWEST INDIAN RIDGE

SOUTHEAS

TROPIC OF CAPRICORN

KEY FACTS

About the
INDIAN

TOTAL AREA
29,400,000 square miles (76,200,000 sq km)

AVERAGE DEPTH
12,990 feet (3,960 m)

DEEPEST POINT
Java Trench: -23,376 feet (-7,125 m)

LARGEST ISLAND
Madagascar

MAURITIUS
Geological evidence suggests there is a lost landmass under Mauritius—a continent formed millions of years earlier than the island itself, which has spewed volcanic debris including zircon into the waters above.

CROZET BASIN

CROZET PLATEAU

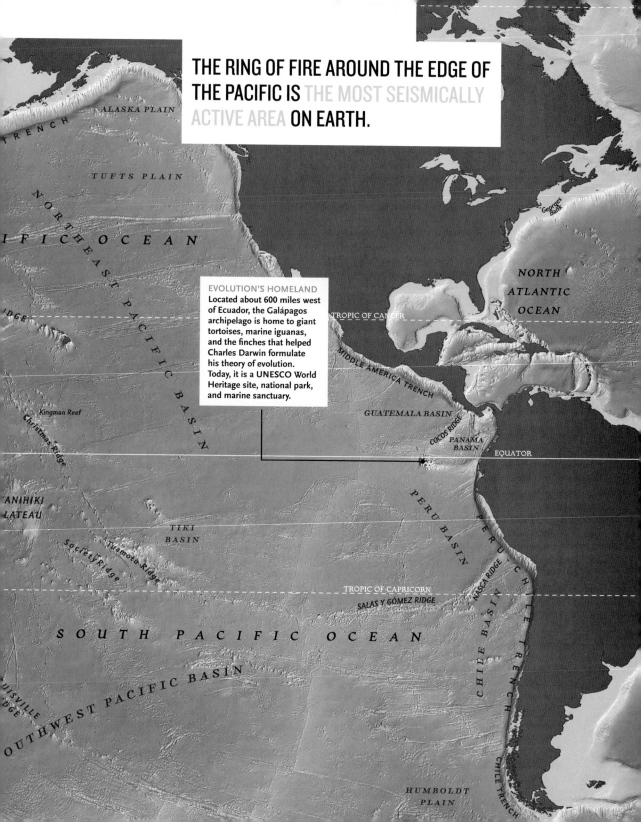

THE RING OF FIRE AROUND THE EDGE OF THE PACIFIC IS THE MOST SEISMICALLY ACTIVE AREA ON EARTH.

TRENCH

ALASKA PLAIN

TUFTS PLAIN

NORTHEAST PACIFIC OCEAN

IFIC OCEAN

IDGE

Kingman Reef

Christmas Ridge

ANIHIKI LATEAU

Society Ridge

Tuamotu Ridge

TIKI BASIN

SOUTH PACIFIC OCEAN

UISVILLE RIDGE

OUTHWEST PACIFIC BASIN

NORTH ATLANTIC OCEAN

Georges Bank

TROPIC OF CANCER

MIDDLE AMERICA TRENCH

GUATEMALA BASIN

COCOS RIDGE

PANAMA BASIN

EQUATOR

PERU BASIN

PERU CHILE TRENCH

NASCA RIDGE

CHILE BASIN

TROPIC OF CAPRICORN

SALAS Y GÓMEZ RIDGE

CHILE TRENCH

HUMBOLDT PLAIN

EVOLUTION'S HOMELAND

Located about 600 miles west of Ecuador, the Galápagos archipelago is home to giant tortoises, marine iguanas, and the finches that helped Charles Darwin formulate his theory of evolution. Today, it is a UNESCO World Heritage site, national park, and marine sanctuary.

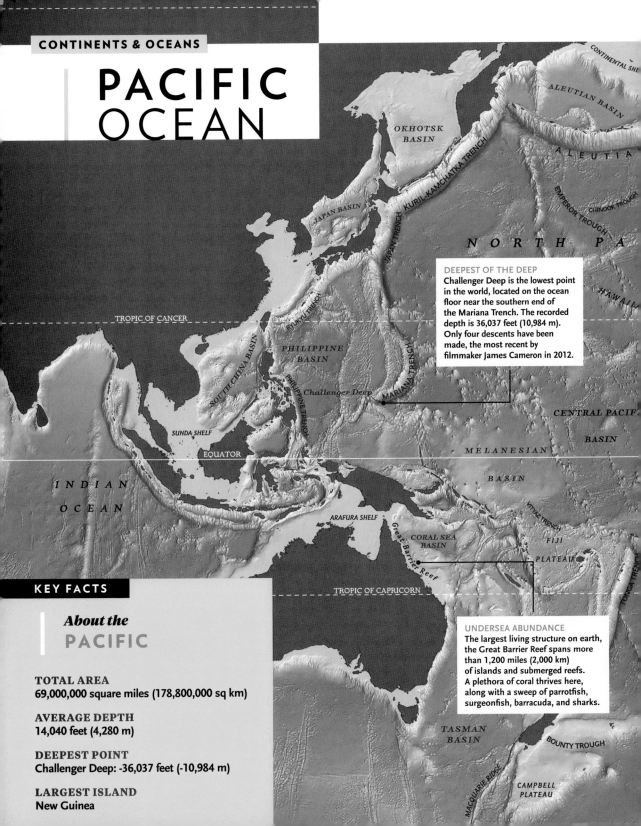

PACIFIC OCEAN

ALEUTIAN BASIN

OKHOTSK BASIN

CONTINENTAL SHE

ALEUTIA

KURIL KAMCHATKA TRENCH

JAPAN BASIN

JAPAN TRENCH

CHINOOK TROUGH

EMPEROR TROUGH

N O R T H   P A

HAWAII

DEEPEST OF THE DEEP
Challenger Deep is the lowest point in the world, located on the ocean floor near the southern end of the Mariana Trench. The recorded depth is 36,037 feet (10,984 m). Only four descents have been made, the most recent by filmmaker James Cameron in 2012.

TROPIC OF CANCER

RYUKYU TRENCH

PHILIPPINE BASIN

SOUTH CHINA BASIN

PHILIPPINE TRENCH

Challenger Deep

MARIANA TRENCH

CENTRAL PACIFIC

BASIN

SUNDA SHELF

EQUATOR

MELANESIAN

I N D I A N

O C E A N

B A S I N

VITYAZ TRENCH

ARAFURA SHELF

CORAL SEA BASIN

Great Barrier Reef

FIJI

PLATEAU

TONGA TRE

TROPIC OF CAPRICORN

UNDERSEA ABUNDANCE
The largest living structure on earth, the Great Barrier Reef spans more than 1,200 miles (2,000 km) of islands and submerged reefs. A plethora of coral thrives here, along with a sweep of parrotfish, surgeonfish, barracuda, and sharks.

KEY FACTS

About the PACIFIC

TOTAL AREA
69,000,000 square miles (178,800,000 sq km)

AVERAGE DEPTH
14,040 feet (4,280 m)

DEEPEST POINT
Challenger Deep: -36,037 feet (-10,984 m)

LARGEST ISLAND
New Guinea

TASMAN BASIN

BOUNTY TROUGH

MACQUARIE RIDGE

CAMPBELL PLATEAU

MANY OF THE WORLD'S GREAT RIVERS DRAIN INTO THE ATLANTIC, INCLUDING THE MISSISSIPPI, THE AMAZON, AND THE NILE.

CONTINENTAL SHELF

GREENLAND

ICELAND PLATEAU

ARCTIC CIRCLE

REYKJANES RIDGE

ROCKALL PLATEAU

CELTIC SHELF

Flemish Cap

MID-ATLANTIC RIDGE
Part of the longest mountain range in the world, this chain is located at the juncture of plates in the Earth's crust and is longer than the Rocky Mountains, the Himalaya, and the Andes combined. In places, the mountain chain rises above sea level to form rocky islands like Iceland.

N O R T H

A T L A N T I C

O C E A N

MID-ATLANTIC RIDGE

TROPIC OF CANCER

PUERTO RICO TRENCH

STREAMING NORTHWARD
A forceful ocean current that flows between Cuba and Florida and then up the southeastern U.S. coastline, the Gulf Stream figures prominently in North American colonial history, as explorers and then slave ships from across the Atlantic rode it northward to their destinations.

A HOME FOR BIRDS
One of the Tristan da Cunha Islands, Gough Island provides breeding grounds for about 20 species of seabirds—albatrosses, petrels, shearwaters—as well as the Inaccessible Island rail, the world's smallest flightless bird. As many as three million pairs of great shearwaters breed on Gough each year.

MID-ATLANTIC RIDGE

S O U T H

A T L A N T I C

WALVIS RIDGE

TROPIC OF CAPRICORN

O C E A N

RIO GRANDE RISE

Agulhas Bank

S O U T H

P A C I F I C

O C E A N

MID-ATLANTIC RIDGE

PATAGONIAN SHELF

UMVOTO RISE

FALKLAND PLATEAU

NORTH SCOTIA RIDGE

SOUTH SANDWICH TRENCH

ATLANTIC-INDIAN RIDGE

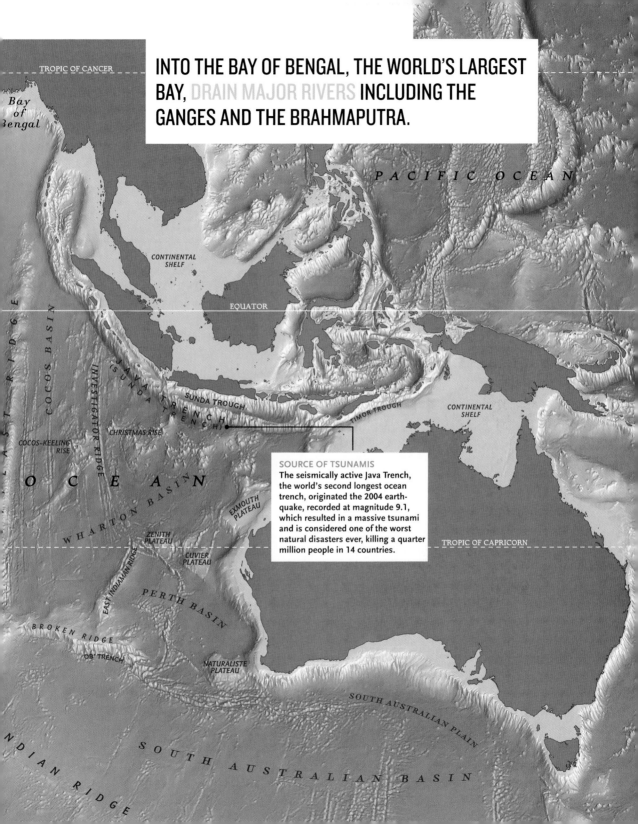

INTO THE BAY OF BENGAL, THE WORLD'S LARGEST BAY, DRAIN MAJOR RIVERS INCLUDING THE GANGES AND THE BRAHMAPUTRA.

TROPIC OF CANCER

Bay
of
Bengal

PACIFIC OCEAN

CONTINENTAL
SHELF

EQUATOR

COCOS BASIN

EAST RIDGE

INVESTIGATOR RIDGE

JAVA TRENCH (SUNDA TRENCH)

SUNDA TROUGH

TIMOR TROUGH

CONTINENTAL
SHELF

CHRISTMAS RISE

COCOS-KEELING
RISE

O C E A N

WHARTON BASIN

EXMOUTH
PLATEAU

ZENITH
PLATEAU

CUVIER
PLATEAU

TROPIC OF CAPRICORN

SOURCE OF TSUNAMIS
The seismically active Java Trench, the world's second longest ocean trench, originated the 2004 earthquake, recorded at magnitude 9.1, which resulted in a massive tsunami and is considered one of the worst natural disasters ever, killing a quarter million people in 14 countries.

EAST INDIAMAN RIDGE

PERTH BASIN

BROKEN RIDGE

OB' TRENCH

NATURALISTE
PLATEAU

SOUTH AUSTRALIAN PLAIN

INDIAN RIDGE

SOUTH AUSTRALIAN BASIN

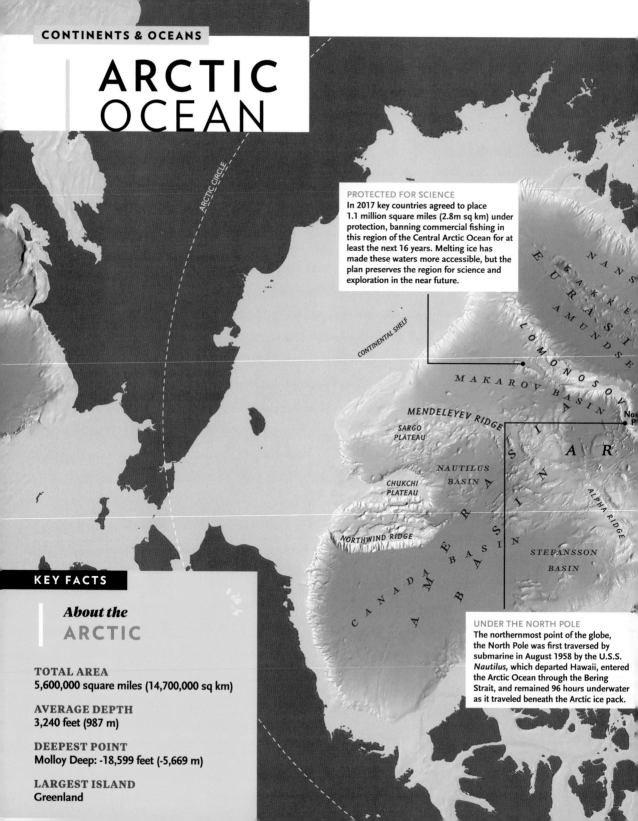

ARCTIC OCEAN

ARCTIC CIRCLE

PROTECTED FOR SCIENCE
In 2017 key countries agreed to place 1.1 million square miles (2.8m sq km) under protection, banning commercial fishing in this region of the Central Arctic Ocean for at least the next 16 years. Melting ice has made these waters more accessible, but the plan preserves the region for science and exploration in the near future.

CONTINENTAL SHELF

NANSEN-GAKKEL

EURASIA

AMUNDSE

LOMONOSOV

MAKAROV BASIN

MENDELEYEV RIDGE

SARGO PLATEAU

North P

SIBERIA

CHUKCHI PLATEAU

NAUTILUS BASIN

ALPHA RIDGE

NORTHWIND RIDGE

BASIN

AMERASIAN

STEPANSSON BASIN

CANADA BASIN

UNDER THE NORTH POLE
The northernmost point of the globe, the North Pole was first traversed by submarine in August 1958 by the U.S.S. *Nautilus*, which departed Hawaii, entered the Arctic Ocean through the Bering Strait, and remained 96 hours underwater as it traveled beneath the Arctic ice pack.

KEY FACTS

About the
ARCTIC

TOTAL AREA
5,600,000 square miles (14,700,000 sq km)

AVERAGE DEPTH
3,240 feet (987 m)

DEEPEST POINT
Molloy Deep: -18,599 feet (-5,669 m)

LARGEST ISLAND
Greenland

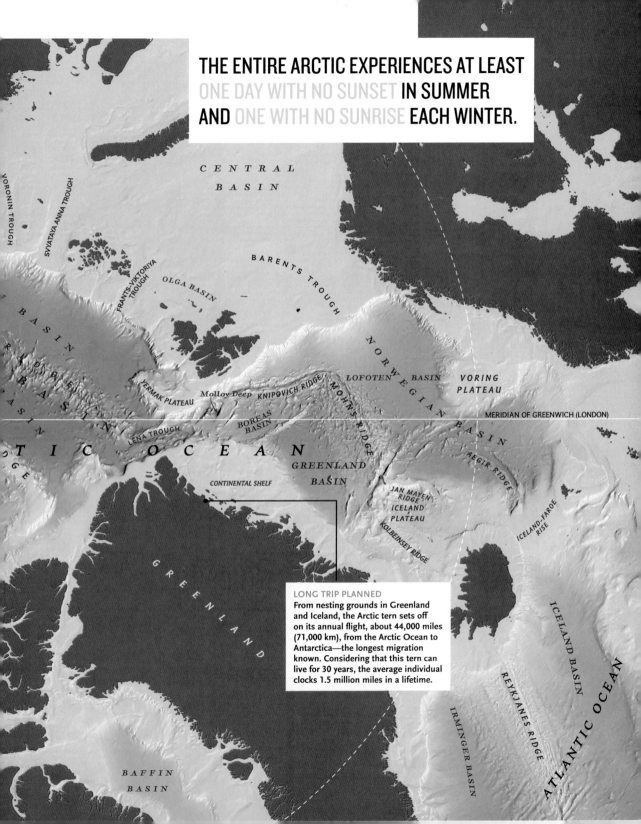

THE ENTIRE ARCTIC EXPERIENCES AT LEAST ONE DAY WITH NO SUNSET IN SUMMER AND ONE WITH NO SUNRISE EACH WINTER.

CENTRAL
BASIN

VORONIN TROUGH

SVYATAYA ANNA TROUGH

BARENTS TROUGH

FRANTS-VIKTORIYA TROUGH

OLGA BASIN

BASIN

BASIN

N O R W E G I A N

LOFOTEN BASIN

VORING
PLATEAU

YERMAK PLATEAU

Molloy Deep

KNIPOVICH RIDGE

MOHNS RIDGE

MERIDIAN OF GREENWICH (LONDON)

LENA TROUGH

BOREAS
BASIN

B A S I N

AEGIR RIDGE

T I C   O C E A N

DGE

GREENLAND
BASIN

CONTINENTAL SHELF

JAN MAYEN
RIDGE

ICELAND
PLATEAU

ICELAND-FAROE
RISE

KOLBEINSEY RIDGE

G R E E N L A N D

ICELAND
BASIN

LONG TRIP PLANNED
From nesting grounds in Greenland and Iceland, the Arctic tern sets off on its annual flight, about 44,000 miles (71,000 km), from the Arctic Ocean to Antarctica—the longest migration known. Considering that this tern can live for 30 years, the average individual clocks 1.5 million miles in a lifetime.

REYKJANES RIDGE

IRMINGER BASIN

ATLANTIC OCEAN

ATLANTIC OCEAN

BAFFIN
BASIN

OCEAN AROUND
ANTARCTICA

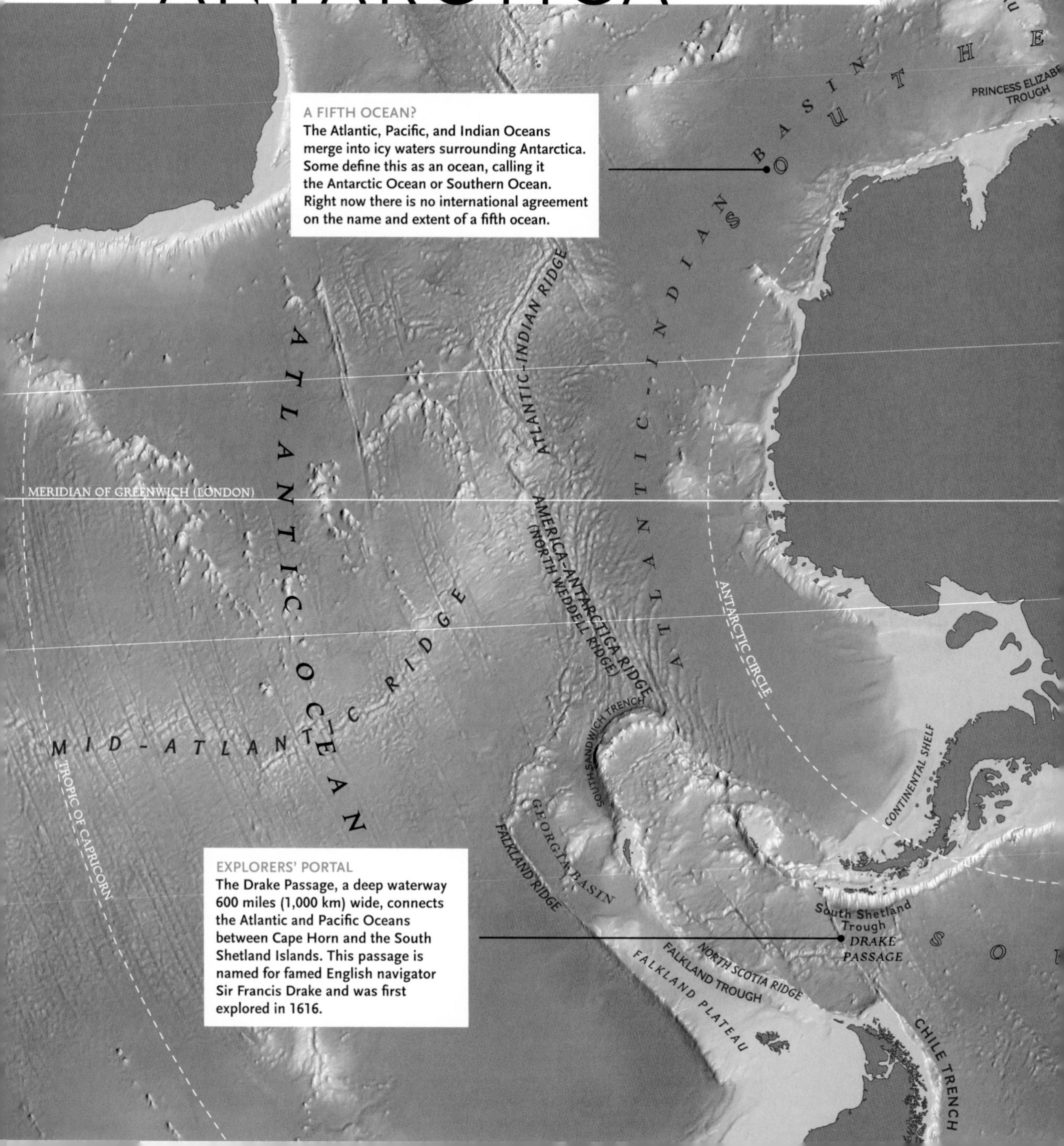

KERGUELEN PLATEAU

INDIAN

SOUTH

BASIN

PRINCESS ELIZABETH TROUGH

A FIFTH OCEAN?

The Atlantic, Pacific, and Indian Oceans merge into icy waters surrounding Antarctica. Some define this as an ocean, calling it the Antarctic Ocean or Southern Ocean. Right now there is no international agreement on the name and extent of a fifth ocean.

ATLANTIC-INDIAN RIDGE

ATLANTIC-INDIAN

ATLANTIC

ANTARCTIC CIRCLE

ATLANTIC OCEAN

MERIDIAN OF GREENWICH (LONDON)

AMERICA-ANTARCTICA RIDGE
(NORTH WEDDELL RIDGE)

MID-ATLANTIC RIDGE

TROPIC OF CAPRICORN

SOUTH SANDWICH TRENCH

GEORGIA BASIN

FALKLAND RIDGE

CONTINENTAL SHELF

South Shetland Trough

EXPLORERS' PORTAL

The Drake Passage, a deep waterway 600 miles (1,000 km) wide, connects the Atlantic and Pacific Oceans between Cape Horn and the South Shetland Islands. This passage is named for famed English navigator Sir Francis Drake and was first explored in 1616.

DRAKE PASSAGE

NORTH SCOTIA RIDGE

FALKLAND TROUGH

FALKLAND PLATEAU

CHILE TRENCH

SOUTH

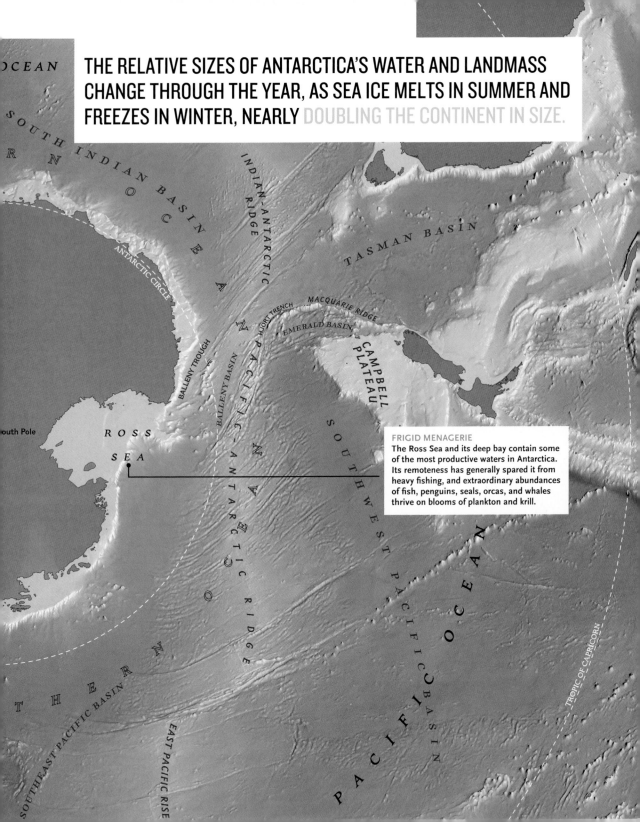

THE RELATIVE SIZES OF ANTARCTICA'S WATER AND LANDMASS CHANGE THROUGH THE YEAR, AS SEA ICE MELTS IN SUMMER AND FREEZES IN WINTER, NEARLY DOUBLING THE CONTINENT IN SIZE.

OCEAN

SOUTH INDIAN BASIN

SOUTHERN OCEAN

ANTARCTIC CIRCLE

INDIAN-ANTARCTIC RIDGE

TASMAN BASIN

HJORT TRENCH

MACQUARIE RIDGE

BALLENY TROUGH

BALLENY BASIN

EMERALD BASIN

CAMPBELL PLATEAU

South Pole

ROSS SEA

PACIFIC-ANTARCTIC RIDGE

SOUTHWEST PACIFIC BASIN

PACIFIC OCEAN

FRIGID MENAGERIE
The Ross Sea and its deep bay contain some of the most productive waters in Antarctica. Its remoteness has generally spared it from heavy fishing, and extraordinary abundances of fish, penguins, seals, orcas, and whales thrive on blooms of plankton and krill.

SOUTHEAST PACIFIC BASIN

EAST PACIFIC RISE

PACIFIC BASIN

TROPIC OF CAPRICORN

BEST OF @NATGEO

OUR FAVORITE PHOTOGRAPHS OF THE OCEANS

@daviddoubilet | DAVID DOUBILET
An ocean swell reveals the thriving Opal Reef, part of the
Great Barrier Reef in Queensland, Australia.

@franslanting | FRANS LANTING
Stromatolites, among the oldest evidence of life on Earth,
are exposed at low tide in Western Australia.

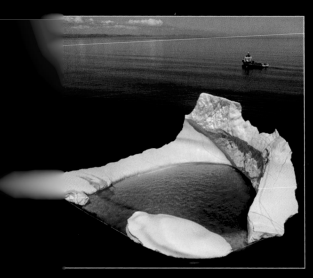

@randyolson | RANDY OLSON
A ship moves a large piece of ice away from an oil platform
off of Newfoundland, Canada.

@cristinamittermeier | CRISTINA MITTERMEIER
A bed of sea grass ripples in the water near the Mosquitia
Reef in Honduras.

> **" HOW INAPPROPRIATE TO CALL THIS PLANET EARTH WHEN IT IS CLEARLY OCEAN."** —ARTHUR C. CLARKE, SCIENCE FICTION AUTHOR

@kengeiger | KEN GEIGER
Hammocks flutter over knee-deep jade waters of Mexico's
Yucatán Peninsula.

@paulnicklen | PAUL NICKLEN
Along the coast of Svalbard, Norway, spring ice breaks up
along the water's surface.

@ brianskerry | BRIAN SKERRY
Nearly birdlike in its motion, a manta ray arcs up out of the
water near the Mexican coastline.

@ladzinski | KEITH LADZINSKI
Waves crash on the rocky shores of Pfeiffer Beach near
Big Sur, California, in the early morning.

FLAGS OF THE WORLD

EACH OF TODAY'S 195 COUNTRIES FLIES AN HONORED AND SYMBOLIC FLAG

AFGHANISTAN

AREA 251,826 sq mi
(652,230 sq km)
POPULATION 34,125,000
CAPITAL Kabul

ALBANIA

AREA 11,100 sq mi
(28,748 sq km)
POPULATION 3,048,000
CAPITAL Tirana

ALGERIA

AREA 919,590 sq mi
(2,381,741 sq km)
POPULATION 40,969,000
CAPITAL Algiers

ANDORRA

AREA 181 sq mi
(468 sq km)
POPULATION 86,000
CAPITAL Andorra la Vella

ANGOLA

AREA 481,351 sq mi
(1,246,700 sq km)
POPULATION 29,310,000
CAPITAL Luanda

ANTIGUA AND BARBUDA

AREA 171 sq mi
(443 sq km)
POPULATION 95,000
CAPITAL St. John's

ARGENTINA

AREA 1,073,512 sq mi
(2,780,400 sq km)
POPULATION 44,293,000
CAPITAL Buenos Aires

ARMENIA

AREA 11,484 sq mi
(29,743 sq km)
POPULATION 3,045,000
CAPITAL Yerevan

AUSTRALIA

AAREA 2,988,885 sq mi
(7,741,220 sq km)
POPULATION 23,232,000
CAPITAL Canberra

AUSTRIA

AREA 32,383 sq mi
(83,871 sq km)
POPULATION 8,754,000
CAPITAL Vienna

AZERBAIJAN

AREA 33,436 sq mi
(86,600 sq km)
POPULATION 9,961,000
CAPITAL Baku

BAHAMAS

AREA 5,359 sq mi
(13,880 sq km)
POPULATION 330,000
CAPITAL Nassau

BAHRAIN

AREA 293 sq mi
(760 sq km)
POPULATION 1,411,000
CAPITAL Manama

BANGLADESH

AREA 55,598 sq mi
(143,998 sq km)
POPULATION 157,827,000
CAPITAL Dhaka

BARBADOS

AREA 166 sq mi
(430 sq km)
POPULATION 292,000
CAPITAL Bridgetown

BELARUS
AREA 80,154 sq mi
(207,600 sq km)
POPULATION 9,550,000
CAPITAL Minsk

BELGIUM
AREA 11,787 sq mi
(30,528 sq km)
POPULATION 11,491,000
CAPITAL Brussels

BELIZE

AREA 8,867 sq mi
(22,966 sq km)
POPULATION 360,000
CAPITAL Belmopan

BENIN

AREA 43,483 sq mi
(112,622 sq km)
POPULATION 11,039,000
CAPITALS Porto-Novo (constitutional),
Cotonou (seat of government)

BHUTAN

AREA 14,824 sq mi
(38,394 sq km)
POPULATION 758,000
CAPITAL Thimphu

BOLIVIA

AREA 424,162 sq mi
(1,098,581 sq km)
POPULATION 11,138,000
CAPITALS La Paz (administrative),
Sucre (constitutional)

BOSNIA AND HERZEGOVINA

AREA 19,767 sq mi
(51,197 sq km)
POPULATION 3,856,000
CAPITAL Sarajevo

BOTSWANA

AREA 224,606 sq mi
(581,730 sq km)
POPULATION 2,215,000
CAPITAL Gaborone

BRAZIL

AREA 3,287,594 sq mi
(8,514,877 sq km)
POPULATION 207,353,000
CAPITAL Brasília

BRUNEI
AREA 2,226 sq mi
(5,765 sq km)
POPULATION 444,000
CAPITAL Bandar Seri Begawan

> ## " PRIDE AND INDUSTRY."
> ### —NATIONAL MOTTO OF BARBADOS

BULGARIA

AREA 42,810 sq mi
(110,879 sq km)
POPULATION 7,102,000
CAPITAL Sofia

BURKINA FASO

AREA 105,869 sq mi
(274,200 sq km)
POPULATION 11,467,000
CAPITAL Ouagadougou

BURUNDI

AREA 10,745 sq mi
(27,830 sq km)
POPULATION 11,500,000
CAPITAL Bujumbura

CABO VERDE

AREA 1,557 sq mi
(4,033 sq km)
POPULATION 561,000
CAPITAL Praia

CAMBODIA

AREA 69,898 sq mi
(181,035 sq km)
POPULATION 16,204,000
CAPITAL Phnom Penh

CAMEROON

AREA 183,567 sq mi
(475,440 sq km)
POPULATION 24,995,000
CAPITAL Yaoundé

CANADA

AREA 3,855,081 sq mi
(9,984,670 sq km)
POPULATION 35,624,000
CAPITAL Ottawa

CENTRAL AFRICAN REPUBLIC

AREA 240,534 sq mi
(622,984 sq km)
POPULATION 5,625,000
CAPITAL Bangui

CHAD

AREA 486,180 sq mi
(1,259,200 sq km)
POPULATION 12,076,000
CAPITAL N'Djamena

CHILE

AREA 291,931 sq mi
(756,102 sq km)
POPULATION 17,789,000
CAPITAL Santiago

CHINA

AREA 3,705,386 sq mi
(9,596,960 sq km)
POPULATION 1,379,303,000
CAPITAL Beijing

COLOMBIA

AREA 439,733 sq mi
(1,138,910 sq km)
POPULATION 47,699,000
CAPITAL Bogotá

COMOROS

AREA 863 sq mi
(2,235 sq km)
POPULATION 808,000
CAPITAL Moroni

CONGO

AREA 132,046 sq mi
(342,000 sq km)
POPULATION 4,955,000
CAPITAL Brazzaville

COSTA RICA

AREA 19,730 sq mi
(51,100 sq km)
POPULATION 4,930,000
CAPITAL San José

CÔTE D'IVOIRE

AREA 124,503 sq mi
(322,463 sq km)
POPULATION 24,185,000
CAPITALS Abidjan (administrative),
Yamoussoukro (legislative)

CROATIA

AREA 21,851 sq mi
(56,594 sq km)
POPULATION 4,292,000
CAPITAL Zagreb

CUBA

AREA 42,803 sq mi
(110,860 sq km)
POPULATION 11,147,000
CAPITAL Havana

CYPRUS

AREA 3,572 sq mi
(9,251 sq km)
POPULATION 1,222,000
CAPITAL Nicosia

CZECHIA (CZECH REPUBLIC)

AREA 30,451 sq mi
(78,867 sq km)
POPULATION 10,675,000
CAPITAL Prague

DEMOCRATIC REPUBLIC OF THE CONGO

AREA 905,350 sq mi
(2,344,858 sq km)
POPULATION 83,301,000
CAPITAL Kinshasa

DENMARK

AREA 16,639 sq mi
(43,094 sq km)
POPULATION 5,606,000
CAPITAL Copenhagen

DJIBOUTI

AREA 8,958 sq mi
(23,200 sq km)
POPULATION 865,000
CAPITAL Djibouti

DOMINICA

AREA 290 sq mi
(751 sq km)
POPULATION 74,000
CAPITAL Roseau

DOMINICAN REPUBLIC

AREA 18,791 sq mi
(48,670 sq km)
POPULATION 10,734,000
CAPITAL Santo Domingo

ECUADOR

AREA 109,483 sq mi
(283,561 sq km)
POPULATION 16,291,000
CAPITAL Quito

EGYPT

AREA 386,660 sq mi
(1,001,450 sq km)
POPULATION 97,041,000
CAPITAL Cairo

EL SALVADOR

AREA 8,124 sq mi
(21,041 sq km)
POPULATION 6,172,000
CAPITAL San Salvador

EQUATORIAL GUINEA

AREA 10,830 sq mi
(28,051 sq km)
POPULATION 778,000
CAPITAL Malabo

ERITREA

AREA 45,405 sq mi
(117,600 sq km)
POPULATION 5,919,000
CAPITAL Asmara

ESTONIA

AREA 17,463 sq mi
(45,228 sq km)
POPULATION 1,252,000
CAPITAL Tallinn

ETHIOPIA

AREA 426,370 sq mi
(1,104,300 sq km)
POPULATION 105,350,000
CAPITAL Addis Ababa

FIJI

AREA 7,056 sq mi
(18,274 sq km)
POPULATION 921,000
CAPITAL Suva

FINLAND

AREA 130,558 sq mi
(338,145 sq km)
POPULATION 5,518,000
CAPITAL Helsinki

FRANCE

AREA 248,572 sq mi
(643,801 sq km)
POPULATION 67,106,000
CAPITAL Paris

GABON

AREA 103,346 sq mi
(267,667 sq km)
POPULATION 1,772,000
CAPITAL Libreville

GAMBIA

AREA 4,361 sq mi
(11,295 sq km)
POPULATION 2,051,000
CAPITAL Banjul

GEORGIA

AREA 26,911 sq mi
(69,700 sq km)
POPULATION 4,926,000
CAPITAL Tbilisi

GERMANY

AREA 137,846 sq mi
(357,022 sq km)
POPULATION 80,594,000
CAPITAL Berlin

GHANA

AREA 92,098 sq mi
(238,533 sq km)
POPULATION 27,500,000
CAPITAL Accra

GREECE

AREA 50,949 sq mi
(131,957 sq km)
POPULATION 10,768,000
CAPITAL Athens

GRENADA

AREA 133 sq mi
(344 sq km)
POPULATION 112,000
CAPITAL St. George's

GUATEMALA

AREA 42,042 sq mi
(108,889 sq km)
POPULATION 15,461,000
CAPITAL Guatemala City

GUINEA

AREA 94,925 sq mi
(245,857 sq km)
POPULATION 12,414,000
CAPITAL Conakry

GUINEA-BISSAU

AREA 13,948 sq mi
(36,125 sq km)
POPULATION 1,792,000
CAPITAL Bissau

GUYANA

AREA 83,000 sq mi
(214,969 sq km)
POPULATION 738,000
CAPITAL Georgetown

HAITI

AREA 10,714 sq mi
(27,750 sq km)
POPULATION 10,647,000
CAPITAL Port-au-Prince

HONDURAS

AREA 43,278 sq mi
(112,090 sq km)
POPULATION 9,039,000
CAPITAL Tegucigalpa

HUNGARY

AREA 35,918 sq mi
(93,028 sq km)
POPULATION 9,851,000
CAPITAL Budapest

ICELAND

AREA 39,768 sq mi
(103,000 sq km)
POPULATION 340,000
CAPITAL Reykjavík

INDIA

AREA 1,269,212 sq mi
(3,287,263 sq km)
POPULATION 1,281,936,000
CAPITAL New Delhi

INDONESIA

AREA 735,354 sq mi
(1,904,569 sq km)
POPULATION 260,581,000
CAPITAL Jakarta

IRAN

AREA 636,368 sq mi
(1,648,195 sq km)
POPULATION 82,022,000
CAPITAL Tehran

IRAQ

AREA 169,234 sq mi
(438,317 sq km)
POPULATION 39,192,000
CAPITAL Baghdad

IRELAND

AREA 27,132 sq mi
(70,273 sq km)
POPULATION 5,011,000
CAPITAL Dublin

ISRAEL

AREA 8,019 sq mi
(20,770 sq km)
POPULATION 8,300,000
CAPITAL Jerusalem

ITALY

AREA 116,347 sq mi
(301,340 sq km)
POPULATION 62,138,000
CAPITAL Rome

JAMAICA

AREA 4,244 sq mi
(10,991 sq km)
POPULATION 2,991,000
CAPITAL Kingston

JAPAN

AREA 145,913 sq mi
(377,915 sq km)
POPULATION 126,451,000
CAPITAL Tokyo

JORDAN

AREA 34,495 sq mi
(89,342 sq km)
POPULATION 10,248,000
CAPITAL Amman

KAZAKHSTAN

AREA 1,052,084 sq mi
(2,724,900 sq km)
POPULATION 18,557,000
CAPITAL Astana

KENYA

AREA 224,080 sq mi
(580,367 sq km)
POPULATION 47,616,000
CAPITAL Nairobi

KIRIBATI

AREA 313 sq mi
(811 sq km)
POPULATION 108,000
CAPITAL Tarawa

KOSOVO

AREA 4,203 sq mi
(10,887 sq km)
POPULATION 1,895,000
CAPITAL Pristina

KUWAIT

AREA 6,880 sq mi
(17,818 sq km)
POPULATION 2,875,000
CAPITAL Kuwait City

KYRGYZSTAN

AREA 77,201 sq mi
(199,951 sq km)
POPULATION 5,789,000
CAPITAL Bishkek

LAOS

AREA 91,428 sq mi
(236,800 sq km)
POPULATION 7,127,000
CAPITAL Vientiane

LATVIA

AREA 24,938 sq mi
(64,589 sq km)
POPULATION 1,945,000
CAPITAL Riga

LEBANON

AREA 4,015 sq mi
(10,400 sq km)
POPULATION 6,230,000
CAPITAL Beirut

LESOTHO

AREA 11,720 sq mi
(30,355 sq km)
POPULATION 1,958,000
CAPITAL Maseru

LIBERIA

AREA 43,000 sq mi
(111,369 sq km)
POPULATION 4,689,000
CAPITAL Monrovia

LIBYA

AREA 679,358 sq mi
(1,759,540 sq km)
POPULATION 6,653,000
CAPITAL Tripoli

LIECHTENSTEIN

AREA 62 sq mi
(160 sq km)
POPULATION 38,000
CAPITAL Vaduz

LITHUANIA

AREA 25,212 sq mi
(65,300 sq km)
POPULATION 2,824,000
CAPITAL Vilnius

LUXEMBOURG

AREA 998 sq mi
(2,586 sq km)
POPULATION 594,000
CAPITAL Luxembourg

MACEDONIA

AREA 9,928 sq mi
(25,713 sq km)
POPULATION 2,104,000
CAPITAL Skopje

MADAGASCAR

AREA 226,657 sq mi
(587,041 sq km)
POPULATION 25,054,000
CAPITAL Antananarivo

MALAWI

AREA 45,747 sq mi
(118,484 sq km)
POPULATION 19,196,000
CAPITAL Lilongwe

MALAYSIA

AREA 127,354 sq mi
(329,847 sq km)
POPULATION 31,382,000
CAPITAL Kuala Lumpur

MALDIVES

AREA 115 sq mi
(298 sq km)
POPULATION 393,000
CAPITAL Male

MALI

AREA 478,838 sq mi
(1,240,192 sq km)
POPULATION 17,885,000
CAPITAL Bamako

MALTA

AREA 122 sq mi
(316 sq km)
POPULATION 416,000
CAPITAL Valletta

MARSHALL ISLANDS

AREA 70 sq mi
(181 sq km)
POPULATION 75,000
CAPITAL Majuro

MAURITANIA

AREA 397,953 sq mi
(1,030,700 sq km)
POPULATION 3,759,000
CAPITAL Nouakchott

MAURITIUS

AREA 788 sq mi
(2,040 sq km)
POPULATION 1,356,000
CAPITAL Port Louis

MEXICO

AREA 758,445 sq mi
(1,964,375 sq km)
POPULATION 124,575,000
CAPITAL Mexico City

MICRONESIA

AREA 271 sq mi
(702 sq km)
POPULATION 104,000
CAPITAL Palikir

MOLDOVA

AREA 13,070 sq mi
(33,851 sq km)
POPULATION 3,474,000
CAPITAL Chisinau

MONACO

AREA 0.8 sq mi
(2.0 sq km)
POPULATION 31,000
CAPITAL Monaco

MONGOLIA

AREA 603,905 sq mi
(1,564,116 sq km)
POPULATION 3,068,000
CAPITAL Ulaanbaatar

MONTENEGRO

AREA 5,333 sq mi
(13,812 sq km)
POPULATION 643,000
CAPITAL Podgorica

MOROCCO

AREA 172,413 sq mi
(446,550 sq km)
POPULATION 33,987,000
CAPITAL Rabat

MOZAMBIQUE

AREA 308,641 sq mi
(799,380 sq km)
POPULATION 26,574,000
CAPITAL Maputo

MYANMAR (BURMA)

AREA 261,227 sq mi
(676,578 sq km)
POPULATION 55,124,000
CAPITAL Nay Pyi Taw

NAMIBIA

AREA 318,259 sq mi
(824,292 sq km)
POPULATION 2,485,000
CAPITAL Windhoek

NAURU
AREA 8 sq mi
(21 sq km)
POPULATION 10,000
CAPITAL Yaren

NEPAL
AREA 56,827 sq mi
(147,181 sq km)
POPULATION 29,384,000
CAPITAL Kathmandu

NETHERLANDS
AREA 16,040 sq mi
(41,543 sq km)
POPULATION 17,085,000
CAPITAL Amsterdam

NEW ZEALAND
AREA 103,363 sq mi
(267,710 sq km)
POPULATION 4,510,000
CAPITAL Wellington

NICARAGUA
AREA 50,336 sq mi
(130,370 sq km)
POPULATION 6,026,000
CAPITAL Managua

NIGER
AREA 489,189 sq mi
(1,267,000 sq km)
POPULATION 19,245,000
CAPITAL Niamey

NIGERIA
AREA 356,667 sq mi
(923,768 sq km)
POPULATION 190,632,000
CAPITAL Abuja

NORTH KOREA
AREA 46,540 sq mi
(120,538 sq km)
POPULATION 25,248,000
CAPITAL Pyongyang

NORWAY
AREA 125,020 sq mi
(323,802 sq km)
POPULATION 5,320,000
CAPITAL Oslo

OMAN
AREA 119,498 sq mi
(309,500 sq km)
POPULATION 3,424,000
CAPITAL Muscat

PAKISTAN
AREA 307,372 sq mi
(796,095 sq km)
POPULATION 204,925,000
CAPITAL Islamabad

PALAU
AREA 177 sq mi
(459 sq km)
POPULATION 21,000
CAPITAL Ngerulmud

PANAMA
AREA 29,120 sq mi
(75,420 sq km)
POPULATION 3,753,000
CAPITAL Panama City

PAPUA NEW GUINEA
AREA 178,703 sq mi
(462,840 sq km)
POPULATION 6,910,000
CAPITAL Port Moresby

PARAGUAY
AREA 157,047 sq mi
(406,752 sq km)
POPULATION 6,944,000
CAPITAL Asunción

PERU
AREA 496,222 sq mi
(1,285,216 sq km)
POPULATION 31,037,000
CAPITAL Lima

PHILIPPINES
AREA 115,830 sq mi
(300,000 sq km)
POPULATION 104,256,000
CAPITAL Manila

POLAND
AREA 120,728 sq mi
(312,685 sq km)
POPULATION 38,476,000
CAPITAL Warsaw

PORTUGAL
AREA 35,556 sq mi
(92,090 sq km)
POPULATION 10,840,000
CAPITAL Lisbon

QATAR
AREA 4,473 sq mi
(11,586 sq km)
POPULATION 2,314,000
CAPITAL Doha

ROMANIA
AREA 92,043 sq mi
(238,391 sq km)
POPULATION 21,530,000
CAPITAL Bucharest

RUSSIA
AREA 6,601,631 sq mi
(17,098,242 sq km)
POPULATION 142,258,000
CAPITAL Moscow

RWANDA
AREA 10,169 sq mi
(26,338 sq km)
POPULATION 11,901,000
CAPITAL Kigali

SAINT KITTS AND NEVIS
AREA 101 sq mi
(261 sq km)
POPULATION 53,000
CAPITAL Basseterre

SAINT LUCIA
AREA 238 sq mi
(616 sq km)
POPULATION 165,000
CAPITAL Castries

SAINT VINCENT AND GRENADINES
AREA 150 sq mi
(389 sq km)
POPULATION 102,000
CAPITAL Kingstown

SAMOA
AREA 1,093 sq mi
(2,831 sq km)
POPULATION 200,000
CAPITAL Apia

SAN MARINO
AREA 24 sq mi
(61 sq km)
POPULATION 34,000
CAPITAL San Marino

SÃO TOMÉ AND PRINCIPE
AREA 372 sq mi
(964 sq km)
POPULATION 201,000
CAPITAL São Tomé

SAUDI ARABIA
AREA 829,995 sq mi
(2,149,690 sq km)
POPULATION 28,572,000
CAPITAL Riyadh

SENEGAL
AREA 75,954 sq mi
(196,722 sq km)
POPULATION 14,669,000
CAPITAL Dakar

SERBIA
AREA 29,913 sq mi
(77,474 sq km)
POPULATION 7,111,000
CAPITAL Belgrade

SEYCHELLES
AREA 176 sq mi
(455 sq km)

POPULATION 94,000
CAPITAL Victoria

SIERRA LEONE

AREA 27,699 sq mi
(71,740 sq km)
POPULATION 6,163,000
CAPITAL Freetown

SINGAPORE

AREA 269 sq mi
(697 sq km)
POPULATION 5,889,000
CAPITAL Singapore

SLOVAKIA

AREA 18,932 sq mi
(49,035 km)
POPULATION 5,446,000
CAPITAL Bratislava

SLOVENIA

AREA 7,827 sq mi
(20,273 sq km)
POPULATION 1,972,000
CAPITAL Ljubljana

SOLOMON ISLANDS

AREA 11,157 sq mi
(28,896 sq km)
POPULATION 648,000
CAPITAL Honiara

SOMALIA

AREA 246,199 sq mi
(637,657 sq km)
POPULATION 11,031,000
CAPITAL Mogadishu

SOUTH AFRICA

AREA 470,691 sq mi
(1,219,090 sq km)
POPULATION 54,842,000
CAPITALS Pretoria (Tshwane) (administrative),
Cape Town (legislative), Bloemfontein
(judicial)

SOUTH KOREA

AREA 38,502 sq mi
(99,720 sq km)
POPULATION 51,181,000
CAPITAL Seoul

SOUTH SUDAN

AREA 248,775 sq mi
(644,329 sq km)
POPULATION 13,026,000
CAPITAL Juba

SPAIN

AREA 195,123 sq mi
(505,370 sq km)
POPULATION 48,958,000
CAPITAL Madrid

SRI LANKA

AREA 25,332 sq mi
(65,610 sq km)
POPULATION 22,409,000
CAPITALS Colombo (administrative),
Sri Jayewardenepura Kotte (legislative)

SUDAN

AREA 718,719 sq mi
(1,861,484 sq km)
POPULATION 37,346,000
CAPITAL Khartoum

SURINAME

AREA 63,251 sq mi
(163,820 sq km)
POPULATION 592,000
CAPITAL Paramaribo

SWAZILAND

AREA 6,704 sq mi
(17,364 sq km)
POPULATION 1,467,000
CAPITALS Mbabane (administrative),
Lobamba (legislative and royal)

SWEDEN

AREA 173,859 sq mi
(450,295 sq km)
POPULATION 9,960,000
CAPITAL Stockholm

SWITZERLAND

AREA 15,937 sq mi
(41,277 sq km)
POPULATION 8,236,000
CAPITAL Bern

SYRIA

AREA 71,498 sq mi
(185,180 sq km)
POPULATION 18,029,000
CAPITAL Damascus

TAJIKISTAN

AREA 55,251 sq mi
(143,100 sq km)
POPULATION 8,469,000
CAPITAL Dushanbe

TANZANIA

AREA 365,753 sq mi
(947,300 sq km)
POPULATION 53,951,000
CAPITAL Dar es Salaam

THAILAND

AREA 198,116 sq mi
(513,120 sq km)
POPULATION 68,414,000
CAPITAL Bangkok

TIMOR-LESTE (EAST TIMOR)

AREA 5,743 sq mi
(14,874 sq km)
POPULATION 1,291,000
CAPITAL Díli

TOGO

AREA 21,925 sq mi
(56,785 sq km)
POPULATION 7,965,000
CAPITAL Lomé

TONGA

AREA 288 sq mi
(747 sq km)
POPULATION 106,000
CAPITAL Nuku'alofa

TRINIDAD AND TOBAGO

AREA 1,980 sq mi
(5,128 sq km)
POPULATION 1,218,000
CAPITAL Port of Spain

TUNISIA

AREA 63,170 sq mi
(163,610 sq km)
POPULATION 11,404,000
CAPITAL Tunis

TURKEY

AREA 302,533 sq mi
(783,562 sq km)
POPULATION 80,845,000
CAPITAL Ankara

TURKMENISTAN

AREA 188,455 sq mi
(488,100 sq km)
POPULATION 5,351,000
CAPITAL Ashgabat

TUVALU

AREA 10 sq mi
(26 sq km)
POPULATION 11,000
CAPITAL Funafuti

UGANDA

AREA 93,065 sq mi
(241,038 sq km)
POPULATION 39,570,000
CAPITAL Kampala

UKRAINE

AREA 233,031 sq mi
(603,550 sq km)
POPULATION 44,034,000
CAPITAL Kiev

UNITED ARAB EMIRATES

AREA 32,278 sq mi
(83,600 sq km)
POPULATION 6,072,000
CAPITAL Abu Dhabi

UNITED KINGDOM

AREA 94,058 sq mi
(243,610 sq km)
POPULATION 64,769,000
CAPITAL London

UNITED STATES

AREA 3,794,079 sq mi
(9,826,675 sq km)
POPULATION 323,996,000
CAPITAL Washington, D.C.

URUGUAY

AREA 68,037 sq mi
(176,215 sq km)
POPULATION 3,360,000
CAPITAL Montevideo

UZBEKISTAN

AREA 172,741 sq mi
(447,400 sq km)
POPULATION 29,749,000
CAPITAL Tashkent

VANUATU

AREA 4,706 sq mi
(12,189 sq km)
POPULATION 283,000
CAPITAL Port-Vila

VATICAN CITY (HOLY SEE)

AREA 0.2 sq mi
(0.4 sq km)
POPULATION 1,000
CAPITAL Vatican City

VENEZUELA

AREA 352,143 sq mi
(912,050 sq km)
POPULATION 31,304,000
CAPITAL Caracas

VIETNAM

AREA 127,880 sq mi
(331,210 sq km)
POPULATION 96,160,000
CAPITAL Hanoi

YEMEN

AREA 203,848 sq mi
(527,968 sq km)
POPULATION 28,037,000
CAPITAL Sanaa

ZAMBIA

AREA 290,586 sq mi
(752,618 sq km)
POPULATION 15,972,000
CAPITAL Lusaka

ZIMBABWE

AREA 150,871 sq mi
(390,757 sq km)
POPULATION 13,805,000
CAPITAL Harare

COUNTRIES OF THE WORLD

UNITED NATIONS

IN SEARCH OF A PEACEFUL WORLD

The UN works to maintain international peace, develop friendly relations among nations, and achieve international cooperation in solving world problems.

In 1945, the 51 original Member States represented more than 80 percent of the world's population.

MORE OF THE WORLD

BEYOND COUNTRY STATUS

There are 195 countries, 36 dependencies, and five other political units that make up the world today. Of those, 14 are U.S. territories, also considered dependencies, and are listed on page 323.

FIVE OTHER POLITICAL ENTITIES EXIST TODAY: GAZA STRIP, NORTHERN CYPRUS, TAIWAN, WEST BANK, AND WESTERN SAHARA.

A mountain road twists up Denmark's Faroe Islands, in the North Atlantic between Norway and Iceland.

THE WORLD

Dependencies Listed by SOVEREIGNTY

AUSTRALIA
Christmas Island, Cocos (Keeling) Islands, Norfolk Island

DENMARK
Faroe Islands, Greenland (Kalaallit Nunaat)

FRANCE
French Polynesia, New Caledonia, Saint-Barthélemy, Saint Martin, Saint-Pierre and Miquelon, Wallis and Futuna

NETHERLANDS
Aruba, Curaçao, Sint Maarten

NEW ZEALAND
Cook Islands, Niue, Tokelau

UNITED KINGDOM
Anguilla, Bermuda, British Virgin Islands, Cayman Islands, Falkland Islands, Gibraltar, Guernsey, Isle of Man, Jersey, Montserrat, Pitcairn Islands, Saint Helena and Dependencies, Turks and Caicos Islands

FUTURE OF THE PLANET

TAKING EARTH'S TEMPERATURE

The temperature is rising across the planet. The Arctic has seen the greatest change, largely because of its lower albedo rates—how much solar radiation is reflected back into space. Heat waves are becoming more common, often with deadly consequences. In many areas, the ocean is also warming. But in other areas, oceans are cooling because changing currents—the effect of warming elsewhere—are bringing colder water up from the deep.

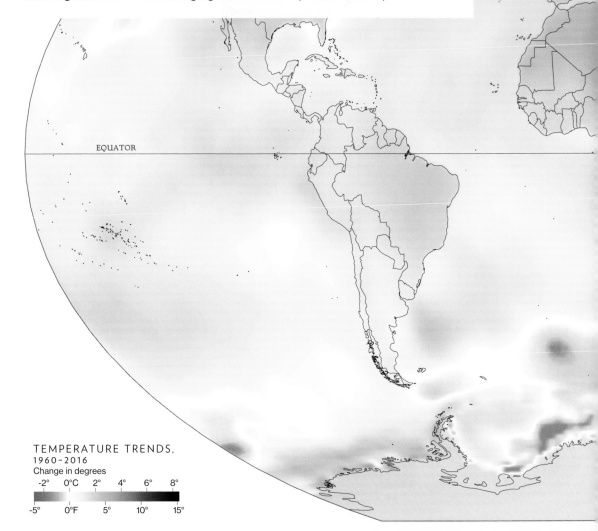

EQUATOR

TEMPERATURE TRENDS,
1960-2016
Change in degrees

-2°	0°C	2°	4°	6°	8°
-5°	0°F	5°	10°	15°	

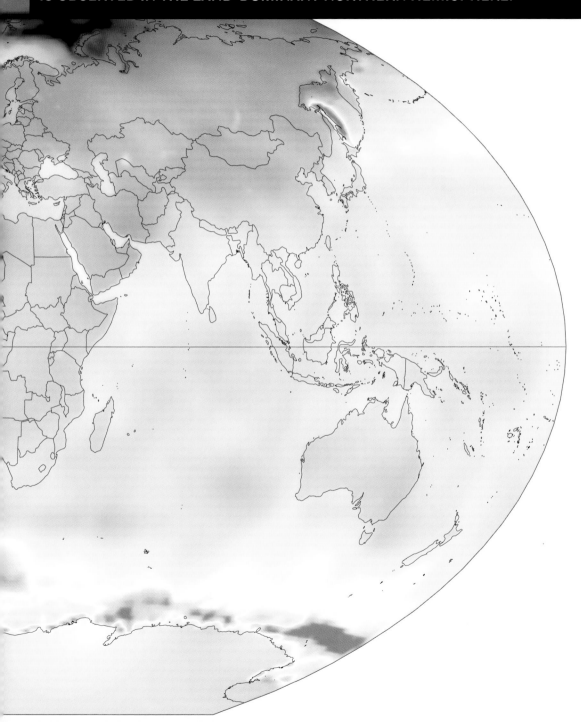

LANDMASSES WARM FASTER THAN OCEANS, AND SO THE MOST HEATING IS OBSERVED IN THE LAND-DOMINANT NORTHERN HEMISPHERE.

FUTURE OF
THE WILD ON EARTH

OUR IMPACT ON NATURE

Humans first began altering Earth's ecology with their use of fire and hunting. Clearing lands for agriculture generated even greater changes in ecology and allowed human populations to expand. Yet the most rapid changes caused by humans began in the 1800s with the industrial revolution, when humans acquired an unprecedented ability to exploit energy, especially fossil fuels, and thereby manipulate the environment.

Graph Key
- Urban
- Mixed settlements
- Rice villages
- Irrigated villages
- Rainfed villages
- Pastoral villages,
- Residential irrigated croplands
- Residential rainfed croplands
- Populated croplands
- Remote croplands
- Residential rangelands
- Populated rangelands
- Remote rangelands
- Residential woodlands
- Populated woodlands
- Remote woodlands
- Inhabited treeless and barren lands
- Wild woodlands
- Wild treeless and barren lands

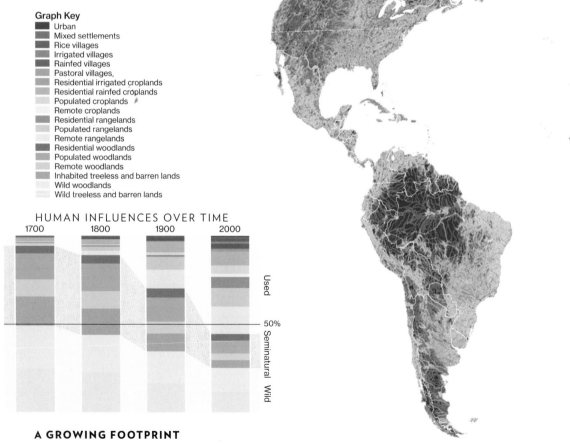

HUMAN INFLUENCES OVER TIME

1700   1800   1900   2000

50%

Used

Seminatural Wild

A GROWING FOOTPRINT

Before the industrial revolution, less than half of Earth's land felt the impact of humans. But with industrialization, the human influence on the biosphere changed as urban centers grew, agriculture developed, and forestry intensified.

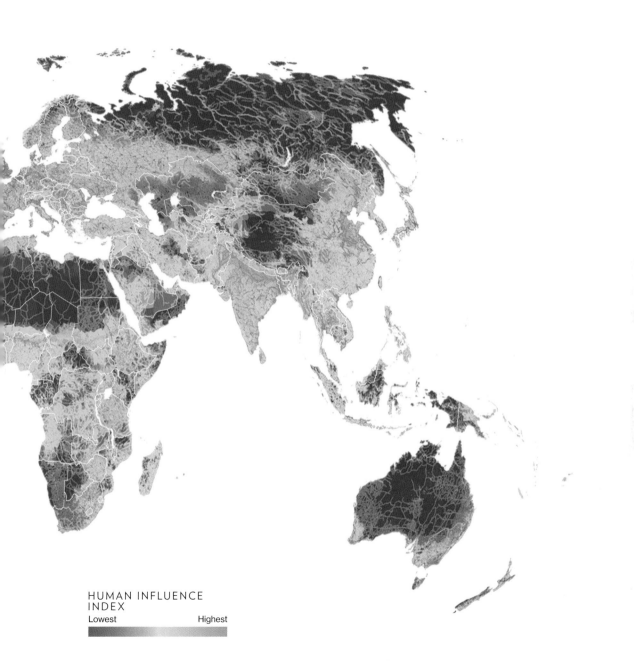

HUMAN INFLUENCE
INDEX
Lowest   Highest

FUTURE OF
HUMANS ON EARTH

SHIFTING DEMOGRAPHICS

In the coming decades, some countries are predicted to grow whereas others will experience population decreases.

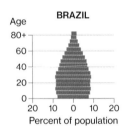

BRAZIL

Age

Percent of population

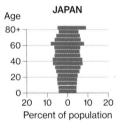

JAPAN

Age

Percent of population

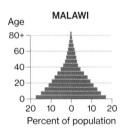

MALAWI

Age

Percent of population

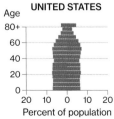

UNITED STATES

Age

Percent of population

POPULATION PYRAMIDS

Divided by sex and age ranges, population pyramids portray demographic trends. Malawi's pyramid, with a wide base and narrow top, indicates a young population with fast growth. A pyramid with a wider top, such as Japan's, represents an aging population.

THE UNITED NATIONS ESTIMATES THAT THE WORLD POPULATION WILL REACH EIGHT BILLION BY THE YEAR 2023.

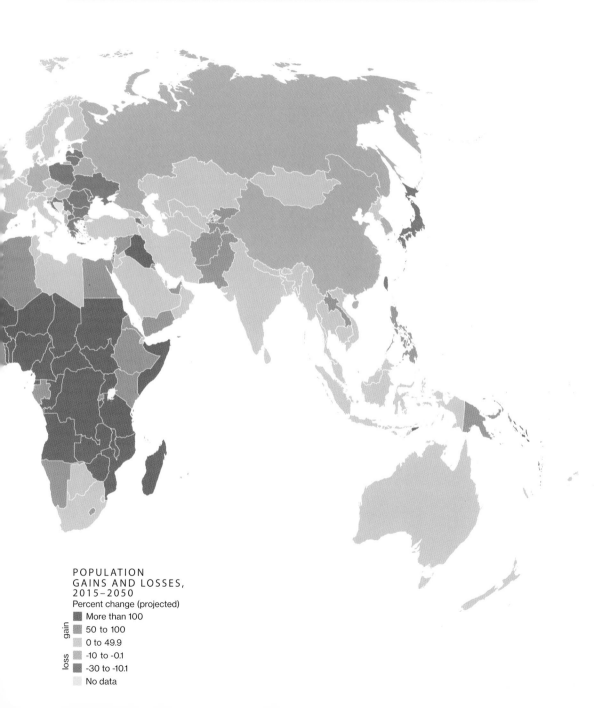

POPULATION
GAINS AND LOSSES,
2015–2050
Percent change (projected)

gain
- More than 100
- 50 to 100
- 0 to 49.9

loss
- -10 to -0.1
- -30 to -10.1

No data

FURTHER

MANY HANDS MAKE A COMMUNITY

Hundreds stretch out to reach the *dahi handi*—a pot full of yogurt, part of the days-long joyous festivities during Krishna Janmashtami, the birthday of the Hindu god Krishna. The practice harks back to a story that as a boy, Krishna and friends stood on one another's shoulders to reach a gourd full of butter hanging above their heads. Stories, beliefs, and traditions mix with music, costume, and color to unite people through this and many other celebrations around the world.

A Hindu celebration becomes a symbol of world unity.

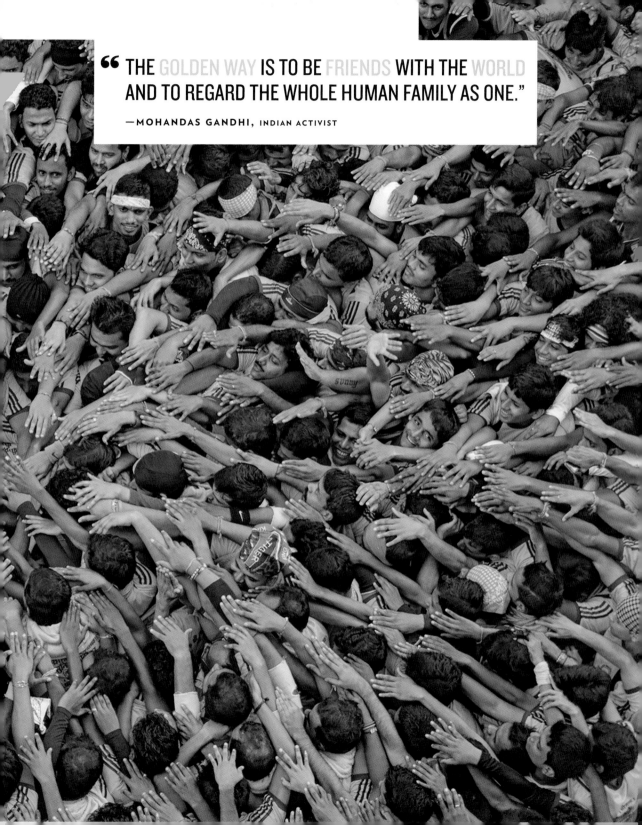

> **"THE GOLDEN WAY IS TO BE FRIENDS WITH THE WORLD AND TO REGARD THE WHOLE HUMAN FAMILY AS ONE."**
>
> —MOHANDAS GANDHI, INDIAN ACTIVIST

CREDITS

Science Source; 114 (3e), Science Stock Photography/Science Source; 114 (4a), National Museum of Natural History, Smithsonian Institution; 114 (4b), National Museum of Natural History, Smithsonian Institution; 114 (4c), Nadezda Boltaca/Shutterstock; 114 (4d), Scientifica/Getty Images; 114 (4e), National Museum of Natural History, Smithsonian Institution; 114 (5a), carlosdelacalle/Shutterstock; 114 (5b), National Museum of Natural History, Smithsonian Institution; 114 (5c), Vitaly Raduntsev/Shutterstock; 114 (5d), National Museum of Natural History, Smithsonian Institution; 114 (5e), Juraj Kovac/Shutterstock; 115, Greg Stewart/SLAC National Accelerator Laboratory; 116, Enric Sala; 117 (UP), NG Maps; 117 (LO), Rebecca Hale, NG Staff; 118-19, Iwan Baan/Reportage by Getty Images; 120-21, Wil Tirion; 121, Courtesy Andrew Fazekas; 122-3, Wil Tirion; 124, Brown Reference Group; 125, Wally Pacholka/Barcroft Media/Getty Images; 126 (UP LE), Davis Meltzer/National Geographic Creative; 126 (UP CTR LE), "The Emperor Julius Caesar" (oil on panel), Rubens, Peter Paul (1577-1640)/Private Collection/Photo © Christie's Images/Bridgeman Images; 126 (UP CTR RT), Atlas Photo Bank/Science Source; 126 (UP RT), NASA, ESA, J. Hester, A. Loll (ASU); 126 (CTR), NASA Images/Shutterstock; 126 (LO LE), © The British Library/The Image Works; 126 (LO RT), NASA/JPL-Caltech; 126-7, Brian Lula; 127 (UP LE), Larry Landolfi/Science Source; 127 (UP CTR LE), Library of Congress/Getty Images; 127 (UP CTR RT), Rolls Press/Popperfoto/Getty Images; 127 (UP RT), NASA/JPL/Cornell University/Maas Digital; 127 (LO LE), Royal Astronomical Society/Science Source; 127 (LO CTR LE), NASA/Johns Hopkins University Applied Physics Laboratory/Southwest Research Institute; 127 (LO CTR RT), National Air and Space Museum/Smithsonian Institution; 127 (LO RT), NASA/JHUAPL/SwRI; 128-9, NASA/JPL; 130, NASA; 131, Everett Historical/Shutterstock; 132-5, NG Maps; 136-7, NASA/JPL-Caltech; 138, © Walt Disney Studios Motion Pictures/Lucasfilm Ltd./Courtesy Everett Collection; 138-9, NASA/JPL; 139, NASA/JPL/DLR; 140 (UP LE), Donny Fallgatter; 140 (UP RT), Ira Block; 140 (LO LE), Babak Tafreshi, The World at Night; 140 (LO RT), Diego Rizzo; 141 (UP LE), Pete McBride; 141 (UP RT), Abhishek Deopurkar; 141 (LO LE), Paul Nicklen/National Geographic Creative; 141 (LO RT), Grant Collins/National Geographic Your Shot; 142-3, Graphic by Jason Treat, NG Staff; 144, Archives & Special Collections, Vassar College Library, Ph.f6.93; 145, Linda Davidson/The Washington Post via Getty Images; 146, FOX via Getty Images; 146-7, Tom Abel and Ralf Kaehler, Stanford KIPAC; 148-9, Radio image by Natasha Hurley-Walker (ICRAR/Curtin) and the GLEAM Team, MWA tile and landscape by John Goldsmith, Celestial Visions (composite of two images); 150, Steve Schapiro/Corbis via Getty Images; 150-51, Pobytov/Getty Images; 151 (ALL), PHL @ UPR Arecibo; 152, Ryan Lash; 153, NASA, ESA, S. Baum & C. O'Dea (RIT), R. Perley & W. Cotton (NRAO/AUI/NSF), and the Hubble Heritage Team (STScI/AURA); 154-5, NASA, ESA, and J. Lotz and the HFF Team (STScI); 156-7, Paul Nicklen/National Geographic Creative; 158 (UP LE), Courtesy Cara Santa Maria; 158 (UP RT), A-Digit/Getty Images; 158 (CTR LE), Sunny studio/Shutterstock; 158 (CTR RT), monticello/Shutterstock; 158 (LO LE), AVIcon/Shutterstock; 158 (LO CTR), nobeastsofierce/Shutterstock; 158 (LO RT), Corey Ford/Stocktrek Images/Getty Images; 159 (UP LE), nektofadeev/Shutterstock; 159 (UP RT), Jeff Stamer/Shutterstock; 159 (CTR), Svetlana Iakovets/Shutterstock; 159 (LO), Matt9122/Shutterstock; 160 (UP LE), Szasz-Fabian Jozsef/Shutterstock; 160 (UP CTR), Illustration of a page of text showing music-making angels around two united reptiles around a circle from Historia Naturalis, by Pliny the Elder (vellum)/Biblioteca Nazionale Marciana, Venice, Italy/Roger-Viollet, Paris/Bridgeman Images; 160 (UP RT), The Picture Art Collection/Alamy Stock Photo; 160 (LO LE), Portrait bust of male, copy after a Greek fourth-century B.C. original (marble), Roman, (first century A.D.)/Museo Archeologico Nazionale, Naples, Campania, Italy/De Agostini Picture Library/A. Dagli Orti/Bridgeman Images; 160 (LO CTR LE), Wellcome Library, London; 160 (LO CTR RT), Granger.com – All rights reserved; 160 (LO RT), International Mammoth Committee, photo by Francis Latreille; 160-61, vitstudio/Shutterstock; 161 (UP LE), Stocktrek Images/Science Source; 161 (UP RT), Eric Isselee/Shutterstock; 161 (CTR LE), Joe Tucciarone/Science Source; 161 (CTR RT), Nata-Lia/Shutterstock; 161 (LO LE), 3D4Medical/Science Source; 161 (LO CTR LE), Daniel Prudek/Shutterstock; 161 (LO CTR RT), Michael Nichols/National Geographic Creative; 161 (LO RT), John Weinstein/Field Museum Library/Getty Images; 162 (UP LE), Dennis Kunkel Microscopy/Science Source; 162 (UP CTR), Dennis Kunkel Microscopy/Science Source; 162 (UP RT), Eye of Science/Science Source; 162 (LE), Kateryna Kon/Shutterstock; 162 (LO RT), Tatiana Shepeleva/Shutterstock; 163 FUNGI: (UP LE) Denis Vesely/Shutterstock, (UP RT) Passakorn Umpornmaha/Shutterstock; 163 PLANTS: (UP LE) surajet.l/Shutterstock, (UP RT) Mizuri/Shutterstock, (LO LE) Alexandra Lande/Shutterstock, (LO RT), Mike Ver Sprill/

Shutterstock; 163 ANIMALS: (UP LE) Ondrej Prosicky/Shutterstock, (UP RT) frantisekhojdysz/Shutterstock, (LO LE) Claudia Paulussen/Shutterstock, (LO RT) Abeselom Zerit/Shutterstock; 164, Mark Thiessen, NG Staff; 164-5, Eye of Science/Science Source; 166-7, Art: Davide Bonadonna; Graphic: Lawson Parker, NG Staff; Samantha Welker; 167, Mark Thiessen, NG Staff; 168 (LE), © MCA/Courtesy Everett Collection; 168 (RT – ALL), Jared Travnicek; 168-9, Dr. Steven Salisbury; 170, Dorling Kindersley/Getty Images; 171 (UP), Jacana/Science Source; 171 (LO LE), John Gerrard Keulemans; 171 (LO RT), Joel Sartore/National Geographic Creative; 172 (UP LE), Tim Laman/National Geographic Creative; 172 (UP RT), Paul Nicklen/National Geographic Creative; 172 (LO LE), Stefano Unterthiner; 172 (LO RT), Steve Winter/National Geographic Creative; 173 (UP LE), Christian Ziegler/National Geographic Creative; 173 (UP RT), Frans Lanting/lanting.com; 173 (LO LE), Peter Essick; 173 (LO RT), Corey Arnold; 174, Jared Travnicek; 174-5, Jim and Jamie Dutcher/National Geographic Creative; 175, Jim and Jamie Dutcher/National Geographic Creative; 176 (UP), Joel Sartore/National Geographic Photo Ark, photographed at Miller Park Zoo; 176 (LO), Joel Sartore/National Geographic Photo Ark, photographed at Catholic University of Ecuador; 177, Britt Griswold; 178, Christian Ziegler/National Geographic Creative; 179, Manuel Canales, NGM staff; Meg Roosevelt; Art: Shizuka Aoki; 180 (UP), Joel Sartore/National Geographic Photo Ark, photographed at Night Safari, Singapore; 180 (CTR), Joel Sartore/National Geographic Photo Ark, photographed at Lincoln Children's Zoo; 180 (LO), Joel Sartore/National Geographic Photo Ark, photographed at Indianapolis Zoo; 181 (UP LE), jeep2499/Shutterstock; 181 (UP RT), Joel Sartore/National Geographic Photo Ark, photographed at Gladys Porter Zoo; 181 (LO LE), Joel Sartore/National Geographic Photo Ark, photographed at Lowry Park Zoo; 181 (LO RT), Mark Thiessen, NG Staff; 182, Science Source/Getty Images; 182 (INSET), Omikron/Science Source; 183, National Library of Medicine/Science Source; 184 (UP LE), Joel Sartore/National Geographic Photo Ark, photographed at Dallas World Aquarium; 184 (UP RT), Paul Nicklen/National Geographic Creative; 184 (LO LE), Keith Ladzinski; 184 (LO RT), Cristina Mittermeier; 185 (UP LE), Tim Laman; 185 (UP RT), David Doubilet/National Geographic Creative; 185 (LO LE), Jennifer Hayes/National Geographic Creative; 185 (LO RT), Brian Skerry/National Geographic Creative; 186-7, David Doubilet/National Geographic Creative; 187, Source: ARC Centre of Excellence for Coral Reef Studies; 188-9 (ALL EXCEPT LO), Brian Skerry/National Geographic Creative; 189 (LO), Mauricio Handler/National Geographic Creative; 190 (3e), Carlyn Iverson/Science Source/Getty Images; 190 (4d), 190 (ALL OTHERS), Jared Travnicek; 190-91, Paul Nicklen/National Geographic Creative; 192-3, Fernando G. Baptista and Daniela Santamarina, NGM staff; Mesa Schumacher; internal structure illustrations: Shizuka Aoki; 194 (UP LE), Tim Laman/National Geographic Creative; 194 (UP RT), Anand Varma/National Geographic Creative; 194 (LO LE), Peter Essick; 194 (LO RT), Paul Nicklen/National Geographic Creative; 195 (UP LE), Keith Ladzinski; 195 (UP RT), Kirsten Luce; 195 (LO LE), Ronan Donovan; 195 (LO RT), Robert Clark; 196 (1a), Diane Pierce; 196 (1b), Diane Pierce; 196 (1c), Peter Burke; 196 (1d), H. Douglas Pratt; 196 (1e), Michael O'Brien; 196 (2a), H. Douglas Pratt; 196 (2b), H. Douglas Pratt; 196 (2c), Diane Pierce; 196 (2d), Michael O'Brien; 196 (2e), David Beadle; 196 (3a), Diane Pierce; 196 (3b), N. John Schmitt; 196 (3c), Donald L. Malick; 196 (3d), H. Douglas Pratt; 196 (3e), H. Douglas Pratt; 196 (4a), H. Douglas Pratt; 196 (4b), Donald L. Malick; 196 (4c), H. Douglas Pratt; 196 (4d), H. Douglas Pratt; 196 (4e), H. Douglas Pratt; 196 (5a-5e), H. Douglas Pratt; 196-7, swedewah/Getty Images; 197, Thomas R. Schultz; 198-9, Monica Serrano, NGM staff; Mesa Schumacher. Art: Vlad Rodriguez; 200-201, Corey Arnold; 201, Courtesy Noah Strycker; 202, Jared Travnicek; 203 (1a), John Serrao/Science Source; 203 (1b), John Flannery (https://creativecommons.org/licenses/by-sa/2.0/legalcode); 203 (1c), J.T. Chapman/Shutterstock; 203 (1d), John Flannery/flickr (https://creativecommons.org/licenses/by-sa/2.0/legalcode); 203 (2a), Steve Byland/Shutterstock; 203 (2b), Arthur V. Evans; 203 (2c), Carolina Birdman/Getty Images; 203 (2d), Steven Russell Smith Photos/Shutterstock; 203 (3a), Claudia Steininger/Getty Images; 203 (3b), Leena Robinson/Shutterstock; 203 (3c), John Flannery/flickr (https://creativecommons.org/licenses/by-sa/2.0/legalcode); 203 (3d), Sari ONeal/Shutterstock; 203 (4a), Paul Reeves Photography/Shutterstock; 203 (4b), Betty Shelton/Shutterstock; 203 (4c), Steven Russell Smith Photos/Shutterstock; 203 (4d), Matt Jeppson/Shutterstock; 204-205, Joel Sartore/National Geographic Creative; 206 (UP LE), Farmers at Work, Northern Song Dynasty, 960-1279 (wall painting)/Mogao Caves, Dunhuang, Gansu Province, NW China/Bridgeman Images; 206 (UP CTR LE), Time Life Pictures/Mansell/The LIFE Picture Collection/Getty Images; 206 (UP CTR RT), SuperStock/Getty

INDEX

National Geographic Partners
1145 17th Street NW
Washington, DC 20036-4688 USA

Get closer to National Geographic explorers and photographers, and connect with our global community. Join us today at nationalgeographic.com/join

For information about special discounts for bulk purchases, please contact National Geographic Books Special Sales: specialsales@natgeo.com

For rights or permissions inquiries, please contact National Geographic Books Subsidiary Rights: bookrights@natgeo.com

ISBN: 978-1-4262-1981-8
ISBN: 978-1-4262-2016-6 (UK ed.)

Printed in the United States of America

18/WOR/1

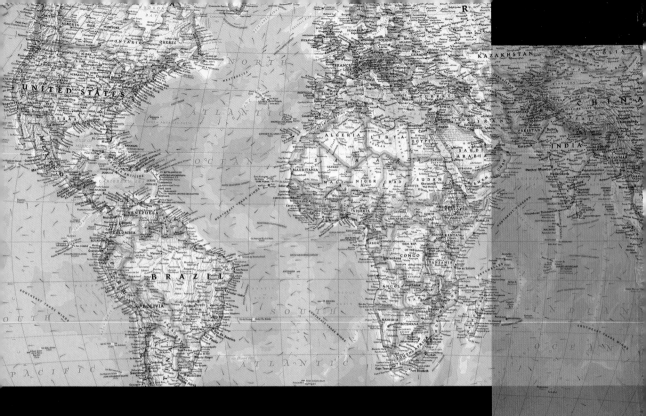

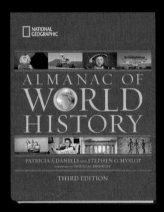